The Faces of Social Policy

A STRENGTHS PERSPECTIVE WITHDRAWN

CAROLYN J. TICE
Ohio University

KATHLEEN PERKINS
Louisiana State University

D1411367

BROOKS/COLE

THOMSON LEARNING

Australia • Canada • Mexico • Singapore • Spain • United Kingdom • United States

BROOKS/COLE

✦

™

THOMSON LEARNING

Executive Editor: *Lisa Gebo*
Assistant Editor: *Shelley Gesicki*
Marketing Team: *Caroline Concilla,*
  Megan Hansen, and *Laura Hubrich*
Editorial Assistant: *Sheila Walsh*
Project Editor: *Mary Anne Shahidi*
Production Service: *Shepherd Inc.*
Manuscript Editor: *Jeanne Patterson* and
  Jane Morgan

Permissions Editor: *Sue Ewing*
Interior Design: *Adriane Bosworth*
Cover Design: *Roger Knox*
Cover Photos: *PhotoDisc and Eyewire*
Photo Researcher: *Mary Reeg*
Print Buyer: *Jessica Reed*
Typesetting: *Shepherd Inc.*
Printing and Binding: *Transcontinental*
  Interglobe

For more information about this or any other Brooks/Cole products, contact:
BROOKS/COLE
511 Forest Lodge Road
Pacific Grove, CA 93950 USA
www.brookscole.com
1-800-423-0563 (Thomson Learning Academic Resource Center)

For permission to use material from this work, contact us by
www.thomsonrights.com
fax: 1-800-730-2215
phone: 1-800-730-2214

Printed in Canada

10 9 8 7 6 5 4 3 2 1

Library of Congress Cataloging-in-Publication Data

Tice, Carolyn J.
    The faces of social policy : a strengths perspecitve / Carolyn J. Tice, Kathleen Perkins.
        p. cm.
    Includes bibliographical references and index.
    ISBN 0-534-34502-6
    1. United States—Social policy. 2. Social policy. I. Perkins, Kathleen. II. Title.

HN57 .T53 2001
361.6'1'0973—dc21   2001043599

To my brother and friend, George Tice, Jr.
—CJT

In memory of Zack, my beloved feline.
—KP

Contents

Chapter 3

Early America: A Time of Need   35

Chapter 4

Social Realities in the Developing Nation   49

Chapter 5

American Industrialization: The Policy of Development   67

Chapter 6

Social Reform in the Progressive Era   99

Chapter 10

A Turn to the Right   207

Preface

THE GOAL

This book has been written because of the continuing challenge for social work educators to connect policy to practice in such a way that policies, past and present, come alive for students, stimulating their critical thinking from a different perspective. Social policy provides the foundation for social work practice by defining who are clients, what are services, who are service providers, and how services are funded. It reflects the values of the nation, depicts the tension between the people with power and those on the fringe of society, and maps the course by which government distributes resources. By defining domestic and international principles for action, social policy defines the way life ought to be for the nation and the world. Most often, social policy is a dreaded required course for social work students who are interested in helping people but see little relevance to policy analysis and practice across client systems. Sparking that interest in social policy for students is the goal of this text.

This text is intended for use in schools of social work, specifically to be used in the required policy courses for both undergraduate and graduate education, and does not require prior knowledge of social welfare. The book can also be used as a supplementary text in diversity and history courses.

FOR THE STUDENT

While the majority of policy texts encourage critical thinking by a problem-centered approach to policy formation, it is the goal of this text, *The Faces of Social Policy: A Strengths Perspective,* to highlight policy through a strengths lens. The benefit for students is that they will be introduced to the history of social policy in the United States from a strengths perspective and challenged to think critically about the influence of historic themes on issues in social welfare today.

When there is an intense focus on problem definition and assessment, policy analysis is deficit and pathology oriented. For example, the policies and programs associated with the 1996 Welfare Reform Bill center attention on the problems of poverty, dependency, and fraud. Correspondingly, welfare recipients are labeled in negative terms that suggest individual weakness or character flaws and essentially blame the victim. Environmental conditions, such as lack of employment opportunities and inadequate education, receive much less attention. The book's strengths perspective highlights common human needs rather than social problems. Stories of the people whose policies are aimed to serve illustrate new ways of viewing those policies and portray the strength of people as they overcome barriers, personally and through programs, to identify opportunities and resources to meet their needs.

FOR THE INSTRUCTOR

This text is replete with poems, speeches, and narratives from various time periods and some music; for example, a history of rap. Each chapter begins with a photograph of the era to set the stage for content. The benefit of this text for instructors is that by putting a face on the people who are being served by social workers and giving them a voice, there is a shift in how social policy is studied—from abstract notions to realities of living through particular events such as the New Deal or under certain conditions including poverty. These unique concepts will help stimulate the students' interest in the subject.

Another feature that is useful for instructors and students is the book's focus on themes. *The Faces of Social Policy: A Strengths Perspective* emphasizes that themes in social welfare policy are relevant not only to historical periods but contemporary society. Themes involve responses to needs and correspond to the fabric of American society. For example, the work ethic in the context of the deserving and nondeserving poor is a theme that runs throughout many social welfare policies beginning with Elizabethan Poor Laws to present-day welfare reform. Understanding this theme and others helps students to analyze critically governmental responses to need while assessing future policy direction and implications.

Divided into twelve chapters, *The Faces of Social Policy: A Strengths Perspective* begins with an introduction of the strengths perspective for social policy, comparing and contrasting the differences between the more traditional problem-solving method of policy development and the nontraditional strengths approach. The remaining book chapters move through periods of history, define emerging themes, and include personal narratives, stories, diaries, letters, and records to illustrate the strengths of people in the context of social policy and issues. The development of social work as a profession is integrated throughout this book, as is an emphasis on disadvantaged people including people of color, women, children, and immigrants.

In many ways, *The Faces of Social Policy: A Strengths Perspective* ends where it begins—with an understanding of the role of social work in influencing social policy. It is incumbent on social workers in whatever area they practice to help develop policies that build on the strengths of people rather than on perceived limitation. Policies designed to empower clients and to preserve their freedom, capacity, and dignity are sorely needed.

C. Tice and K. Perkins

I am a white anti-racist. The journey I have taken to get here has been profound, exciting, and life-changing. Upon arriving in the South 12 years ago, I was stunned at the depth and breadth of racism, and shocked into taking a stand. I grew up in the Northwest, and moved to Louisiana after 4 years in Philadelphia. Of course, there is racism in the North, but I was looking at it through different lenses then. In retrospect, what I realize is that racism is more covert outside of the South. In the South it is in-your-face, overt, and everywhere. While I was shocked at the overtness, my African American friends and colleagues assured me that they much prefer it this way: to be able to see the enemy head on, so to speak.

I first got into "Undoing Racism" four years ago when my church, Unitarian Universalist, sponsored a curriculum called Journey to Wholeness, putting forth the concept. From there I was led to "The People's Institute for Survival and Beyond: Undoing Racism," a New Orleans based group that has been in existence for 20 years. The Institute provides "Undoing Racism" training and community organizing training and technical assistance nationally and worldwide.

This book is written from an anti-racist perspective as well as from a strengths perspective. As a social work educator, I find that most of our textbooks tend to reflect the white point of view as well as white history. We have brought "color" to *The Faces of Social Policy: A Strengths Perspective.* This was done intentionally with two goals in mind: that people of color would be able to see themselves, their faces, in a social work policy textbook; and to better educate/inform white students of the richness of different races and diversity.

K. Perkins

ACKNOWLEDGMENTS

We would like to first extend our appreciation to Rosemary Kennedy Chapin from the School of Social Welfare at the University of Kansas, who provided us with inspiration for this book with the publication of her article: "Social Policy Development: The Strengths Perspective," which appeared in *Social Work* in 1995 (Volume 40, Number 4). Dr. Chapin, along with other faculty at KU, have been at the forefront of promoting the strengths approach to practice, research, and teaching and have been generous with their encouragement in our continued work in the area. We would especially like to acknowledge

Charlie Rapp and Dennis Saleebey for the time and kindness they have extended to us over the years. We'd also like to thank the following reviewers for their helpful comments and suggestions: Hazel Arthur, David Lipscomb University; Joel Blau, SUNY-Stony Brook; Janine Mariscotti, LaSalle University; Katherine Shank, Northwestern University; Dale Smith, Western Kentucky University; and Joseph Wronka, Springfield College. (C. J. Tice and K. Perkins)

I would also like to thank David Billings of the People's Institute who has not only been an inspiration to me in my anti-racist work, but who read my chapters as I produced them, offering critical input and lavishing high praise on my efforts. I am grateful to Barbara Major, executive director of the St. Thomas Health Clinic, for giving me the opportunity to work alongside her and the fine staff at the clinic to assist in developing a culturally competent, anti-racist, mental health curriculum for health care providers.

My work on this book was aided greatly by the assistance of several graduate students who served, in part, as my researchers, digging deep to find interesting tidbits and factual information that helped to bring many of the events in the book alive. I'm grateful to Gina Abbott for her work on Chapters 5 and 6; Alice Collier, Chapter 6; Leah Patin, Chapters 6 and 9; and Julie Latimer, Chapters 11 and 12. I'm especially indebted to Charlie Mann, a graduate student who worked long and hard for one entire summer to assist me with Chapters 10, 11, and 12. He deserves the accolade, "the conqueror of large jobs," because he responded to my every need for more, and more, and more details. His dedication to this project enabled me to meet my deadline. And, last but not least, I wish to thank Shad Duplessis, yet another graduate assistant, who worked tirelessly over his summer break to help me track down the endless sources that required permission to go into the book. (K. Perkins)

Andrea Glass, a student in the Department of Social Work at Ohio University, offered me considerable assistance throughout the writing of this book. She was my proofreader and editor on numerous drafts. I greatly appreciated her words of encouragement.

Kendra Mitchell, a graduate of the Department of Social Work, conducted various research and provided me with a great deal of support during the early phases of the book.

David Reese, a graduate student in the new Master of Social Work Program at Ohio University, typed many a page for me and helped to keep my classes, especially Social Work 101, in order. Whatever I requested, David was there with a smile and a pleasant word.

Hannah and Hank, my dear friends, added joy to the extensive time necessary to complete this project by sitting patiently by my side as I worked on my computer in Morton Hall or greeting me with enthusiasm when I returned home. And, of course, a special word of appreciation to my parents, Jeanne C. Tice and the late George Tice, Sr., along with Victoria Howell who inspire me to keep moving forward. (C. J. Tice)

SOCIAL POLICY FROM A STRENGTHS PERSPECTIVE

Social work practice is greatly influenced by social policies. Social policies define who clients are, as well as what services will be delivered by whom and for how long. Undergraduate and graduate social work students study social policy and the nation's network of social services to understand the foundation

We would like to thank Rebecca Chaisson, Louisiana State University, for carefully reading this chapter and providing valuable feedback.

of social programs. This chapter defines and explores social policy from a strengths perspective. The relevance of this material highlights the impact social policy has on social work practice and on the lives of individuals, groups, communities, and organizations.

Explicit in the discussion are themes of social policy and the influence of political systems on policy development. Policy themes, as used in this book, are recurring patterns of governmental action that respond to human needs and reflect societal values. Examples of policy themes are the designation of categorical services for the poor and nonpoor, the expansion and reduction of government intervention, and the relationship between the public and private sector. Political systems reflect liberal, moderate, and conservative ideology in the framework of a capitalistic economy. Because social policy is shaped by these ideologies, it is important to understand political systems in order to analyze existing policy and develop new social policy.

WHAT IS SOCIAL POLICY?

T. H. Marshall (1965), a founder of social policy theory, defines social policy as the actions of government that have a direct impact on the welfare of people by providing services and income. As principles of action, policies translate our government's sense of responsibility to us, its citizens. Thus, policy reflects societal values, ideals, and a vision of what the world should look like. Other social policy include the following:

- Guidelines that support a decision-making process.
- Methods of explaining the people's actions.
- Boundaries that define the relationships and obligations of government to citizens.
- Processes that produce programs, services, or interventions.
- Responses to societal needs and political pressures.
- Corrections of inequities to improve the conditions of disadvantaged people.
- Measures to distribute power.

Social policy is the basis of social work practice because it defines, finances, and implements social programs. Three premises support this statement:

1. Policy specifies the rules and regulations that govern developing and operating social programs. Such rules and regulations are contained in legislation and are revised periodically to reflect changes in public attitude and in the political and economic environment.
2. Policy determines the mechanisms for financing services. This involves a relationship between the local, state, and federal government. For

example, the Personal Responsibility and Work Opportunity Act of 1996, the latest version of public assistance for poor people, gave states the right to use federal block grants in a variety of experiments and innovations to assist needy people.

3. Policy outlines employment opportunities for social workers. For example, when the 1935 Social Security Act—the foundation of the American welfare state—was implemented, the number of social work positions increased from 40,000 in 1930 to 70,000 in 1940 (Wenocur & Reisch, 1989). Social case work was adaptable to new public agencies that screened, referred, and provided assistance to many poor people who used New Deal programs. At the same time, psychiatric social workers continued to provide services to the various private agencies that existed during the 1930s (Jansson, 2001).

DEVELOPING SOCIAL POLICY

The Problem-Centered Approach

Social welfare policies regulate the provision of benefits to people to meet basic needs, including employment, income, food, housing, health care, and relationships. Social policies are often society's response to social problems. In traditional, problem-centered policy development, problem definition is considered the cornerstone of policy design (Chapin, 1995). The problem-centered approach involves a series of processes intended to address an entanglement of problems and combined to make policy development a complex web of activities. This is opposed to the nontraditional, strengths-centered approach, which literally assesses the strengths of the people and the environment as part of the process of policy development.

Social policy making occurs on many levels. Most social welfare programs are a result of government choices and decisions. To understand the implications and effects of social welfare policies and to influence the development of those decisions, social workers must be familiar with the policy-making process from the traditional, problem-focused method. Once that method is put into perspective, the strengths approach to social policy development will be examined.

Identifying the Policy Problem Social welfare policy is often developed as a response to social problems (Chambers, 1986, 1993; Jansson, 2001; Chapin, 1995). However, the relationship between social problems and social welfare is not simple, and not all social problems generate social welfare policies. Policy makers label a condition or situation a "problem" to be corrected or, in some instances, a source of future problems. A social problem, in this sense, is a condition that affects the quality of life for large groups or is of concern to economically or socially powerful people. Social welfare policies are shaped by a set of social and personal values that reflect the preference of those in decision-making capacities. Thus, labeling a condition as a problem is based partly on analysis and partly on the beliefs and values of people in decision-making positions.

Careful definition of the problem that a social policy is intended to address creates a source of knowledge that can be used in assessing the appropriateness of current social policy trends and in implementing new policies and programs. In addition, problem definition is basic to the process by which the general public develops consensus that a need, such as health care or housing, deserves the attention of elected officials.

The definition of social problems and the subsequent development of social welfare policies are shaped by sets of social, political, professional, and personal values. Social values are organized through ideology, the framework of commonly held beliefs through which we view the world (Karger & Stoesz, 1998), for example, liberal (democrat) and conservative (republican). Ideology is a set of assumptions about how the world works: what has value, what is good and bad, and what is right. An understanding of the relationship between values, social and economic instability, and social welfare policy is provided by Francis Fox Piven and Richard Cloward (1971) who attribute the cyclical nature of social welfare programs to periods of social unrest. Their view is further discussed in Chapter 9. The Social Security Act of 1935 provides an example of policy and programs designed in the midst of social and economic instability.

Liberal and conservative ideologies reflect values that are often at the opposite end of the spectrum. A liberal position supports active intervention by the federal government. Social welfare policies are regarded as being so important that they should be legislated by the government. Conservative ideology generally opposes government intervention because it regards such involvement as a waste of taxpayers' money. Implicit in the liberal view is the idea that the welfare of society cannot be left to operate without some controls. Liberal ideology views the government as both a referee to ensure fairness and a provider to correct imbalances and inequities. Conservatives, on the other hand, view social programs as either providing benefits to those who need them, or creating a dependency that encourages people to stop caring for themselves.

In addition to political values, we add to the mix principles and values associated with social work including fostering self-determination on the part of clients and promoting the general welfare of society. These professional values demonstrate that social workers are obligated to advocate for social welfare policies and programs that promote social justice, respect diversity, and improve social conditions. This is seldom an easy task, especially when focusing on social need as a problem, or a deficit.

The Strengths Approach

The discussion on social, political, and professional values is a good place to introduce some of the tenets of the strengths approach to policy development.

The strengths perspective supports the belief, or value, that many of the barriers people face in meeting basic needs for food, shelter, and positive community participation "tend to come from educational, political, and economic exclusion based on demographics rather than individual characteristics" (Chapin, 1995; Rappaport et al., 1975, p. 526). In order to foster self-determination for the people we serve, social workers are challenged to identify individual and community resources that create opportunities for inclusion or provide alternatives that nurture the growth and capabilities of people in their environments. Thus, deficits shift away from the central focus of policy development. Rather, the need for clients' perceptions of the situation to be clearly understood by policy makers is underscored.

For social policy to reflect the reality of its intended recipients, and if the right for self-determination is indeed tantamount, the recipients must be directly affected by the policy. If a purpose of social policy is the distribution of resources (Chambers, 1986) and clients are viewed in the context of their strengths, then their inclusion in problem definition and policymaking is more likely. In this scenario, social workers have the responsibility to (a) ensure that clients' voices are heard and understood by policy makers (b) work for inclusion of clients in policy making, and, (c) focus on client strengths and common need rather than deficits (Chapin, 1995).

Values are personal. Taking a position on social welfare can also depend on a personal system of values. Because values are often conflicting and contradictory, the development and acceptance of social welfare policies and programs are always filled with controversy when people and personalities are involved. Conflicting positions demonstrate how powerful the disagreement about social values and ideologies can be. Major conflicts between values are often at the root of disagreement over public policies. Usually social welfare policies reflect some public consensus regarding social values. When those values change over time, however, policies seem outdated and become the subject of public debate.

Driving while under the influence of alcohol, teen pregnancy, and HIV-AIDS are current examples of conditions, interfaced with values, that have became social policies and then social programs. In Society became aware of the social problem of driving while under the influence of alcohol, largely as a result of parents, particularly mothers, who experienced the death of a child as a result of a drunk driver. When considering the problem, interested parties discovered that driving while under the influence of alcohol arose from a number of circumstances: happy hours at bars where liquor was served without regard to intoxication levels, lenient fines for drunk driving, and limited education on the affects of alcohol and driving.

Mothers Against Drunk Driving (MADD), a private organization, developed a multidimensional campaign to educate the general public on the results of drunk driving, lobby for revisions in the law, and monitor cases against drunk drivers. Schools and establishments that sold alcohol also developed strategies to minimize the number of drunk drivers on the road by offering alternative transportation, sponsoring nonalcohol events, and encouraging the appointment of designated drivers. Although problems associated with driving under the influence are not solved, some policies and programs were implemented that reduced the number of accidents and casualties associated with drunk driving. It should be noted that the MADD approach, while highly effective, is not perceived as a poor, or person-of-color phenomenon; however, the issue of teenage pregnancy is often racialized.

In a manner similar to MADD, advocates for those experiencing teen pregnancy and HIV-AIDS have successfully lobbied to develop policies, programs, and services to help address and prevent the problems. With assistance from private and public funds, a network of education, prevention, and supportive services has been developed in communities across the nation. The following example of teen pregnancy and HIV-AIDS assistance would be confronted using a strengths approach. Compared to other population groups, a disproportionally higher number of African American pregnant teens and folks suffering from HIV-AIDS exists. Taking a strengths approach to this social need for assistance (policy), social workers would go into the African American community and seek their vantage point on the problem (collaboration). Social workers would identify individuals in the community from whom they could obtain information before proceeding. The strengths approach and teen pregnancy is covered in detail in Chapter 10.

Formulating Policy Alternatives

There are different means by which social policy is formulated. One of those is through the pressure of special interest groups. The efforts of Mothers Against Drunk Drivers exemplify the formation of policy by an interest group. Policy proposals are also formulated by policy-planning organizations, government bureaucracies, Congress, and the President. The process of formulating policy alternatives involves gathering and providing decision makers with the information needed to make decisions more rationally with respect to stated goals.

Knowledge is essential in formulating policy alternatives. To gain knowledge, policy related information can be obtained from government agencies, congressional offices, professional associations, and policy research groups. Many of these publications must be secured directly from their issuers, and are not available in libraries. By viewing the gathering of knowledge from a strengths approach, we could tap various communities in need and gain information of them by use of narrative or story-telling by the people directly involved. This approach takes it from the professional to the people, forming a collaborative relationship.

Daily newspapers, such as *The New York Times* and *Washington Post* are excellent sources of information on pending polices and policy alternatives. These papers are indexed and the indices are available in book form and on computer databases. For news related to business and economic events, the *Wall Street Journal* provides detailed accounts.

The Cable-Satellite Public Affairs Network (C-SPAN), a private, nonprofit network, televises proceedings from the House of Representatives and the Senate. Coupled with newspapers, C-SPAN provides a good foundation for understanding policy issues, examining policy alternatives, and tracking policy from design to implementation.

Many federal departments and agencies compile data and develop analysis of social welfare policy concerns. For example, the Office of Family Assistance, an agency under the Department of Health and Human Services, keeps statistics in public assistance programs and publishes reports under request (Segal & Brzuzy, 1998). The Centers for Disease Control and Prevention, an agency under the National Institute of Health, publishes quarterly statistics on health and morbidity that are available free through subscription.

In addition to government sources, a great deal of policy information can be acquired from professional associations and policy research groups. Many professions have national offices in Washington, D. C. that are responsible for tracking legislation relevant to its membership. For example, the National Association of Social Workers (NASW) is one of the many professional organizations with a legislation affairs office. Other professional organizations such as the American Medical Association and the American Psychological Association also have legislative affairs offices. Policy institutes, such as the Brooking Institution and the Heritage Foundation, provide technical expertise to legislatures and governmental organizations upon request. It should be noted that in keeping linked to the consciousness of strengths, social workers must be diligent in making sure that the people who are to be affected be policy also have a voice.

Organizations such as the National Association for the Advancement of Colored People (NAACP), the National Organization of Women (NOW), and the National Gay and Lesbian Task Force (NGLTF) provide current information on policies affecting their constituent groups. Nonprofit organizations produce extensive social welfare policy material on special populations. An example is the Children's Defense Fund that publishes numerous books and reports assessing the social needs of children in poverty.

As in problem definition, values are influential when exploring policy alternatives. Two social values, social responsibility and personal responsibility, have influenced the creation of social welfare policies alternatives. They are often contradictory and have been supported by differing groups at various times.

Social responsibility maintains that the public should help individuals who are perceived as less fortunate, but the recipients must be deemed worthy of that assistance. Although this distinction may appear straightforward, it is difficult to distinguish between people who are needy and those who are not. When is a service an assistance and does a service maintain a person in his or her position of need?

The values of independence and providing for oneself are reflected by the high regard associated with individualism in America. The notion that people are responsible for their position in society permeates social policy debates. For example, is a person poor and needy because of economic or social barriers that make is difficult to obtain gainful employment or is the person's preference not to work? With individual achievement regarded so highly, policy alternatives that promote social responsible and collective achievement, are difficult to promote and almost nonexistent.

Legitimizing Policy

Legitimizing policy includes all of the activities associated with passing policy into law. Figure 1.1 describes the process of legitimizing policy.

Two primary groups are involved in the legislative phase: the legislature and special interest groups. Much policy work is completed by legislators who are appointed to committees and subcommittees on the basis of their particular interests. Of particular significance to social welfare policy are the Senate Financial Committee (with the Medicaid and Health Care for Low-Income Families subcommittee) and the House of Representatives Ways and Means Committee (with the Social Security subcommittee). Committees are the loci of testimony on issues, and legislative hearings provide an opportunity for official testimony from the public. The process is buffered, however, by the intermediaries and gatekeepers.

Special interest groups can be divided into two groups, according to the nature of their activities. Political action committees (PACs) influence the composition of legislatures prior to elections. Lobbyist exert pressure between elections to ensure that their interests gain legislative attention. Examples of special interest groups include the American Medical Association (AMA), the National Education Association (NEA), the National Association of the Mentally Ill (NAMI), and the National Rifle Association (NRA).

Social welfare advocacy groups usually have limited funds and rely on volunteers as lobbyists (Karger & Stoesz, 1998). Despite their disadvantages, social welfare advocacy groups are often successful in defeating some policy proposals and gaining support for others. For example, in the 1980s the American Association of Retired Persons (AARP) launched an effective campaign

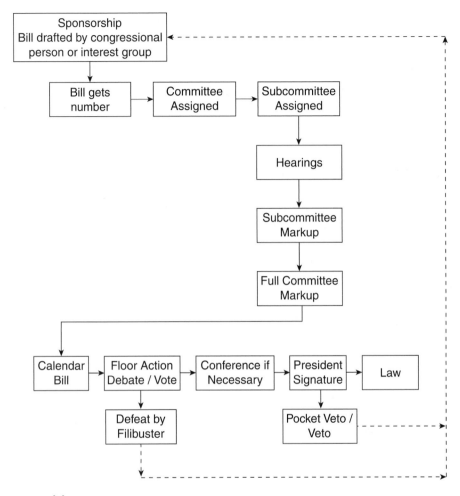

FIGURE **1.1**

The Legislative Process Path from Bill to Law

against cutbacks in Social Security benefits. Under the Clinton administration, the Children's Defense Fund (CDF) was successful in extending Medicaid benefits to cover more uninsured children.

Legitimizing a policy is an evolutionary process that changes with implementation. Consequently, what develops as a policy differs from the actual program or service that is implemented. Often the policy decisions of politicians are vague and represents a general consensus because there are so many differing views to be considered. Also, policy makers do not have the responsibility for actually putting the ideas into practice. This often leaves a gap between interpretations and values. What makes political sense in a policy passed by Congress, a state legislature, or a local board may not address the interests of communities or population groups. Thus it is important to recognize and understand the difference between what was planned by a social welfare policy and what the actual policy consequences are in terms of programs and services.

The Problem-Centered Approach in Perspective

As described, the problem-centered approach to social policy development begins with a problem definition that is translated into social policy and in turn, programs and services. The value-laden process of policy development has led to the examination of social problems by various stakeholders and has generated debates about the existence and roots of problems.

Unfortunately, the problem definitions of many current social policies and programs emphasize individual pathologies and deficits. Specifically, the Personal Responsibility and Work Opportunity Reconciliation Act of 1996 mandates work and establishes time limits to welfare benefits with the underlying public idea that welfare mothers will become "dependent on the system" and are unwilling to work unless forced to do so.

In the Personal Responsibility and Work Opportunity Reconciliation Act or other public assistance policies, structural barriers—including lack of jobs, inadequate day care, and poor educational preparation—receive little or no attention. The popular press provides numerous examples of punitive policy proposals aimed at people with acquired immune deficiency, pregnant teenagers, and people with alternative lifestyles. Those proposals all build on problem definitions that Ryan (1971, p. 5) says essentially blame the victim. "The miserable health care of the poor is explained away on grounds that the victim has poor motivation and lacks health information. The problems of slum housing are traced to the characteristics of tenants who are labeled as 'Southern rural migrants' not yet 'acculturated' to life in the big city." Ryan's theory is discussed further in Chapter 9 and more fully in Chapter 10.

Although a problem-centered approach to social development could focus on institutional rather that individual factors, Rappaport, Davidson, Wilson, and Mitchell (1975), conclude that the substitution of "environmental blaming" is often no more helpful in developing and guiding intervention (Chapin, 1995). Both blaming approaches focus on the "causes" of the pathological or deficit behavior rather than on identifying the strengths of and resources in the individuals and their environments. In other words, it is disempowerment by design. It cannot by fixed unless it is known why it is broken.

Other biases inherent in the knowledge-building process shape problem definitions even when problem definition does not reflect a predisposition to blame the victim or the environment. When knowledge is sought to ultimately predict or control a social problem, the acquisition and protection of the knowledge is fundamentally political. Understanding the relationship between social problems and knowledge production encourages social workers to examine methods of policy development that incorporate the views and realities of disenfranchised groups and others who experience social problems as a part of daily living.

A Strengths Perspective for Developing Social Policy

The problem-centered approach to social policy development, much like social work and other human service professions, unravels the complexities of social issues according to stark divisions between problem and solution, deserving and nondeserving, and deficit and strength (Tice & Perkins, 1996). Although social work has a bias toward theoretical structures that define and labels problems, the profession has not ignored the importance of individual and environmental strengths. Bertha Reynolds (1951) suggested, "Our first question to the client should not be 'What problem bring you here today?' but rather, 'You have lived thus far, how have you done it?' " (p. 125). The structure and principle of Perlman's (1957) problem-solving model presented a departure from Freudian-based psychodynamic "diagnostic" social work practice of diagnosing or labeling that emphasized pathology (Turner, 1986).

Functional theory, pioneered by Jesse Taft and Virginia Robinson of the School of Social Work at the University of Pennsylvania, highlighted the significance of client choice and self-determination (Robinson, 1930). Ruth Smalley applied functional theory to principles of practice based on purposive choices and decisions made by the person being helped. More recent writers, including Shulman (1979), Germain and Gitterman (1980), Hepworth and Larsen (1990) have stressed the importance of expanding assessments to include a focus on individual strengths and included the client as an active participant in the change process.

Saleebey (1992) advanced the assessment of strengths by articulating a strength perspective for social work practice. According to Saleebey, the strengths perspective is represented by a collation of ideas and techniques rather than theory or a paradigm (Tice & Perkins, 1996). It "seeks to develop abilities and capabilities in clients" and "assumes that clients already have a number of competencies and resources that may improve their situations" (Saleebey, 1992, p. 15). Tice and Perkins (1996) developed the strengths model of social work further by applying it to mental health and older adults.

The Policy Process from a Strengths Approach

Towle's (1945/1987) *Common Human Needs* is a logical companion piece to the strengths approach, providing a foundation to the policy problem component of the policy-making process. According to Towle:

> We give hesitantly and grudgingly—that is, fearfully—the nurturing services which would seem to foster dependence. We fail to comprehend the interrelatedness of man's needs and the fact that frequently basic dependency needs must be met first in order that he may utilize opportunities for independence. Accordingly, funds are appropriated for school lunches and school clinics less willingly than for schoolbooks. (1945, p. 5)

In the basic needs tradition of Towle (1945/1987) social policy is a tool for helping people met basic needs including food, shelter, education, and participation in community life. Emphasis on human needs presents social workers with several considerations:

- People with similar needs are nevertheless confronted with different barriers in meeting their needs.
- Highlighting common needs instead of social problems eliminates labels based on deficits or pathologies.
- With human needs as the basic criteria, people do not have to be described as deficient to justify receiving benefits and services.
- The social work values of self-determination and respect for worth and dignity are operationalized by focus on human needs.
- Recognizing common human needs supports the conceptual core of the strengths perspective whereby social workers collaborate with people as opposed to exerting the power of knowledge or institutions.
- Human needs involves communities as a resource that offer opportunities for growth and development. (Towle, 1945/1987; Salleebey, 1992; Chapin, 1995; Tice & Perkins, 1996).

Table 1.1 illustrates how the traditional problem-centered process of policy development can be infused with the nontraditional, strengths approach. In the strengths approach, common human needs and barriers to meeting these needs are emphasized as opposed to problem definition and analysis (Chapin, 1995).

The policy development process infused with the strengths approach differs from the traditional problem-centered process. The strengths approach negotiates needs and barriers by soliciting input from people who are disadvantaged in meeting their needs and who are searching for opportunities and resources. This is accomplished through the worker/client and educator/student relationship, knowledge development, linking people with existing services and advocating for services when they do not exist. Thus, social welfare policy becomes more representative by considering problems from the per-

TABLE 1.1
COMPARISON OF THE PROBLEM–CENTERED AND STRENGTH APPROACHES TO POLICY DEVELOPMENT

Policy Process	Problem Centered	Strengths
Identify the Problem	• A condition or situation is labeled as a "problem" to be corrected • "Problem" impacts the quality of life for a large group of the economically/socially powerless • Definition of problem is shaped by sets of values • Political ideology affects problem identification	• Identifies barriers associated with meeting common needs • Problem definition is negotiated with all parties involved • Stories and observation of ordinary people are included in the definition • Recognition given to peoples' methods of coping and confronting barriers
Formulate Policy Alternatives	• Knowledge accumulation is essential • Federal departments/agencies compile data • Professional associations provide sources of data • Professional policy–maker is considered the expert	• Knowledge accumulation focuses on the strengths of the individuals • Alternatives are considered as tools to assist people to meet their needs • Consumers of services are collaborators in policy development
Legitimize Policy	• Involves organized activities on legislatures and elected officials • Special interest groups influence the process of passing bills into law • Social welfare advocacy groups endorse or confront issues/programs	• Environment is scanned for support of policy that supports individuals in their environments • Program consumers introduce formal and informal resources into policy implementation • Considers if client needs are met
Evaulate Policy	• Involves relatively scientific methods • Provides a pool of information • Universities and government entities participate in conduct and evaluate studies	

sonal through the external environment, interweaving these two dimensions in a circular fashion (Gutierrez, Parsons, & Cox, 1998). When working with people of color, social workers need to keep in mind that the individual has less emphasis than the community as a whole, and his or her history, culture, and power must be addressed.

The strengths approach assumes that social problems occur in all tiers of multilevel systems and exist in groups with varying degrees of power and conflicting interests (Gutierrez, Parsons, & Cox, 1998; Gutierrez, 1994; Parsons, Jorgensen, & Hernández, 1994; Rees, 1991). One aspect of the strengths approach is to identify opportunities for people and communities to gain access to resources to meet common needs. Closely connected to this is empowerment, the process by which people, families, and groups or communities gain power. Gutierrez, Parsons, and Cox (1998, pp. 4–5) associated the following components with empowerment:

- *Attitudes, Values and Beliefs.* Beliefs that people can direct their lives and promote an environment conducive to their growth and well-being.
- *Collaborative Experiences.* By sharing experiences and realizing commonalties, people contribute to a collective view that "reduces self-blame, increases the tendency to look beyond personal failure as the cause of the problem at hand, brings about a sense of shared fate, and raises consciousness" (Gutierrez, Parsons, & Cox, 1998, p. 5).
- *Critical Thinking and Knowledge.* As people share their perspectives and gain an understanding of common human needs, they begin to identify macro-level structures that impede access to information and services. The process of macro-level problem analysis reduces self-blame and helps individuals examine the root of social problems to see that their problems are similar to those of others. Also, self-empowerment can be accomplished in communities of color by organized resistance.
- *Action.* From program design to outcome assessment, individuals can develop action strategies and cultivate resources, knowledge, and skills necessary to influence internal and external structures. Further, they learn to assume responsibility for their actions and to engage in collective action to attain common goals and social change.

What becomes apparent in the strengths approach is that policy experts do not design policy and inform the public of policy goals. Rather, voice is given to the public to participate in and influence the entire process. Thus, the strengths approach challenges current government decision making by including lower socioeconomic groups in decision making. It is important to realize that recent attempts to include disadvantaged groups in decision making have not been well received. Specifically, the War on Poverty included Community Action Programs that supported "maximum feasible participation" throughput program administration (Karger & Stoesz, 1998). Threatened by the redistribution of power and disturbed by the militancy of poor people, maximum feasible participation was eliminated in social service programs for all practical purposes. Currently, clients and poor people might serve on advisory committees, but their influence and control is minimal at best.

The purpose of introducing the strengths approach is not to suggest that it is the truth and the problem-centered policy development is wrong. Actually, the problem-focused approach more clearly reflects the current process of social welfare policy development. However, considering the strengths approach is useful for social workers because of the "values implicit in the model, expected outcomes of the use, and the direction offered to social workers who engage in the policy process" (Chapin, 1995, p. 510).

The social work values of respect for clients and their right to self-determination compliment the strengths approach. These values are reinforced by understanding the power of social relationships and collective action on structural barriers to needs. To insure that this happens, social workers need to be participants in the process and not just observers. Negotiating policy consensus in light of the clients' view of reality empowers people to use knowledge, skill, and power to make effective change in their lives and environment. The emphasis of the strengths approach on searching the environment for opportunities and resources challenges social workers to articulate the political nature of personal problems through such activities as lobbying. Furthermore, this approach works to make policy development more democratic in origin, implementation, and evaluation.

PROFILES IN SOCIAL POLICY: GIVING RECIPIENTS A FACE AND A VOICE

Perhaps the most exciting potential of the strengths perspective is its usefulness in shaping social policies more relevant to the immediate needs of people. This book provides a historical account of social welfare policy development by exploring how people coped with barriers to address their needs. The book's premise is that understanding barriers to needs, resources people need to survive, and people's coping skills leads to more relevant and effective policy design.

The book uses social art and people's stories or nonfiction accounts including personal narratives, letters, and historical documents to give them a face and a voice. Using social art and people's stories as a tool of policy development supports a strengths approach by insuring that the general public's common needs are heard and seen by policy makers in agencies as well as at the legislative level. Forms of art and personal narratives add a new dimension to policy development by introducing those sensibilities, feelings, inarticulate thoughts. The outcome draws on creative resources that allows people to experience a place in time, society, and politics beyond their own (Tice & Perkins, 1994). Further, when policy makers see or hear the experiences of others, a new constituency profile often emerges, one that views people as cocreaters of social policy (Tornstam, 1992). The art and stories of survival and strength, rather than the misconceptions about people's difficulties or social problems, may then become the linchpin for action (Chapin, 1995; Weick et al., 1989).

For social workers attempting to understand the historical context of social welfare development, stories and art bring alive people and conditions of days gone. In much the same way, art and nonfiction accounts also provide direction by searching the environment for resources and opportunities that can enhance current life chances (Chapin, 1995). For example, the social art of the 1950s and 1940s embraces a huge body of socially conscious art reflecting the social, economic, and political climate of the times. The aesthetic conditions, as indicated by the work of Gotlieb's *Drillers* (1930) and Siporin's *The Homeless* (1939), were created to document and comment on conditions related to human needs such as housing, employment, and health care in a manner that would be understood by ordinary people (Braufman, 1997). At the same time, the art provided visual support the social insurance programs under the Social Security Act of 1935 including Old Age, Survivors, and Disability Insurance (OASDI) and Unemployment Insurance (UI).

The use of social art and nonfiction contained in this book illustrates social welfare policy in such a way that students can transfer the world of others into their world to understand, more fully, Towle's (1945/1987) perspective on common human needs. Through art and nonfiction, students examine social evidence and commentary on the complexities of life from a human perspective. Moreover, relevant art and nonfiction enhances a holistic evaluation of social welfare policy because such work reflect the times, tensions, and cultures of society from the perspective of the general public.

IMPLICATIONS FOR POLICY PRACTICE

The efficiency of the strengths approach in policy formulation will be judged on its effect on policy practice and on the people's common good. Policy practice is fundamental to social work practice in every setting and whether working legislatively, interorganizationally, or within their own agencies, social workers influence social policies that shape clients' lives (Chapin, 1995).

The strengths perspective can be used to conceptualize a new understanding of the relationship between the helper and those who are helped and the accountability of both to the collective. When policy makers go beyond considering themselves as experts, the nature of their work will change. For example, it is expected that more attention will be spent in outreach to increase the interest of diverse groups in the policy decision-making agenda.

When policies are developed, key elements of any effort to evaluate their merit should involve the extent to which they reflect the ideas of the people most clearly affected by the policies and the outcomes that can be expected to result. Social workers are challenged to develop strengths not only in people but in communities. In this way, the strength approach leads social workers to see the potential of effective government policy and involvement of the corporate community as well as the voluntary community.

In many cases, during the early years of government, there was a void of social welfare policies, and it was through the sheer strength of the people and the resources in their communities that they survived. This profound lack of adequate response to need was indeed challenging. Hence, the book's focus: recapping the history of social welfare policy by looking at the peoples' strengths.

SUMMARY

While the problem-centered approach is the policy development model used most often, the strengths approach described in this chapter provides social workers with a new perspective that builds on the values of self-determination and dignity for the individual. Based largely on the work of Towle (1945/1987), the strengths approach highlights common human needs, shifting the thrust of policy focus from pathology and deficits to strength building in the people and communities.

The chapter introduces the use of art and nonfiction as a means of exploring the effects of policy on the lives of ordinary people. Creative and personal pieces of work will be introduced throughout the book to encourage students to rethink social situations. Thus, the synergistic power of words and art in the context of social welfare policy development supports the strengths approach by allowing us to listen and observe how people have met their survival needs.

REFERENCES

Braufman, S. B. (1997). When artists became workers: The people's art movement of the 30's and 40's. *American Art Review.* Vol. IX, No. 1, 96–103.

Chambers, D. (1986). *Social policy and social programs.* New York: Macmillan.

Chambers, D. (1993). *Social policy and social programs* (2nd ed.). New York: Macmillan.

Chapin, R. K. (1995). Social policy development: The strengths perspective. *Social Work, 40*(4), 506–514.

Germain, C., & Gitterman, A. (1980). *The life model of social work practice.* New York: Columbia University Press.

Gutierrez, L. (1994). Beyond coping: An empowerment perspective on stressful life events. *Journal of Sociology and Social Welfare, 21*(3), 201–220.

Gutierrez, L., Parsons, R. J., & Cox, E. O. (1998). *Empowerment in social work practice: A sourcebook.* Pacific Grove, CA: Brooks/Cole.

Hepworth, D., & Larsen, J. A. (1990). *Direct social work practice: Theory and skills* (3rd ed.). Pacific Grove, CA: Brooks / Cole.

Karger, H. J. & Stoesz, D. (1998). *American social welfare policy.* New York: Longman.

Jannson, B. S. (2001). *The reluctant welfare state.* 4th ed. Pacific Grove, CA: Brooks/Cole.

Marshall, T. H. (1965). *Social policy.* London: Hutchman.

Parsons, R., Jorgensen, J. D., & Hernandez, S. H. (1994). *The integration of social work practice.* Pacific Grove, CA: Brooks/Cole.

Perlman, H. H. (1957). *Social casework: A problem-solving process.* Chicago: University of Chicago.

Piven, F. F. and Cloward, R. (1971). *Regulating the poor.* New York: Vintage.

Rappaport, J., Davidson, W., Wilson, M., & Mitchell, A. (1975). Alternatives to blaming the victim or the environment: Our places to stand have moved the earth. *American Psychologist, 30,* 525–528.

Rees, S. (1991). *Achieving power.* North Sydney, Australia: Allen & Unwin.

Reynolds, B. (1951). *Social work and social living: Explorations in philosophy and practice.* Silver Spring, MD: National Association of Social Workers.

Robinson, V. P. (1930). *A changing psychology in social casework.* Chapel Hill: University of North Carolina.

Ryan, W. (1971). *Blaming the victim.* New York: Random House.

Saleebey, D. (1992). *The strengths perspective in social work practice.* New York: Longman.

Segal, E. A. & Brzuzy, S. (1998). *Social welfare policy, programs, and practice.* Itasca, IL: F. E. Peacock Publishers, Inc.

Shulman, L. (1979). *The skills of helping individuals and groups.* Chicago, IL: F.E. Peacock.

Tice, C. (1993). Using literature to illustrate social work theories. *Arete, 18*(1), 48–52.

Tice, C. J. & Perkins, K. (1994). A focus on community: Integrating literature in HBSE curriculum. *Arete, 19*(2), 52–59.

Tice, C. J. & Perkins, K. (1996). *Mental health issues and aging: Building on the strengths of older persons.* Pacific Grove, CA: Brooks/Cole.

Tornstam, L. (1992), The quo vadis of gerontology: On the scientific paradigm of gerontology. *Gerontology, 32,* 318–326.

Towle, C. (1987). *Common human needs.* Silver Spring, MD: National Association of Social Workers. (original work published 1945).

Turner, E. J. (1986). *Social work treatment: Interlocking theoretical approaches.* New York: Macmillan.

Weick, A., Rapp, C., Sullivan, W. P., & Kisthardt, W. (1989). A strengths perspective for social work practice. *Social Work 37,* 350–354.

Wenocur, S. & Reisch, M. (1989). *From charity to enterprise: The development of American social work in a market economy.* Urbana: University of Illinois Press, 115–135.

THE LEGACIES OF ANTIQUITY AND MEDIEVAL SOCIETY

The nation's social welfare system reflects our society's historical values. Like other institutions that comprise American government, social welfare mirrors traditions, influences, and practices of the Old World. As social workers, we cannot understand or change the current policies and programs that help people in need without first comprehending their historical foundations. Because the practice of assisting people in need as we know it in the United States did not originate in this country, it is necessary to go back in time to understand social welfare.

Studying social welfare policy history demonstrates that the basis of all current programs and services can be found in the earliest recorded history. The purpose of this chapter is to explore aspects of antiquity and medieval society that underpin current social policies. As a result, social workers will gain an understanding of fundamental concepts of social welfare that will help them design and administer new programs.

ANTIQUITY: THE POOR AND TRADITIONS OF CHARITY

Greek and Roman Society

From a purely chronological standpoint, world history is commonly divided into antiquity (from earliest times to the dissolution of the Roman Empire), Middle Ages (from the fourth century to the discovery of America), the modern times (from the 15th century to the French Revolution), and most modern times (from the 18th century onwards) (Beer, 1929). Each of these periods has specific social, economic, and intellectual features. In antiquity, blood relationships connected people to clans or tribes. These communities lived in common, on the basis of equality, with customs and habits dominating their simple, mostly nomadic, life (Beer, 1929). The art of writing was unknown and the clans or tribes did not describe their social institutions. We are dependent on travelers who orally conveyed traditions for our knowledge of this period.

It is important to note that the majority of travelers were men. Because women were confined to the home where their work went unnoticed, much of their voice has been lost. They could not inherit their husband's property or incur debt, and their legal actions were nonbinding (Day, 1997). Girls were first married at the age of 14, and many died during childbirth. Consequently, generalizations were often made about Greece and the Roman Empire supported by male-dominated evidence. These men related primarily to lands stretching from the Black Sea and the Rhine and Danube regions to North Africa.

During antiquity, the ideals associated with democracy and philanthropy essential to Western social welfare emerged. Protection and hospitality were traditions of antiquity that relate to social welfare practices. For example, Hammurabi, the famed ruler of Babylonia some two thousand years before Christ, decreed the protection of widows and orphans, and the weak against the powerful. Similarly, Buddhism, founded in 400 B.C., taught that all other forms of righteousness "are not worth the sixteenth part of the heart through love and charity" (Trattner, 1999, p. 1).

In ancient Greece and Rome it was common for villagers to provide both shelter and food to travelers in exchange for stories from far off lands. Such cooperation with fellow men followed the words of Aristotle (384–322 B.C.) who spoke that it was more blessed to give than to receive. Aristotle used words such as "philanthropy" and "charity" to describe concepts of love and humanity while the famed Roman, Cicero (106–43 B.C.), urged for universal justice and equal treatment of rich and poor people.

Acts of charity were ways of acquiring honor within the social and political arenas of Greek and Roman life. Linked to charity was the Greek and Roman notion of poverty. The "poor" were defined as the vast majority of people in any city-state who, having no claim to the income of a large estate, lacked the degree of independence regarded as essential to a life of leisure. A distinction was made between poor people and *ptochos,* the Greek term for beggars (Hands, 1968, 63–64). As suggested by Plutarch's quotation, neither the Greeks nor the Romans felt obligated to provide charity to beggars:

> But if I give to you, you would proceed to beg all the more; it was the man who gave to you in the first place who made you idle and so is responsible for your disgraceful state.

The commodities commonly distributed to poor people were corn, oil, and cash. Commodity distributions, which were seen as "doles" for people in particular need, were made in response to special events, including emergencies related to the food supplies. Detailed distribution processes provided for a set of officers to oversee the lending of money, the purchase of the corn or oil, and the enforcement of special provisions for people who were traveling or ill at the time of distribution (Jones, 1940).

The distribution of food is currently used in the United States as a method to relieve distress as are other forms of assistance used by the Greeks and Romans including pensions for people with physical disabilities and institutions for orphans and other people who require custodial care. However, other commonly used methods such as infanticide, concubinage and slavery are anathema to the American social welfare system.

Jewish Traditions

Perhaps more important for the history of American philanthropy and social welfare are the Jewish doctrines that teach the duty of giving and the right of those in need to receive. Charity, justice, and loving kindness are the basic precepts of Judaism (Van Wormer, 1997). To honor and respond to people in need is to honor God. These concepts are codified in the Talmud, the second great collection of Jewish scripture after the Torah, and form the basis of Judaic altruism (Day, 1997). Sensitivity in giving was traced directly to the Scriptures and rules for sparing the embarrassment of the poor were derived in Rabbinical literature of the early centuries and middle ages from the verses:

> Blessed is he that considereth the poor:
> The Lord will deliver him in the day of evil.
>
> Psalm 12:1

> You shall give to him (your brother) freely, and your heart shall not be grudging when you give to him because for this the Lord your God will bless you in all your work and in all that you undertake.
>
> Deuteronomy 15:7–10

Jews displayed consideration for the poor by discouraging begging from door to door and by refusing to force poor people to draw tickets from an urn to receive relief (Abrahams, 1896). Rather, a common form of charity was the purchase of food to be retailed to the poor at cost prices in times of scarcity. The distribution of food in this manner was gradually superseded by methods such as receiving poor travelers in the homes of the rich, providing food in communal inns or hostelries, and encouraging benevolent societies to fed the poor.

The Talmud prescribes exactly how charitable funds are to be collected and distributed, including the appointments of *gabbaim,* or tax collectors, to administer the system (Trattner, 1999). Collections were made periodically and each person was expected to contribute according to his or her means. No one escaped from this duty, including children and women. Even the poor were taxed for relief since charity was considered a universal duty.

The Talmud distinguished between alms, which meant a gift of money or property, and charity of love, which meant a gift of one's self. The following passage from the Mishnah (Peah, i) describes charity kindliness:

> These are things the fruit of man enjoys in his world, while the stock remains for him for the world to come; viz.: honouring father and mother, the practice of charity, timely attendance at the house of study morning and evening, hospitality to wayfarers, visiting the sick, dowering the bride, attending to the dead to the grave, devotion in prayer, and making peace between man and his fellow; but the study of the Law is equal to them all.

In terms of charity, Jews contributed to the poor box and relief on special occasions such as marriages and seder anniversaries. This tradition was so regular that it could not be considered voluntary. Gifts of a more voluntary nature included funds accumulated from legacies. Charity of love often pertained to one's family which had priority over other poor people. This obligation for family members to aid each other was accepted as unconditional principle. The obligation of financial support involved the raising of relative orphans and arranging for their marriages (Katz, 1993).

Islamic Philanthropy

Islam was founded by the prophet Muhammad who died in 632 A.D. Information on social welfare in the ancient Islamic world is sketchy. Although Arabic, Persian, and Turkish literature contain references to philanthropic individuals and institutions, there is no comprehensive history of Islamic social services (Stillman, 1975). The prophet Muhammad was orphaned at a young age. The scriptures that he brought to the Arabs, the Koran, commands believers to demonstrate charity to widows, orphans, wayfarers, and the unfortunate, and specifies "right" ways of giving (Sura, 1337). Almsgiving is one of the Five Pillars of Islam, and those that are charitable are promised paradise (Stillman, 1975; Trattner, 1999).

The mosque was the principal Islamic institution that supported social services and charity to the poor. Much like the synagogue in Judaism, the mosque represented far more than a house of worship. Public lavatories and water basins for ablutions and public drinking were located in mosques and supported socialization of Muslims in the city-states. On occasion, mosques provided temporary housing, served as hospitals, and distributed food (Hamarneh, 1962).

Similar to the Greeks, Romans, and Jews, individual acts of charity were prevalent in the classical Islamic world. At the conclusion of the month of Ramadan, every believer who possessed more than the bare necessities of life distributed food to the less fortunate (Stillman, 1975). In addition, families of means had a long-term commitment to a needy family and would provide charitable gifts on specific dates throughout the year (Lane, 1923).

Christianity

Christianity reflects a blending of Greek thought, Jewish teachings, and resurgence of ideas on class and gender equality. Jesus reminded Jewish society of its prophetic past and spiritual teachings regarding the poor and oppressed people. Both men and women served as his disciples. As the spiritual leader of Christianity, Jesus revised marriage laws to give women protection against divorce, enforced monogamy on men and women, and regarded women as spiritual beings.

The care of the needy became a major activity in Christian churches. Slaves, widows, orphans, and prisoners were provided aid. Women were actively engaged in charitable works, opening hospitals and religious communities. Christian charity was organized and church members were expected to give regular donations to the poor box.

Christianity became legal in 361 A.D. with the conversion of the Roman emperor Constantine who believed that religion should be responsible for the needy. Under Constantine's reign, state, church, and voluntary social welfare functions overlapped in an attempt to releave the poor of need. Endowed foundations provided interest for charitable use and the relationship between good works and salvation was strengthened through religious doctrine including scripture from the Bible:

> Thus, when you give alms, sound no trumpet before you, as the hypocrites do in the synagogues and in the streets, that they may be praised by men. Truly, I say to you, they have their reward. But when you give, do not let your left hand know what your right hand is doing, so that your alms may be in secret; and your Father who sees in secret will reward you.
>
> Matthew 6:2–4

Themes Emerging from Antiquity

Several themes begin to emerge from the review of social welfare in antiquity. First, charity supported by individuals and developing institutions, was linked to religious duty. People with means were expected to give to people in need who were to receive assistance without guilt. Second, charitable acts were organized at the local level and distributed primarily to people from the area. Third, in both Greece and Rome, distinctions were made between the poor and beggars. The poor included people who attempted to support themselves and fell short due to circumstances such as age or infirmity. Beggars, in contrast, made little attempt to be self-sufficient. Finally, the giver's actions were often self-regarding in the sense there was the expectation of some sort of return in the form of favor from the gods, an outstanding reputation, or everlasting salvation.

It is difficult to analyze Greek and Roman societies from a strengths perspective. Although religions worked ceaselessly to alleviate the misery of the poor, the ruling elite maintained a politic and economic structure of oppression. Poor people had no means to negotiate their needs or influence their environment. As humankind moved toward an economy based on class stratification and gender oppression, religion and politics converged to control rather than to assist the poor. Social welfare did not reflect the needs and wants or poor people but rather served as a means to support structures that perpetuated oppression.

MIDDLE AGES SOCIETY

The Middle Ages, from the fall of the Roman Empire until the Industrial Revolution, seem remote from our contemporary world. However, as we study the social welfare traditions of this period, we come to understand its influence on our modern world and the social work profession.

For social workers, the study of medieval poor law sheds light on the relationship between religious, political, and economic developments. In particular, church law is critical to understanding medieval attitudes and responses to poverty. Church tenets were essential to England, the country most influential in American social welfare. Consequently, England and English Poor Law are the primary focus of this section.

The Church and Social Welfare

By the sixth century, both men and women had established religious orders whose primary duty was to care for the disadvantaged. Their monasteries and abbeys evolved into medieval hospitals, which provided medical assistance but also housed and cared for travelers, widows, orphans, the aged, and the poor. By the eighth century all church members were required to tithe in support of the bishop, the parish clergy, church upkeep, and the poor.

Women were increasingly involved in services to the poor under church auspices. They cared for elderly and indigent patients in convents and abbeys. In time, nuns provided refuges for unmarried women and women intellectuals (Day, 1997). Since the church considered women to have spiritual inadequacies, the activities of nuns were restricted to convents; however, some were permitted to engage in community work. Whether in convents or involved in community work, nuns took vows of poverty and served the poor in both urban and rural areas.

The cannon law books and the writings of canonists are critical to the investigation of medieval poor law. In particular, the Decretum, a compilation of papal decrees, cannons of the church council, and commentaries of church lawyers codified in the twelfth century is considered the authoritative source of law for Christians. According to the Decretum, Christian social welfare resembled Hebrew doctrine. Specifically, the underlying principal of both Christian and Hebrew indicated that poverty was not a crime and evidence of need overrode all other concerns. Further, the needy or *miserabiles personae*, "wretched persons" had a right to assistance, and those who had the means had a duty to provide it (Tierney, 1959; Trattner, 1999).

By the 13th century, the rich had to support the poor by law. Poverty was not considered a crime but a life condition. Rich people were obligated to care for the poor as society in general and the church in particular became increasingly critical of private wealth.

Feudal Society

William the Conqueror introduced feudalism to England when he invaded in 1066 (Van Wormer, 1997). Feudalism, a system of government in which those who possessed landed estates also held political power, was firmly in place by the eleventh century. The majority of people lived on feudal manors as serfs, protected by lords or masters against the hardships of life including infirmities, famines, and old age. In strict law, serfs were incapable of possessing property; their earnings were their master's. Thus, serfs were bound to the soil. They were distinctly above the slave, yet no less distinctly below the freeman (Coulton, 1931). Figure 2.1 shows a typical serf's cottage. The following excerpt from Aelfric's Colloquy, written in 1005 by a monk of Canterbury, describes the daily tasks of various occupations under feudalism. The format is a dialogue between a master and his several pupils:

> *M: What do you say plowman, how do you do your work?*
> *N: Oh sir, I work very hard. I go out at dawn, driving the oxen to the field, and I yoke them to the plough; however hard the winter I dare not stay at home for fear of my master; but, having yoked the oxen and made the plough-share and coulter fast to the plough, every day I have to plough a whole acre or more.*
> *O: Have you any companions?*
> *P: I have a boy who drives the oxen with the goad, and he is even now hoarse with cod and shouting.*
> *Q: What more do you do in the day?*
> *R: A good deal more, to be sure. I have to fill the oxen's cribs with hay, and give them water, and carry the dung outside.*
> *S: Oh, oh, it is hard work.*
> *T: Yes, it is hard work, because I am not a free man.*

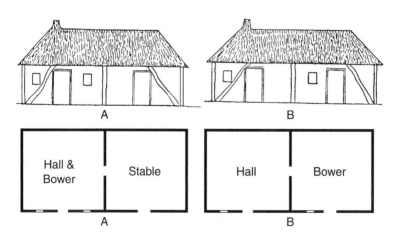

FIGURE 2.1

Sketches of a Serf's Cottage

The diagram depicts two different types of cottages. Cottage A suggests that the hall and bower comprised a single room separated by a partition and door for a stable inhabited by animals such as sheep and cows. Cottage B comprises two rooms. The animals shared the hall with serfs.

Both cottages contained 30 feet in length and 14 feet in width, with corner-posts, three doors and two windows (Coulton, 1931).

If this is the self-description of the ploughman what was the expectations of the lord in terms of duties of the serf? *Fleta* (Henley, 1510), the late 13th century manual, provides such descriptions. The following excerpt describes a role assigned to women, that of dairymaid:

> The dairymaid should be chaste and honest and faithful, laborious in her dairy duties, wise and neat-handed; not lavish but of a thrifty nature. For she must not suffer any man or woman to come to her in the dairy and carry aught away which might make her render the less perfect account. Now it is her work to receive the vessels proper for her office with a written indenture when she leaves, and in this record it must be noted on what day she began work. She must receive the milk tallies, and make cheese and butter according to the tale of the gallons; she must keep ward over the poultry, and render to the Bailiff and Reeve frequent account of the profits arising therefrom; nor will some Auditors allow her to account for less than twelve pence a year for every goose and four pence for every hen. Moreover it is her duty to winnow or sift, to cover up the fire, and to do such little petty works when she can find time for them.

(Henley, 1510, 94–95)

The description of serf's work highlights the conformity of medieval society. People were born into a position, knew their tasks and obligations and were expected to remain loyal to their master. Serfs lived in small and elected village members to negotiate with the bailiff matters pertaining to animals and the farming (Snell, 1982).

The relationship between serfs and their masters or noblemen was based on mutual obligation. Noblemen provided food and other necessities for life in return for the labor and loyalty of serfs. Families were responsible for the care of children, aging people, and persons with mental and physical infirmities. When family resources were inadequate or depleted the church provided food and lodging. Based on canon law, the rights of the poor to receive care was upheld through the collection of tithes. Thus, medieval society assumed a nonpunitive approach to relief of poverty.

Hospitals were an important source of aid to the needy during the Middle Ages. Medieval hospitals provided medical assistance to the ill, sheltered travelers, and served as a home for orphans, older people, and destitute people. Often situated in close proximity to monasteries, hospitals were found along main routes of travel. Eventually they were located in cities and were administered by municipal authorities, establishing a formal relationship between ecclesiastical and secular charity (Trattner, 1994).

Feudalism Gives Way to Capitalism

Ecclesiastical charity worked tolerably well until the mid-14th century. However, problems arose that drew the secular government into providing for the poor. For one thing, changes in the economic environment, spurred by a developing international market, affected both commerce and agriculture. A greater number of the population earned their living as craftsmen, working for wages in towns. As crafts such as cloth making moved from home industry to organized production, people of all ages, including children were hired as pieceworkers in their homes. For women, cloth making took on an added importance in commerce with the invention of the spinning wheel and "piecing out" became a way of life for poor women. Spinning was so identified with women that the female side of the family was known as the "distaff side" or the "spindle side" (Gies & Gies, 1978).

Although the majority of people still lived by agricultural means, changes occurred in rural life associated with the breakup of the manorial system. As in commerce, agriculture was developing a money economy and the beginnings of capital investment, credit, interest, and rent (Tierney, 1959). The dissolution of feudalism and the manorial system increased individual freedom, but agricultural laborers experienced mounting uncertainty and serious hardship.

Another problem that increased secular involvement in charity was the Industrial Revolution and the subsequent development of the factory system. The Industrial Revolution brought the decline of rural handicrafts and the rise of urban masses with limited skills. For the first time workers experienced cyclical unemployment over which they had little control.

The difficult employment situation was further complicated by England's Black Death, or bubonic plague, which occurred in 1348–1349 after sweeping across Continental Europe. By 1400 the population of England was reduced by approximately 50%; the result was an unprecedented shortage of labor. However, the decrease in population also led to a decrease in trade, so many localities experienced temporary unemployment in the midst of a shortage of workers (Tierney, 1959). Available workers seized the opportunity to demand higher wages and release from work contracts. The tension between workers and employers produced widespread peasant unrest and increased vagrancy as people wandered from town to town searching for better conditions.

In response to the mounting economic and social strife, major secular statues were introduced. The Ordinance of Laborers of 1349 prevented laborers wandering away from their work to seek higher wages. To enforce this act, the giving of alms to able-bodied beggars was prohibited. An act of 1388 specified rules that prevented laborers from leaving their place of work and provided for punishment of able-bodied beggars who were forbidden to wander as vagrants. Three years later, in 1391, a statue specified the role of the secular government to secure effective enforcement of existing cannon law:

> Because divers damages and hindrance sometimes have happened, and daily do happen to the parishioners of divers places by the appropriation of benefices of the same places, it is agreed and assented . . . that the diocesan of the place upon appropriation of such churches shall ordain, according to the vague of such charities, a convenient sum of money to be paid and distributed yearly . . . to the poor parishioners of the said churches, in aid of their living and sustenance for ever; and also that the vicar be well and sufficiently endowed.

(Richard II,c.6. Cited by Hartridge, Viscarages, p. 157)

In the 15th century, the enclosure movement further complicated the economic situation by increasing the number of wandering vagrants. This movement was tied to the growth of the woolens industry. Specifically, as the demand and price for wool increased, landowners responded by turning fields into pastures and raising sheep. This shift in land usage reduced the feudal system of tillage and led to the destruction of rural homesteads forcing people into wage labor.

In 1517, Martin Luther, a Catholic priest, posted 95 theses on the door of a church in Wittenberg, Germany. Luther's action resulted in his excommunication and a revolution against the corruption of the church. The Protestant Reformation dissolved the monasteries and other church property held by Henry VIII, forcing the people who had lived or had been employed in ecclesiastical institutions into the ranks of wanderers and vagabonds.

On the secular side, the Act of 1531 enacted severe penalties against vagrants and required justices of the peace to register the names of poor, aged, and impotent people (Tierney, 1959). This was followed in 1536 with the act that provided for regular collections dedicated to the poor in parish churches and specified what parish funds should be used for in regard to relief. Although not a new feature of ecclesiastical responsibilities, the overlay of an act of Parliament with canon law was indeed significant. Further new departures from secular law were found in the act of 1552 that denounced to the bishop people who refused to give contributions to the poor and in Elizabeth's act of 1563 that provided for a compulsory contribution if the bishop's exhortations were unsuccessful. Thus, by the 16th century, acts of parliament were widely used to provide for regular compulsory contributions to the poor and to denounce uncooperative parishioners to ecclesiastical authorities. In taking over the system of poor relief, the state acknowledged that society had to provide for the poor through public authority.

Elizabethan Poor Law of 1601

New social contracts were established to mitigate life's hardships and to stabilize community life. In the 1590s, between one fourth and one third of the populations of most English towns could not find work, and many starved or froze to death (Day, 1997). It was in this context that the modern institution of social welfare emerged by way of the renowned Elizabethan Poor Law of 1601 that was officially called an Act for the Relief of the Poor. These laws legalized and formalized England's responsibility for the poor by defining social welfare as part of the national labor policy. The environment of the famous statue reflects the conditions of the 1590s, a period marked by food scarcity, inflation, and social disorder. Fearful of insurrection, with no standing army to provide a sense of security, Parliament was forced to act.

It was estimated that by 1587 over 10,000 persons roamed the highways and countryside, out of work and often engaged in crime to live (Fletcher,

1970). In response, poor law legislation was passed in 1597–1598. The act of 1597 placed the care of the poor under the duties of the churchwarden and four overseers appointed by the justice of the peace in each town or parish. These five people were required to seek out the poor, provide housing for them, estimate their expenses, and tax the local residents accordingly (Fletcher, 1970). Taxpayers were forced to pay taxes or face imprisonment. The able-bodied poor, if found, were required to work. If they refused to do so, they were sent to the House of Correction.

In 1598, a companion act of legislation addressed the problems of the able-bodied unemployed. The whipping provision was punishment for those vagrants found begging. For beggars thought to be dangerous, the law provided for the deportation of those "rogues (who) shall appear to be dangerous to the inferior sort of people where they shall be taken, or be such as will not be reformed of their roguish kind of life" (Fletcher, 1970; 11).

The Elizabethan Poor Laws of 1601 combined the 1597 and 1598 statues to meet the needs of the poor and to stabilize the country. The laws introduced no measures that had not been introduced in legislation in a half-century, but they did provide a guideline for system of relief that England would follow until the mid-19th century. Of particular interest to social workers is Section VII of the laws which states:

> And be it further enacted, That the father and grandfather, and the mother and grandmother, and the children of very poor, old, blind, lame an impotent person, or other poor person not able to work, being of a sufficient ability, shall, at their own charges, relieve and maintain every such poor person in that manner, and according to that rate, as by the justices of peace of that county where such sufficient persons dwell, or the grater number of them, at their general quarter-sessions shall be assessed; (2) upon greater pain that every one of them shall forfeit twenty shillings every month which they shall fail therein.
>
> (An Act for the Poor, 43 Elizabeth, 1601)

This section specifies the measures to relieve want and suffering in the family unit. Parents had the obligation to support their children and grandchildren from poverty. In return, children were responsible for the care of their parents. According to Leiby (1987), critical features of the law included:

- Defining the role of the parish or local government in providing relief to those in need.
- Establishing overseers of the poor to relieve suffering and to monitor aid.
- Giving overseers the power to raise funds for the poor.
- Defining government relief as the measure of last resort used only after assistance has been provided by family and friends.
- Describing the worthy poor as people who were sick, aged, orphaned or disabled.

- Establishing workhouses and deportation in response to those people who appear to have the wherewithal to support themselves through their work.

Thus, the Elizabethan Poor Law contained harsh, regressive features such as requiring vagrants to work, and if they refused, placing them in a house of correction. However, there were constructive measures including state responsibility to relieve want and suffering of the poor. It also concluded that helpless persons deserved assistance. In addition, categories of dependency were defined-children, and the impotent and authorized services for each category: apprenticeships for children; and home (outdoor) or institutional (indoor) relief for the "worthy" poor (Trattner, 1999).

Institutions, including orphanages, almshouses, workhouses, and prisons, were constructed and operated in a similar manner. Comprising little more than shed-like structures divided into small rooms, most institutions had neither heat nor insulation. Sanitation facilities were limited, and the daily menu offered little more than watery gruel. Health and medical services were virtually nonexistent and disease ran rampant. House overseers or managers who received a flat fee plus room and board in exchange for their work ran the institutions. The vast majority of institutions were not well run and as a result became cluttered with unwanted or undesirable people.

A Strengths Perspective

The Elizabethan Poor Laws of 1601 merged the secular and ecclesiastical principles of centuries. Threatened by increased social and economic instability, the statue's first purpose was one of social control; control of the poor, ablebodied, unemployed, and vagrants. Measures of control included institutions, forced work, and residency requirements. Labeling the deserving and nondeserving poor controlled, through stigma, the perceptions of people and their needs. Fear of deportation, harsh punishment, and public humiliation added elements of control to the duties of local public officials. And the measure did not contain appeal procedures for recipients of relief if they left unfairly treated.

In contrast to a strengths perspective, the Elizabethan Poor Laws neglected to:

1. Place the problems associated with poverty in their proper context. The environment and working conditions of poor people were overlooked. Rather, conditions of poverty were institutionalized so that levels of support could be established, costs of food, clothing and shelter monitored, and work behavior closely supervised.

2. View the social dimensions of resource distribution. Instead of enabling people to move beyond the limitations of their situations, the character of poor people was of central concern. Poor people were either "deserving" and required supervision or "nondeserving" and constitutionally defective.

3. Mobilize resources to move beyond the problems associated with poverty. Private donors, churches, foundations, and guilds augmented the poor laws through charities, but they were restricted from giving indiscriminately so that the poor could leave local employment. Whipping or imprisonment was the punishment for people who would not work under conditions specified by the government.

There were, however, strengths or positive aspects associated with the Poor Laws. Unemployment relief was provided, as was in-kind assistance such as food, clothing, and wood. The statue made public the needs of the poor resulting in an increase in charitable contributions. Thus, whether motivated by the feudal Catholic traditions or the Protestant emphasis on giving as a moral duty, affluent persons gave money to many charities, including 800 hospitals in England (Jansson, 2001).

The Elizabethan Poor Laws provided the framework of the welfare system in England and eventually in the United States. The statute defined basic concepts related to relief; namely, family responsibility, settlement or residency requirements, and local responsibility. Of the three concepts perhaps the most complex is local responsibility because it is here that questions about moral behavior and personal freedom are raised.

That the concepts included in the Elizabethan Poor Laws have endured as legislation and as central issues in social welfare policy, is indicative of the central importance given to the family unit. The emphasis on local responsibility is reflective of the enduring belief that each community knows best how to handle its own problems. Settlement concepts—belonging to a parish, residence with intent to remain, and citizenship in a country—continued to reflect fear of those who may be somehow different in color, life-style, or values.

SUMMARY

Social work students might consider antiquity and medieval society as remote periods of history in relation to social work practice. However, this chapter connected relief measure of the ancient world and medieval society with concepts of today's social welfare system. Concepts such as deserving and nondeserving poor, indoor and outdoor relief, residency requirements, family responsibilities, and local control are as relevant to discussions of poor relief in the 21st century as they were centuries ago.

The Elizabethan Poor Laws specified the role and responsibilities of overseers, the forerunners of social workers. Much like social workers of today, overseers requested funds from local government officials to address the needs of the poor. They were also responsible for the care of the poor, especially those people who could not care for themselves, such as children, older persons, and people with significant physical and mental challenges. Overseers met on a regular basis to discuss poor relief and to report back to local officials on perceived needs. Thus, overseers, similar to current social workers, were committed to the poor but obligated to public officials.

The emerging social welfare system did not attempt to eliminate certain kinds of difference, those defined or created by people in power. Rather, in contrast to a strengths perspective, social welfare emphasized and assigned social status to a person's deficits, differences, and defects. By doing so, opportunities and motivations for far-reaching change were suppressed.

REFERENCES

Abrahams, I. (1896). *Jewish life in the middle ages.* Philadelphia: The Jewish Publication Society of America.

Beer, M. (1929). *Social struggles in antiquity.* New York: International Publishers.

Coulton, G. G. (1931). *The medieval village.* Cambridge, UK: Cambridge University Press.

Day, P. J. (1997). *New history of social welfare.* Needham Heights, MA: Allyn & Bacon.

Fletcher, J. L. (1970, Spring). Enlightenment England: The background and development of its poor law system. *Enlightenment Essays, 1–2,* 1–13.

Gies, F. & Gies, J. (1978). *Women in the Middle Ages.* New York: Barnes & Noble.

Hands, A. S. R. (1968). *Charities and social aide in Greece and Rome.* Ithaca, NY: Cornell University Press.

Henley, W. (1510). Extracts from *Fleta.* In F. H. Cripps-Day, *The Manor Farm.* (1931). London: Bernard Quaritch, LTD.

The Holy Bible. Deuteronomy. The text conformable to that of the edition of 1611. Philadelphia: N. J. Holman Co.

Hamarneh, S. (1962, July). Development of hospitals in Islam. *Journal of the History of Medicine and Allied Sciences.* 367–374.

Jansson, B. S. (2001). The reluctant welfare state. Belmont, CA: Brooks/Cole.

Jones, A. H. M. (1940). *The Greek City from Alexander to Justinian.* Oxford: The Claredon Press.

Katz, J. (1993). *Traditions and crisis: Jewish society at the end of the Middle Ages.* New York: New York University Press.

Lane, E. W. (1923). *The manners and customs of the modern Egyptians.* London. Methuen.

Leiby, J. (1987). History of social welfare. In A. Minahan et al. (Eds.), *Encyclopedia of social work*, 18th ed. Silver Spring, MD: NASW Press. 755–777.

Mollat, M. (1986). *The poor in the Middle Ages.* New Haven, CT: Yale University Press.

Richard II,c.6. Cited by Hartridge, Viscarages. p. 157.

Stillman, N. A. (1975, Spring). Charity and social services in medieval Islam. *Societas, 5,* 105–16.

Snell, K. D. M. (1985). *Annals of the laboring poor: Social change agrarian England, 1660–1900.* Cambridge, UK: Cambridge University Press.

Sura 2:215, 234,240: 13:22 and 35:29. Egyptian edition of 1337 A.H.

Tierney, B. (1959). *Medieval poor law: A sketch of canonical theory and its application in England.* Berkley: University of California Press.

Trattner, W. I. (1999). *From poor law to welfare state: A history of social welfare in America.* New York: The Free Press.

Van Wormer, K. (1997). *Social welfare a world view.* Chicago: Nelson-Hall Publishers.

Early America:
A Time of Need

Early America, from colonial times to the America Revolution, is often described in terms of economic opportunity and social mobility. However, a careful look at social conditions questions the validity of this popular opinion. Studies present clear evidence that poverty was a major problem in 18th century America, especially in villages and towns (Nash, 1976). For example, between 1630 and 1645, Plymouth Colony reported 57 permanent relief cases in a population ranging from 500 to 700 persons (Abramovitz, 1989; p. 75). Frequent wars with Native Americans; recurring epidemics of yellow fever, small pox, and dysentery; the hazards of fishing and the consequent loss of life at sea all gave rise to economic need. Severe weather patterns and isolation also threatened physical well being and economic prosperity.

Since gender profiles of the poor are rarely described, it is not widely known that the povertization of women dates to colonial time. In some towns women comprised from one third to one half of the town's paupers (Abramovitz, 1996). The poverty associated with women was based largely on martial status and lack of economic opportunities. Adult white women faced poverty if they did not marry, married a poor man, or were widowed. In such cases, women frequently relied on family members or the town for support. Most African American women were enslaved at this time, though a small group of the free African American population secured some means.

Influenced by English statues, religious doctrine, and Old World traditions, colonial leaders accepted the presence of poverty and the obligation of family and community to aid the poor. The colonial response to hardships mirrored the principles of the Elizabethan Poor Law of 1601 and the Settlement Act of 1662: local responsibility, and the residency requirement of legal settlement (Axinn & Levin, 1992). Recipients of relief were most often the sick, the disabled, widows with children—all essentially unemployable.

This chapter examines Colonial America and its social welfare system. For social workers, this period of history is significant because the prevailing attitudes and practices toward the poor were quite different from those Americans eventually came to adopt. For the most part, the colonists accepted the prevalence of poverty as more a life condition than an individual shortcoming. The colonists, relatively small in number, needed one another for success in enterprises and, therefore, had a stake in the contribution and well being of each other. As a matter of individual self-interest, colonists maintained a watch over neighbor and community affairs. Local officials, without apparent fear of fraud or dependency, provided for those who could not care for themselves.

COLONIAL AMERICA'S RESPONSE TO NEED

The Colonists

The majority of English colonists migrated to America to escape the life of a peasant in Europe, seek fortune or adventure, or gain religious freedom. Resources in America were plentiful but labor was scarce, so concerted efforts were made to populate the colonies. By 1640, thousands of English colonies were established in New England. Caves or primitive houses served as homes because colonists did not have the tools or skills necessary to turn logs into lumber. It was expected that all family members would work in the house and with crops as needed. Strenuous work was promoted by religion, for idleness was considered a sign of Satan. In Massachusetts and other colonies, a wife's refusal to labor obediently and frugally was considered grounds for divorce.

Immigrant family groups settled New England and Pennsylvania, setting the stage for community democracies such as public meetings. People familiar with the English manor system settled the South. They readily accepted the burden of *noblesse oblige*, taking government and public responsibility (Day, 1997). The ideal of serfs and lords was also imported, making the concept of slavery easy.

By the late 1600s, approximately 90% of the colonists were farmers who tended small, isolated farms. Farming families were self-sufficient supplying their own food, clothing, and equipment, education, entertainment, and health care. Based on a patriarchal hierarchy, all family members were expected to offer contributions to the family upkeep. Large families were a necessity; consequently, childbearing was viewed as a productive contribution to the family economy. In the case of the husband's death, the wife assumed the economic support of the family.

According to Abramovitz (1996), women constituted about a third of the early immigrants to North America. Many of the women were kidnapped, providing the new country with much-needed wives and laborers. Married white women could own property and sue in courts, and judges often defended them against personal abuse. Women could also receive land grants as head of families.

Free African Americans and slaves comprised the colonial African American population. For a brief period, the colonial leaders tolerated the increase of a free African American population and treated Africans similarly to white indentured servants. Free African Americans voted, mingled with whites, held elective offices, owned property and became slave owners (Abramovitz, 1989).

Colonial law held slaves to be the property and responsibility of their masters, and free African Americans relied largely on themselves or their own self-help systems of support. Most colonial towns attempted to protect themselves against the cost of maintaining members of the African American population. Some masters provided their freed slaves with land or other resources; other could not afford this and simply freed dependent or unproductive slaves to avoid the cost of care.

Interracial coupling, rather widespread in colonial America, threatened to make African Americans dependent on the town. The intermingling of the races occurred across class lines but was especially great among African American slaves and indentured servants who often worked in close proximity. White leaders gradually banned interracial couples because it was considered a threat to white supremacy and to the institution of slavery. Laws punishing interracial coupling proliferated in the early 18th century for these reasons but also to reduce the number of mulatto children born outside of marriage who might need support from the town.

The Presence of Poverty

Those people who came to the colonies were of moderate or poor means. Once in America, life was full of hardship and deprivation so that many people lived in poverty. As a result, each colony soon had to address an array of needs associated with poverty such as lack of food, shelter, clothing, and medical care.

Poverty in Colonial America was closely related to urbanization. After 1740, as immigration increased population growth, the number and needs of the poor became more observable. For example, one recent study of the social structure of colonial Boston found the class of laborers without land increasing twice as rapidly as population as a whole (Henretta, 1965). Similarly, Philadelphia, the largest colonial city after 1750, experienced the negative social effects of rapid urban growth including poverty and associated factors including disease and crime.

Nash's (1976) study on poor relief in Philadelphia provides detailed information on poverty in Colonial America based on data contained in the Philadelphia Poor Records. As presented in Table 3.1, poverty did not become a serious problem in Philadelphia until the Seven Years War. During the war, the city experienced wartime boom with full employment, but when the war ended so did much of the prosperity.

The result was a sudden decrease in trade and the onset of a period of economic depression. The depression was compounded with thousands of new-

| TABLE 3.1 | POOR RELIEF IN PHILADELPHIA, 1717 TO 1775 |

Year	Population	Poor Tax	Expenditures	Expense/ 1,000 Pop.	No. Recipients	No. Poor/ 1,000 Pop.	Expense/ Recipients
1709	2,500	1 1/2d*	£ 158	£ 59	13	4.8	£ 12–0
1739	9,100	3d	800	83	[80]	[8.3]	[10–0]
1756–1758	15,600	3d	1,175	72	[110]	[6.7]	[10–9]
1765	18,100	5d	2,385	123	310	16.0	7–14
1768–1771	19,700	6d	3,681	175	590	28.1	6–5
1772–1775	22,300	6d	3,868	163	720	30.3	5–7

*d = denarius or one penny

Nash, G. B. (1976). Poverty and poor relief in Pre-Revolutionary Philadelphia. *William and Mary Quarterly,* 33 (January), p. 9.

comers to Philadelphia each year and the unusually cold winter of 1761–1762 (Williams, 1973). In response to this dire environment, Quaker merchants established a "Committee to Alleviate the Miseries of the Poor" (Nash, 1976). The committee record listed 329 "objects of Charity who received wood, blankets, and stockings in the southern half of the city" (Nash, 1976, p. 13).

By the end of the 17th century, it was quite evident not only that poverty was a natural product of the human situation and an inevitable concomitant of urban growth, but also that it would get worse (Trattner, 1999). Although the poor increased in number and skilled administration was lacking, most communities expressed genuine sympathy for the needy and tried to improve their methods and facilities for helping them.

Colonial Social Welfare

In response to the economic and physical conditions of the colonists, the principles of English Poor Law including local responsibility, family responsibility, and settlement laws became the cornerstones of Colonial America's relief system. Local responsibility stipulated that relief was the duty of small government units. For example, acting on orders from the colony's new proprietor, New York initiated a comprehensive legal code called the "Duke's Laws" (Mohl, 1969). The code did several things including: a) dividing the New York City area (called Yorkshire) into parishes; b) selecting eight overseers of the poor and two churchwardens within each parish; and c) stipulating public taxation to support the poor (Mohl, 1969; Axinn & Levin, 1992).

Throughout the colonies, provincial legislation established the framework for the Poor Law administration. Local overseers were appointed to determine methods of relief, investigate applicants for assistance, distribute aid to the needy, and enforce the settlement laws. Poor people were often required to wear badges of blue or red cloth with large letters, designating their dependent status and indicative of the social stigma attached to public poor relief.

The family as a social entity was not recognized as a unit to be helped. Rather, the provisions of relief established categories to serve children, people who were old, people with physical and mental disabilities, and able-bodied individuals. Axinn and Levin (1992) suggest that "family responsibility" is a misinterpretation of Poor Law intent for the laws designated relative, rather than family, responsibility for support. Families that were not self-sufficient were not simply considered unsuccessful but a threat to the economic and moral good of society. It was thought that such families could not be expected to prepare and educate children. The colonists, therefore, provided for the placement of children as apprentices for "better educating of youth in honest and profitable trades and manufactures, as also to avoyd (sic) sloath and idleness wherewith such young children are easily corrupted" (Henning, 1823, p. 6).

Settlement Laws flourished throughout the 13 colonies and designated a period of residence as a standard requirement for the receipt of public assistance. The decision to establish local settlement as an eligibility condition for relief reflected the interests of the landed gentry. In supporting this interest the government satisfied the town's concern for minimizing local costs. Also, by limiting the mobility of poor people, the government responded to the interest of landowners and industrialists in maintaining law and order.

Outdoor Relief

The settlement laws reduced the number of poor persons qualified to receive public aid, but towns were still required to provide for poor persons. The assistance available to poor white people varied widely but was generally familial and neighborly. These characteristics coincide with the small size of towns and the centrality of the family to the colonial society but also the absence of other care taking institutions (Abramovitz, 1996; Day, 1997). In most small towns the overseer of the poor knew those in need and could assess the ability of family members to provide care. At the same time, the colonial officials distinguished between the deserving and nondeserving poor based on their compliance with prevailing work and family norms.

Families were the first line of defense against poverty, and colonial poor laws held families responsible for supporting their immediate relatives. Parents and grandparents were required to provide for adult children and to support their elderly parents. The local government assumed responsibility only when these family members could not.

During this early period, the most common method of aiding the poor was "outdoor relief," the provision of aid to people in their own or a neighbor's home. Outdoor relief went primarily to the deserving poor women, who were aged, sick, or disabled. According to Morris (1935), documentation from mayors' court and the records of the vestrymen and church wardens reveal that outdoor relief took many forms: money, firewood, food and provisions, shoes and clothing, and funeral expenses. In many colonies a physician was maintained as "Doctor of the Poor" to provide medical care for the sick poor.

The receipt of outdoor relief enabled deserving poor women to continue to fulfill their responsibilities in the confines of their home. By continuing their work as homemakers, women maintained the family structure at a relatively low cost to the colonial economy (Abramovitz, 1996).

Indoor Relief

The undeserving poor were forced to work in exchange for a place in the poorhouse. Colonial welfare legislation stressed the provision of "indoor relief," that is, care offered in homes other than one's own and, in time, institutions. Patterned after the family, yet considered a place of last resort, the almshouse was typical of all eighteenth-century service institutions. The actual structure, often located well within town boundaries, lacked a distinctive architecture and specially designed administrative procedures. In some localities, almshouses were not constructed. Rather, a local farmhouse or building was bought by the government and used with minor or no renovations.

The family model dominated the almshouse's interior arrangements and its daily routine (Rothman, 1971). The almshouse keeper and his family lived in the house with its residents as they would in a family. Instead of a uniform, residents wore everyday clothing, of ordinary color and make, and similar to what other people in the community would wear. Much like people in a crowded and poor family, sleeping arrangements often involved several people, probably segregated by gender, in a single bed with several beds in one room. The residents of the almshouse ate together with the keeper and his family.

Hospitals

According to Rothman (1971) hospitals for sick people functioned in a similar fashion as almshouses, and in many places the almshouse became an infirmary. The Pennsylvania Hospital, founded in 1751 in Philadelphia, was the first designated hospital in the thirteen colonies. Supported by Benjamin Franklin and a group of Quaker merchants, the hospital assisted Philadelphia's relief system by providing care for the sick-poor of Pennsylvania. The founders of the hospital designated that the institution would first house the ailing poor, who experienced difficulty locating and paying for lodging in Philadelphia. Hospitals also admitted poor residents, whose physical conditions were too involved for family and community care. In time, hospitals became a focal point for illness, physicians became regular and salaried attendants, and soon students were trained there (Rothman, 1971).

Philadelphians were receptive to the idea of a voluntary hospital because the Quaker city recognized the growing number of sick paupers (Williams, 1973). The desire to improve medical practice and knowledge also supported new hospitals. John Bellers (1714), a Quaker who was active in creation of voluntary hospital movement, highlighted the potential of hospitals in the field of medical education, as did Benjamin Franklin's *Gazette* when it discussed that hospitals:

> . . . not only render the physicians and surgeons who attend them still more expert and skillful . . . but afford such speedy and effectual instruction to the young students of both professions, who come from different and remote parts of the country for improvement, that they return with a more ample stock of knowledge in their art, and become blessings to the neighbors in which they fix their residence. (Franklin, 1751, p. 40)

To assure that the Pennsylvania Hospital's purpose to provide for the "useful and laborious" poor was upheld, prospective patients were required to complete a screening process that necessitated each prospective patient to procure a letter signed by an influential person describing his/her case (Williams, 1973). Patients who had recommendations from hospital contributors were given first preference to the hospital's limited beds. Those sick and poor people who were denied hospital admission more than likely turned to the almshouse for assistance.

Prisons

The American colonists addressed criminal behavior with severe and complex measures. Guided by religious definitions and concepts of community, colonists employed punishments that ranged from warning out strangers to capital sentences for multiple offenders (Rothman, 1971). However, just as almshouses and hospitals were not the typical place of services and support, so too the jail was not the primary focus in treating the criminal.

Eighteenth-century criminal codes defined a wide range of punishments such as fines, whippings, stocks, pillar, public cage, banishment, and the gallows. Institutionalization of criminals was rarely ordered alone. Rather, punishments were administered in pairs with fines and whippings the most common consequence for deviant behavior.

The 1770 Walnut Street Jail of Philadelphia, typical of Colonial institutions, resembled a household in both routine and structure. Following the household model, the keeper and his family occupied a room in the jail with the prisoners living in other rooms together. According to Rothman (1971), prisoners did not wear uniforms, cuffs or chains. Since security in the jail was not a priority, escapes were frequent.

Religious and Humanitarian Contributions to Social Welfare

Unlike the churches of England, the religious institutions of Colonial America were too poor and too fragmented to provide very much assistance to the needy. Perhaps the Protestant Church was the most influential religious organization that reflected Colonial American attitudes toward poverty and dependency. Led by the clergy, the Protestant Church attempted to confront poverty with temporary relief. During religious services, sermons included content on the poor, charitable giving, and notions of ministries to the less fortunate.

From a religious perspective, poverty in Colonial America was neither feared nor ignored. Religious organizations considered incidences of poverty as natural and its relief as obligatory and right. Ministers concluded that the poor would always be present in society. Further, they concluded that the presence of poor people was an opportunity for more fortunate people to do good on behalf of others. Poverty actually was a blessing, in that it permitted people to act as the stewards of God's wealth.

In the Quaker colonies along the Delaware, the religious organization spent an enormous amount of time, effort, and money aiding the needy (James, 1963). Founded in England in 1647 by George Fox, the Quakers, looking upon themselves as bound together by love and fellowship, kept informed of worldwide problems of need, first providing assistance to their own, but then to others as well. Quaker meeting houses or congregations maintained a permanent poor fund for use by members. In time of general need or suffering, Quakers were often among the first to raise additional funds for distribution to those in need, whoever or whatever they happened to be (Trattner, 1999).

In 1766 a group of wealthy Quaker merchants proposed a new system of relief for the poor. At the time, Philadelphia was supporting a record 220 paupers in the city's overcrowded almshouse; poor rates were burdensome; and the linen manufactory was proving unprofitable (Nash, 1976). The Quakers proposed to incorporate a group of private citizens who would raise a substantial sum for construction of a large new almshouse and workhouse, and in return, would be given nearly complete control over the management of the poor. Calling themselves the "Contributors to the Relief and Employment of the Poor the City of Philadelphia, Southwark, Moyamensing, Passyunk and the Northern Liberties," the promoters of this organization modeled it on the Hospital for the Sick (Nash, 1976). The "Bettering House" as it was called, consisted of an almshouse for the aged and disabled and a workhouse for the able-bodied poor. It represented Colonial America's attempt to combine an act of charity with a practical approach to reduce the costs associated with providing for the poor. Table 3.2 shows the number of patients admitted to the Bettering House from 1768 to 1776.

In additional to the religious organizations, numerous "friendly societies" with humanitarian interests supplemented the relief efforts of the municipal government. The Scots Charitable Society, organized in 1657 by 27 Scotsman living in Boston provided relief for its members and other people in need. By 1690, the society had 180 members, including several wealthy merchants in Boston and elsewhere (Trattner, 1999). Still a functioning organization, The Scots Charitable Society served as a model for similar organizations that emerged during Colonial America and continued in the 18th and succeeding centuries. The Episcopal Charitable Society of Boston, founded in 1754, provided relief to its members as did the 1767 Charitable Irish Society of Boston. Like the other friendly societies that appealed to nationality, self-interest, and compassion, the French Benevolent Society and the German Society of New York cared for sick or distressed members, their families and newly arrived countrypersons.

TABLE
3.2
ADMISSIONS TO THE BETTERING HOUSE AND HOSPITAL FOR THE POOR AND SICK, 1768 TO 1776

	Bettering House Admissions	Hospital Admissions	Total
1768–1769	428	336	764
1769–1770	389	338	727
1770–1771	495	349	844
1771–1772	395	315	710
1772–1773	398	374	772
1773–1774	309	361	670
1774–1775	368	393	761
1775–1776	427	268	695

Nash, G.B. (1976). Poverty and poor relief in Pre-Revolutionary Philadelphia. *William and Mary Quarterly, 33* (January), p. 23.

Occupational groups also formed for mutual relief, a trend especially apparent in the 1760s when organizations such as the Society of House Carpenters (1767) and the Marine Society (1769) appeared (Mohl, 1969). Benefit theater performances in New York provided funds for charities including schools and jails. Bequests and individual donations encouraged other humanitarian causes as did benevolent groups as varied as Free Masons and Sons of Liberty (Mohl, 1969).

Associative patterns of private humanitarianism became more pronounced in the post-Revolutionary years, providing not only relief for poor people but establishing the foundation for labor organizations. The General Society of Mechanics and Tradesmen, founded in 1785, designated overseers of the poor and a loan committee to assist needy members. The members of these various philanthropic activities were undoubtedly motivated by an array of factors; proving themselves worthy, respectable citizens, interacting with distinguished citizens, supporting national heritage, and controlling the growth of relief dependency.

It is obvious from the charitable giving that many Colonial Americans held genuine concern for others. However, it was an age of humanitarianism not only in America but also in much of the western world. According to Trattner (1999) the Great Awakening, which began in the late 1720s and continued for approximately 15 years, rested on faith, repentance, regeneration, or being born again based on human responsibility rather than the work of God alone (pp. 36–37). Proponents of the movement claimed that the Great Awakening nurtured humane attitudes at all levels of society and fostered philanthropy that focused on the less fortunate.

During a similar time frame, the so-called Enlightenment gained momentum from growth of science and John Locke's treatises on psychology both of which challenged Calvinism by advocating that people possess reason and had the capacity for being good. In this context poverty was not something to be tolerated with resignation. Rather, its elimination, along with that of other injustices and inequities, should be a goal for society (Trattner, 1999).

In concert with the Great Awakening, the Enlightenment began to change how poverty and poor people were treated. The American Revolution intensified the sense of humanitarianism and reform. The Declaration of Independence, with its emphasis upon reason and human equality, naturally tended to call attention to the need to improve the common person's lot. Independence in the New World, where abundant resources offered Americans the opportunity, if not the obligation, to root out old errors and vices and erect a society that would be a beacon to the world. And so, even the states became an instrument for advancing the welfare of the entire population, resulting in many reforms, including the separation of church and state.

COLONIAL SOCIAL WELFARE: A STRENGTHS PERSPECTIVE

The poor relief and private charity of Colonial America indicated a new energy for the alleviation of human misery. However, neither public nor private benevolence or the municipal government's responsibility for the poor succeeded in preventing, eliminating or even reducing the incidence of poverty in families and communities. In part this was due to the prevailing thought that poverty was linked to deficit morals in terms, intemperance, immorality, irreverence to religion, and lack of the work. Consequently, with the exception of the occasional employment scheme, few relief proposals attempted to solve the social and economic problems from an environmental perspective. Rather, most programs concentrated on ridding the poor of their supposed vices. Education might have helped, but the majority of its promoters supported the idea that schooling should serve primarily as the agent of morality and social control (Mohl, 1969). Colonial America's tendency to moralize about the poor thwarted reforms and solutions to poverty.

Although Colonial social policies reflected many of the harsh features of 17th and 18th century England, what were the emerging strengths and resources of America?

1. The Constitution of the United States specifically designated that states were responsible for the social welfare needs of families and individuals, much as it had been the responsibility of the separate colonies. This permitted more local government and individualized responses to need.

2. The Poor Law tradition of reluctant governmental intervention meant that individual assistance largely remained the responsibility of voluntary, charitable endeavors. Citizens were aware of poverty and its impact on daily life.
3. The tradition of private philanthropy led to an array of private and public ventures including the development of libraries, support for educational programs, and community organizations such as fire fighting and emergency services. The needs of people in their communities were addressed.
4. Slaves and indentured servants received no recognition by or received no assistance from colonial social welfare. These groups developed their own informal self-help mechanism, demonstrating the resiliency to surmount and overcome adversity.
5. In early colonial America, free African immigrants were not considered racially inferior. In time they accumulated wealth and position, often used to assist those in slavery.
6. Slavery, viewed as a moral imperative because it saved slaves from destitution, gave rise to racism. However, slaves engaged in regular uprisings and maintained a strong sense of family membership against the odds of a hostile environment.
7. Women, subjugated to male domination, empowered themselves as they doctored and nursed their families. Others gained membership in the community by opening schools and achieving status as midwives and apothecaries. Through successful collaborations, women accumulated capital and opened small stores and taverns.
8. Colonial America has an abundance of natural resources. It held reservoirs of energy, talent, ideas, and tools on which to draw.

The importance and usefulness of recognizing the strengths of Colonial America lies in knowing America's political and economic direction could be changed in response to the needs and wants of its growing and diverse population. Although equality was a component of the colonial period, patterns of equality emerged as people made gradual inroads into the racist, sexist, classist society.

SUMMARY

The social policy created during the colonial era reflected conflicting tendencies. On the one hand the poor law institutions reflected positive responses to social problems. On the other hand such institutions categorized people and separated people in need from their communities.

To varying degrees social policies sharpened class differences in Colonial America. A wealthy, elite, even aristocratic class had evolved that possessed a weaker notion of social obligations than did their English counterparts (Axinn and Levin, 1992). As self-made individuals, they often believed that the economic success they enjoyed was available to all persons. Beneath this class emerged a group of middle class farmers, artisans, small tradesmen, and laborers. A counterpart to this group was an individual who owned no property. The subjugation of persons of color and the lack of a large class of landless people exerted little pressure on public officials to develop policies that redistributed land or resources (Jansson, 2001).

The Colonial Americans found widespread economic opportunity and the advantages of a mobile society; however, the needs of poor people were often overlooked. However, if Colonial America had few poor people, why were there heavy relief expenditures and overcrowded almshouses? If human needs were being met, why the proliferation of mutual aid societies and humanitarian organizations? If economic opportunity was a reality for all, how does one account for large numbers of unemployed on the poor lists (Nash, 1976). Social workers should be mindful that colonial society, especially the urban areas, requires closer scrutiny before the concept of America as the land of opportunity can be accepted at face value.

REFERENCES

Ambramovitz, M. (1996). *Regulating the lives of women.* Revised Edition Boston, MA: South End Press.

Axinn, J., & Levin, H. (1992). *Social welfare: A history of the American response to need.* New York: Longman.

Bellers, J. (1714). An essay towards the improvement of physick in twelve proposal (London), passim; Owen, D. (1964). *English philanthropy, 1660–1960.* (University of Cambridge Press. Cambridge, MA), 40.

Day, P. J. (1997). *A new history of social welfare* (2nd ed.). MA: Boston, MA: Allyn & Bacon.

Franklin, B. (1751, August 8). *Pennsylvania Gazette.*

Act XXVII, October 1646 in The Statutes at Large. Being a Collection of all the Laws of Virginia from the First Session of the Legislature in the Year 1619. William Walker Henning, ed. (New York: 1823): 1:336.

Henretta, J. A. (1965, January). Economic development and social structure in Colonial Boston, *William and Mary Quarterly, 23,* 85.

James, S. V. (1963). *A people among peoples: Quaker benevolence in eighteenth century America.* Cambridge, MA: Harvard University Press.

Jansson, B. S. (2001). *The reluctant welfare state: American social welfare policies: Past, present, and future.* Pacific Grove, CA: Brooks/Cole.

Mohl, R. A. (1969, January). *Poverty in early America, a reappraisal: The case of eighteenth New York City, New York History, 50,* 5–27.

Morris, R. B. (Ed.). (1935) Select cases of the mayor's court of New York City, 1674–1784. Washington, 67–71.

Nash, G. B. (1976, January). Poverty and poor relief in Pre-Revolutionary Philadelphia, *William and Mary Quarterly, 33,* 3–30.

Rothman, D. J. (1971). *The discovery of the asylum: Social order and disorder in the new republic.* Boston: Little, Brown and Company.

Trattner, W. I. (1999). *From poor law to welfare state: A history of social welfare in America* (6th ed.). New York: The Free Press.

Williams, W. H. (1973, October). The "industrious poor" and the founding of the Philadelphia Hospital. *Pennsylvania Magazine of History and Biography,* 431–443.

Social Realities in the Developing Nation

The American Revolution created new hardships for the independent states held together in a loose confederation of governance. In February 1784, New York City's population totaled about 12,000. One newspaper estimated that more than 1,000 families were supported by public and private charities (*Independent Journal*, 1784). Outdoor relief assisted thousands of indigent persons, especially during periods of epidemic or depression, and during winter months when unskilled day laborers could find no employment. Heavy immigration in the post-Revolutionary period had a direct relation to the increasing relief burdens. For example, the New York Commissioners of Alms House reported in 1795 that 44% of poor house residents came from immigrant stock (Mohl, 1969).

Officials described the almshouse in 1795 as full of paupers "subject to rheumatisms, ulcers and palsie and to fits which impair their reason and elude all the forces of medicine" (Minutes of the Commissioners of Alms Houses, 1791–1797, p. 185). Some of the poor people were transients who received short-term relief while others were not. John Sullivan, for example, was born blind in the poor house in 1759 and remained a resident in the institution until his death in 1819.

Although the Articles of Confederation had promised a "perpetual union" of the states, the post-Revolutionary War disorganization and poverty highlighted the need for more effective political organization. A new constitution for the states and the United States government was drafted by the Federal Convention, which sat at Philadelphia from May 25 to September 17, 1787 (Axinn & Levin, 1992). The new government began to function on March 4, 1789, with the commencement of the first presidential term.

The preamble of the Constitution of the United States stated that "general welfare" was one reason for the new government. However, social welfare concerns were not enumerated in the powers of Congress, the government's legislative body. The Constitution reserved to the states such powers that were not delegated to the central government. Consequently, providing for the social welfare needs of families and individuals remained the responsibility of separate states, much as it had been the responsibility of separate colonies. Individual relief, in keeping with the Poor Law tradition of reluctant governmental intervention, largely remained the responsibility of voluntary charity.

FEDERAL WELFARE FOR REVOLUTIONARY WAR VETERANS

As the government began to operationalize the Constitution of the United States, the houses of Congress passed, by overwhelming majorities, the 1818 Revolutionary War Pension Act. The act, combining features of a pension plan and poor law provisions, provided $96 a year for privates and $240 annually for officers who served at least nine months in a Continental line and who swore that they were "in reduced circumstances: and "in need of assistance from [their] country for support" (Annals of Congress, 1817–1818, pp. 2518–19). Thus, fueled by sentimentality toward Revolution veterans and a growing national spirit in the wake of the War of 1812, Congress shattered nearly 40 years of resistance against providing lifetime pensions for completing military service by launching the first federal effort to aid some of the nation's poor.

The Revolutionary War Pension Act is a significant social welfare measure for several reasons. The most important reason is that it created the first military pension plan and established a precedent for later veteran programs. In 1820, in response to the flood of applicants, Congress introduced a means test to the program whereby veterans wishing to enroll in the program had to report their residence, income, debts, employment and an inventory of assets to the War Department (Resch, 1982). Therefore, a second critical feature of the Act was its inclusion of an unofficial national poverty line that produced a national survey of poverty conditions experienced by a large number of older men. Finally, the act resulted in the largest relief effort until the 20th century.

The 20,000 claims made under the act provide a rich source of demographic information. For example, Table 4.1 illustrates claimants residing in the West reported the lowest per capital wealth while claimants from the New England states had the highest, although the differences were minimal (Resch, 1982). Regardless of the region, veterans appeared to share a meager portion of the nation's wealth. Table 4.2 demonstrates that a hierarchy existed among all types of households. The highest levels were extended households that functioned as refuges for the veteran's kin or housed nonrelatives. Solitary veterans had the lowest level with an average of $20 (Resch, 1982). According to the case studies of veterans, illness, the death of a spouse, departure of children, the burden of children with handicaps, and indebtedness increased the incidence of poverty and dependence. Often the support of family and friends was a major factor in thwarting poverty. Poverty was best prevented in households where there were healthy children because they offered household support, attracted help from family, or relieved financial demands on the

---

TABLE 4.1 AVERAGE PER HOUSEHOLD AND PER CAPITA WEALTH FOR EACH REGION

Region	Court-Assessed Wealth		Applicant-Assessed Wealth	
	Average per Applicant Household ($)	Average per Capita	Average per Applicant Household ($)	Average per Capita
New England	160	47	81	23
Middle Atlantic	95	30	47	15
South	112	35	110	34
West	102	27	53	14

Adapted from Resch, J. P. Federal welfare for Revolutionary War veterans. *Social Service Review, 56.* (June 1982), p. 175.

TABLE 4.2	WEALTH DISTRIBUTION BY TYPE OF HOUSEHOLD (AVERAGE WEALTH)	

Type of Household	Court-Assessed Wealth ($)	N
Solitary	20.00	132
Conjugal	105.00	233
Nuclear	141.00	400
Extended:		
Applicant living with kin	64.00	21
Kin living with applicant	279.00	78
Nonrelatives living with applicant	500.00	13

Adapted from Resch, J. P. Federal welfare for Revolutionary War veterans. *Social Service Review, 56.* (June 1982), p. 177.

household by leaving. Older veterans who were penniless had to resort to direct support from friends and town. A case in point was Asher Russell who experienced total destitution. In 1818 at the age of 62, Russell received his pension. Prior to that time he was supported, for ten years, by the town of Wetherfield, Connecticut (Revolutionary War Pension File, S35378).

The Revolutionary War Pension Act demonstrates that American social welfare is based not only on the Elizabethan poor law traditions but also on new practices that combine features of a pension plan and poor law provisions. The distinction is significant because it illuminates the complexity of American social welfare. On one hand, traditional practices create a net to catch worthy and deserving individuals who are unable to support themselves. On the other hand, American welfare includes practices that, in effect, invite individuals to apply for assistance from the nation in recognition of their membership in a group identified with particular cultural ideals.

POPULATION GROWTH, GEOGRAPHIC EXPANSION

The poverty experienced by veterans of the Revolutionary War became more apparent in the general public with population growth and the intensification of urban poverty during the last two decades of the eighteenth century. Specifically, in 1790, the year of the first United States Census, the country's total population numbered 3,929,000. By 1800 the population had risen by 34% to about 5,297,000, of whom 1,002,000—19%—were nonwhite and 322,000—6%—lived in urban areas (Axinn & Levin, 1992, p. 35). From 1800–1860 the population had multiplied six times, in part as a result of massive migrations.

And as the population increased, the country had become more urban. In 1800, only 6% of the population lived in urban areas, by 1860, almost 20% of American resided in cities.

Of the total of 1,427,337 immigrants to the United States during the decade 1840–1849, 874,917 came from Ireland and 395–434 from Germany (Axinn & Levin, 1992, p. 35). Almost all of the immigrants landed at entry points between Baltimore and Boston, and almost all remained in the northern section of the country, where they congregated in cities and were viewed as a threat to Native Americans. Not only were immigrants foreign, with different languages and customs, but also many were Catholic in an essentially Protestant country. The dramatic increase in available workers altered the relationship between American labor and industry. In a similar fashion, immigrants placed demands on the nation's emergency financial aid that caused animosity toward them.

Territorial expansion complimented the nation's population growth. By 1860, the country's northern and southern borders were fixed and settlement expansion extended to the Pacific Ocean. The original 13 colonies had increased to 33 states. In 1860 half of the population lived in trans-Appalachian regions, despite the Northeast urbanization.

The increased population and territorial expansion combined with the accelerated growth of manufacturing combined. By 1830, factories supported by the spinning jenny and the power loom, appeared across the New England landscape and mid-Atlantic rivers. The 1793 invention of the cotton gin provided the southern economy with an economic base where slavery was a profitable form of labor.

Their economic bases led the South and New England to different labor supplies. In the South laborers were largely represented by slaves who had no right to public social welfare programs. Both free blacks and slaves employed self-help practices to support one another and to address common needs. Slaver owners also had some stake in maintaining their property to ensure a steady rate of production.

Poverty in the New England states was more directly related to urbanization, industrialization, and development of the factory system. The process of industrialization necessitated a family's mobility to find employment and gain a regular wage in order to maintain family solvency. Travel and distance often strained kinship ties; with people working out of home on a daily basis, family members gradually became more dependent on services supplied from sources outside the family unit.

The perils associated with the developing market economy in which families depended on wages in a competitive marketplace kept a series of economic depressions—one, 1815 to 1821; another, 1837 to 1843; still another, 1857 to 1859. The long stretch between 1815 and 1859 was a difficult time for individuals and families who were not physically or psychologically free to move to the open lands and opportunities of the West. These people included immigrant families physically and financially exhausted by their journey; disabled veterans of the War of 1812, the Mexican War, and the Indian Wars; the ill and disabled; children who had been orphaned or abandoned; older people who had no children or spouses to support them and who found themselves forced into involuntary retirement because if ill health or employment.

REFORM MOVEMENTS

"Reform activities" dominated the response to unemployment and inadequate income. Based on the view that the nation's economic structure was sound, reform movements ushered in new ideas about the ability of people to change. Social structures, in the form of labor unions, patriotic and political groups, and humanitarian associations, became more pronounced after the Revolutionary War. For example, the Mechanics' Union trade association was formed in 1827 in Philadelphia. By the 1837 depression there were at least five national trade unions: cordwainers (shoemakers), comb makers, carpenters, weavers, and printers. One of the most important labor organizations was the General Society of Mechanics and Tradesmen, founded in 1785. Its structure contained overseers of the poor and a loan committee to assist needy members and families.

The Tammany Society and the Order of Cincinnati, both political organizations, engaged in some charitable work, as did the fraternal society of free Masons. The Society for the Relief of Distressed Doctors (1787), which became the Humane Society in 1803, and the City Dispensary (1791), provided free medical care for poor people. Education for poor children flourished with the development of new religious school. The Religious Society of Friends, the Quakers, regarded charity as an expression of God and used the concept of family solidarity to justify mutual aid (James, 1963). The Quaker Meeting assumed responsibility for widows, fatherless children, the sick, and kept watch over the treatment of apprentices, and supported the aged.

The election of Andrew Jackson to the presidency in 1828 launched Jacksonian democracy symbolized by the notion that common people had the opportunity to succeed with hard work and determination. The optimism of change swept the country. The victorious Jackson, believed to have been born in a log cabin, seemed to provide living proof of the possibility of egalitarianism.

George Caleb Bingham (1811–1879), one of America's greatest painters, captured the feelings of Jacksonian democracy with paintings that depicted life and personalities as simple and hearty as rivers and country scenes. The peaceful "Fur Traders Descending the Missouri" (1845), considered Bingham's masterpiece, depicts the early West when the white population was sparse and Europeans had traded—often in furs—and intermixed with Native Americans; as large numbers of settlers and the agrarian economy assumed a presence in the 19th century. Among Bingham's cast of Western characters, fur traders and squatters fall near the mid-point on a continuum between savagery and civilization, being neither settled and agrarian, nor wholly nomadic (Shapiro et al, 1990, pp. 58–59). Fur traders, like scouts and hunters such as Daniel Boone, served in literature and the visual arts as convenient symbols of the coming civilization, its advance guard breaching the wilderness. (The flowing river bearing the canoe in Bingham's painting characterizes the trappers' easy passage between two conditions the remote with the urban. Water serves as a mirror of the sky, of the landscape, and of man. (Shapiro et al, 1990, pp. 58–59).

Renowned as "the Missouri painter," Bingham is admired today as an artist whose paintings and drawings combine aesthetic merit with informative documentation of American social history, especially regarding works depicting the election process. As a whole, his art framed a pictorialized collective history of his region and everyday activities of people. In his election series "Country Politian" (1849, "Canvassing for a Vote" (1851–1852), "The County Election" (1852), "Stump Speaking" (1853–1854), and "Verdict of the People" (1854–1855), Bingham made sure that all his election canvases could be regarded, at least initially, as exemplars of the American system—persuasive monuments to democracy intended to boast the ideals of the nation. The political series is enriched because Bingham the politician and Bingham the historian were mutually engaging. What proves intriguing about "The Country Election" is that it does not seem to convey serious ideals of democracy, documentable chicanery or even violence at the polls (Shapiro et al, 1990, pp. 58–59). Neither the battered man to the right of the painting nor the unconscious drunk being lugged to the polling place provide admirable models of democracy in action. Bingham offered no comment on the lack of women or African American subjects in his paintings. Rather, he painted the scenes as seen by his eyes.

As illustrated by Bingham's work, democracy captured the American white male spirit. In this context, all individuals had the potential to participate and to achieve. It was in this national mood that reform movements emerged. Areas of reform activity included the extension of suffrage, temperance, more effective poor relief, humane treatment for the insane, rehabilitation of criminals, child saving and, efforts to abolition slavery. Also, free public education became a focal point for egalitarianism and democracy. Reformers linked moral deficits to indigence or in the words of the 1860 Annual Report of the New York Association for Improving the Conditions of Poor People (AICP) "one of the primal and principal causes of poverty and crime is the want of early mental and moral culture" (New York Association for Improving the Conditions of the Poor, 1860).

An example of a reform movement charged with moral issues is The American Society for the Promotion of Temperance founded in 1826. Whiskey became abundant and cheap in America with the growth in corn production by the pioneer farmers of the Ohio River Valley and the burgeoning distilling industry of the east (Axinn & Levin, 1992). In time men, women, and children developed a national pastime for drinking as a form of relaxation, celebration, and ritual. As a result, in the first three decades of the 19th century, annual per capital consumption increased to more then five gallons. The temperance movement's purpose was to educate the general public against intemperance through social and political activities including pamphlets, rallies, public speakers, and demonstrations.

In 19th-century America, middle-class women were relegated to a "separate sphere" of domesticity and morality, charged with protecting family life and rearing their children into respectable citizens (Skocpol, 1995). In this designated role, women became deeply involved in civic affairs. The temperance movement, in particular the transdenominational Women's Christian Temperance Union (WCTU), expressed the sentiments of many women with the motto, "Woman will bless and brighten every place she enters, and will enter every place," (Rothman, 1978). The WCTU was comprehensive in nature, organizing against prostitution, operating kindergarten classes for working women, and participating in election campaigns.

The temperance movement in general, and the Women's Christian Temperance Union in particular, addressed the economic costs of drinking and reflected the crusading nature of the period. The ideal citizen was democratic, educated, temperate, and spiritual. Reform activity was determined to achieve this level of perfectibility. Although the temperance movement would become more vocal and politically stronger after the Civil War, the attention given to the problem during the prewar period was evidence of a growing concern about the relation of drinking to unemployment and to financial and moral poverty.

METHODS OF CARING FOR THE INDIGENT

Although there were differences of opinion about the principle and mode of relief for the poor, the majority of reform activities during the pre–Civil War period focused on the reform of individuals rather than reforms of systems. The effort was to find an environment in which individual changes might be encouraged. As a result, the Senate and Assembly of the State of New York charged that the secretary of state study and report on cost of operating the

Poor Laws in New York for the purpose of suggesting improvements in the New York welfare system. In February 1824, Secretary John V. N. Yate's submitted his report that discussed the four major means being used to care for the needy: the contract system, auction of the poor, the almshouse, and relief in the home—commonly referred to as "outdoor relief" (Coll, 1969). Further, Yates divided the poor of the state into "the permanent poor," that is those who received support regularly during the year, and "the occasional poor," that is, those who received help during part of the year such as during the autumn and winter months (Axinn & Levin, 1992).

For Yates and a number of others, the almshouse appeared to be the best alternative to for the permanent and occasional poor. Josiah Quincy concluded:

> That of all modes of providing for the poor, the most wasteful, the most injurious to their morals and destructive to their industrious habits is that of supply to their own families. That the most economical mode is that of Alms Houses; having the character of Work Houses, or Houses of Industry in which work is provided for every degree of ability in the pauper; and thus the able poor made to provide, partially, at least for their own support; and also to the support, or at least the comfort of the impotent poor.

> (Massachusetts, General Court, Committee on Pauper Laws: 1821)

By instituting a poorhouse plan, Yates estimated that New York would save approximately $250,000 yearly, a reduction of 50% of allocated expenditures. In addition, almshouses would alter people from seeking assistance and people residing in almshouses would learn to work, improve their morals, stop consuming alcohol, and become upstanding citizens.

The Yates report is significant because of the widespread attention it gained and because it established almshouses as the major approach to the relief of the poor in the United States. In the cities along the eastern seaboard, almshouses were often free hospitals that served immigrant populations. In fact some of the nation's renowned public hospitals including New York's Bellevue, Brooklyn's Kings County Hospital, Philadelphia's General Hospital, and Baltimore City Hospitals were originally almshouses. (Coll, 1969)

Advocates of almshouses assumed that the majority of inmates would be able-bodied men. During the winter, the population of almshouses did have an increase in the number of people who could work because of layoffs in farming, shipbuilding, and other outdoor employment. However, as indicated by Table 4.3, which describes the population in the Philadelphia Blockley Almshouse in 1848, only 12% of the total 192 men and women were capable of working (Coll, 1969, p. 25).

The almshouse was the preferred method of caring for the poor people during this period, however, several aspects challenge this generalization. For example, almshouses addressed the needs of the medically indigent, people who would not be considered paupers today. The 19th century institutions also

<table>
<tr><td>TABLE 4.3</td><td>CLASSIFICATION OF PERSONS
BLOCKLEY ALMSHOUSE, PHILADELPHIA 1848</td></tr>
</table>

Total White Persons: 1,509

Children	111
Hospital and lunatic	718
Old men's infirmary and incurable section	188
Male working wards	79
Mechanics' wards	42
Old women's asylum and incurable	256
Women's working ward	71
Nursery with women	21
Nursery with children	23

Coll, B. D. (1969), *Perspectives in public welfare*, p. 25.

housed the mentally ill, the mentally retarded, and homeless children in large numbers. Older people and people physically unable to care for themselves aroused sympathy in many except for those who claimed that the indigent aged should have saved for old age or misfortune.

For all their proliferation, almshouses did not receive universal support; in fact within a relatively short time, the public began questioning their value. Arguments presented by the opponents of almshouses suggested that the idea of deference was extreme and would keep the deserving from entering the house, but the "vicious and ideal" would not hesitate (Coll, 1969). Others stated that it was cruel, especially in rural communities where people were accustomed to natural settings, to force them into congregate living. Some opponents considered the almshouse system as costly and contended that dependent persons could reside with friends or relatives for a significantly lower cost to the public.

In 1832, opposition to almshouses developed when the conditions in the county almshouses were revealed. Specifically, information about such conditions was published in a committee report of the 1838 State Assembly. The report's first section described shocking conditions at the Genesee County almshouse. Since the faculty buildings were dilapidated, the almshouse offered not only poor shelter but also overcrowded conditions. A room measuring 18 × 17 feet contained 5 beds occupied by 12 women and children (Coll, 1969). Sick people mingled with the healthy, and people with mental illness were housed with older, fragile people.

When the democrats gained power in 1856, they ordered the investigation of 55 poorhouses, in New York City and Kings County. The findings revealed appalling conditions and the committee report strongly condemned almshouses:

> The poor houses throughout the state may be generally described as badly constructed, ill-arranged, ill-warmed, and ill-ventilated. The rooms are crowded and inmates . . . In some cases, as many as forty-five inmates occupy a single dormitory, with low ceilings, and sleeping boxes arranged in three tiers one above another. Good health is incompatible with such arrangements. (Breckenridge, 1857/1957)

ASYLUM MOVEMENT

As the story goes, Dorothea Lynde Dix, an elite Bostonian lady with wealth, education, and social standing, visited the East Cambridge Massachusetts jail, where, on a winter's night in 1841, she supposedly first witnessed the suffering of a handful of insane inmates. In a sudden flash of inspiration, she resolved to take up their cause. By 1843, Dix had submitted a petition to the Massachusetts General Court about the despicable condition for poor people who were mentally ill throughout the state by county and town. Her *Memorial to the Legislature of Massachusetts* (1848) described people with mental illness, "in cage, closets, stalls, pens! Chained, naked, beaten with rods, and lashed into obedience" (Dix, 1848, p. 4). The *Memorial,* eloquent and impassioned, written by women with no political background and few humanitarian efforts, launched the American asylum movement and remains a distinctive piece of Jacksonian reform literature (Gollaher, 1993).

The conditions in asylums are vividly captured in the first-person accounts of women; and a poem by an unnamed woman inmate appeared in the first volume of the 1842 *Asylum Journal* (Appendix A). In their writings, the women recalled the persecution they experienced from their families when they attempted to exercise religious freedom or violated what was perceived to be "acceptable behavior," (Geller, Harris, & Chesler, 1994). Elizabeth T. Stone (incarcerated 1840–42, in Massachusetts) describes the mental asylum as "a system that is worse then slavery." Adriana Brinkle (1857–85 in Pennsylvania) describes the asylum as a "living death," filled with "shackles," "blackness," "handcuffs, straight-jackets, balls and chains, iron rings and other such relics of barbarism," (Geller, Harris, & Chesler, 1994, p. xv).

The asylum movement involved a stirring call to halt the abuses of the state's fragmented community-based approach to social welfare. Dix called for the establishment of two types on asylums: one for people who were thought to be chronic or the "incurable" cases and the other for those with a high likelihood of "being restored to reason" then discharged (Gollaher, 1993, p. 438).

Dix's conviction was that individuals were capable of self-perfection, but they required treatment in a setting that afforded dignity. According to Dix, "The confinement of the criminal and the insane in the same building is subversive of that good order and discipline which should be observed in every well-regulated prison (p. 30).

Dix delivered to legislatures all around the country exhaustive data on the details of inmates' diets, measurements of their living quarters, and facts concerning their daily routine. In 1848, she appealed to Congress for 5 million acres of public land to be given to the construction of institutions for the insane. Dix's request was a challenge to the federal government to support reform on a national level. After a period of time, Congress passed a bill that allocated 10 million acres for building sites for people who were insane, blind, or deaf (Axinn & Levin, 1992). President Pierce denied the federal government's responsibility for social welfare:

> I readily and, I trust, feelingly acknowledge the duty incumbent on us all as men and citizens, and as among the highest and holiest of our duties, to provide for those who, in the mysterious order of providence, are subject to want and to disuse of body or mind; but I can not find any authority in the Constitution for making the Federal Government the great almoner of public charity throughout the United States. . . . (Pierce, 1854)

The Pierce veto reinforced the pattern of state responsibility and of the role private charity in social welfare. The federal government maintains direct responsibility only for veterans as a group of disabled citizens. Pierce's refusal to allow the federal government to provide social services established a precedent that continued for the next 75 years in social welfare policy development.

CHILD SAVING

Soon after the Yates report appeared, there was public dissatisfaction with the care children received or in institutions caring for children. A prime example of institutional care is The House of Refuge of Philadelphia, which first opened its doors in late 1828. The House was established by a group of benevolent citizens who wanted to remove children from adult prisons because until the 19th century, children accused of crimes were, if found guilty, were placed in adult jails.

When the House of Refuge of Philadelphia was first opened, there were no requirements that the inmates be of any particular race. However, after the first year, no black child was admitted to the house; rather, youthful offenders were placed in adult prisons. In 1850, the House of Refuge For Colored Children was opened in Philadelphia, the only time in the 19th century that a northern state opened an institution designed specifically for African Americans (Frey, 1981).

Social control was an implicit element of the original House and the later one. This idea suggests that reformers of the 19th century were motivated to socially control any perceived deviant elements of the increasingly heterogeneous society (Frey, 1981). As a way to address disturbing social and economic conditions, and to maintain "a sense of community to urban America, moralist succeeded benevolence, public aid and private charity were transformed into mechanism for social control" (Trattner, 1974, p. 67).

The program for inmates in Philadelphia presented social control to house managers. They maintained control through a program comprising three primary components: (a) schooling that offered basic instructions in reading, writing, and numbers; (b) teaching of the ethics of Protestantism; and, (c) work (Frey, 1981). For children in the House of Refuge For Colored Children, the program of education and work reflected the racism and prejudice of the times exemplified by the statement of Elisha Swinney, superintendent of the House in 1860:

> . . . we have difficulties to meet that are not found among white children. To a white boy, inducements may be held out to make efforts to elevate himself to some important position in life. Not so with these colored children. We cannot say, you may attain to such a high calling or position in life; to that of a physician, lawyer, legislator, governor. . . . There are few given them whereby they might prove themselves capable of filling higher positions. (Thirty-Second Annual, Report, 1860)

Despite the increase in specialized institutions for children, the unquestioned acceptance of institutional child care began to decline during the 1850s, in part because of the inability to build a sufficient number of specialized institutions for the growing number of dependent, homeless, orphaned, and delinquent children. As economic uncertainty increased, so did the capacity to support children. Charles Loring Brace, the famous critic of institutional life, advocated for a change in the care of the children, especially poor children. In 1853, Brace made public the idea of "placing-out" children in homes rather than institutions by creating the Children's Aid Society (CAS).

Conceptually, Brace contended that children should be placed in rural homes rather than institutions. His beliefs were largely based on anti-urban, anti-immigrant, and anti-Catholic sentiments (Hacsi, 1995). The fact that farm labor was in demand in the West, and that large numbers of children could be absorbed there fit neatly with a romantic conception of country life. During the 12-year period, 1853–1814, the Children's Aid Society for New York placed 4,614 children with Western farmers (Axinn & Levin, 1992). An even larger number was placed during the decade following the Civil War.

Children came to CAS in a variety of ways. Some were swept off the street by agents, others were brought by staff from orphan asylums and infant asylums. The CAS "orphan trains" became famous. Placements were similar to those made in asylums, aside from the distance children traveled. Approximately 90% of the 200,000 children who were "placed out" between 1853 and

1930 were sent to Michigan, Ohio, Indiana, Illinois, Iowa, Missouri, and Kansas (Douglas, 1995).

Expectations about how much a child should work and about the relative importance of emotional ties between parent and child shaped views about how children should be treated in placement homes (Cook, 1995). Older children were expected to work to earn their keep. Younger children also worked, but ideally they were thought to be taken into homes for love. All the children were denied information and contact with their biological parents.

Brace and the CAS highlighted three debates related to the child saving movement (Katz, 1986). The first focused on the role of parents and asked the question, "Should poor children be taken from their destitute parents?" The second concerned the merits of institutions as settings for dependent children, and the third highlighted the role of government in the care of children.

DEVELOPING SOCIAL WELFARE FROM THE STRENGTHS PERSPECTIVE

As the nation developed, so did social welfare policies. During the period between the Revolutionary War and the Civil War when the American economy shifted from an agrarian to primarily an industrial base, many people considered social problems a threat to moral standing and social order and associated problems with immigrant populations, industrialization, and urbanization. Thus, there were few attempts to identify individual and community resources that could be used to create opportunities for inclusion or to provide alternatives that bypassed the predominate system.

Although the Poor Laws provided the fundamental structure for relief, local officials needed more comprehensive responses to conditions such as mental illness, orphaned children, and the rising crime rate. Institutions, such as almshouses, asylums, and houses of refuge were constituted to care for people in an environment that provided rehabilitation, discipline, and a model for citizenship. At the core of the institutional care was the belief that individual behavior resulted in social problems. Deficits were the central focus of social welfare policy development. Fueled by religious and moralistic perspectives, the emphasis was on "fixing the person" rather than evaluating the environment. Supported by the concept of rugged individualism, people were thought to determine their success through hard work coupled with America's resources and opportunities. In sharp contrast to the strengths perspective, poverty was an individual condition and responsibility. People who were poor and unemployed were viewed with suspicion and received harsh and controlling treatment. With an emphasis on social problems and labeling, it was necessary for people to be portrayed as deficient or deviant to justify receiving benefits and services.

In keeping with the idea of a strengths perspective in social policy, the question becomes: What were the barriers in the developing nation that thwarted poor and unemployed people from meeting their basic needs, food, clothing, shelter, and participation in the life of a community? This chapter pinpoints several barriers including living conditions associated with rapid urbanization, the nation's uncertain economy, and discrimination against immigrants (Jansson, 2001). Perhaps the nature of the population of inmates is even more telling. Although estimates vary widely, there is general agreement that more than half the inmates were foreign-born. The probability is that most people agreed with Brace who said that these inmate were "dangerous classes" and that fear rather than concern was the mark of public opinion.

The physically disabled aside, public and private sources generally agreed that the causes of poverty were to be found in individual character flaws and in organizations that encouraged and promoted decency. The New York Society for the Prevention of Pauperism was founded to investigate and as far as possible remove the causes of mendicity, to devise plans for ameliorating the condition of the poor and wretched, and to secure their successful operations (Axinn & Levin, 1992).

The agreement that pauperism could be prevented and cured only by erecting "barriers against the encroachments of moral degeneracy" fostered a review of contemporary relief practices and a search for barriers that could, at one and the same time, save the poor from pauperism and the rich from taxation. Voluntary organizations such as the New York Society for the Prevention of Pauperism and the Associates for Improving the Conditions of the Poor that developed later in several larger cities, sought "to remove the various causes of mendicity" primarily through friendly advice. These efforts at personalized attention foreshadowing the more persistent operation of the Charity Organization Societies (COS) were aimed at raising the needy above the need for relief by bringing about a change in character. But also like the COS, these early voluntary organizations attempted to effectuate governmental provision for bettering the circumstances of the poor and, thus, to lend encouragement to individual and family effort.

SUMMARY

With the emerging capitalist economy, the period before and after the Revolutionary War was one in which many Americans thought that moral behavior and hard work could eliminate poverty. Individual responsibility, personal achievement, and the notion of self-help dominated responses to poverty and other social issues.

There were few changes in social welfare from Colonial America. The continued importance of state rights, limited central government, and the separation of church and state, suggested that private citizens were still responsible for the poor through individual acts and voluntary associations. Charity work became associated with social status and served mostly poor women and their children, leaving persons on the margins of society to the care of institutions (Abramovitz, 1996). Almshouse care remained the dominant form of care for the poor until the Progressive Era of the late 19th century.

REFERENCES

Abamouitz, M. (1996). *Regulating the lives of woman.* Boston, MA: South End Press.

Annals of Congress, 15th Congress, 1st session. 1817–1818, pp. 2518–19.

Asher Russell. Revolutionary War Pension File, S35378.

Axinn, J. & Levin, H. (1992). *Social welfare: A history of the American response to need.* New York: Longman.

Coll, B. D. (1969). *Perspectives in public welfare.* U.S. Department of Health, Education, and Welfare. Washington, DC: U. S. Government Printing Office.

Cook, J. F. (1995, January–February). A history of placing-out: The orphan trains. *Child Welfare, 74* (1), 181–197.

Dix, D. L. (1843). Memorial, *"Praying A Grant of Land for the Relief and Support of the Indigent Curable and Incurable Insane in the United States,"* Miscellaneous Senate Document No. 150, 30th Cong., 1st sess., June 27, 1848, p. 213. Reprinted in *Poverty, U.S.A., On Behalf of the Insane Poor* (New York: Arno Press and *New York Times,* 1971).

Douglas, B. J. A. (1995). The orphans trains of 1853–1930 and their effect on the development of adoption policies and practices. *Social Work Perspectives, 5* (1), 36–42.

Frey, C. P. (1981, Spring). The house of refuge for colored children. *The Journal of Negro History,* 10–25.

Geller, J. L., Harris, M. & Chesler, P. (1994). Women of the asylum. New York: Doubleday.

Gollaher, D. L. (1993, Spring). Dorothea Dix and the English origins of the American Asylum movement. *Canadian Review of American Studies, 23,* 149–175.

Hacsi. T. (1995, January–February). From indenture to family foster care: A brief history of child placing. *Child Welfare, 74,* (1), 162–180.

Independent Journal (New York), February 18, 1784; Pomerantz, New York, p. 328.

James, S. V. (1963). A people among people: Quaker benevolence in eighteenth century America. Cambridge, MA: Harvard University Press.

Jansson, B. (2001). The reluctant welfare state. Pacific Grove, CA: Brooks/Cole.

Katz, M. B. (1986). Child-saving. *History of Education Quarterly, 26* (3), 413–424.

Massachusetts, General Court, Committee on Pauper Laws, Report of the Committee to Whom was Referred the Consideration of the Pauper Laws of the Commonwealth (Josiah Quincy, Chairman). (1821). In C. Pumphrey & H. Pumphrey, Heritage of American Social Work (p. 63).

Minutes of the Commissioners of Alms Houses. (1791–1797). In New York City Municipal Archives and Records Center, p. 185.

Mohl, R. A. (1969). Poverty in early America, a reappraisal: The case of eighteenth-century New York City. *New York History, 50,* 5–27.

New York Association for Improving the Conditions of the Poor. (1860). *Seventeenth Annual Report* (p. 31). New York: Author.

President Franklin Pierce (1854). "Veto message-An act making a grant of public lands to several states for the benefit of indigent insane persons," May 3. In Axinn, J. & Lewin, H. 1992. Social Welfare: A history of the American (1957). Response to need. New York: Longman pp. 80–84.

Report of Select Senate Committee to Visit Charitable and Penal Institutions, (1957). "New York Senate Document" No. 8, 1857. In 'Sophonisba P. Breckenridge. *Public welfare administration in the United States: Select documents,'* (pp. 150–51, 152).

Resch, J. P. (1982, June). Federal welfare for Revolutionary War veterans. *Social Service Review, 56,* 171–95.

Rothman, S. (1978). *Women's proper place.* New York: Basic Books.

"Scenes in a private mad-house," *Asylum Journal, I* (1842): I.

Shaprio, M. E., Groseclose, B., Johns, E., Nagel, P. C., & Wilmerding, J. (1990). *George Caleb Bingham.* New York: Harry N. Abrams, Inc., a Times Mirror Company, in association with The Saint Louis Art Museum.

Skocpol, T. (1995). *Social policy in the United States: Future possibilities in historical perspective.* Princeton, NJ: Princeton University Press.

Trattner, W. (1974). *From poor law to welfare state.* New York: Free press, a Division of Macmillan Co.

Twenty-Eight Annual Report of the Board of Mangers of the House of Refuge (Philadelphia: Ashmead, 1856) to Thirty-Second Annual Report of the Board of Managers of the House of Refuge (Philadelphia: Ashmead), 1860.

APPENDIX 4–A

Scene in a Private Mad-House

Stay, jailor, stay, and hear my woe!
　　She is not made who kneels to thee,
For what I'm now, too well I know,
　　And what I was, and what should be.
I'll rave no more in proud despair,
　　My language shall be mild, though sad;
But yet I'll firmly, truly swear,
　　I am not mad, I am not mad!

My tyrant husband forged the tale
　　Which chains me in this dismal cell;
My fate unknown my friends bewail—
　　Oh, jailer, haste that fate to tell!

Oh, haste my father's heart to cheer!
　　His heart at once will grieve and glad,
To know, though kept a captive here,
　　I am not mad, I am not mad!

He smiles in scorn and turns the key!
    He quits the grate—I kneel in vain!
His glimmering lamp still, still, I see!
    'Tis gone—and all is gloom again.
Cold! bitter cold—no warmth! No light!
    Life, all thy comforts once I had!
Yet here I'm chained this freezing night,
    Although not mad! no, no, not mad!

'Tis sure some dream—some vision vain!
    What! I, the child of rank and wealth!
Am I the wretch who clanks this chain?
    Bereft of freedom, friends and health!
Ah! while I dwell on blessings fled,
    That never more my heart must glad,
How aches my heart, how burns my head—
    But 'tis not mad! no, tis not mad!

Hast thou, my child, forget ere this,
    A mother's face, a mother's tongue?
She'll ne'vr forget your parting kiss,
    Nor round her neck how fast you clung;
Nor how with me you sued to stay,
    Nor how that suit your sire forbade;
Now how—I'll drive such thoughts away—
    They'll make me mad—they'll make me mad!

His rosy lips, how sweet they smiled—
    His mild blue eyes, how bright they shone;
None ever bore a lovelier child—
    And art thou now forever gone?
And must I never see thee more,
    My pretty, pretty, little lad?
I will be free—unbar the door—
    I am not mad, I am not mad?

O hark—what mean those dreadful cries?
    His chains some furious madman breaks—
He comes—I see his glaring eyes—
    Now, now, my dungeon grate he shakes—
Help—help—he's gone. Oh fearful woe,
    Such screams to hear, such sights to see!
My brain, by brain—I know, I know
    I am not mad, but soon shall be.

Yes, soon—for lo, now—while I speak,
    Mark how yon demon's eyeballs glare!
He sees me—now with dreadful shriek,
    He whirls a serpent high in air!
Horror—the reptile strikes his tooth
    Deep in the heart, so crushed and sad!
Aye, laugh, ye fiends—I feel the truth—
    Your task is done—I'm mad, I'm mad!

"Scene in a Private Mad-House," *Asylum Journal,* 1 (1842):1.

AMERICAN INDUSTRIALIZATION: THE POLICY OF DEVELOPMENT

This chapter begins with a review of Civil War history and then proceeds to a more in-depth discussion of reconstruction policies and the events and actions surrounding the time—for example, the Freedman's Bureau, the suffrage movement, and the Seneca Falls Declaration. As Jansson (1997) tells us, "Americans' responses to [most of] these . . . events can be understood as a lost opportunity for social reform" (p. 83).

EMANCIPATION WITHOUT FREEDOM

Note that emancipation without freedom (Zinn, 1995) is played out as we chronicle the history of the end of slavery without the accompanying benefits of freedom. In other words, slavery ended but racism and discrimination did not. In the United States, slavery was an economic practicality supported by the government. In 1860, a million tons of cotton were produced yearly, up from a thousand tons in 1790. In the same time period, the number of slaves was 4 million, up from 500,000. The slaves lived in 15 southern states, comprising about one third of the southern population. The great majority of them were directly involved in agriculture such as growing tobacco—mostly in Maryland, Virginia, North Carolina, Kentucky, and Tennessee; raising sugar in Louisiana; cultivating rice in South Carolina and Georgia; and raising hemp in Kentucky. By far, the greatest number were involved in cotton farming in South Carolina, Georgia, Florida, Alabama, Mississippi, Louisiana, Texas, and Arkansas. Slave rebellions and conspiracies resulted in the development of networks of controls in the southern states that were backed by the laws, courts, armed forces, and race prejudice of the nation's political leaders (Levine, 1996; Zinn, 1995).

Slaves were not just field hands, however. The larger plantations had more specialized labor forces. On the bigger plantations, for example, many slaves worked as domestic servants, blacksmiths, carpenters, weavers, nursemaids, millers, gardeners, and coachmen. On the bigger estates, however, every slave was sent into the fields during high times of cotton picking and sugar harvesting. As the plantation system grew, more slaves were needed. In spite of the illegalities of slave importation, deemed illegal in 1808, it is estimated that 250,000 slaves were imported illegally before the Civil War. While the conditions of slaves varied, many historians believed that the American version of slavery was even more repressive than slavery in other countries (i.e., South America, the West Indies). Slaves in the United States were reduced to chattel; and, lacking support from church, government, and legal institutions, slaves were wholly at the mercy of their masters (Jansson, 1997; Levine, 1996).

The transportation of the slaves to America on slave ships was equally cruel and horrific. Thomas Pringle, the son of Scottish farmers in South Africa, wrote a haunting poem entitled "The Slave Dealer," suggesting the torment suffered by a man who had spent years on board a slave ship and contributed to the cruel death of many slaves (Pringle, 1834, pp. 91–93):

> From ocean's wave a Wanderer came,
>   With visage tanned and dun:
> His Mother, when he told his name,
>   Scarce knew her long-lost son;
> So altered was his face and frame
>   By the ill course he had run.
> There was hot fever in his blood,
>   And dark thoughts in his brain;
> And oh! to turn his heart to good
>   That Mother strove in vain,

For fierce and fearful was his mood,
    Racked by remorse and pain.
And if, at times, a gleam more mild
    Would o'er his features stray,
When knelt the Widow near her Child,
    And he tried with her to pray,
It lasted not—for visions wild
    Still scared good thoughts away.
'There's blood upon my hands!' he said,
    'Which water cannot wash;
My soul from murder's dye;
    Nor e'en thy prayer, dear Mother, quash
That Woman's wild death-cry!
    'Her cry is even in my ear,
And it will not let me pray;
    Her look I see—her voice I hear—
As when in death she lay,
    And said, 'With me thou must appear
On God's great Judgment-day!'
    'Now, Christ from frenzy keep my son!'
The woeful Widow cried;
    'Such murder foul thou ne'er hast done—
Some fiend thy sould belied!'—
    '—Nay, Mother! the Avenging One
Was witness when she died!
    'The writhing wretch with furious heel
I crushed—no mortal nigh;
    But that same hour her dread appeal
Was registered on high;
    And now with God I have to deal,
And dare not meet His eye!'

History is replete with stories and accounts of what slavery was like. Economists tried to assess slavery by estimating the cost of food and medical care for the slaves. This, however, falls enormously short of the reality of the human beings trapped into the life of slavery. A former slave, John Little, wrote:

> They say slaves are happy, because they laugh, and be merry. I myself and three or four others, have received two hundred lashes in the day, and had our feet in fetters; yet, at night, we would sing and dance, and make others laugh at the rattling of our chains. Happy men we must have been! We did it to keep down trouble, and to keep our hearts from being completely broken: that is as true as the gospel! Just look at us—must not we have been very happy? Yet I have done it myself—I have cut capers in chains. (Zinn, 1995, p. 168)

A poem, also written by a slave, entitled "To a Slave-Holder" follows:

Canst thou, and honor'd with a
    Christian's name,
Buy what is woman born, and feel
    no shame?

Trade in the blood of innocence, and
  plead
Expedience, as a warrant for the
  deed!
So may the wolf, whom famine has
  made bold
To quit the forest and invade the
  fold:
So may the ruffian, who with ghastly
  glide,
Dagger in hand, steals close to your
  bedside;
Not he, but his emergence, forc'd the
  door—
He found it inconvenient to be poor.

(Campbell, 1897, p. 4)

Only a full-scale slave rebellion or a full-scale war could end the deeply entrenched plantation system. History went the way of a war, with its organizers in control of the consequences rather than the smaller-scale rebellion. Abraham Lincoln was the hero, not John Brown, an abolitionist from the north, who was hanged in 1859 for his attempts to end slavery. Several years later, Lincoln would end slavery by large-scale violence (Zinn, 1995).

John Brown and Abraham Lincoln can both be described as men who fought for the end of slavery; however, their moral and philosophical views were vastly divergent. John Brown was a white abolitionist who put his life on the line to end slavery; he had the wild scheme to seize the federal arsenal at Harper's Ferry, Virginia, and then set off a revolt of slaves through the South. The plan failed, and Brown, lying wounded, under interrogation by the governor of Virginia, said, "You had better—all you people of the South—prepare yourselves for a settlement of this question. . . . You may dispose of me very easily—I am nearly disposed of now, but this question is still to be settled,—this Negro question, I mean; the end of that is not yet" (Du Bois, quoted in Zinn, 1995, p. 181). DuBois, in his book *John Brown,* says of Brown's actions:

> Picture the situation: An old and blood-bespattered man, half-dead from the wounds inflicted but a few hours before; a man lying in the cold and dirt, without sleep for fifty-five nerve-wrecking hours, without food for nearly as long, with the dead bodies of his two sons almost before his eyes, the piled corpses of his seven slain comrades near and afar, a wife and a bereaved family listening in vain, and a Lost Cause, the dream of a lifetime lying dead in his heart. . . . (Zinn, 1995, p. 181)

The state of Virginia, with the approval of the national government, executed John Brown. The national government weakly enforced the law ending the slave trade, while at the same time sternly enforcing laws that provided the return of fugitives to slavery. This era of government, under Andrew Jackson's administration, collaborated with the South to keep abolitionist literature from the people; and, the Supreme Court in 1857 refused to allow the slave Dred Scott to sue for his freedom stating he was not a person, but property. This was a government that could not accept an end to slavery by rebellion but, rather, would end slavery under controlled conditions by whites (Zinn, 1995).

There were other abolitionists in the North besides John Brown. The northern antislavery sentiment increased steadily after 1815 as more ministers, editors, and other leaders of public opinion spoke out against the evils of the slavery institution. In Ohio in 1817, Charles Osborn published *The Philanthropist,* an antislavery paper, in Jonesboro, Tennessee; in 1820, Elihu Embree was publishing *The Emancipator* in Greensboro, North Carolina, and William Swaim was expressing the opposition of Quakers to slavery; and in 1821, Benjamin Lundy began editing *The Genius of Universal Emancipation.* Lundy set forth a program for the emancipation and colonization of blacks. Within 10 years, the abolitionist became more militant, demonstrated by the publication of David Walker's "Appeal," the appearance of William Lloyd Garrison's *Liberator,* and the insurrection of Nat Turner (Franklin & Moss, 1994). Nat Turner was a slave preacher who lead a slave revolt in 1831 that killed 60 whites, including his master and family. With this revolt lead by a seemingly obedient, pious slave, along with the emergence of a new, militant abolitionist movement, southerners were more fearful than ever of rebellions (Levine, 1996).

David Walker was a free black man who spoke out passionately, calling upon blacks to rise up and throw off the yoke of slavery. The country was startled at reading the words of this black man who urged fellow blacks to resist, with force if necessary, the oppression of white masters. For a generation, Garrison was the spokesman for nonviolent militant abolition. In his first newspaper, he invoked the Declaration of Independence, claiming that the black man was as much entitled to the "life, liberty, and the pursuit of happiness" as the white man. The only solution, from his point of view, was immediate and unconditional abolition of slavery. The efforts of the abolitionists lead to the organization of the New England Anti-Slavery Society in 1831 and the American Anti-Slavery Society in Philadelphia in 1833 (Franklin & Moss, 1994).

The anti-slavery movement was multifaceted. There were many blacks with a strong abolitionist doctrine who had been preaching for the end of slavery long before Garrison was born. The Massachusetts General Colored Association was created in 1826, and the *Freedman's Journal,* the first black newspaper in the United States, was founded by John Russwurm and Samuel E. Cornish in 1827. Of the 63 delegates to the founding convention of the American Anti-Slavery Society, 3 were black, and 6 blacks served on the organization's board of managers, the most prominent among them Robert Purvis. Sojourner Truth, Harriet Tubman, and Sarah Parker Remond were among the black women in the abolitionist movement. There was conflict between Garrison's nonviolence approach and those who pushed for more militant, violent action; and there were those who opposed the anti-slavery movement all together. However, the abolitionist movement remained a strong faction pushing to end slavery (Franklin & Moss, 1994; Levine, 1996).

POLITICS AND THE ECONOMY

Unlike John Brown, Abraham Lincoln was a politician wanting to end a war and pull the nation together economically. Lincoln, by combining the needs of business and the political ambition of a newly formed Republican Party, along with the rhetoric of humanitarianism, was able to appease abolitionists and maintain a practical political advantage. Lincoln skillfully blended the interests of the very rich and the interests of the blacks at a time in history when such interests met. He also linked these two with a growing section of America— the white, up-and-coming, economically ambitious, politically active middle class. As Richard Hofstadter described it:

> Thoroughly middle class in his ideas, he spoke for those millions of Americans who had begun their lives as hired workers—as farm hands, clerks, teachers, mechanics, flatboat men, and rail-splitters—and had passed into the ranks of landed farmers, prosperous grocers, lawyers, merchants, physicians, and politicians. (Zinn, 1995, pp. 182–183)

Lincoln passionately argued against slavery on moral grounds, while acting cautiously in practical politics. He believed slavery was founded on injustice and bad policy but said that the promulgation of abolition doctrines tended to increase rather than abate its evils (Zinn, 1995). "Lincoln read the Constitution strictly, to mean that Congress, because of the Tenth Amendment (reserving to the states powers not specifically given to the national government), could not constitutionally bar slavery in the states" (p. 183).

Lincoln, refusing to publicly denounce the Fugitive Slave Law, wrote to a friend: "I confess I hate to see the poor creatures hunted down . . . but I bite my lips and keep quiet" (Zinn, 1995, p. 183). Lincoln opposed slavery but did not view slaves as equals, with his approach being to free the slaves and to send them back to Africa. In 1849, as a congressman, he did propose a resolution to abolish slavery in the District of Columbia but accompanied the resolution with a section requiring local authorities to arrest and return fugitive slaves coming into Washington. Depending on the views of his audience, Lincoln spoke differently. In his 1858 campaign speech in Illinois for the Senate race, he said:

> Let us discard all this quibbling about this man and the other man, this race and that race and the other race being inferior, and therefore they must be placed in an inferior position. Let us discard all these things, and unite as one people throughout this land, until we shall once more stand up declaring that all men are created equal. (Zinn, 1995, p. 185)

In Charleston, Illinois, just two months later, he told his audience:

> I will say, then, that I am not, nor ever have been, in favor of bringing about in any way the social and political equality of the white and black races [applause]; that I am not, nor ever have been, in favor of making voters or jurors of Negroes, nor of qualifying them to hold office, nor to intermarry with white people. . . .
>
> And inasmuch as they cannot so live, while they do remain together there must be the position of superior and inferior, and I as much as any other man am in favor of having the superior position assigned to the white race. (Zinn, 1995, p. 184)

Republican Victory and the Civil War

There is controversy among historians about the origins of the Civil War. Research suggests that it can be attributed to multiple factors. A long series of policy clashes between the South and the northern business elite lay behind the secession of the South from the Union. Contrary to conventional thinking, the clash was not over slavery as a moral institution. With the exception of the abolitionists, most northerners did not care enough about slavery to make sacrifices for it; and it was not a clash of peoples. More to the point, it had to do with wealth. Most northern whites were poor, not politically powerful, and most southern whites were poor farmers, not decision makers. The northern elite wanted economic expansion in the form of free land, free labor, a free market, a high protective tariff for manufacturers, and a bank of the United States. The slave interests opposed it all, seeing Lincoln along with the Republican Party as making continuation of their pleasant and prosperous way of life impossible in the future (Zinn, 1995).

Because of the abolitionist movement during the 1850s, the North and South drifted further apart, each feeling increasingly threatened by the other. There was outrage by northerners over the Supreme Court's *Dred Scott v. Sanford* decision. Part of the decision declared that Congress had no more power to ban slavery in the territories than it did in the states. Northerners believed this ruling was in line with the most extreme proslavery views in the South. Furthermore, they believed that the Democratic Party was dominated by pro-southern elements and were able to convince many free-state whites that slaveholding interests were running the national government. In the meantime, southerners grew increasingly convinced that slavery was in mortal danger as long as the South remained in the Union. Even more drastic laws were passed to protect slavery. Between 1855 and 1860, Virginia, Florida, Alabama, and other states passed laws allowing them to reenslave themselves, hoping to reduce the number of free blacks. Some states considered expelling free blacks (Levine, 1996; Jansson, 1997).

The southern sentiment continued to spread, especially after the election in 1860 of Republican candidate Abraham Lincoln without a single southern vote. The southern advocates for secession from the Union gained newfound strength. From December through the spring of 1861, 11 of the 15 slave states left the Union and the Civil War was set in motion shortly after a new president was elected (Levine, 1996).

By the time President-Elect Lincoln arrived in Washington the end of February 1861, the nation was rapidly falling apart. It seemed there was no pleasing either side. Lincoln perceived that his most important and difficult task was stemming the tide of national disintegration. In his inaugural address, he condemned the southern citizens who were in insurrection, but the abolitionists were not encouraged. They felt that the time for words was over; they wanted action in bringing an end to the institution of slavery against which the Republican Party had taken a stand during the election campaign (Franklin & Moss, 1994). President Lincoln laid out his priorities for the war, stating in 1862:

> My paramount object in this struggle is to save the Union and is not either to save or to destroy slavery. . . . What I do about slavery, and the colored race, I do because I believe it helps to save the Union: and what I forbear, I forbear because I do not believe it would help to save the Union. (Levine, 1996, p. 83)

Lincoln did not believe that the Constitution gave him the authority to abolish slavery in the states; therefore, he would consider emancipation only if it seemed a military necessity. There were other reasons that the president gave no support to emancipation early in the war. He believed that the Confederacy could be quickly defeated; that emancipation of the slaves would prolong the war; that the Confederate states would fight harder; that it would antagonize pro-Union elements in the Confederacy; and that it might undermine the loyalty of the five slave border states, Delaware, Maryland, Kentucky, Missouri, and West Virginia; as well as because workers in the North feared emancipation believing the freed slaves would flood the area and work for wages below existing rates. This fear was fueled when white laborers tried to raise their wages by striking and saw the willingness of employers to use black strikebreakers. There were riots in New York in 1862 when a group of black women and children working in a tobacco factory were mobbed. In time, however, various developments pushed for federal policy for emancipation and the use of black soldiers (Levine, 1996; Zinn, 1995).

By late 1861, Lincoln began to develop an emancipation program. This was done carefully, trying not to offend the slave states in the Union and public opinion in general; and it was not an easy, straightforward process. He began in November 1861 by proposing to the Delaware legislature a gradual emancipation plan over a 30-year period with the government partly compensating the masters. Delaware rejected this. Then, in March 1862, Congress was convinced to offer financial help to any state that adopted a gradual emancipation plan. There were no takers. Lincoln then tried to develop a colonization plan to send slaves abroad after emancipation, but the great majority of blacks rejected it. Finally, in April, slavery in Washington, D.C., was abolished; and, two months later, Lincoln signed a bill ending slavery in the territories (Levine, 1996).

In the summer of 1862, Lincoln went further and attacked slavery in the Confederate states. The war effort faulted, with mounting fears of a long war. The Confederate campaign against Richmond failed; the flow of Union volunteers had almost stopped; and public opinion, still with opposition, moved in favor of freeing and then arming the slaves. Lincoln signed the Emancipation Proclamation on January 1, 1863, justifying it as a military necessity, not as an act of liberation; and he signed it as the commander in chief of the armed forces, not as president. Since it was a military measure, it did not cover the border states that had remained in the Union or the Union-occupied areas of Tennessee, Louisiana, and Virginia, accounting for about one million slaves. The proclamation did cover the near 3 million slaves in Confederate territory, which was an invitation for them to cross over to the Union side. Even with its limitations, the proclamation represented a death blow to the institution of slavery, providing that the North won the war (Levine, 1996).

While slaves in the Confederate territory were not free to celebrate, word spread among them. Blacks throughout the Union were joyous, celebrating at meeting after meeting. A black man, at a gathering in Washington, D.C., expressed the feelings of others:

> Once, the time was that I cried all night. What's the matter? What's the matter? Matter enough. The next morning my child was to be sold, and she was sold, and I never 'pected to see her no more 'till the day of judgment. Now, no more that! No more that! No more that! With my hands against my breast I was going to my work, when the overseer used to whip me along. Now, no more that! No more that! No more that! (Levine, 1996, pp. 85–86)

There were songs of emancipation, too, which tended to focus on the benevolence of the government for their freedom. The songs were joyous, heralding the coming of the "Jubilee," or day of freedom, and they were sung in dialect. The following song (Crawford, 1977), "Sixty-three Is the Jubilee," was written by J. L. Greeneand in 1863:

> Oh, darkeys hab ye heered it,
> Hab ye heerd de joyful news?
> Uncle Abram's gwine to free us,
> And he'll send us where we chuse;
> For de Jubilee is comin',
> Don't ye sniff it in de air!
> And Sixty-three is de Jubilee
> For de darkeys eberwhere!

The proclamation led to a policy of the federal government taking seriously the recruiting of black soldiers. Prior to that, there were some black units, but now the president ordered the enrollment of four regiments of black infantry, as well as a battalion of mounted scouts; and recruitment headquarters were set up in New York and New Orleans. The War Department, in May 1863, formed the Bureau of Colored Troops to handle all matters relating to black units. Black troops numbered nearly 180,000, almost three quarters from the slave states. The black men served in 166 all–black units led almost entirely by white commissioned officers. The breakdown was 145 infantry, 7 cavalry, 12 heavy artillery, one light artillery, and one engineer, with more than 37,000 men losing their lives (Levine, 1996).

Despite black soldiers' great contributions, they were not treated as equals. There was a Board of Examiners within the Bureau of Colored Troops who tried to select white officers who supported the use of black soldiers, but there were seldom any blacks selected as high commissioned officers. Blacks received lower pay than whites—$10 a month with $3 going to clothing. Whites received $13 a month with nothing held out for clothing. After some protests, Congress was moved in 1864 to mandate equal pay for blacks. In the Civil War, black troops played a greater role than in the American Revolution, with their performance modifying the antiblack views of some whites (Levine, 1996).

There were many poems produced related to the Civil War. Black poet and novelist Paul Laurence Dunbar (Marius, 1994) sings the praises of the black troops' performance in "The Colored Soldiers":

> And their deeds shall find a record,
> In the registry of Fame;
> For their blood has cleansed completely
> Every blot of slavery's shame.
> So all honor and all glory
> To these noble Sons of Ham—
> To the gallant colored soldiers,
> Who fought for Uncle Sam!

and in "The Unsung Heroes":

> A song for the unsung heroes who stood the awful test,
> When the humblest host that the land could boast
> went forth to meet the best;
> A song for the unsung heroes who fell on the bloody sod,
> Who fought their way from night to day and struggled up to God.

Their valiant service for the Union became a strong argument in behalf of equal rights for blacks after the Civil War (Levine, 1996).

SOCIAL WELFARE AND RECONSTRUCTION

More American lives were lost, percentage-wise, during the Civil War than during World War II. The battlefield causalities reflected but one portion of the human toll. People by the millions were dislocated during and after the war, and freed slaves were cast into a society with few economic or social supports. Enormous relief problems were created for wounded and disabled soldiers, as well as for bereaved families who lost their male breadwinners, and for displaced slaves. The devastation in the South was great. Cities were in ruin; transportation lines were destroyed; and fields were barren. Money was not available for seeds, machinery, or livestock, with near famine occurring because of drought and the lack of organized workers. The first concern for the southern states was getting artificial limbs and cash payments to veterans, enabling them to work, and second was provisions for war orphans. The war aroused the charitable energies of the American people with public officials and private citizens responding as never before (Jansson, 1997; Trattner, 1999).

The social welfare issue of dislocated persons in the wake of the Civil War received only secondary attention, and these people were addressed improvisationally. As it turned out, the northern Union army was the major instrument of social welfare because of its presence in the South. At issue was the support of the vast numbers of African Americans who had left plantations either because the Union Army had conquered southern territory, or because slaves fled behind Union lines. Many camps were constructed and maintained with former slaves being placed in barracks or tents and given food and health care. The surroundings provided by the camps were harsh, with roughly 25% of their occupants dying of disease (Jansson, 1997).

Black people were not the only victims of disease and death. Because the first contingents of the northern troops were hurried into battle, few provisions were made for their sanitary or medical care and thousands of men died unnecessarily in the absence of medical supplies. As a result, concerned citizens organized the U.S. Sanitary Commission in 1861, representing the nation's first public health group. Numerous local voluntary relief societies were united into a national organization that would supplement the work of governmental agencies in meeting the physical and spiritual needs of the men in uniform (Trattner, 1999). There were legions of volunteers in the North sent to assist refugees behind Union lines. There were provisions such as clothing, food, and medical supplies and the development of some schools. In the South, there were various government departments developing programs for assistance (Jansson, 1997).

There was a difference, however, between the services provided for the Union troops and those provided for the freed slaves. It was the view of some military administrators of the camps and most citizens that the freed slaves were intrinsically lazy; and, consequently, many were placed on work details on camp fortifications or they worked under contract labor on plantations in conquered territories. The War Department operated the camps for the freed slaves, with the Treasury Department controlling the lands that had been confiscated from Confederate landowners (Jansson, 1997).

Even with the different treatment that existed between the freed slaves and the Union troops, the social and economic changes arising from the Civil War were completely interwoven with other consequences of the war, making

the black-white issues inseparable. For example, while the South did not experience great industrial development during the war, the North did; and the
forces let loose were so powerful that they affected the entire course of Reconstruction (Franklin & Moss, 1994). "The political changes that began with the
secession of the southern states affected the whole nation, but the economic
transformation brought on by numerous changes in production and distribution demanded the attention of every practical-minded person in the United
States" (p. 220).

Reconstruction must be studied in its setting to grasp the full understanding of its impact on history. The history is not of "Negro rule," as many
historians have dubbed the period of Radical Reconstruction; nor is it merely
southern. It is an integral part of the national history where we can find explanations for events in Alabama not only in the activities of people in that state
but in the movements and transactions of Boston, New York, or Philadelphia
citizens as well. The United States, from 1865 to the end of the century, was
picking up the threads of its social, political, and economic life, which were so
abruptly cut in 1861, and attempting to weave them into a new pattern. The
political life in South Carolina after 1865 was not just affected by the presence
of blacks in the state legislature or in other positions of public trust; it was also
affected by the dynamic changes of a nationwide economic reconstruction
(Franklin & Moss, 1994). Between 1865 and 1900, America underwent a spec-
tacular expansion of productive facilities and output that was without parallel
in the world's history. The growth did not proceed uniformly; nor was it distributed equally among industries, among regions of the country, or among
population groups (Axinn & Levin, 1997; Trattner, 1999).

White southerners traveling in the North after the Civil War were stunned
by the changes that a few years had wrought in the section's economic life.
Pressing military needs, extensive inflation of Union currency, and the stimulating effort of protective tariff legislation all had conspired to industrialize the
North. Events were taking place that would have strained the imagination two
decades earlier. For example, steel factories were producing much more than
what was needed to sustain the war effort; railroads were rapidly connecting
the North and the West in one large community, and hundreds of technologi-
cal developments made possible the production of commodities. With the
almost unlimited new forms of economic organization that emerged, with possibilities for expansion throughout the nation and the world, leaders were
filled with a desperate anxiety to create monopolies and reap huge profits.
Northerners willingly sold to ex-Confederates as they did to northerners. It
became apparent to the most discerning white southern that the new order of
things was the result of the triumph of industrialism over the agrarian way of
life. The symbols of triumph were the new and old bustling cities, while the
wasted and abandoned lands of the South signified the defeat of the old agrar-
ianism. White southerners soon saw that if their section was not careful, its

economic and psychological defeat would be as complete as its military downfall (Franklin & Moss, 1994).

In the period after the Civil War, the political situation was much disturbed; the problem of the reorganization of the seceded states was only part of the unsettled state of political affairs. The president had wielded many powers during the war that would not be tolerated in peace, and even before the war's end Congress was anxious to restore the balance of the three branches of government (Franklin & Moss, 1994). Many difficult choices faced Lincoln. One of these choices was supporting policies that would guarantee freed slaves the right to vote, give them access to public accommodations, and give them access to federal courts where they were harassed by local citizens. Also, to prevent the restoration of racist policies, Lincoln could have excluded former Confederate officials from local, state, or federal government; but he chose a course of caution, deferring to the southern states and restoring their power as quickly as possible. He did this, in part, because he did not want to stiffen the resolve of the South to fight to the bitter end. Military governors were appointed in each state and promised a return to civilian and southern rule with the requirement that 10% of the white population vote their loyalty to the Union and agree to end slavery. The passivity of the federal government allowed southern states to retain laws that prohibited African Americans from voting, as well as infringing on other civil liberties. This stance was strongly opposed by many abolitionists, who feared that the South would soon return to a system of quasi-slavery giving black nominal freedom but no land, resources, or the vote. The abolitionists' arguments went unheeded by Lincoln who was solely intent on restoring order in the South on terms that were acceptable to southern leadership (Jansson, 1997). History went the way of Reconstruction rather than radical reform.

The emancipation of the slaves did not change white racism in the North or in the South. It is doubtful, had Lincoln lived, that he could have imposed enlightened policies on southerners toward the freed slaves, because most of them were antagonistic to African Americans, just as most northerners were (Jansson, 1997). The unexpected accession of Andrew Johnson to the presidency merely complicated matters, making Congress more determined than ever to have a full share in governing the country. As we study the politics of the period, we cannot overlook certain factors such as the fear the Republicans had of losing political control, the pressure of new industrialists for favorable legislation, and conflicting philosophies of Reconstruction (Franklin & Moss, 1994).

President Johnson's term of office was a disaster for freed slaves. He was an unabashed southerner who not only detested blacks but also bitterly disliked the southern aristocracy. His goal was to develop a political base among white monied interests in the postwar South. His policies went so far as to embolden southern white leaders to develop "Black Codes" that would limit black's ability to move around the countryside, restrict their rights of assembly and free speech, and subject them to whippings for discourteous behavior (Jansson, 1997). Black children fell victim to the Codes, too; for example, in Mississippi in 1865, all black people under 18 years of age who were orphans, or whose parents were unable to support them, were declared available for apprenticing. Former masters were given preference, and the children were not afforded guarantees in regard to food, clothing, and education as were white children who were written into indenture ship agreements (Axinn & Levin, 1997).

These Codes bore a remarkable resemblance to the antebellum Slaves Codes and can hardly be described as measures that respected the rights of freed blacks. Nonetheless, of great concern to southerners was the problem of controlling blacks. Ugly rumors abounded of a general uprising in which blacks would take vengeance on whites. While most southern whites were willing to concede the end of slavery, they were convinced that laws should be speedily enacted to curb blacks and to ensure their role as a laboring force in the South (Franklin & Moss, 1994).

Friends of African Americans refused to accept Johnson's sanctioning of white home rule in the South, which bore a striking similarity to that existing before the Civil War. Abolitionists demanded that blacks be enfranchised and a harsher policy adopted toward the South. Republicans, fearing the political consequences of a South dominated by Democrats, became convinced that black suffrage in the South would aid in the continued growth of their party. Industrialists were fearful that the old agrarian system would be resurrected by the Democrats, diminishing markets without cheap labor. The groups pooled their interests with the intent of substantially modifying Johnson's policy of Reconstruction. In December 1865, when Congress met, it was determined to take charge of Reconstruction (Franklin & Moss, 1994).

Johnson was defeated in the congressional election about the same time that northerners demanded passage of a succession of civil rights act. In 1865, the northern states ratified the Thirteenth Amendment to the Constitution, which abolished slavery. Under the Military Reconstruction Act of 1867, southern states were required to include universal suffrage in their constitutions before they could be readmitted to the Union, allowing the army to serve as a protector of civil rights by bypassing local courts. In 1868, the Fourteenth Amendment was ratified, rescinding the provision in the Constitution that had counted each African American as only three fifths a person, required that all citizens be given equal protection under the law, and stipulated that all persons be accorded the protection of due process. In 1870, the Fifteenth Amendment established universal suffrage of adult males, but it did not exclude the use of poll taxes and literacy tests, which southern jurisdictions eventually utilized to disenfranchise black Americans. Civil rights acts were enacted, one in 1870 that limited the ability of states to enforce discriminatory legislation and one in 1875 that outlawed segregation in public facilities and schools. The southern states reeled in the light of this onslaught of federal legislation, which was enforced only by the North's imposition of laws and troops (Jansson, 1997). History tells us that this did not last long; through various untoward tactics, equality was blocked for African Americans, and racism and discrimination continued.

Because of the excesses of "white reconstruction," Congress saw fit to require the Confederate states to call state conventions to create more representative state governments and to ratify the Fourteenth Amendment to the Constitution. This was to be a prerequisite for readmission into the Union. This was in 1867; and, by 1870, all the southern states had complied. There was no requirement of redistribution of land, and little was achieved. The role of state government was enlarged in matters of expenditures for social welfare and education for black and whites with the evolution of a pattern of separate institutions for the races. There was considerable discussion of state responsibility, but no comprehensive programs of state welfare emerged. Each state followed its own limited design in building orphanages, mental hospitals, and almshouses with local responsibility for relief being endemic (Axinn & Levin, 1997).

As the Civil War came to an end, the acute problem of aiding the freed men and women faced the nation. There were several million people who were largely uneducated, unskilled, and unprepared for their abrupt change in status; and all would be in search of employment and assistance, primarily in the South. This was a national problem, since, for the most part, the southern communities and states had neither the resources nor the desire to deal with it. Two months before the war ended, in March 1865, Congress established—in the U.S. War Department—the Bureau of Refugees, Freedmen, and Abandoned Lands—known as the Freedmen's Bureau—in essence, the nation's first federal welfare agency (Trattner, 1999).

A precursor to the Freedmen's Bureau was the Port Royal Experiment of 1862. In South Carolina, when faced with the Union army's advance, whites abandoned the plantations of the Port Royal area, leaving 10,000 slaves to fend for themselves. Their distress led to the establishment, without funding, of the experimental relief and rehabilitation program. Volunteer organizations, the National Freedmen's Relief Association of New York and the Boston Education Commission, supplied most of the labor and funding. These several hundred volunteers saw to the distribution of food and clothing and the rehabilitation of abandoned and pillaged homes. They also established schools for black children and attempted to use free labor in large-scale cotton cultivation. The experiment was considered a success, but the needs of the South were beyond the resources of volunteer organizations—hence, the congressionally established Freedmen's Bureau (Axinn & Levin, 1997).

The only criterion for eligibility was need; consequently, thousands of white southerners, as well as other freed people, relied on the Freedmen's Bureau for relief. Because of the great displacement caused by the war, there were no residence requirements. The services to families were comprehensive in nature, providing food, shelter, and clothing; counseling to restore family relationships; advocacy for children; and free medical care and employment services, including training. The Bureau also distributed land and building materials at minimal amounts; established institutions for the orphaned and older adults; and opened more than 4,000 schools for children of both races. As it evolved, the Bureau became an agency for civil rights advice and advocacy. It distributed 18.3 million rations in its first 3 years, about 5.2 million going to white people. Twenty-one million rations had been distributed by the end of its fourth year with 6 million going to white people. As an education agency, it not only encouraged the founding of African American schools but also provided them with financial aid, supporting universities, such as Howard, Atlanta, and Fisk; Hampton Institute; and Talladega College (Day, 1989).

The Bureau was renewed in 1866 over Presidents Johnson's veto and extended until 1872. The Freedmen's Bureau demonstrated that the federal government could provide for the welfare of people on a large scale when poverty and hardship could not be treated locally. It seems, though, that the Bureau was ahead of its time, as its impact on the social welfare policies of the era—public and private—was nil (Trattner, 1999).

THE STATE OF AFFAIRS OF WOMEN

The colonial period, with the doctrine of separate spheres, led to the cult of domesticity, which consigned women to household and familial functions. The professions and businesses were reserved for males. With the importance attached to child rearing, the economic roles of women were further constrained. The roles of married women were predominately raising children and administering their households, with few rights to own or manage property. It was rare for a married, middle- or upper-class woman to work outside the home, and many working-class women avoided external work when possible. Of course, female slaves were given no choice. This prohibition against labor did not extend to single women who dominated work as domestics and live-in servants. The working conditions for these women were harsh with low wages, and only one day off each week, and many were ill-treated by employers. Some women who sought more independence found scarce jobs in factories in New England, but they, too, experienced the same harsh conditions as domestic servants—long hours and low pay (Jansson, 1997).

The post–Civil War era saw the status of women change. Middle-class women, with their expanded affluence offering more independence and leisure, sought to establish a proper place for themselves more nearly equivalent in significance and power to that of men. While women participated in the abolition movement, the drive for women's rights ceased as they became engaged in wartime tasks. They took on war-related services that the government had not been prepared for; they took jobs vacated by men going off to battle; they worked in industries and businesses, on farms and plantations, and in the professions. Working at the bench and loom, teaching and nursing, organizing and managing, some women thought this was proof of equality with men and were shocked with the passage and ratification of the Fourteenth Amendment, which explicitly defined voters as men. Another rebuff came with the passage and ratification of the Fifteenth Amendment, extending suffrage to include black men while excluding women (Axinn & Levin, 1996).

Women were expected to quietly return home at the end of the war; but, because of the very economic, industrial, and social advances that were stimulated by the war, this never happened. This was a time for the advancement of women with white, middle- and upper-class career women forming a new generation of educated women, with Vassar being founded in 1865, Smith in 1871, and Bryn Mawr in 1885. Of those women who graduated from college before 1900, 75% remained single with large numbers moving into settlement work or casework. Freed from homemaking by new technologies such as indoor plumbing, electric lighting, washing machines, vacuum cleaners, nonfire cookers, canned food, and bread that was cheaper to buy than bake, middle-class women aspired to paid work, social reform, and college. Married women, too, began entering the workplace in great numbers; and, by 1890, women comprised 18 percent of the labor force (Day, 1999; Axinn & Levine, 1996).

Professional women, ethnic women, African American women, and working women across the nation formed thousands of clubs and by the late 1880s coalesced into national organizations, for example, the National Council of Clubs and the General Federation of Women's Clubs. The General Federation of Women's Clubs had nearly a million members by 1920 who were active in improving the social environment; investigating sanitation and government corruption; and raising money for worthy causes like hospital, schools, and homes for the aged. These clubs also became involved in the labor struggles of wage-earning women. The African American counterpart consisted of clubs that supported the new class of working black women by giving them places to live, a community of safety, and emotional and spiritual help. There were 2.7 million black women over the age of 10, with a million working for wages, nearly 39% in agriculture, 30.8% in domestic service, 15.6% as laundresses, and 2.8% in manufacturing. Discrimination was present, but many still managed to enter some professions. Charlotte E. Ray (1850–1911) was the first African American woman lawyer to practice in the United States. She received her law degree from Howard University. Prejudice eventfully forced her from practice, and she went into teaching. Others were Caroline V. Still, a doctor; Anna J. Cooper, a teacher in Washington, D.C.; and Fannie Barrier Williams, who founded the first school for African American nurses (Day, 1989).

The first truly national women's organization, the Women's Christian Temperance Union (WCTU), was born in 1874. The women saw as their mission the fight against alcohol use and abuse, seeing it as an evil that permeated all aspects of society. However, before this strong women's movement, during the colonial era, the Seneca Falls Convention in 1848 paved the way for women's voices to be heard. Seeds of discontentment among women were sown at the convention in Seneca Falls, New York, which issued a Declaration of Sentiments modeled after the Declaration of Independence (Jansson, 1997). The meeting was called to consider the social, civil, and religious conditions and rights of women, with one advertised speaker, Lucretia Mott, of Philadelphia. She was widely known for her anti-slavery speeches and as a Quaker "minister." However, Elizabeth Cady Stanton was the impelling force behind the meeting. The two women had met in London eight years earlier at the World's Anti-Slavery Convention where they witnessed the exclusion of all the female delegates from the convention (Schneir, 1992). Based on the discrimination against women at the London convention, Stanton later wrote that the experience "stung many women into new thought and action" (Schneir, 1992, p. 77). In her memoirs, she wrote:

> My experiences at the World's Anti-Slavery Convention, all I had read of the legal status of women, and the oppression I saw everywhere, together swept across my soul, intensified now by many personal experiences. . . . [I]n this tempest-tossed condition of mind I received an invitation to spend the day with Lucretia Mott. . . . I poured out the torrent of my long-accumulating discontent with such vehemence and indignation that I stirred myself, as well as the rest of the party. (pp. 77–78)

It was then that the decision was made to call a women's rights meeting. Just prior to the convention, Stanton, with Lucretia Mott and others, drew up the Seneca Falls Declaration of Sentiments and Resolutions (Schneir, 1992).

So we see that the discontentment of the colonial era women rose not only from the treatment women received as abolitionists and the unjust labor laws of the time but also from the World's Anti-Slavery Convention in London. Indeed, women who were abolitionists working to end slavery in America also saw what Stanton and Mott encountered at the London convention, quickly recognizing a similar incongruity between the equal rights doctrines of their nation and their own limited legal and social roles. American women experienced similar discrimination in their work as abolitionists, not just from male abolitionists, who sought to limit their roles to those in the background, but also from the public, who often objected to women speaking in public (Jansson, 1997).

There were almost 300 persons who attended the Seneca Falls Convention, with eleven resolutions being adopted. The twelfth one, pertaining to granting women elective franchise, passed only by a narrow margin after Frederick Douglass defended it from the floor (Jansson, 1997; Schneir, 1992). The signed document, in part, declared: "We hold these truths to be self-evident that all men and women are created equal" and "have the duty to throw off such government" that visits on them "a long train of abuses and usurpation." This was a remarkable and prescient document with the signing attacking the cult of domesticity and the prevalent notion that women were intellectually and legally inferior to men. The persons involved demanded suffrage, access to the professions, and legal rights—for example, the right to hold property while married. There were similar conferences that followed this convention, roughly one each year between 1849 and the outbreak of the Civil War in 1861 (Jansson, 1997).

More of this history can be told through the use of letters, editorials, speeches, and personal narratives. Frederick Douglass (1817–1895) was born a slave in Maryland and had been a free man for 10 years at the time of the Seneca Falls meeting. He lived in Rochester, New York, where he was the editor of a weekly abolitionist newspaper, *The North Star*. In his autobiography, he wrote:

> When the true history of the antislavery cause shall be written, women will occupy a large space in its pages, for the cause of the slave has been peculiarly woman's cause. . . . Observing woman's agency, devotion, and efficiency in pleading the cause of the slave [he added], gratitude for this high service early moved me to give favorable attention to the subject of what is called "woman's rights" and caused me to be denominated a woman's-rights man. I am glad to say that I have never been ashamed to be thus designated. (Schneir, 1992, p. 83)

Not only was Douglass present at Seneca Falls, but the following decades saw him as a frequent participant in many other woman's rights conventions. While most Americans reacted to the founding of a woman's movement with a storm of ridicule and abuse, Douglass printed the following editorial in *The North Star*, July 28, 1848:

> One of the most interesting events of the past week was the holding of what is technically styled a Woman's Rights Convention at Seneca Falls. The speaking, addresses, and resolutions of this extraordinary meeting were almost wholly conducted by women; and although they evidently felt themselves in a novel position, it is but simple justice to say that their whole proceedings were characterized by marked ability and dignity. . . . We should not do justice to our own convictions, or to the excellent persons connected with this infant movement, if we did not . . . offer a few remarks on the general subject [pertaining to the] Convention. . . . [The] contemptuous ridicule and scornful disfavor is likely to excite against us the fury of bigotry and the folly of prejudice. It is in their estimation, to be guilty of evil thoughts, to think that woman is entitled to equal rights with man. Many who have at last made the discovery that the negroes have some rights as well as other members of the human family, have yet to be convinced that women are entitled to any. . . . We go farther, and express our conviction that all political rights which it is expedient for man to exercise, it is equally true of

woman; and if that government only is just which governs by the free consent of the governed, there can be no reason in the world for denying to woman the exercise of the elective franchise, or a hand in making and administering the laws of the land. Our doctrine is the "right is of no sex." We therefore bid the women engaged in this movement our humble Godspeed. (Schneir, 1992, pp. 83–85)

William Lloyd Garrison (1805–1879), the creator and editor of the antislavery newspaper *The Liberator*, became, like Douglass, a vigorous supporter of the woman's movement. He too attended the World's Anti-Slavery Convention in London and, upon learning that the female delegates for the United States had been barred from taking their rightful place at the proceedings, declined to take his own seat or to participate in the meeting, declaring: "After battling so many long years for the liberties of African slaves, I can take no part in a convention that strikes down the most sacred rights of all women" (Schneir, 1992, p. 86). Other men lent their names and voices to the feminist conventions: Thomas Wentworth Higginson, Wendell Phillips, Theodore Parker, and Parker Pillsbury (Schneir, 1992).

In Cleveland in 1853, the Seneca Falls Declaration of Sentiments was criticized from the audience by a male speaker who thought the document unfairly blamed men for the condition of women. Garrison, who could not brook such an approach, took the floor, saying:

> It was this morning objected to the Declaration of Sentiments, that it implied that man was the only transgressor . . . and our eloquent friend, Mrs. Rose, who stood on this platform . . . told us she did not blame anybody, really, and did not hold any man to be criminal. . . . For my own part, I am not prepared to respect that philosophy. I believe in sin, therefore in a sinner; in theft, therefore in a thief; in slavery, therefore in a slaveholder; in wrong, therefore in a wrong-doer; and unless the men of this nation are made by woman to see that they have been guilty of usurpation, and cruel usurpation, I believe very little progress will be made. . . . I, too, believe things are done through misconception and misapprehension, which are injurious, yes, which are immoral and unchristian; but only to a limited extent. There is such a thing as intelligent wickedness, a design on the part of those who have the light to quench it, and to do the wrong to gratify their own propensities, and to further their own interests. So, then, I believe, that as man has monopolized for generations all the rights which belong to woman, it has not been accidental, not through ignorance on his part; but I believe that man has done this through calculation, actuated by a spirit of pride, a desire for domination which has made him degrade woman in her own eyes, and thereby tend to make her a mere vassal.
>
> It seems to me, therefore, that we are to deal with the consciences of men. . . . The men of this nation, and the men of all nations, have no just respect for women. They have tyrannized over her deliberately, they have not sinned through ignorance, but theirs is not the knowledge that saves. . . . Is not the light all around us? Does not this nation know how great its guilt is in enslaving one-sixth of its people? Do not the men of this nation know ever since the landing of the pilgrims, that they are wrong in making subject one-half of the people? . . .

How has this Woman's Rights movement been treated in this country, on the right hand and on the left? This nation ridicules and derides this movement, and spits upon it, as fit only to be cast out and trampled underfoot. This is not ignorance. They know all about the truth. It is the Natural outbreak of tyranny. It is because the tyrants and usurpers are alarmed. They have been called to judgment, and they dread the examination and exposure of their position and character. . . . (Schneir, 1992, p. 89)

Two French feminists wrote a letter addressing the Second National Convention at Worcester in 1851 expressing their joy at the Seneca Falls Declaration of women's rights (Schneir, 1992, pp. 91–92):

June 15, 1851

Dear Sisters:

Your courageous declaration of Women's Rights has resounded even to our prison, and has filled our souls with inexpressible joy. In France, reaction has suppressed the cry of liberty of women. . . . The darkness of reaction has obscured the sun on 1848, which seemed to rise so radiantly. Why? Because the revolutionary tempest, in overturning at the same time the throne and the scaffold, in breaking the chain of the black slave, forgot to break the chain of the most oppressed of all—of Woman, the pariah of humanity. . . .

But, while those selected by half of the people—by men alone—evoke force to stifle liberty and forge restrictive laws to establish order by compulsion, women, guided by fraternity, foreseeing incessant struggles, and in the hope of putting an end to them, make an appeal to the laborer to found liberty and equality on fraternal solidarity . . . the laborer recognizes the right of women, his companion is labor.

The delegates of a hundred and four associations, united, without distinction of sex, elected two women with several of their brothers to participate equally with them in the administration of the interests of labor and in the organization of the work of solidarity. . . .

It is in the name of law framed by man only . . . that the Old World . . . has shut up within the walls of a prison . . . those elected by the laborers. . . .

Sisters of America! Your socialist sisters of France are united with you in the vindication of the rights of woman to civil and political equality. We have, moreover, the profound conviction that only by the power of association based on solidarity—by the union of the working classes of both sexes to organize labor—can be acquired, completely and pacifically, the civil and political equality of woman, and the social right for all.

It is this confidence that, from the depths of the jail which still imprisons our bodies without reaching our hearts, we cry to you, Faith, Love, Hope, and send to you our sisterly salutations.

                                                Jeanne Deroin and Pauline Roland

Another leader in this movement was Sojourner Truth (1795–1883), born into slavery in New York State and freed in 1827 when that state emancipated its slaves. She was "called by the Lord" at age 46 to travel up and down the land testifying to the sins against her people. She dropped her slave name, Isabella, and took the symbolic name of Sojourner Truth. She spoke wherever she could get an audience, and by mid century she was well known voice in both anti-slavery circles and abolitionist gatherings. From the early years of the women's movement, she consistently and actively identified herself with the feminist cause. She was the only African American women in attendance at the First National Woman's Rights Convention in Worcester, Massachusetts, in 1850. There were still a million and a half African American women of the South still in slavery, and they were not forgotten at the convention. A resolution was adopted that referred to these women as "the most grossly wronged and foully outraged of all women" and vowing that, "in every effort for an improvement in our civilization, we will bear in our heart of hearts the memory of the trampled womanhood of the plantation, and omit no effort to raise it to a share in the rights we claim for ourselves" (Schneir, 1992, p. 93).

The next year at the woman's convention at Akron, Ohio, Sojourner Truth spoke over the protests of a male clerical presence who opposed the granting of freedom to women, and of some of the women in attendance who feared that their cause would be mixed with abolition:

> Well, children, where there is so much racket there must be something out of kilter. I think that 'twixt the negroes of the South and the women of the North, all talking about rights, the white men will be in a fix pretty soon. But what's all this here talking about?
>
> That man over there says that women need to be helped into carriages, and lifted over ditches, and to have the best place everywhere. Nobody ever helps me into carriages, or over mud-puddles, or gives me any best places! And ain't I a women? Look at me! Look at my arm! I have ploughed and planted, and gathered into barns, and no man could head me! And ain't I a woman? I could work as much and eat as much as a man—when I could get it—and bear the lash as well!! And ain't I a women? I have borne thirteen children, and seen them most all sold off to slavery, and when I cried out with my mother's grief, none but Jesus heard me! And ain't I a woman?
>
> Then they talk about this thing in the head; what's this they call it? [Intellect, someone whispers.] That's it, honey. What's that got to do with women's rights or negro's rights? If my cup won't hold but a pint, and yours holds a quart, wouldn't you be mean not to let me have my little half-measure full? Then that little man in black there, he says women can't have as much rights as men, 'cause Christ wasn't a woman! Where did your Christ come from? Where did your Christ come from? From God and a woman! Man had nothing to do with Him. If the first woman God ever made was strong enough to turn the world upside down all alone, these women together ought to be able to turn it back, and get it right side up again! And now they is asking to do it, the men better let them.
>
> Obliged to you for hearing me, and now old Sojourner Truth ain't got nothing more to say. (Schneir, 1992, pp. 94–95)

Truth never learned to read or write, and her speech was not officially recorded but survives because it was written down by Frances Gage, without the heavy dialogue. The simple moving words of Truth had an effect on the gathering that Gage described as "magical." Gage went on to say that the speaker had "taken us up in her strong arms and carried us safely over the slough of difficulty turning the whole tide in our favor" (Schneir, 1992, p. 94).

The women's property measure was defeated in 1854, and it was six years before another opportunity presented itself for an all-out effort in the New York State Legislature. Susan B. Anthony, a confidante and supporter of Elizabeth Cady Stanton, told her that the salvation of the women in the state depended upon her power to move "the hearts of our law-makers at this time." Stanton described their joint efforts in her upcoming speech to the legislature as well as in dozens of other writings. "In thought and sympathy we were one, and in the division of labor we exactly complemented each other. I am the better writer, she the better critic. She supplied the facts and statistics, I the philosophy and rhetoric, and, together, we have made arguments that stood unshaken through the storms of long years; arguments that no one has answered. Our speeches may be considered the united product of our two brains." Speaking on the very eve of the Civil War, Stanton asserted that "The prejudice against color . . . is no stronger than that against sex" (Schneir, 1992, p. 117).

After the Civil War, a division and regrouping occurred in the women's movement as women suspended their activities for women's rights to devote full energy to the Union cause. Women's contributions to the war effort were great with them serving in nursing services, fund-raising, and even some brave military exploits. It was during this time that a National Woman's Loyal League was formed under the leadership of Anthony and Stanton, which, in effect, functioned as an arm of the Republican Party's radical wing. They collected hundreds of thousands of petition signatures calling for abolition of slavery. The women were bitterly disillusioned when the proposed Fourteenth Amendment to the Constitution omitted any preference to women. It was the widely held view that this was "the Negro's hour," and that women had no decent course available but to stand aside and wait their turn (Schneir, 1992).

Lucy Stone, a faithful feminist, was torn in her loyalties, writing: ". . . woman has an ocean of wrong too deep for any plummet," yet "the Negro too has an ocean of wrong that cannot be fathomed." On the other hand, Stanton and Anthony openly opposed the constitutional amendments which guaranteed suffrage to the black man but not to women. Stanton argued that "The demand of the hour is equal rights to all" (Schneir, 1992, p. 129).

Sojourner Truth came forward to stand alone for the all but forgotten black woman and was greeted by a cheering audience.

> My friends, I am rejoiced that you are glad, but I don't know how you will feel when I get through. I come from another field—the country of the slave. They have got their liberty—so much good luck to have slavery partly destroyed; not entirely. I want it root and branch destroyed. Then we will all be free indeed. I feel that if I have to answer for the deeds done in my body just as much as a man, I have a right to have just as much as a man. There is a great stir about colored men getting their rights, but not a word about the colored woman; and if colored

men get their rights, and not colored woman theirs, you see the colored men will be masters over the women, and it will be just as bad as it was before. So I am for keeping the thing going while things are stirring; because if we wait till it is still, it will take a great while to get it going again. White women are a great deal smarter, and know more than colored women, while colored women do not know scarcely anything. They go out washing, which is about as high as a colored woman gets, and their men go about idle, strutting up and down, and when the women come home, they ask for their money and take it all, and then scold because there is not food. I want you to consider on that, chil'n. I call you chil'n, you are somebody's chil'n, and I am old enough to be mother of all that is here. I want women to have their rights. In the courts women have no right, no voice; nobody speaks for them. I wish woman to have her voice there among the petti-foggers. If it is not a fit place for women, it is unfit for m en to be there . . . (Schneir, 1992, pp. 129–30).

The two factions of the American woman's movement were reunited as the National American Suffrage Association in 1890. Stanton was not totally in agreement with this stance, fearing that it so narrowed the platform to the single issue of suffrage that the movement would henceforth cease to "point the way." She wrote, "It is germane to our platform to discuss every invidious distinction of sex . . . covering the whole range of human experience." Despite the basic disagreement of goals, she was elected first president (Schneir, 1992, p. 155).

We end this section of this important woman's movement of the 19th century with excerpts from two of Stanton's last speeches given to the 1890 and 1892 convention respectively.

Some men tell us we must be patient and persuasive; that we must be womanly. My friends, what is man's idea of womanliness? It is to have a manner which pleases him—quiet, deferential, submissive, approaching him as a subject does a master. He wants no self-assertion on our part, no defiance, no vehement arraignment of him as a robber and a criminal . . . while every right achieved by the oppressed has been wrung from tyrants by force; while the darkest page on human history is the outrages on women—shall men still tell us to be patient, per-suasive, womanly? (p. 155).

And, "The point I wish plainly to bring before you on this occasion is the individuality of each human soul . . . In discussing the rights of women, we are to consider, first, what belongs to her as an individual, in a world of her own, the arbiter of her own destiny, an imaginary Robinson Crusoe with her woman Friday on a solitary island. Her rights under such circumstances are to use all her faculties for her own safety and happiness . . . " (p. 157)

LOOKING AT THE ERA FROM A STRENGTHS PERSPECTIVE

Having the power, or capacity, to influence the forces which affect one's life space for one's benefit is an essential, psychological component affecting all aspects of life. The flip side, of course, is powerlessness and the incapacity to exert such influence (Pinderhughes, 1983). Both the African Americans, during slavery and after, and women of that time period, to a large extent, were powerless to exert much influence over their lives. But they struggled, and many survived their oppression. How? The women gathered strength in numbers and a collective voice through organizing and speaking out publicly. For African Americans, the journey took a different course. One of the barriers for African Americans was the fact that social welfare and social reform did not really begin in earnest until the turn of the century, primarily because the larger society chose to pay little attention to their suffering.

CHALLENGES TO SOCIAL WELFARE

To set the stage for the discussion on the strengths of the slave culture, a critique of the Gilded Age is provided. The 19th century comprises three central experiences—the frontier, the Civil War, and industrialization—each posing different social welfare challenges. Many persons were benefited by each, and each created social casualties. For example, the frontier displaced Native Americans, Spanish-speaking persons, destitute farmers, and exploited laborers; the Civil War freed slaves and poor white refugees; and industrialization's casualties were workers who were unemployed, underpaid, or disabled (Jansson, 1997).

Americans glamorized the successes of the Gilded Age (extending from the Civil War to the end of the 19th century) and paid relatively little attention to the casualties, choosing not to construct policies to alleviate suffering. "The nation virtually pursued a policy of genocide toward Native Americans and Spanish-speaking persons. Asian and Latino laborers were deprived of their fundamental rights and subjected to virulent racism in local communities" (Jansson, 1997, p. 105). Freed slaves were given scant assistance and were left to wander in a racist society as they made the difficult transition from slavery to freedom. Industrialists were left unchecked in their exploitation of workers, which included women and children who were often placed in dangerous working environments (Jansson, 1997).

Americans were strikingly similar in their interpretations of each: the frontier was idealized as a place where Christian religion and values were defended against savages; industrialization was viewed as an American success story, whereby self-made men rose to prominence by dint of hard work; and the Civil War was perceived as the triumphs of morality over the greed of shareholders and of nationalism over the renegade southern secessionists. Furthermore, the negative outcomes of these three experiences were interpreted by many Americans in a manner that blamed their victims rather than American social institutions and values. For example, in the case of slavery, it was believed by most Americans that, once freed, the slaves were given the same "fair shake" that had been extended to white immigrants; personal short-comings were commonly attributed to their lack of economic success and not to the racism of society or the intrinsic difficulties in making a transition from slavery (Jansson, 1997). A closer look at history tells a much different story.

RESISTANCE AND RESILIENCY OF THE SLAVE CULTURE

Lacking the power to influence the forces that affected their lives for their benefit, the slaves possessed tremendous inherent strengths that helped them survive the atrocities that beset them. Resistance and resiliency are indeed strengths; and, through these strengths, many slaves survived their bondage. Among the freed slaves and other blacks, leadership emerged. Some of the leaders became well known and are mentioned in present-day literature for their work in Reconstruction; others were local community leaders who had been slaves (Magdol, 1974). In the absence of social welfare policies, the black leadership brought about alternative means to help with the staggering transition from slavery.

Whites, in theory, had almost absolute power over their slaves. In reality, however, bondspeople found many ways—short of open revolt—to get better treatment and preserve their self-respect. They discovered how to put pressure on their masters if they failed to fulfill their responsibilities. For example, a Mississippi planter warned an overseer that if he did not feed the slaves adequately, they would steal. If slaves were mistreated, their reactions included staging work slowdown, doing work badly, and destroying tools and other property. On one plantation, the slaves were able to trick the master into firing a harsh overseer by not chopping weeds but merely covering them up. Thus, there was an unspoken understanding that developed about the mutual obligations of masters and slaves on some plantations. One former slave said, "White folks do as they please, and the darkies do as they can" (Levine, 1996, p. 62).

Slaves did much more, however, than react to abusive treatment. They had forged their own semi-independent societies by the 19th century wherein they developed rules, values, a sense of self-respect, and a spirit of solidarity that, in turn, helped them to survive both physically and psychologically. The remarkable result was that they did not simply draw on the culture of the dominant white society but, rather, blended West African and American practices and values creating an African American culture that met their needs (Levine, 1996). From a strengths perspective, we begin to see that for African Americans, strength equates to their culture and how it is embraced.

Slave families, too, survived many obstacles to their preservation, developing their own values and practices to suit their circumstances, defying the notion that slavery had destroyed the African American family. Typically, slave marriages were not recognized, masters often violated male-female slave relationships by raping the females, and man and woman could suddenly be separated by sale (Levine, 1996). A man wrote to his wife who, along with his children, had been sold away from him: "Send me some of the children's hair in a separate paper with their names on the paper. . . . I had rather anything to had happened to me most than ever to have been parted from you and the children. . . . Laura, I do love you the same . . ." (Zinn, 1995, p. 174). Hurdling these obstacles as best they could, slave families were still able to form families and the two-parent family prevailed. One way this was done was to consider it acceptable for a husband and wife to remarry if they were separated. Also, slaves preserved the West African tradition of large, extended families strongly bound by mutual obligations. If a family was broken up and children were separated from their parents, they were raised by relatives; and, barring that, strangers would step in to act as "grandparents," "aunts," and "uncles" (Levine, 1996). When his sister died leaving three children, a southern, black farmer recalls his father proposing sharing their care, "That suits me, Papa. . . . Let's handle em like this: don't get the two little boys, the youngest ones, off at your house and the oldest one be at my house and we hold these little boys apart and won't bring em to see one another. I'll bring the little boy that I keep, the oldest one, around to your home amongst the other two. And you forward the others to my house and let em grow up knowin that they are brothers. Don't keep em separated in a way that they'll forget about one another. Don't do that Papa" (Zinn, 1995, p. 174).

This preservation of family was a remarkable achievement given that the larger, white society did not recognize it and, in fact, did much to undermine it. The documentation of the preservation further defies the claim that the black condition was blamed on family frailty, when in fact it was poverty and prejudice (Levine, 1996; Zinn, 1995).

There were other strengths—religion, storytelling, and music, to name some. The slaves adopted Christianity but carved out of it what was important for them, for example, that all were equal before God, regardless of earthly status; and that every life was significant; and that all those with faith, whatever their position in society, could attain salvation. They added African religion to their practices, which included communal call-and-response-style worship, drumming, and clapping, all of which strengthened their solidarity. Whites generally did not care for independent African American worship and tired to prevent their services, but the slaves managed to assemble on their own anyway, sometimes slipping into the woods or swamps if necessary. The shaping of their own religious practice helped them to assert an independent spiritual identity that enabled them to be free from within, although enslaved from without (Levine, 1996).

Storytellers were important people in the slave community, offering stories with hidden messages that told of how the weak could triumph over the strong by using their wits. The use of stories helped relieve the anger that slaves felt toward their masters by providing at least imaginary victories and offering guidance on how to survive in an unfriendly world. Musicians were also important people among slaves. Group singing was most often used and was usually improvised. The singing fostered the union of the individual with the slave community, promoting solidarity. Work songs helped ease the burden of toil, and other songs contained messages of protest and, particularly in the spirituals, hope (Levine, 1996).

The following is an example of the creativity of stories and songs:

> We raise de wheat,
> Dey gib us de corn;
> We bake de bread,
> Dey gib us de crust,
> We sif de meal,
> Dey giv us de huss;
> We peel de meat,
> Dey gib us de skin;
> And dat's de way
> Dey take us in;
> We skim de pot,
> Dey gib us liquor,
> An say dat's good enough for nigger.

(Zinn, 1995, pp. 174–175)

This piece illustrates a complex mixture of mockery, adaptation, and rebellion (Zinn, 1995).

Leadership Emerged

"The chief witness in Reconstruction," wrote W. E. B. DuBois, "the emancipated slave himself, has been almost barred from court" (Magdol, 1974, p. 81). There were many lower-class blacks who furnished leadership and wielded their influence, trying to make Reconstruction a success in their local communities in the absence of more stringent welfare programs. The information gathered about this leadership comes from the 1871 congressional inquiry into the Ku Klux Klan, investigating violence in six states. The findings have several limitations. For instance, the testimony deals with the terrorism by the Klan that rose up after the passage of the Reconstruction acts and on into the summer of 1871 but provides no information from the period up to 1877, the traditional end of the Reconstruction era, and little of what happened in the two years from emancipation in 1865 to the passage of the acts. Also, the hearings were concerned almost exclusively with testimony relating to some rural counties in only five states (Georgia, Alabama, South Carolina, Florida, and Mississippi) with little information about local black leadership in cities. Further, the hearings were intended primarily to probe political matters with little investigation by the committee of social conditions. This information, however, was gathered from the congressional resolution establishing the commit-tee, which was set up to inquire into "the condition of the late insurrectionary states," with occasional glimpses furnished during the hearings on economic and social discussions. These glimpses were adequate enough that some pro-filing could be done on leadership, which was characterized as the roles the men played and, more strictly, the influence they were able to exert in moving others to attain group goals (Magdol, 1974, pp. 83–84).

Leadership of the freedmen is defined by a variety of organized social and political activities. There emerged, in these leadership roles, 16 members of the state legislature, 6 men who had reputations as "leaders among colored people," 5 militia company officers, and 4 identified as presidents of Union League or Loyal League clubs. (The Union League was established nationally in May 1863, organized to rally support for the U.S. government during the Civil War. After the war, the League became a partisan political group, an arm of the Republican Party.) These former slaves, identified as leaders, were mostly artisan or laborer class, with little or no schooling, but in contrast more literate than most freedmen and were the principal victims of Klan retaliation against black political equality. They were viewed by most whites as threats of social equality (Magdol, 1974).

Some of the specific roles/tasks were:

- Union League leader, 300–500 members
- register of election
- 1868, representative of Macon County in lower house
- 1869, elected to lower house Alabama legislature
- state senator since 1867
- leader of men regarding working contracts
- member of Georgia State Central Committee
- led voters to election in Aberdeen
- speech for arming blacks
- removing city officers, "or burn the town down"
- served on a committee to see governor
- leader of meeting
- 1871, authorized by sheriff to get colored men for a guard
- member of county board of supervisors
- president of Union League Club
- census taker, and distributor of ballots on election day
- 1870, brought voters to polls

In spite of the limitations of the information gathered from the congressional inquiry, the relationships between village and urban artisans and farm and plantation laborers enlarge our understanding of the 19th-century leadership role of the black American craftsman. Above all else, it was demonstrated that black people wanted stability in order to live in peace ("to live like humans"), to have land and schools, independence, and self-support. The actions of these men also heavily go against the Stanley Elkins thesis of slave infantilization (Magdol, 1974).

It would be unrealistic to suppose that all this activity proved successful; however, the black leadership that emerged help in the understanding of black communities in countless southern villages and plantations. They can take us back and help to explain the world of slavery, and they can take us forward to the farmers' alliances and the populist upsurge. "They are among our chief witnesses of Reconstruction social history" (Magdol, 1974, p. 110).

There were African American female heroines/leaders as well. Sojourner Truth and Josephine S. Pierre Ruffin became recruiters of black troops for the Union army. Harriet Tubman raided plantations, leading black and white troops, with one expedition freeing 750 slaves. Tubman was also a conductor on the Underground Railroad that transported slaves to freedom in the 1850s. Frances Ellen Watkins Harper was involved in helping rebuild the postwar South. She was born free in Baltimore, was self-supporting, was an abolitionist lecturer, read her own poetry, and spoke all through the southern states after the war. She also participated in the 1866 Women's Rights Convention and founded the National Association of Colored Women. She wrote the first novel published by a black woman in 1890 entitled *Iola Leroy or Shadows Uplifted* (Zinn, 1995).

Other Notable People

Women moved with "colored" regiments that grew as the Union army marched through the South. They helped their husbands, enduring terrible hardships, and suffered the loss of many of their children on the long military treks. The women suffered the same fate as soldiers in a massacre by the Confederate troops at Fort Pillow, Kentucky, in 1864. The Union soldiers, black and white, had surrendered but nonetheless lost their lives along with women and children in an adjoining camp (Zinn, 1995). One of the Civil War poems speaks to the massacre. Entitled "A Second Review of the Grand Army," written by Bret Harte (1836–1902), it tells of his dream of a grand review of the Union army in which black soldiers were allowed to participate, which, in real life, they were not allowed to do:

> . . . and, marching beside the others,
> Came the dusky martyrs of Pillow's fight,
> With limbs enfranchised, and bearing bright.

(Crawford, 1977)

Before the war, black Americans in the North and South grew more militant as the tension grew. In a speech delivered by Frederick Douglass in 1853, the words remained apropos throughout Reconstruction and, indeed, still apply to the struggles of today:

Let me give you a word of the philosophy of reforms. The whole history of the progress of human liberty shows that all concessions yet made to her August claims have been born of struggle. . . . If there is no struggle there is no progress. Those who profess to favor freedom and yet deprecate agitation, are men who want crops without plowing up the ground. They want rain without thunder and lightning. . . . The struggle may be a moral one; or it may be a physical one; or it may be both moral and physical, but it must be a struggle. Power concedes nothing without a demand. It never did and it never will. (Zinn, 1995, p. 179)

Women's Struggle for Rights

White women, too, were very courageous during this period of time and exhibited enormous strengths as they fought for their rights during a time of oppression. We learned of some of their struggles, their gains and their losses, earlier in the chapter. Not only were most men perplexed by the demands of women, they were not supportive. The same could be said for masses of women. There were many avant-garde women who were content to seek access to the professions and to positions in teaching within the old framework consisting of separate spheres and the cult of domesticity; they did not agree with the feminist movement that was seeking an array of public and political reforms (Jansson, 1997).

The hard work, courage, and strength of these 19th-century women clearly paved the way for women through the ages as the struggle for equal rights continued. A quote from Stanton's last speech provides a fitting end to this discussion: "Nothing strengthens the judgment and quickens the conscience like individual responsibility. Nothing adds such dignity to character as the recognition of one's self-sovereignty; the right to an equal place, merit, not an artificial attainment of inheritance, wealth, family and position . . . the responsibilities of life rest equally on men and women . . . [and] they need the same preparation for time and eternity (Schneir, 1992, pp. 158–159).

SUMMARY

Social policy just was not happening in this era of American history. Few Americans envisioned any major or ongoing social policy role for the federal government. With no tradition of federal intervention, Americans were disinclined to regulate the emerging industrial order or to develop federal policies to distribute free lands to impoverished persons. The conservative consensus continued to embrace a moralistic and punitive stance toward persons in poverty and saw social problems as temporary rather than endemic, favoring limited government. The inability of most Americans to support compensatory strategies to help populations that needed special assistance was staggering. Throughout American history, no group possessed such desperate need as the freed slaves whose economic problems stemmed so clearly from the horrors of slavery. The lack of compensatory strategies in cases of such obvious need represents a legacy of lost opportunity that has influenced social welfare to this day (Jansson, 1997).

So, while the federal government cannot be attributed with tapping into people's strengths, nor providing the necessary assistance to adequately meet the human needs of the time, the people filled the void as best they could by using their collective strengths for the betterment of the whole.

REFERENCES

Axinn, J., & Levin, H. (1997). *Social welfare: A history of the American response to need* (4th ed.). New York: Longman.

Campbell. (1897, January 26). "To a Slave-Holder." *The Sutfolk Gazette*, p. 4. [On-line]. Available: http://www.lihistory.com

Crawford, R. (1977). *The civil war songbook.* New York: Dover.

Day, P. J. (1989). *A new history of social welfare.* Englewood Cliffs, NJ: Prentice Hall.

Day, P. J. (1999). *A new history of social welfare* (3rd ed.). Boston, MA: Allyn & Bacon.

Du Bois, W.E.B. *John Brown.* New York: International Publishers, 1962.

Franklin, J. H., & Moss, A. A. (1994). *From slavery to freedom: A history of African Americans* (7th ed.). New York: McGraw-Hill.

Jansson, B. S. (1997). *The reluctant welfare state* (3rd ed.). Pacific Grove, CA: Brooks/Cole.

Levine, M. L. (1996). *African Americans and civil rights: From 1619 to the present.* Phoenix, AZ: The Oryx Press.

Magdol, E. (1974, Spring). Local black leaders in the South, 1867–75: An essay toward the reconstruction of Reconstruction history. *Societas, 2,* 81–110.

Marius, R. (Ed) (1994). *The Columbia book of Civil War poetry.* New York: Columbia University Press.

Pringle, T. (1834). The slave dealer. *African Sketches.* London: E. Moxon, pp. 91–93.

Schneir, M. (1992). *Feminism: The essential historical writings.* New York: Vintage Books.

Trattner, W. I. (1999). *From poor law to welfare state: A history of social welfare in America* (6th ed.). New York: The Free Press.

Zinn, H. (1995). A people's history of the United States: 1492–present. New York: Harper Perennial.

CHAPTER 6

SOCIAL REFORM IN THE PROGRESSIVE ERA

The Progressive Era was an exciting time for the social work profession. This was a time when social work blossomed as a profession, making a profound imprint on the society through its work in social welfare. The birth of the charity organizations and the settlement house movement occurred during this time. African American social work also has it roots in this time period. The history for this era is rich for the profession; we use it for the backdrop in this chapter to explore social welfare legislation—the resistance to it as well as the advancements.

AFTERMATH OF THE CIVIL WAR

The development of social welfare after the Civil War was slow and fraught with dissension. Many Americans considered the social problems of the new nation as a pestilence that threatened its moral and social order. The social problems of the time were generally seen as emanating from the moral defects of citizens. This was particularly true for immigrants in the rapidly expanding cities. Reformers were not sympathetic and failed to recognize that the structural factors such as the nation's uncertain economy, the blighted conditions of its cities, or discrimination against its immigrants were largely responsible for causing social problems. Rather, they tried to develop institutions that could purge these defects from stigmatized groups—people with mental disorders, criminals, paupers, and delinquent youth; or they imposed preventive strategies including temperance and moral instruction through the Sunday School movement or the expanding network of public schools (Jansson, 1997).

The nation was deprived of alternative perspectives by the lack of strong reform and political organizations that could represent the policy needs of the lower class. The nation also failed to develop expansive notions of social obligation for social programs. Most reformers believed social programs should concentrate only on the provision of institutional and social services to individuals who were truly destitute and ill but not to a broader range of citizens. History tells us that most services were to be provided by local governments and private philanthropic organizations, whereas Americans accorded the federal government virtually no social welfare roles except for maintenance of some institutions for the deaf and a small program of pensions for veterans (Jansson, 1997).

Much of the dissension surrounding reform in the Progressive Era arose from Social Darwinism and the Populist Democratic/Socialist movement. Social Darwinism defined the worthy and moral as those who succeeded economically, with its followers claiming it to be a "scientific" ideal. The Populists mobilized farmers in the Midwest and the South to protest low agricultural prices, high interest rates, excessive charges by granaries and railroads, and profiteering by food processors. They got the attention of bankers, Wall Street, and corporations; were able to obtain a variety of regulatory measures in local and state jurisdictions and developed cooperative storage facilities. The Populist reform movement was short-lived, however, when farm prices improved, limits were placed on rates of railroads, and cooperatives were developed. Populism, though, was a rural movement having negligible impact on urban reform (Day, 1999; Jansson, 1997).

It was not until the turn of the century that urban reform took place, known as Progressivism. Progressivism was not a focused reform movement but embraced a variety of issues, such as antimonopoly, city beautification, civil service, government, and social reforms, and at the same time advocated prohibition, laws to outlaw prostitution, and efforts to limit immigration, along with policies to limit child labor, correct unsafe working conditions, and obtain unemployment insurance. With so many projects included in the movement, it is difficult to establish a profile of the typical Progressive reformer. Included were middle-class Americans, many bewildered by the emergence of massive corporations; big-city bosses; and large, urban immigrant populations. Many affluent Americans, political machines, and trade unions, however, supported various Progressive reforms. Progressivism was not dominated by members of the Democratic or Republican Parties. In spite of the amorphous nature, Progressivism was the first sustained reform movement in the United States that addressed a variety of urban issues (Jansson, 1997).

THE EVOLUTION OF REFORM

What with the political power of corporations, Social Darwinism, and the national preoccupation with upward mobility in 1900, it seemed unlikely that Americans would develop a major reform movement to address social problems. This was an era dominated by parties and lobbyists, presidents, and governors who were relatively weak figures and tended not to initiate legislation but, rather, to acquiesce in decisions fashioned in smoke-filled rooms. Even if social programs could be developed, it seemed that government could not implement or enforce their regulation (Jansson, 1997).

Efforts to develop social reform were further thwarted by patterns of party support. Complicated sectional and ethnic traditions dictated voting patterns, with neither Democrats nor Republicans focused on the needs of the working class. The South was dominated by the Democrats; in New England, the Republicans held considerable strength; and, in the Midwest and West, the two parties divided the votes. It was local tradition, not their positions on social issues, that prompted various ethnic groups to support the two political parties (Jansson, 1997).

Other factors influenced reform, such as the depression of 1893, which lingered for three years with a decisive effect on the nation. The depression brought discontentment with the Democratic government (President Grover Cleveland), blaming it for the economic downfall; and it also brought widespread disenchantment with corporate tycoons who were poised for the unlimited prosperity promised from the script of the Gilded Age. Through the untoward practices of corporate executives, for example, the willingness to fire workers and shut down plants, their flamboyant lifestyles came to be resented when more than a quarter of adult males were unemployed in many areas (Jansson, 1997).

Some social unrest stirred about this time with the emergence of fringe organizations such as the Socialist Party and the Industrial Workers of the World. They were radical and vocal and represented a new phenomenon in the nation, which was certainly a contrast from the millions of immigrant workers providing the cheap labor for the American industry. Most of the workers were relatively tranquil despite their appalling working and living conditions. They did not speak English, lacked citizenship, often hoped to return to Europe, feared unemployment, and were unlikely to engage in militant protest. The leaders of the fringe organizations espoused ideas that departed from the conventional political beliefs of the nation, with many advocating political organization of the working class; supporting national strikes; favoring the nationalization of some industries; and calling for a national minimum wage. The fringe parties, however, had scant success in obtaining political offices, except at the mayoral level. They did, nonetheless, constitute a political threat because the unskilled labor force that they sought to organize was so huge (Jansson, 1997).

EARLY REFORM EFFORTS OF THE ERA

During the Progressive Era, reform began with regulations. These reforms regulated the political process, banking and economic institutions, conditions of employment, food and drugs, employment of immigrants, and housing. Most regulations were enacted in local jurisdictions, but they also gave state and federal governments new policy roles. During this time period, there were few social controls on corporations and political and social institutions. Without public regulations, corporations could make products, establish working practices, and subject workers to hazardous conditions. Without public scrutiny, politicians could accept bribes, hire relatives, and tamper with elections. The move for many of these regulations came about only after exhausting political battles. For example, those fighting for child labor laws were up against those who argued that these laws violated parental rights, that immigrants needed the earnings of their children to survive, and—even more outlandish—that child labor prevented the overcrowding of schools. Those who sought to reform federal labor laws were told that the Constitution did not give the federal government jurisdiction in social reform (Jansson, 1997).

The regulatory reforms supplemented the efforts to rationalize a social services system that would develop a social work profession, which we talk about in detail later in this chapter. The reformers viewed with great disdain the provision of services by amateurs and political appointees (Jansson, 1997). It was determined that a system of well-coordinated voluntary organizations staffed by people who would keep accurate records of applicants and distribute aid honestly and carefully, while uplifting the needy, seemed the better way to meet the problem. It was thought that this would ensure that welfare remained a charity rather than an entitlement and would bind the lower to the upper classes, thus avoiding potential conflict (Trattner, 1999).

Public outdoor assistance had been abandoned by 1900 in New York; Baltimore; St. Louis; Washington, D.C.; San Francisco; Kansas City; New Orleans; Louisville; Denver; Atlanta; Memphis; Charleston, S.C.; Cincinnati; Indianapolis; Pittsburgh; and elsewhere. The abolition of public home relief did not eliminate the forces that drove people to dependency. Evidence suggests the opposite, that elimination of such assistance led to a significant increase in the breaking up of families, in the placing of children in institutions, and in the formation of private charitable agencies. As it turned out, public authorities only cared for dependents and defectives who required confinement in asylums, almshouses, and other like institutions. A vast majority of those in need remained outside the public institutions with "the county" being their last resort (Trattner, 1999).

The needy reluctantly and anxiously turned to the "official" private charitable agencies in the community and then only when other resources were either exhausted or unavailable. They first sought out family, kin, and neighbors for aid, including the landlord, who sometimes deferred the rent; the local butcher or grocer, who frequently carried them for a while by allowing bills to go unpaid; and the local saloon keeper, who often came to their aid by providing loans and outright gifts, including free meals and occasionally temporary jobs. They also looked to various agencies in the community—those of their own devising, such as churches and religious groups, social and fraternal associations, mutual aid societies, local ethnic groups, and trade unions (Trattner, 1999.)

Nevertheless, private charitable agencies continued to proliferate as public home relief was abolished; they grew so rapidly that their directories took as many as 100 pages to list and describe the numerous voluntary agencies that sought to alleviate misery. For example, in 1878, in Philadelphia, as many as 800 such groups were in existence. This proliferation of agencies created an excess of relief and chaos in the way in which charity was distributed. An argument ensued for cessation of all public outdoor aid and for the improvement of all relief operations, especially by paying more attention to the individual needs of those helped. It was argued that charity work needed to be organized along scientific lines to make it more rational and efficient, which gave rise to the so-called charity organization movement, or "scientific charity" (Trattner, 1999).

THE INFLUENCES ON REFORM

The two leading social reform efforts of the time were the Charity Organization Society (COS) and the settlement house movement. Charity organization societies were influenced by Social Darwinism, relying on the emerging science of genetics, sociology, administrative management, and psychology. The settlement house movement was inspired by Populism (Day, 1999). The polarization of the influences of these two movements put them at either end of a continuum: The settlement house movement looked toward environmental factors as causes of problems of the individual, whereas the COS placed the blame for the problems on the individual.

Charity Organization Societies

The purpose of charity organization societies was to organize all charities in an area so that needy people could be served but would be unable to get help from more than one charity. Central case registries and forums were developed in which all agencies, including the police, could work closely together on cases. Applications for charity would be investigated by paid staff, and volunteers would personally interview applicants in what would become casework practice. Eligibility would be determined by volunteer boards who would set grants on a case-by-case basis (Day, 1999).

In addition to eliminating fraud and duplicity in the field, organized charity was also about devising a constructive method of dealing with or treating poverty. One worker said, "We sought to organize the charitable impulses and resources of the community" to "develop the special capacities of each [need] individual." The movement, in part, hoped to treat poverty by guarding against overlapping but, more important, by having "friendly visitors" look into each case, to diagnose causes of destitution. The keystone of treatment was investigation, comparable to a physician not prescribing medicine until after a diagnosis. Friendly visiting was the second aim, which was to serve as a substitute for alms. Registration, cooperation, and coordination formed the basis of the "science" of social therapeutics that was supposed to relieve philanthropy of sentimentality and indiscriminate almsgiving, making it a matter of the head as well as the heart, thereby eradicating pauperism. If friendly visitors did their job well, said the movements founder, "all avoidable pauperism would soon be a thing of the past, and an age of good will would be ushered in, when the poor would regard the rich as their natural friends and not, as now, fair object of their deceit and imposition" (Trattner, 1999, p. 93).

Keeping in mind that there were influences other than philanthropy and benevolence during this time, there were those who did not look favorably on public assistance for the needy. Social Darwinism was very much present, and between 1870 and 1890 an English philosopher, Herbert Spencer, became its spokesman, saying:

> If they are not sufficiently complete to live, they die, and it is best they should die. . . . The whole effort of nature is to get rid of such, to clear the world of them, and make room for better. (Day, 1999, p. 219)

Further, he argued that poor laws provided:

> artificial preservation of those least able to take care of themselves. The poverty of the incapable, the distresses that come from the imprudent, the starvation of the idle, and those shoulderings aside of the weak by the strong were "the decrees of a large far-seeing benevolence." (Day, 1999, p. 219)

This line of thought clearly expressed a class bias: Social aid removes people from the labor market, makes them unavailable for work, and thereby undermines the God-given reward—wealth—of nature's fittest (Day, 1999).

Darwinists argued that government should confine itself to ensuring liberty for individual citizens by protecting them from assault upon their persons and property. There was no place in their belief of things for public support of education, sanitary regulation, a public mail system, nor regulation of business or trade. Spenserians claimed that competition was the law of life and that there was no remedy for poverty other than self-help. The needy were considered unfit by virtue of being poor and had to pay the price exacted by the decrees of benevolence. It was thought pointless and hazardous to interfere in their behalf, whether undertaken by the state or by unwise philanthropists. The protection of the ill-favored who struggled for existence would only permit them to multiply and could lead to no other result than a disastrous weakening of the species and interfere with nature's plan of evolutionary progress toward higher forms of social life. Spencer believed that "the unfit must be eliminated as nature intended [and that] the principle of natural selection must not be violated by the artificial preservation of those least able to take care of themselves" (Trattner, 1999, p. 89).

These arguments to justify inequality and condone misery never went completely unchallenged; nonetheless, the theory that poverty was caused by personal frailty was not easily supplanted. It was endowed with a new aura of authority and retained a loyal following for a long time. Most Americans, however, did not carry the idea to its logical extreme. America was a Christian nation with a strength of conviction and held on to its charitable impulse and tradition (Trattner, 1999).

The Positives and Negatives of Charity Organization Societies   The COS movement had an explicit goal, which was to restore the "natural order" of class stratification. It was not coincidental that the movement began at a time of economic turmoil, with massive unemployment, low wages, and the displacement
of people from the war. Social disruption was everywhere, and the burgeoning
wealth of the upper classes was salt in the wounds of those without enough to
eat. The end of the Civil War brought production layoffs at the same time that
the labor market was flooded with returning soldiers, new immigrants, war widows, and freed slaves. Unemployment was a national problem for the first time
in history. More than altruism was at stake, however, with charity organization
societies that were developed and maintained by the elite (Day, 1999).

Heredity could not be changed, but it was thought that "moral" environments and treatment could alleviate some of the results of bad heredity. Casework was used to dispense moral advice, although workers were told not to
make moral judgments. Only as a last resort would outdoor relief be given
because it was seen as material rather than spiritual and "demoralized the
poor." People were encouraged to work even though there was no work to be
found, and severe work tests were given the able-bodied, though at a fair
wage. Women and children were helped by COSs only if the breadwinner died
and then only if the friendly visitor felt it better to keep the family together.
Institutionalization was preferred, with mothers sent to poorhouses and children to orphanages to "train them away" from the heritage of pauperism. The
families of drunkards were only helped if the drunkard left; thus, the wives
were considered widows. On the other hand, deserted families received no
help, the logic being not to encourage other men to desert (Day, 1999).

Scientific charity was built on the pessimistic view of human nature, at
least the poor's—the notion that no members of the lower class would exert
themselves if they felt secure. The founder of the New York Charity Organization Society, Josephine Shaw Lowell, who was also the leader of the movement, believed that the poor had to be forced to endure deprivation to be kept
at work and that deprivation was the essential incentive. Furthermore, her
position was that the poor needed supervision rather than alms to help them
combat or overcome intemperance, indolence, and improvidence. Their
motto was, "not alms but a friend," with critics charging that its mottos should
be "neither alms nor a friend" (Trattner, 1999, p. 96).

The charity organization societies relied on their corps of friendly visitors
to carry out their work. The visitors investigated appeals for assistance, distinguished between the worthy and unworthy poor, and then provided the needy
with the proper amount of moral exhortation. A *Manual for Visitors Among
the Poor*, written by the Reverend R. E. Thompson, stated, "The best means
of doing the poor good is found in friendly intercourse and personal influence." He believed that gifts of alms were not needed but, rather, "sympathy,
encouragement, and hopefulness." Mary Richmond agreed, saying, "If you are

going to be a *friend,* fertile in helpful suggestions, sympathetic and kind, you cannot be a almoner too" (Trattner, 1999, pp. 96–97).

There were severe critics of the charity organization societies, especially among the more reform-minded, radical individuals of the time. For example, the founder of Hull House, Jane Addams, in Chicago felt the COS agents were cold, unemotional, too impersonal, and stingy and that they were pervaded by a negative pseudoscientific spirit. She argued that their vocabulary was one of "don't give," "don't act," "don't do this or that," saying all they give the poor was advice. Poet-reformer John Boyle O'Reilley of Boston said, "The organized charity scrimped and iced, in the name of a cautious, statistical Christ"; and the Reverend James O. S. Huntington of New York condemned the movement for its predilection to judge individuals and for establishing standards of truthfulness and labor for the poor that were not applied to the more affluent. John Reed referred to the COSs as "deadening and life-sapping" agencies that were "unnecessarily cruel . . . [and] uncomprehending" (Trattner, 1999, p. 97).

The COSs, however, remained undaunted by these attacks. As they saw it, no incompatibility existed between their profession of being scientific and their reliance upon voluntary service. For the services of the voluntary friendly visitor to work, they believed, it had to regenerate character, which involved the direct influence of kind and concerned, successful and cultured, middle- and upper-class people upon the dependent. Because friendly visiting assumed the right and the duty of intervention in the lives of the poor by their social and economic betters, there were charges of meddling, to which Mary Richmond replied, "Some question our right to go among the poor with the object of doing good, regarding it as an impertinent interference with the rights of the individual. But . . . [we] *must* interfere when confronted by human suffering and need. Why not interfere effectively?" Ironically, despite the distrust they felt for the poor and the belief that poverty was mainly a consequence of moral failing, many charity organizers felt a sincere responsibility to serve the needy (Trattner, 1999, p. 98).

Over time, friendly visitors began to see that their brand of intervention was not going to affect a poverty rooted in ill health, premature death, substandard wages, involuntary unemployment, and other structural forces in the economy. It was a poverty too deeply rooted and complex to be affected very much by any relief policy, let alone one of benevolent stinginess. The charity workers did not come to this belief because they wanted to but saw it as inevitable. For example, they found great difficulty "in trying to distinguish between the worthy and the unworthy poor when no amount of verbal effort could raise the income of a family to a subsistence level, or when a depression, which occurred like clockwork in 19th- and early 20th-century America, threw several million people out of work" (Trattner, 1999, p. 100).

On a positive note, early COSs lobbied for housing reform and worked to bring disease preventative techniques such as vaccinations into the community.

They also built tuberculosis sanatoriums and fresh air camps for slum children; provided day nurseries and sewing rooms; taught mothers thrift, better health care, and home economics; found employment for men; and lobbied for legislation to discourage vagrancy (Day, 1999).

Systems of accountability were bureaucratized, and COSs kept case records collecting social statistics on poverty, unemployment, wages, family expenditures, disease, and working conditions. Through their investigations and record keeping, they uncovered information that showed that unemployment was involuntary and that there were industrial accidents and low wages that lead to poverty, not intemperance or improvidence. With this new evidence, the preconceived notions about the poor had to be seriously reconsidered or even discarded. Poor people were not all alike, nor were they "dangerous" or "depraved" classes (Trattner, 1999).

The use of untrained, part-time workers became obsolete; and the COS volunteers were eventually replaced by full-time, paid workers with education, experience, and professional discipline. This turn of events led to the creation of training schools for charity workers. By 1892, women workers far outnumbered men and thereafter dominated the leadership and development of the emerging profession of social work (Day, 1999; Trattner, 1999).

The Settlement House Movement

Opposed to Social Darwinism, settlement houses sought to reconcile class differences, unlike the COS who sought to differentiate between the classes. The concept for settlement houses was modeled after a London experience based on the Social Gospel movement that attracted middle-class people to emulate Jesus in living among the poor. In America, the first settlement house was the Neighborhood Guild, established by Dr. Stanton Coit and Charles B. Stover on the Lower East Side of New York. In 1889, Jane Addams founded Hull House in Chicago and Vida Scudder founded the College Settlement, a club for girls, in New York City. Then Lillian Wald established the Henry Street Settlement, where nursing was taught to immigrant women. By 1910, there were 400 settlement houses in America, located mostly in eastern and midwestern cities (Day, 1999).

The settlement house movement was different than the COS movement with the settlement houses run in part by groups that used them with an emphasis on social reform rather than on relief or assistance. In many cases, settlement house residents regarded themselves, and were regarded by others, as friends and neighbors of the poor as opposed to being dispensers of charity. They tended to be more fraternalistic than paternalistic, more objective than judgmental, and more positive than negative. Perhaps the more distinguishing component separating them from COSs was that their work was based upon the needs and desires of the people they were working with rather than on a pattern of behavior prescribed by donors of moral enlightenment. Like the COSs, the work was dominated by women with most of them educated and dedicated to working on problems of urban poverty. Settlement house workers sought to improve housing conditions, organized protests, offered job training, supported organized labor, worked against child labor, and fought against corrupt politicians, with the movement eventually advocating for social reform. The Socialist Party and other political groups used settlement houses as bases of operation (Day, 1999; Trattner, 1999).

Jane Addams and Hull House   Hull House was the most famous settlement house, attracting many powerful women to this work, most notably its founder, Jane Addams. Through her reform work, she became the most famous woman in America and a model of feminine virtue. She was described as a gifted scholar, a brilliant administrator, a shrewd tactician, and a marvel of a business woman. She handled an annual budget of several hundreds of thousands of dollars, and people kept insisting that she was a saint (Day, 1989).

Jane Addams founded Hull House in 1899 to address the problems of the immigrant population. She saw the relationship between forces of social and economic oppression and discontent. Addams believed that cultural differences were important for welfare work and for the nation and encouraged immigrants to retain and be proud of their Old World heritage. Through the efforts of Hull House, second-generation immigrants were taught to be proud of their parents' traditional ways and values that they brought to America. By 1910, Hull House had grown into an imposing complex of 13 buildings, covering nearly a city block. Hull House initiated activities for people of the surrounding immigrant neighborhood; as those activities flourished, Hull House expanded into fully developed, complex programs, each with its own staff of experienced leaders. By 1920, it was estimated that more than 9,000 people came weekly to participate. The residential staff numbered about 65 people (Johnson, 1989, Trattner, 1999).

The staff were people who worked in other parts of the city (i.e., doctors, lawyers, college professors, school teachers, social workers, students, musicians, actors, writers, poets, artists, and politicians), all wanting to live and share their talents with the less-fortunate people of the neighborhood. One of the artists formed an experimental artists' community, using the studio and shops at Hull House for their own work while teaching art classes to interested members of the neighborhood. Professors and teachers offered similar types of classes for educational purposes. Many young people were deeply influenced by their experiences at Hull House and went on to become professional musicians, artists, writers, dramatists, social workers, and educators. A well-equipped Hull House Boy's Club Building offered almost every imaginable activity to boys and men of the surrounding area. Many other clubs were directed by volunteers, with the philosophy of Hull House being to work as much as possible with natural groups from the neighborhood. Hull House used the street gangs, organized by the boys themselves, as a basis for the settlement's various clubs (Johnson, 1989). This is an excellent example of a strengths approach, tapping the community resources to promote self-empowerment.

Addams was motivated, in part, by her "impulse to share the lives of the poor" and spoke for many, indicating that her motivation came from a desire "to make social service . . . express the spirit of Christ." Most of the residents took their religion seriously, a common denominator in the conversion to settlement work and social reform. Addams was influenced by the militant Social Gospel movement, which was concerned with matters of poverty and social justice and aligning with the working rather than the employing classes. Those beginning in settlement work found a sense of mission to God and to mankind; and, rather than entering the ministry, which was mostly closed to women, they chose a life of practical helpfulness to the poor. Addams's life, like that of many of her peers in settlement house work, was a practical substitute for a religious (or educational) vocation, allowing her to translate theory into action, to practice rather than preach (teach) (Trattner, 1999).

Among other things, Addams was a pacifist and wrote on the war, with her views countering the views of mandatory male service to foster values of manliness and discipline. Those who reflected the male values of the time considered her view idealistic, unrealistic, and "womanly"—the ultimate pejorative in the double standard that placed women on the pedestal of the separate sphere as guardians of virtue as they were denied opporuntiy to apply those values in active, public life. Addams defied the norm with her public life involving her in direct pragmatic negotiations with the harsh realities of war and economic violence (Adams, 1991).

Addams's influence extended to Theodore Roosevelt during his presidential campaign in 1912, when she urged him to mount a progressive reform platform. She became active in the Progressive Party, founded the International Society for World Peace, and won the Nobel Peace Prize in 1931 for her work in the peace movement. Because of her work, she became a threat to the national security and was considered the be the most dangerous woman in America by the FBI (Day, 1989), quite a contrast from others' view of her as a saint.

In sum, Hull House, along with the many settlement houses around the nation, not only provided forums and centers for women reformers but also led the way to community organization and group work practice within the profession of social work (Day, 1999).

THE PROFESSIONALIZATION OF SOCIAL WORK

Among postwar trends was the professionalization of social work. Formal training became available for those wanting to do social work. For example, the Children's Aid Society of Pennsylvania began a training program in 1882; the New York Society conducted a course of 12 lectures relating to social problems in 1894; and, in 1890, the Boston Associated Charities paid workers to learn COS techniques, giving lectures on social and philanthropic topics. Mary Richmond was instrumental in the profession's development, defining the practice of casework with the emphasis on "person in situation" (Day, 1989). This era was also influenced by African American pioneer social workers whose legacy is a strengths-based model of contemporary community practice (Carlton-LaNey, 1999), which is discussed further later in this chapter.

Social Work, Casework, and Welfare in the 1920s

The following section is a summarized account of this time period taken from Trattner (1999, pp. 253–262). In an effort to be recognized as professionals, social workers underwent changes in outlook and in practice. With the friendly visitor concept employed by the charity organization societies, the approach to social welfare was personalized. Casework, as it later came to be called, was basically a device for snooping, refusing appeals for help based on "worthiness" or unworthiness," or attempting to control the needy. As we have learned, this method soon came under heavy attack.

In spite of the disfavor, we know that casework endured and was utilized in a variety of settings—for example, the court for probation work, schools for truancy work, hospitals for medical social work, and mental health facilities for aftercare work. Poverty, however, was not dealt with but, rather, pushed into the background. The settlement house effort focused on social and economic problems rather than on needy people. The interest was more in reform and prevention legislation than in individual treatment. In the 1920s, when Mary Richmond's classic book *Social Diagnosis* was published, casework once again came into favor. She spent her lifetime working for the organized charity movement, which believed in the individual cause of poverty and the self-help concept. Eventually, Richmond applied the medical model to social work and conceived of investigation, diagnosis, prognosis, and treatment as a means of treating individuals. *Social Diagnosis*, which implied a pathology or disease, became the first definitive treatise in book form of social casework theory and methods. Casework now overshadowed the settlement house movement of social reform.

Richmond's book was not influenced by the writings or thoughts of Sigmund Freud. *Social Diagnosis* encompassed preceding sociological thought rather than the oncoming psychoanalytical era of thought. The caseworker was described as an artificer in social relations, and Richmond's book emphasized the social environment and financial distress, not psychological factors or intra psychic conflict. Consequently, it soon became outdated.

Even though Richmond was not enthusiastic about social reform, she was not hostile toward it. In fact, she was continually troubled by the antagonism between the social worker and the social reformer and strived for reconciliation between them for the remainder of her career. She said, ". . . I shall spend the rest of my life trying to demonstrate to social caseworkers that there is more to social work than . . . casework."

Still, she believed social reform had failed. Even after preventive social work and social legislation, poverty and need had not been eliminated—nor could they be. The need for individual treatment persisted. It has been said that social action and reform dealt with need in wholesale; casework dealt with need in retail; both were necessary. Richmond preferred the retail method and used the step-by-step process of helping individuals, which again became widely accepted by social workers.

The reason *Social Diagnosis* was so fervently accepted was that it was a 500-page work that guided the reader through every conceivable circumstance to be found in the lives and attitudes of clients, with minute detail on how to gather all the necessary information to determine a final diagnosis. (Her book was meant to include treatment at a later date, but that never happened.) The book came at the same time—1915—that the profession was being attacked by Dr. Abraham Flexner, assistant secretary of the General Education Board and an authority on professional graduate education. He took the adamant stance that social work *was not* a profession. He claimed that social workers were involved in good work that almost anyone could do, seeing social workers as mediators rather than originators of action. Flexner's paper had a profound effect on social work. Social workers were desperate to define and perfect techniques of their own—hence, *Social Diagnosis*. Note that social workers pursued casework with such a singleness of purpose that they virtually blinded themselves to the fact that method was only one test of a profession. The legacy of Flexner's challenge still follow us today. It serves as a constant reminder to strive for excellence and diversity in the field.

Casework was reinforced when America entered into World War I. The American Red Cross established a Home Service Division to provide casework services to displaced soldiers and their families. The Red Cross worked with social workers to train people for the work, specifically providing funds to fifteen colleges and universities to finance the creation and teaching of the courses. Mary Richmond prepared a special casework manual for use in the courses. Another turn of events was the discovery that dealing with people "above the poverty line" did not need to depend on relief funds to help clients. What followed was the validation of casework as a technical service analogous to that performed by lawyers and doctors. Now social workers were dealing with maladies formerly outside social workers' experiences—for example, war neuroses (years later to be called post-traumatic stress disorder [PTSD]). This necessitated working with psychologists and psychiatrists to become well versed in their revelation of the human psyche.

The psychologists, psychiatrists, and physicians in the military service saw in caseworkers specialists in the field of social adjustment, able to work with persons rejected or dismissed because of mental or emotional problems. The war effort served to facilitate the social workers' shift from a social-economic base to an individual-psychological base. In July 1918, Mary Jerrett, chief of social services at Boston's Psychopathic Hospital, and Dr. E. E. Southard, the director, were influential in Smith College, establishing a School of Psychiatric Social Work to train personnel for work with mentally ill patients.

The creation of the school was the first of its kind and began by offering a six-month course for psychiatric aides attached to the Army Medical Service. Its creation also served to further split the social work ranks of settlement house residents/social reformers, who opposed the war and America's involvement in it, with caseworkers supporting it. Jane Addams and many of her colleagues were actively involved in the peace movement, and Mary Richmond and many of her colleagues were actively involved in the Home Service Division of the Red Cross.

With this need for new knowledge brought on from the war effort came the mental hygiene movement in the 1920s. Along with these events came the thirst for psychoanalytic thought. The casework emphasis on the individual-psychological approach fueled growing interest in Freud. Freud provided a theoretical base, as well as a scientific method of treatment, that had previously been lacking. Prior to this, social workers had no systematic way to proceed when personality was the resistant factor. They used common sense and intuition, with success depending more on chance than on any logically conceived process. Many social workers adapted Freud's major discoveries in the language and practice of psychoanalysis to the language and practice of casework. They were then allies with the psychiatric clinical team rather than with social reformers or even social caseworkers. Now, when looking at dynamic human behavior, they threw over environmentalism and the assumption that people are rational beings for the newly found psychiatric "tool" of unconscious motivation.

Psychiatry held the promise of eliminating one of the most serious obstacles to the attainment of professional status by the social worker—the historic link with charity and humanitarianism, which assumed that social work required only a warm heart and a cheerful outlook. Now occupied with psychological rather than economic factors, social workers were allowed to see themselves in a new light. They were no longer dispensers of charity, primarily to the poor, but were now armed with old-time moralism and a vocabulary strewn with psychological and medical terms. Social workers were social physicians concerned with problems of emotional maladjustment that occurred among the upper classes as well as the lower classes.

This surrender to Freud and the clinical orientation further fueled the shift already taking place in social workers' orientation—from the social environment to the individual emotional environment, from poverty and economic problems to personality and emotional problems, and from social reform to individual adjustment (Trattner, 1999, pp. 253–262).

During this same time period, the Chicago School of Civics and Philanthropy, under the direction of Hull House worker Julia Lathrop and Graham Taylor of the Chicago Commons Settlement, was instituted. First called the Institute of Social Sciences in 1903–1904 while under the Extension Division of the University of Chicago, it later became the Graduate School of Social Service Administration with an emphasis on research and social planning. The social work profession continued on these two courses—the COS movement, which looked to individual casework using the medical model for a "cure"; and the settlement house movement, which looked to community action, group work, and social action and reform as remedies to help those in need (Day, 1999).

We begin to chronicle the problem-solving continuum of social work and add to it in remaining chapters as the profession evolves through the decades, leading to the strengths perspective and empowerment at the other end of the continuum (see Figure 6.1). As we progress, note how social policy is the basis of social work practice.

African American Social Work

Also during this era, African American social work came on the scene. Since African Americans were "overwhelmingly excluded from full participation in the U.S. social system and at the same time receiving limited responses from white social workers, [African Americans] developed a dogged determination to take care of their own" (Carlton-LaNey, 1999, p. 312). A review of the *Proceedings* of the National Conference on Charities and Corrections from 1874 through 1945 reveals only brief and infrequent expressions of concern about the staggering problems and inadequate social conditions that faced African Americans during the early decades of the 20th century. For that information, turn to the *Southern Workman*, published by Hampton Normal and Agricultural Institute (now Hampton University) for Negroes and Indians, which was devoted entirely to the improvement of economic, social, and political conditions of African Americans. The mission of the journal was to expose problems,

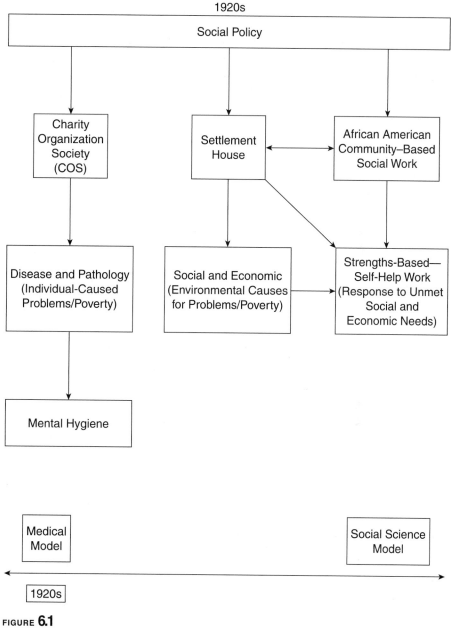

1920s

Social Policy

Charity Organization Society (COS)

Settlement House

African American Community–Based Social Work

Disease and Pathology (Individual-Caused Problems/Poverty)

Social and Economic (Environmental Causes for Problems/Poverty)

Strengths-Based— Self-Help Work (Response to Unmet Social and Economic Needs)

Mental Hygiene

Medical Model

Social Science Model

1920s

FIGURE **6.1**

1920s Social Policy

suggesting and examining strategies for planned change. Many African American social worker pioneers, artists, business men and women, and others relied on the journal as a publishing outlet during the early part of the century. For example, Sarah Collins Fernandis, a settlement house leader and pioneer in the public health movement, depended on the *Southern Workman* as a means of communicating information about settlement work, interracial activities, health, housing, child care issues, and the need for African Americans to help each other. Other efforts to chronicle social services within the African American community included works by W. E. B. DuBois who, through the Atlanta University surveys, published *Some Efforts of American Negroes for Their Own Social Betterment* in 1898 and *Efforts for Social Betterment Among Negro Americans* in 1909. Content in both documents was incomplete but nevertheless reflected the nature of the self-help work going on in the country at the time (Carlton-LaNey, 1999).

The legacy of African American social work is a strength-based practice model of contemporary community practice. The African American pioneer social workers were concerned about individuals' private troubles as well as the larger public issues that affected them. Significant to this pioneering work was the fact that the social workers' reality in relation to that of the community residents they served was not dissimilar. By virtue of race and living in the same community, they shared many of the same societal problems and issues of concern. The African American social workers worked at both the macro and micro levels of practice with intervention designed to bring about planned change in communities and organizations while working to develop, locate, link with, and manage community resources (Carlton-LaNey, 1999).

The concepts of self-help and mutual aid became an institutionalized part of the African American community. Mutual aid, used as a survival technique during enslavement, became a fundamental part of the African American tradition. Mutual aid was essential for the slave community, as it was later for the emancipated freedmen and women who strove to resist the heinous oppression that existed in the aftermath of slavery; and survival was still the objective. The turn of the century saw mutual aid take on the character of community action. Helping each other was the most effective method for African Americans to ameliorate the desperate social conditions in a racially segregated country, at the same time looking to other ways of ensuring open communication. African American reformers established their own literary organs to persuade, encourage, organize, and conjole in the way of newspapers and journals or magazine such as *The Crisis; Opportunity; The New York Age;* a womanish publication, *Women's Era;* and A. Phillip Randolph and Chandler Owen's socialist magazine, *The Messenger. Woman's Era,* initially established in 1894 to serve Boston clubs, became the official organ of The National Association of Colored Women (NACW). The NACW relied on the journal for news about the activities of the growing network of clubs throughout the country. *The*

Messenger, too, served a pivotal role in the creation of the Brotherhood of Sleeping Car Porters, a labor union serving African American male porters working on Pullman cars (Carlton-LaNey, 1999).

Race Pride   Progressive Era African American social workers played a significant role in elevating their race. Race pride, race consciousness, and racial uplift were part of the reform during the era. Race pride was not only encouraged; it was taught, mentored, and role modeled. This reflection of race pride brought tremendous power to the social service work of African Americans. They did not perform a concrete social service so much as encompass the whole person within his or her environment. For example, racial uplift was inseparable from efforts to oppose sexual exploitation. In a two-way effort, reformers provided recreational programs for boys, giving them safe and healthy recreational outlets, with the benefit of protecting girls from assault. Race pride was also the mechanism that facilitated group solidarity and helped to undercut class differences that existed between social workers and the people they served (Carlton-LaNey, 1999).

Social Debt   African Americans who had achieved economic and educational success carried with them a moral, monetary, and service obligation. With an education, African Americans became members of a privileged group with the expectation that education would be used to help the race. DuBois (quoted in Carlton-LaNey, 1999, p. 313) said, "The best of us should give of our means, our time and ourselves to leaven the whole." Education had such particular meaning for African Americans that it became integrated into campaigns for the welfare and betterment of the race with many of the social welfare leaders teaching school at some point in their careers. The importance of education and teaching was such that the pioneer social workers built it into most programs and services of which they were a part. For example, African American social settlements included programs that taught sewing, dressmaking, and child care, as well as public lectures, with literary clubs to stimulate intellectual and political discourse. Colleges and universities with which these pioneers were affiliated advocated education for service and racial uplift (Carlton-LaNey, 1999).

Race Lens   At the pinnacle of the work of African American social work/welfare leaders was the emphasis on working for the "race" or racial uplift. They literally used a "race lens" to carefully assess the problems and issues that confronted the African American community. The "lens" never lost focus on racism as a powerful part of the life experiences of the people. There was never any question for the pioneers that their race was central to their well-being or lack thereof. Part of the work of the leaders of the African American community was gaining respect from white people. It was thought necessary, and in most cases desirable, to have good working relations with white people through interracial cooperation. It was not so much white wisdom that was being sought as it was the reality that that was where the power to change systems lay. There was not agreement among African Americans regarding the role of interracial cooperation; nonetheless, social workers and social welfare leaders continued to tout the importance of race pride and self-reclamation. At the same time, the struggle remained constant to dispel myths and to establish powerful social institutions along with strong role models for African Americans (Carlton-LaNey, 1999).

Social Work Education   The professional training of African American social workers embraced a holistic approach to practice with the National Urban League (NUL), providing the first organized social work course of study for African Americans at Fisk University in 1911. The cofounder and first executive director of the NUL, Dr. George Edmund Haynes, was a leader in the emerging social work profession. Through his work, hundreds of young men and women were introduced to formal social work training through the National Urban League Fellowship program. Haynes strongly believed that knowledge and an appreciation of African American history were essential for any African American student engaging in social work practice, and he developed the first such courses to be taught in any U.S. university. The courses in African American history, along with the courses in economics and sociology, became part of the social work certificate program (Carlton-LaNey, 1999).

George Haynes was extraordinarily astute in his belief that knowledge and an appreciation of African American history were essential. He was perhaps ahead of his time with this thought. As Lerner (1997, p. 199) tells us, "All human beings are practicing historians." Lerner goes on to explain "why history matters." We present ourselves to others through our life story, which changes as we grow and mature. Different, decisive events are stressed that give new meaning to our lives over time. This is called "doing history." One's self-representation, the way he or she defines who he or she is, also takes the shape of the life story that is told. What is remembered, stressed as significant, or omitted serves to define past and present. One's personal history can affect the future; for example, if people are seen as victimized, as powerless and overwhelmed by forces that they cannot understand or control, they may choose to live cautiously, avoiding conflict and evading pain. On the other hand, if the perception is that one is loved, grounded, and powerful, the future is embraced with a sense of accepting the challenges that lie ahead with confidence, and life can be lived more courageously (Lerner, 1997).

For Progressive Era African Americans dealing with the legacy of slavery, an accurate examination of that history can be a powerful tool for healing. As Lerner (1997) explains:

> History, a mental construct which extends human life beyond its span, can give meaning to each life and serve as a necessary anchor for us. It gives us a sense of

perspective about our own lives and encourages us to transcend the finite span of our lifetime by identifying with the generations that came before us and measuring our won actions against the generations that will follow. By perceiving ourselves to be part of history, we can begin to think on a scale larger than the here and now. We can expand our reach and with it our aspirations. It is having a history which allows human beings to grow out of magical and mythical thought into the realm of rational abstraction and to make projections into the future that are responsible and realistic. (p. 201)

Social Work Schools for African Americans Most individuals who practiced social work were not trained professionally, though training was deemed preferable. Two social work schools were established for African Americans in 1920—the Atlanta School of Social Work and the Bishop Tuttle School in Raleigh, North Carolina. The second executive director of the NUL, Eugene K. Jones, accorded professional social work among African Americans a powerful status, stating that Negroes who were effective social workers would tend to raise the level of intelligence, physical vigor, and industrial status of the group. Jones believed social work encompassed all aspects of African American life. The director of the Philadelphia Armstrong Association, Forrester Washington, believed that professional social work required a "humanitarian's impulse," along with the ability to see "the causes of certain problems and [to] know the proper treatment of these problems," and also that "to be master of the process by which social change takes place is the function of the social worker" (Carlton-LaNey, 1999, p. 315). [Carlton-LaNey (1999) provides an enlightening and thorough history of African American social work.]

There are scores of other Progressive Era pioneer African American social work icons whose contributions to social welfare history and the development of social welfare institutions for African Americans and the larger community go unsung. For example, social worker, author, politician, "race woman," and community activist Elizabeth Ross Haynes constantly advocated and agitated not only for the rights of African Americans but for women's rights as well. She put forth a challenge to her contemporaries in 1937 with this question:

> If Frances Perkins (the Honorable Francis Perkins), secretary of labor, can fill one of the most difficult posts in the Cabinet of the President of these United States—and this she had done superbly despite any criticisms—is not the time ripe for women, black and white, to extend and enlarge the opportunity fought for by Susan B. Anthony and Sojourner Truth, especially since the latter could neither read nor write? (Carlton-LaNey, 1997, p. 573)

Haynes served as a role model, involving herself in researching, writing, and speaking about women's labor issues, women's spiritual and Christian growth, women's roles in the political arena, and women's use of all their talents and skills. The exclusion of African American women in history creates gaps in social workers' cognition, distorting the knowledge base. Lost are the "concepts, perspectives, methods, and pedagogues of women's history and women's studies [that] have been developed without consideration of the experience of black women" (Carlton-LaNey, 1997, p. 574). The reason that efforts to uncover African American women's history has failed is due, in part, to the parallel history of the development of feminist theory. The result of this timing is that African American women's history tends to be addressed inside the feminist perspective, which omits the unique experiences of women of color. Generally, African American women have had marginal positions in the feminist movement. There is the misperception that African American women deal either with women's issues or with race issues but not both simultaneously. The stance of most white women is that they did not want to dissipate their energies dealing with race issues because their time could be better spent addressing issues that were important to all (cf. Giddings, 1984; Smith, 1985). This stance, the primacy of female oppression, denies the structured inequalities of race. The other side is that the African American woman's "feminist efforts are directed chiefly toward the realization of the equality of the races, the sex struggle assuming a subordinate place" (Carlton-LaNey, 1997, 574).

Some believe that the term *"feminism"* is partly responsible for the exclusion that African American women feel, because "feminism: puts a priority on gender, not race" (Carlton-LaNey, 1997). Among African American authors (cf. Walker; Hine, 1996; Ogunyemi, 1985), the problem of terminology has been dealt with by the use of the terms *womanish* and *womanism* to describe the African American female experience. It is defined by Walker (Carlton-LaNey, 1997, p. 574) as "a consciousness that incorporates racial, cultural, sexual, national, economic, and political consideration for all people." Among the African American female community, it is believed that *womanism* speaks to a double legacy of oppression and a resistance movement among African American women. Some may find the word uncomfortable, but its ideals are descriptive of the life careers of many African American pioneer social welfare leaders of the Progressive Era—such as Ida B. Wells-Barnett, Janie Porter Barrett, and Birdye Henrietta Haynes. These pioneers knew that their oppressed position in society resulted from both gender and race and that their continued struggle must include both, knowing that they were not fragmented individuals but whole and holistic in both consciousness and purpose (Carlton-LaNey, 1997). For an uplifting, in-depth look at Haynes and her work with women through the Young Women's Christian Association (YWCA) and the U.S. Department of Labor's Women in Industry Service (WIS), as well as her role as an elected leader in Harlem's 21st Assembly District, see Carlton-LaNey (1997).

SOCIAL REFORM ACTIVITIES

The social reform activities most representative of the Progressive Era occurred in the arena of social welfare. The reform movement embraced the new profession of social work. Through research, persistence, and expertise, individual social workers moved to the forefront of advocacy for social legislation. Acting on the commonly held conviction that all citizens were personally responsible for the current state of affairs, Theodore Roosevelt called upon all to contribute to "reform through social work" (Axinn & Levin, 1997, p. 132).

Most persons laboring for social reform were primarily concerned with social justice, striving "to bring the power of the state and national governments into the economic struggle on the side of women, children, and other unprotected groups" (Axinn & Levin, 1997, p. 132). Social workers found common ground for the work that needed doing by balancing themselves between the Charity Organization's mission of working with individuals in their own efforts to cope, and the settlement house conviction to work with the large community and environment. Social workers, along with their natural allies, worked for legislation to regulate tenement and factory construction; to prevent and compensate for industrial accidents and disease; to prohibit child labor and provide for compulsory education; to improve sanitary and health conditions; to provide social insurance as security against unemployment, retirement, or death of the breadwinner; and to protect workers, specifically women, in regard to minimum wages and working hours (Axinn & Levin, 1997).

Mothers' Pension Legislation

Between 1911 and 1919, the mothers' pension movement swept the nation with many states developing programs. Unlike today, with most single mothers being divorced or having children out of wedlock, the progressive period found them to be widowed. Progressive reformers, by focusing on the needs of women who had been widowed, believed that the women would be viewed more sympathetically by governmental agencies than those who had been divorced or deserted. They argued that, without governmental assistance, the single mothers—widowed, divorced, or deserted—would have to work such long hours that they could not adequately care for their children with many having to continue to divide their family by sending some of their children to orphanages (Jansson, 1997).

In 1914, in Denver, Gertrude Vaile made a statement to a local newspaper about administrating mothers' pensions:

> Moreover, it is the democratic thing to do. When the Father dies why should a good mother have to depend upon the alms of her more fortunate neighbor for the opportunity to perform the natural and civic duty of bringing up her children—even if her more fortunate neighbors are willing and able to give alms (Pumphrey & Pumphrey, 1963, p. 673)

This modern welfare consisted of a network of women who fought for and administered these programs, the caveat being that they were mainly white,

Protestant, and middle class so we could view them as both brave and compassionate and frequently blinded by their race and class privilege. Never intended to be universal, the mothers' aid programs were, by design, under funded and reached only a minority of needy single mothers. Every recipient was not only means-tested but also morals-tested, with only 46,000 women being assisted nationally by 1919. The programs were operated with low appropriations, often creating long waiting lists (Gordon, 1998; Jansson, 1997).

The head of New York's Charity Organization Society, Otis Bannard, said, "[Mothers' pensions are] an entering wedge towards state socialism with relief to the able-bodied not far behind" (Ringenback, 1973, p. 182). And his colleague, Edward Devine, said, ". . . [G]overnmental support of abandoned women is an insidious attack upon the family and is an encouragement to abandonment."

This campaign could be considered successful by some. During that decade, 40 states offered pensions to single mothers. A closer look, however, reveals that only women who became single without violating respectability were served—mainly widows. The limitations of the mothers' aid programs most certainly can be explained by the racial and class makeup of its designers. Many were denied assistance because of health problems or poor housing. The programs also discriminated against immigrants and minorities. African Americans constituted only 3% of the recipients, although they were much more in need on average than whites. In the West, Hispanics and Native Americans were usually totally excluded. Furthermore, pensions were so miserly that large numbers of women were forced to work while receiving assistance (Gordon, 1998; Jansson, 1997).

The state mothers' pensions programs hung on by a thread until the Great Depression of the 1930s when they collapsed. The states and localities realized that only the federal government had the tax base and the enforcement power to administer them. We learn in the next chapter that Franklin D. Roosevelt and the New Deal were a blessing, but the blessing came in disguise for some. The SSA institutionalized the role of the state in maintaining families and marked the beginning of the destabilization of the family (Abramovitz, 1996).

Child Labor Legislation

Children moved to center stage in social welfare activities from the mid-19th century through the early 20th century. Reformers included the Association for Improving the Conditions of the Poor (AICP) agents, charity organization society friendly visitors, settlement house residents, and almost every other agency or individual working for social betterment, all seeing in children the possibility for constructive altruism. There were many avenues that the movement pursued—for example, removal of dependent, neglected, and delinquent children from almshouses and other institutions and their placement in private homes. The creation of juvenile courts and probation systems, the passage of compulsory school attendance laws, crusades against child labor, and the provision of mothers' and widows' pensions also were included here, along with a host of other activities (Trattner, 1999).

A real need existed for social work on the behalf of the nation's youngest citizens. The interest in children in trouble is understandable, and they were more numerous than adults in an age when large families were the rule. Among the neglected and needy, they formed one of the largest groups, especially after tens of thousands of youngsters were orphaned or half-orphaned as a result of the Civil War. Of the vast numbers of people needing help during this time, children seemed the most deserving and surely not responsible for their conditions. The social upheaval and family disruption resulting from large-scale immigration, rapid industrial and urban growth, and several severe economic depressions were extremely hard on children. Deprived of one or both parents early in life, along with being affected by the mobility and anonymity of a swiftly changing urban-industrial society, the children were left in strange and often hostile environments and forced into harsh working conditions (Trattner, 1999).

The turn of the century found 1 out of 6 children gainfully employed, comprising 7 million children between the ages of 10 and 15. It is unknown how many children under age 10 worked, especially African American children on southern farms. Of the 60% of farm child laborers, all were employed by people other than their parents. The other jobs held by children were in cotton, woolen, and silk mills; in clothing and tobacco sweatshops; in coal mines and iron mills; and—up to 2.5 million—in street trades (Day, 1989). The underage children, working illegally, were taught to hide from inspectors. There were 120,000 children in mines and mills in Pennsylvania and 92,000 in New York, reportedly. With the move of the textiles mills to the South, child employment increased until children comprised 30% of all textile millworkers. With the advent of new labor laws, such as compulsory education, inroads were made into child labor; and, by 1910 only 2 million were working; by 1920, 1 million; and, by 1930, about 667,000 (Day, 1999).

Mary Harris Jones ("Mother Jones"—1830–1930), was a lifetime advocate against child labor. This Irish immigrant, while supporting a textile mill strike in Pennsylvania in 1903, found that 10,000 of the 75,000 mill workers were children and that a goodly number of them had been maimed by machinery. She publicly spoke out against the plight:

> Eddie Dunphy, a little fellow of twelve, whose job it was to sit all day . . . handing in the right thread to another worker . . . eleven hours a day . . . with dangerous machinery all about him . . . for three dollars a week. And . . . Gussie Ragnew, a little girl from whom all the childhood had gone. Her face was like an old woman's . . . little boys with their fingers off and hands crushed and maimed . . . Philadelphia's mansions were built on the broken bones, the quivering hearts, and drooping heads of these children. (Day, 1989, p. 253)

The U.S. Bureau of Labor published the findings of a national survey of child labor in 1904, tying in the general deterioration to premature employment. The report "referred to young employees as 'worn' and 'run down,' and recounted one worker's impression that 'the millwork used him up.' Senator Beveridge held that veteran employees were 'utterly exhausted and almost worthless' by the age of 17 or 18, but he offered no biomedical explanation" (Derickson, 1992, p. 1286).

Eventually, the nation became aware of the "crime of child labor," and shortly thereafter Pennsylvania passed a child labor law setting a minimum age of 14 for child employment. National intervention in child labor, however, was prohibited by the Constitution; thus, reforms were sought out by the states. Thirty-four states did pass child labor laws, but they had many loopholes and were, for the most part, ineffective. There was a clear paradox here: Labor would be the beneficiary of restrictive child labor, giving more jobs to men. Labor standards for children, however, would raise wages and reduce profit; therefore, although altruism won the day in law, exceptions countered the victory in favor of factory owners (Day, 1999).

Other women—Lillian Wald and Florence Kelly—got involved, and in 1902 they called a meeting of representatives of 32 settlement houses in New York City. Child labor was discussed, and in 1903 the group secured passage of a law regulating street trades. A national child labor committee was formed in 1904 that acted as a clearinghouse against child labor. This committee, with one if its members being Jane Addams, influenced President T. Roosevelt to call the 1909 White House Conference on Child Dependency. It went on record that the Conference favored home care for children rather than institutionalization and recommended the creation of a public bureau to collect and disseminate information on children and child care (Day, 1999).

The Children's Bureau was established in 1912 by William Howard Taft and became a permanent part of the Department of Commerce and Labor. The primary purpose was to protect children from early employment, dangerous occupations, and diseases. A minimum work age of 14 in manufacturing and 16 in mining was advocated, with documented proof of age, an 8-hour workday, and prohibition of night work. With Julia Lathrop as its director, the first 15 social workers were employed to staff it. The bureau's duty was to investigate and report on all matters pertaining to child welfare and child life—infant mortality, birth rates, children's institutions, juvenile courts, desertion, dangerous occupations, accidents and diseases, child labor, and children's legislation. The initial appropriation of about $25,000 was doubled but was still far less than money spent for animal research, with young animals having a lower morality rate than children (Day, 1999).

The struggle was far from over with all child labor reforms called Bolshevik plots to "nationalize" children and families and consistently declared unconstitutional. In 1916, the Keating-Owens bill to control child labor came to Congress but failed to pass. A constitutional amendment was proposed in 1924 but was defeated by a lobby of manufacturers and Catholics who believed it was a threat to family life. Nevertheless, all the states and Washington, D.C., enacted child protections law by 1930 (Day, 1999).

Other Social Reform Issues

We know from history that many more important social reform issues were fought for during this time. Among them were Veterans' welfare, aid to the blind, old age assistance, unemployment insurance, health insurance, juvenile and criminal justice, women's health and suffrage, and worker's compensation. We briefly review the last three.

Women's Reproductive Health   The obstacles to women's sexual freedom persisted. Birth control techniques had expanded to include condoms and diaphragms, but these techniques were learned by word of mouth or vaguely worded advertisements rather than through a public, family-planning clinic (Jansson, 1997). Margaret Sanger (1883–1966) founded the birth control movement, dedicating her book, *Woman and the New Race,* to the memory of her mother, who had given birth to 11 children and who died at age 48. Sanger was a public health nurse who witnessed firsthand the disastrous economic and physical effects on poor women and their families because of uncontrolled fertility. Sanger's life mission was to give every woman the right "to control her own body" (Schneir, 1992, p. 325).

Upon Sanger's return in 1915 from Europe, where she studied the history of birth control, she launched a massive campaign to break down legal barriers to dissemination of contraceptive information and devices by physicians. She believed that birth control was the most important part of the struggle to liberate women and that the right to voluntary motherhood was woman's key to the temple of liberty. In her book, first published in 1920, she says:

> The most far-reaching social development of modern times is the revolt of woman against sex servitude. The most important force in the remaking of the world is a free motherhood. . . . Only in recent years has woman's position as the gentler and weaker half of the human family been emphatically and generally questioned. Men assumed that this was woman's place; woman herself accepted it. It seldom occurred to anyone to ask whether we would go on occupying it forever. . . . [Women] claimed the right of suffrage and legislative regulation of her working hours, and asked that her property rights be equal to those of the man. None of these demands, however, affected directly the most vital factors of her existence. Whether she won her point or failed to win it, she remained a dominated weakling in a society controlled by men. (Schneir, 1992, pp. 325–326)

Sanger opened two clinics upon her return from Europe. The Brownsville Clinic in New York, the first one in 1916, was closed; and Sanger and her sister Ethel Byrne were arrested and spent 30 days in jail for conducting a house-to-house advertising campaign informing women of their services. Her next clinic was opened in 1917 with physicians dispensing diaphragms smuggled in from Europe only to those women whose medical history indicated that another pregnancy would be a health hazard. Several attempts failed to get a license for herself and her physician to distribute contraceptives legally. Finally, by 1927, the clinic's medical director, Dr. Hannah Stone, could demonstrate and prescribe diaphragms, but it was not until 1936 that doctors were allowed to distribute contraceptives. Contraceptives remained illegal, however, until 1938, even though the American Medical Association recognized their importance as a medical topic. Although a court ruling allowed physicians to import, mail, and prescribe devices, the "under-the-counter" racket in contraception remained a $250,000-million-a-year business because doctors were still unwilling to prescribe contraceptives (Day, 1999).

Suffrage We learned in Chapter 5 that suffrage was at the forefront of reform in the women's rights movement with the formation of the National American Women's Suffrage Association (NAWSA) in 1900. Susan B. Anthony was succeeded as president by Carrie Chapman Catt in 1900 and then by Dr. Anna Howard Shaw (1847–1919), a Methodist minister and physician. Shaw was an eloquent orator but had almost no administrative skills and little tact, consequently alienating men in power with frequent attacks on their politics. This lead to the men undermining the women's political support, leaving NAWSA's administration in a shambles; and many of its staunchest women supporters, such as Florence Kelley, resigned. Upon Shaw's resignation, Jane Addams took the presidency in 1911 and held it until 1915 when Carrie Chapman Catt resumed the role (Day, 1999). By this time, the women leaders had developed more sophisticated organizing skills and the reform issues seemed less radical because of women's prominent roles (Jansson, 1997).

This momentum lead to 12 states granting women the vote by 1916. The suffragettes argued that voting women would support progressive reform on education and family instead of emphasizing feminist arguments. The males received this stance favorably, as they were imbued with the 19th-century belief that women's superior moral qualities and temperament best suited them to attend to family matters and children. Also, the limiting nature of a single issue, organization became apparent with other women's groups moving to the fore. For example, the National Consumers' League, the National Women's Trade Union League, and the Young Women's Christian Association became concerned with matters affecting women as women and saw the vote as a way to righting wrongs. This lead to NAWSA broadening its view and, in its publication *The Women's Journal*, supported the garment workers' strike of 1909. This, in part, resulted in an increase of membership, rising to 100,000 in 1910 and to 2 million in 1917 (Axinn & Levin, 1997; Jansson, 1997).

The real breakthrough came during World War I when Woodrow Wilson finally agreed to support the issue. The women leaders threatened to target

Democratic candidates for defeat and argued that suffrage was needed to maintain national unity during the war. In 1920, the 19th Amendment to the Constitution was finally enacted (Jansson, 1997).

Workmen's Compensation Workmen's Compensation was meant to help those injured on the job or the survivors of those killed at work and was first discussed at the American Sociological Association Conference in 1902 and again in 1905 and 1906. The unions vehemently opposed worker's compensation despite the horrendous rate of industrial accidents at the time. They wanted welfare to be a union function and resisted state intervention in union affairs. Eventually, however, the nation moved toward worker's compensation. A high rate of injuries and deaths in industrial accidents occurred yearly—half a million and 15,000 respectively. Employers put the blame on the workers, arguing that they knew the risks involved in the jobs when they took them; and courts generally supported this claim (Day, 1989).

The Federal Employment Act was passed in 1906 (President Theodore Roosevelt), providing a minimum worker's insurance for federal employees; and, in the same year, the National Conference on Charities and Corrections appointed a committee to look into the issue. Shortly thereafter, a National Conference on Worker's Compensation was held in 1909; and, shortly thereafter, a major study was undertaken in Pittsburgh. This study, a comprehensive survey of all labor conditions in the entire city, was one of the most important social research efforts of the era. The survey looked at wages, hours, conditions of labor, housing, schooling, health taxation, fire and police protection, recreation, and land values. The finished report was published and argued that the high rate of industrial accidents would continue as long as employers were not held responsible. Thereafter, 30 states investigated safety conditions in industry. In 1911, 10 of the states enacted worker's compensation laws; and, by 1920, 42 states had adopted the author's (Crystal Eastman) suggestions into law. Included were compensation for workers and their survivors based on economic loss due to industrial accidents; employer responsibility for all accidents regardless of fault; and a voluntary insurance pool under public administration. While it left many people uncovered, with limited benefits, it was a beginning (Day, 1999).

A Strengths Perspective Analysis of the Progressive Era

Much like the Colonial Era, the people moved to fill the vacuum that existed in the absence of federal social policy. The federal government continued its hands-off philosophy to social reform, leaving it to the states who did a slipshod job. Social workers can take much of the credit for the social welfare reform that did take place. The Charity Organization Societies, the settlement house movement, and the formation of African American social work all came about as a response to unmet need. We know from history that social policy is the basis of social work practice; it defines, formulates, and implements social programs. What we had in the Progressive Era was the reverse of this process—social work practice pushing for social policy/reform.

Dual strengths were found in the pioneer social workers: their personal conviction and dedication to the pressing needs of people, and their professional commitment to social change. The social workers saw the basic, common needs of the people—women, children, laborers, freedmen and freed women—and the barriers to meeting their needs—lack of pensions, child labor laws, safeguards and benefits for workers and the exclusion of African Americans from the social system. This identification of common need, as opposed to deficits and social problems, is one of the first tenants in a strengths approach to social policy formation. The next step is a negotiated means, a mutual collaboration, of how to achieve the desired policy. We build on this step, negotiated means, as well as the others, as we proceed through the chapters of the book.

African American Social Work

We use the development of African American social work during the Progressive Era as an example of refocusing, or reframing, the problem definition. In her article on social policy development, Chapin (1995) uses the argument that a social constructionist approach to the understanding of social problems is basic to the use of a strengths perspective. Translated, this means that an understanding of social problems, like all human interaction, is based on sociably and personally constructed views of reality. This is precisely what African American social workers did as they constructed the use of race pride, social debt, and a race lens to view their own, unique reality.

The African Americans' perception of reality was mediated by their culture, language, and the meaning of social conditions (race lens). Their reality was shaped by personal belief (race pride) and consensus. Their view of reality, in contrast to the classic scientific model of knowledge, served to identity and understand the various human situations that needed to be shaped by them, the lookers or observers (social debt).

Using the social constructionist position as an analytical tool, we see that African American social workers were able to understand historical changes in the contexts of welfare and poverty. They were able to grasp the influence of values in the definition of social problems and to understand that reality was multifaceted; they were excluded from the social system and received limited responses from white social workers at a time when their postwar needs were great. Like white social workers of the era, African American social workers' response to need was a reaction to the absence of social policy. The latter-day strengths perspective can be applied here, based on the premise that the barriers people labeled as belonging to a "disadvantaged groups" face in meeting their basic needs tend to originate from the demographic exclusion of educational, political, and economic rather than individual characteristics. The African American social worker pioneers go on to demonstrate that their task was to identify individual and community resources that could be used to create opportunities for inclusion or to provide clear-cut alternatives that bypass the predominate system "in favor of those which work better for a given community" (Chapin, 1995, p. 509). They did not perform a concrete social service so much as they encompassed the whole person within his or her environment.

SUMMARY

Social reform had virtually ended by 1920, with it taking a separate path from social work, which had become a middle-class profession. Governmental reform legislation had bureaucratized county and state departments of public welfare for more accountability with funding. Institutionalization of the poor was markedly decreased, but pensions were far from adequate, nonetheless becoming the trend of the future (Day, 1999).

While some would like to think of this era as one of increasing equality, the reality was that America had lost little of its classism, racism, and sexism. Union gains were primarily for men, and women's secondary status in the job market was confirmed by law in most states. With the polarization of classes, the great wealth of the few insulated and isolated them from the problems of the poor. The era's significance for social work was a crystallization of the scope and method of professional social work, setting it apart from social reform. While the new domain for government became bureaucratization and concern with poverty, for social work it became casework—mental health, psychiatric casework, school social work, medical social work, and so on, for people who could afford the services or who were entitled to them: the worthy (Day, 1999).

REFERENCES

Abramovitz, M. (1996). [Revised]. *Regulating the lives of women: Social welfare policy from colonial times to the present.* Boston, MA: South End Press.

Adams, J. P. (1991). *Peacework: Oral histories of women peace activists.* Boston: Twayne.

Axinn, J., & Levin, H. (1997). *Social welfare: A history of the American response to need* (4th ed.). New York: Longman.

Carlton-LaNey, I. (1997). Elizabeth Ross Haynes: An African American reformer of womanist consciousness, 1980–1940. *Social Work, 42,* 573–583.

Carlton-LaNey, I. (1999). African American social work pioneers' response to need. *Social Work, 44,* 311–321.

Chapin, R. K. (1995). Social policy development: The strengths perspective. *Social Work, 40,* 506–514.

Day, P. J. (1989). *A new history of social welfare.* Englewood Cliffs, NJ: Prentice Hall.

Day, P. J. (1999). *A new history of social welfare* (3rd ed.). Boston, MA: Allyn & Bacon.

Derickson, A. (1992, September). Making human junk: Child labor as a health issue in the Progressive Era. *Public Health Then and Now, 82,* 1280–1290.

Johnson, M. A. (Ed.). (1989). *The many faces of Hull House: The photographs of Wallace Kirkland.* Chicago: University of Illinois Press.

Giddings, P. (1984). *When and where I enter: The impact of black women on race and sex in America.* New York: Bantam Books.

Gordon, L. (1998). How welfare became a dirty word. *Journal of International and Comparative Social Welfare, XIV,* 1–14.

Hine, D. C. (1996). *Speak truth to power.* New York: Carlson.

Jansson, B. S. (1997). *The reluctant welfare state* (3rd ed.). Pacific Grove, CA: Brooks/Cole.

Lerner, G. (1997). *Why history matters.* New York: Oxford University Press.

Oqunyemi, C. (1985). Womanism: The dynamics of the contemporary black female novel in English. *Signs, 11,* 63–80.

Pumphrey, R. E., & Pumphrey, M. H. (Eds.). (1963). *The heritage of American social work.* New York: Columbia University Press.

Ringenback, P. T. (1973). *Tramps and reformers, 1873–1916: The discovery of unemployment in New York.* Westpoint, CT.

Schneir, M. (1992). *Feminism: The essential historical writings.* New York: Vintage Books.

Smith, B. (1985). Some home truths on the contemporary black feminish movement. *Journal of Black Studies and Research, 16,* 4–13.

Trattner, W. I. (1999). *From poor law to welfare state: A history of social welfare in America* (6th ed.). New York: The Free Press.

Walker, A. (1983). *In search of our mother's gardens' Womanist prose.* New York: Harcourt, Brace.

The Emerging
Welfare State

The American story of social welfare rapidly unfolded during 1929 through 1931. Within this short period of time, a succession of events introduced important and dynamic changes in the philosophy, policies, and programs of social work and public welfare. The stock market crash in the fall of 1929 and the long depression that followed influenced the future of the social welfare system by highlighting critical questions pertaining to local, state, and federal governmental responsibilities; the role of private and public agencies in unemployment relief; and federal loans versus grants-in-aid to the states (Brown, 1940).

This chapter reviews the socioeconomic conditions and political environment of the depression and the social welfare policy initiatives of the New Deal. Throughout the chapter, students of social policy are reminded of the unprecedented increase in public relief expenditures in the United States, as well as notable changes in governmental responsibilities and administrative methods that marked this era. A system of local poor relief, which had remained practically unchanged for a century and a half, was now superseded not only by new methods but also by a new philosophy of governmental responsibility for people in need. More progress was made in public welfare and relief during this time frame than in the 300 years after this country was first settled.

Many of the changes in social welfare reflected the ideas of social work pioneers who had a vision for the United States that extended beyond the concept of charity to a society that functioned for the good of all. A. W. McMillen, director of the new Bureau of Social Statistics, University of Chicago, described the shift from private charity to public support for the poor in his comments at the 1929 National Conference for Social Work in San Francisco:

> Whether we like it or not, government is already in the field of social work in a big way—on a scale so colossal, in fact, that even the enormous efforts of the private societies seem dwarfed by comparison. (McMillen, 1929)

SOCIOECONOMIC CONDITIONS OF THE TIMES

The economic state of the nation and subsequent social conditions gave the first warnings of the coming disaster. Unlike previous years, the spring of 1929 did not bring with it the usual seasonal decrease in relief expenditures. Rather, according to the National Industrial Conference Board, the Alexander Hamilton Institute, and the Cleveland Trust Company, there were an estimated 2,860,000 unemployed men and women in the United States (Hopkins, 1933). Figures compiled by the Children's Bureau from 120 cities indicated that expenditures remained ominously higher than the levels of relief during the corresponding months of the preceding year (Kimberly, 1975).

On October 24, 1929, a record 13 million shares were sold on the New York Stock Exchange, and prices dropped further than ever in the history of the exchange (Kimberly, 1975). The great crash signaled economic peril for the nation. During the first months following the stock market crash, the business community and its counterparts across the nation expressed their confidence that the fundamental structure of the country remained sound and that the business slump would soon end. However, the rise in unemployment continued through 1930. By January, there were well over 4 million people out of work, nearly double the 1929 figure. In March, 600,000 more people became unemployed. August proved worse than March, and the early summer seasonal work brought only a slight decrease in the monthly totals. Five million were unemployed in September, nearly 7 million by the end of the year, 8 million by the spring of 1931, and then a steady increase to the peak of 13 to 15 million in the spring of 1933 (McMillen, 1935).

What did the rise in unemployment mean in the lives of people? Studies completed by the Children's Bureau described the conditions that affected the health of children in mining communities of West Virginia, Kentucky, Pennsylvania, Illinois, and a number of other states. The alarming incidents of undernourishment and even starvation and the pitiful inadequacy of relief revealed by these studies led to the request, made in the spring by Mr. Croxton, that the Friends' Service Community go into these counties and feed the children, as they had done in Europe after World War I (Brown, 1946). Later, Mr. Picket, secretary of the American Friends' Service Committee testified at a congressional hearing that their work of feeding children began in September in West Virginia and Kentucky and later extended to southern Illinois, western Pennsylvania, and eastern Ohio (Senate Hearings, 1931).

Working-class families lived with the threats of repossession, overcrowding, abuse, child neglect, marital problems, sickness, and starvation as described in a 1934 short story by Meridel Le Sueur:

> The working-class family is going fast, the lower middle class family is also going, though not so fast. It is like a landslide. It is like a great chasm opening beneath the feet and swallowing the bottom classes first. The worker who lives from hand to mouth goes first, and then his family goes. The family rots, decays and goes to pieces with the woman standing last, trying to hold it together, and then going too. (Le Sueur, 1982, p. 144)

Patterson (1981) states that activist social workers saw the social impact of unemployment and the depression firsthand during their home visits and in social service agencies. Their case entries portray a theme of the resilience of poor people even in the face of desperate circumstances:

> 1920s—The Lovejoy Family: William Lovejoy, a carpenter of Cleveland, is a Negro. The Negro is harder hit in dull times than the white, although differently. During the course of a year, he will have more jobs but also more unemployment than the average white worker. . . . Lovejoy finished grammar school and the first year of high school in Georgia. His wife, too, had a fairly good education at a girls' school. Her mother had been a schoolteacher. Lovejoy's father and older brothers had been carpenters, and he had learned his trade from them. He was forced to join the carpenters' union in 1923. Because union wages were as high for colored workers as for others, his white employers dropped him from the

payroll and hired white help instead. For the past seven years he has depended on odd jobs of any kind. . . .

During spells of unemployment they have lived on next to nothing, so that children (they had nine) have been much undernourished. . . . Often the whole family went hungry, particularly the father and mother. . . . Somehow they managed to exist without calling upon agency help. . . . Through every vicissitude, it has been the family aim to keep the children in school at all costs. . . . (Calkins, 1930, pp. 40–42)

1920s—The Poulos Family: Say that trade shifts oust you. You are Nicholas Poulos of Boston. In the 19 years since you came from Greece, you have worked in shoe factories there. But the shoe industry has increasingly left New England. In your early days you had no work for one month, part time for three months, and full time the rest of the year. Now you work full time for one month, and part time for five, and for the remaining six you do not work at all. Since even for full time you never received more than $25 a week, on which your wife Helen and your three children have had to live, it is thanks to Helen's extraordinary thrift that you made any savings at all. What has the decentralization of the shoe factory done for you?

This is what happened to the Nicholas Poulos family. First they lost two insurance policies. Rent fell in arrears, so the mother, Helen, found work in a laundry. During the weeks in which Mr. Poulos also had work, her weekly earnings of $12 enabled the family to pay back some of the money they owed to their friends.

But Mrs. Poulos worked beyond her strength. In spite of her utmost efforts at management, her children had to be neglected. The youngest was reported by the school as being undernourished and had to be fed at the School Diet Kitchen. She resented her husband's idleness, said he did not try to work. He became inert and fatalistic. They quarreled and were under constant domestic strain. (Calkins, 1930, pp. 28–29)

These two studies highlight that poverty was the result not of a personal weakness or character flaw but, rather, of a consequence of inequitable resource distribution and "an economy insufficiently abundant to provide substance for all the able-bodied" (Patterson, 1981, p. 6). Thus, poverty, during robust or weak economic conditions, could be conceived as a structural element of American society as opposed to a moral issue.

The dimensions of poverty before and during the depression defy precise measurement because there were no official statistics on poverty or unemployment rates. However, by interpolating from vital statistics, it is estimated that 18 million people lived in disadvantaged families with women and children comprising over 50% of all poor people. A sample of 165,000 urban households in 1934 described 20% of these households as having no employable member and that, of the rest, 25% depended on jobs that paid below substance wages (Works Progress Administration, 1936, pp. 50–52). The following social work report illustrates the living conditions of poor people:

1938—Sullivan County, New York: Truly rural slums are worse than city slums. Homes are, almost without exception, old farm or camp buildings on shallow foundations. They are heated by woodburning stoves. In the past few years wood has become scare and almost as costly as coal. Families five to seven members have been obligated to move beds into kitchen and crowd up the best way possible to sleep and keep from freezing. . . . Hardly without exception, roofs leak, plastering is off walls and ceilings, and cracks let in cold air to add to the cold, damp mildewed air of the unheated rooms. (American Association of Social Workers, 1938, p. 18)

In rural and urban areas across the country, the median income of African American families was below that of whites. The 1935 income of the majority of African American families, in comparison to a portion of white families, was less than an emergency budget of $903 a year for a family of four (Sterner, 1943, p. 87). Few African Americans earned the $1,261 maintenance income level. African American unemployment exceeded white unemployment by 30% to 60% (Abramovitz, 1996). According to the Urban League, prior to the depression, African American workers sought "to advance to positions commensurate with their abilities. Now they just hoped to hold the line against advancing armies of white workers intent on gaining and content to accept occupations which were once thought too menial for white hands" (Wolters, 1970, p. 92).

THE RESPONSE OF PRIVATE SOCIAL AGENCIES

The financial demands of the children, the aged, the sick, the disabled, and the unemployed middle-class people were clearly beyond their meager existence caused approximately one third of the nation's private agencies to disappear for lack of funds. In the fall of 1930, the Charity Organization Department of the Russell Sage Foundation called a conference of private family welfare agency representatives to discuss the ways and means of meeting relief needs of the coming winter. The *Survey Midmonthly* carried a report of the discussion, which included the following:

> If private contributions cannot carry the load, the family agencies should push for the establishment of public departments giving both service and relief. Since it has been demonstrated that good standards can be maintained under public auspices, this seems a logical position for them to take in such circumstances, and is the statesmanlike way of forestalling the setting up of temporary emergency relief measures, the results of which often hampered their work for years after the past emergency. (Colcord, 1930)

The conservative attitude toward governmental responsibility for relief prevailed when, in October 1930, President Hoover appointed Colonel Woods to develop a program to address unemployment. Colonel Woods organized the Committee for Employment, which shifted the focus from unemployment to the emergency need for work. The purpose of the Committee was to supplement and encourage the activities of state and local communities upon which was placed the primary responsibility for meeting by:

1. Cooperating with the departments of the Federal Government in their activities concerned with the emergency
2. Pointing out the value of expediting necessary public and semipublic construction already planned in providing employment in the emergency
3. Working with industry to spread employment and otherwise increase employment opportunities, to care for laid-off employees, and to develop stabilizing
4. Indicating specific ways and means by which the individual citizen could personally provide employment for his less-fortunate neighbor
5. Cooperating with national organizations concerned with these problems
6. Supporting publicity and other methods to enable states and communities to provide employment and relief (Hayes, 1936, pp. 3–4)

The Woods Committee asked the Association of Community Chests and Councils to find out what they could about local needs and resources and asked the family Welfare Association of America to study the effects of unemployment on people, deterioration of family morale, and the values and dangers of various types of work. They asked the Bureau of Census to secure figures on relief expenditures for the first three months of 1929 and 1931 to discover the effect of unemployment on the total of obligations assumed. This was the first attempt to secure nationwide relief statistics. The report, published in January 1932, describes what was happening during 1931:

> The total expenditures, including cost of administration, reported by governmental and private organized agencies for family relief (outside of institutions) and for relief to homeless men, in the areas for which returns were received, amounted to $22,338,114 in January, February, and March 1929, and to $72,757,300 during the corresponding period of 1931. The number of families reported as receiving aid averaged 333,861 per month in the first three months of 1929 and 1,287,778 per month in the first three months of 1931. (Brown, 1946, p. 74)

In the midst of mounting public need, the Association of Community Chests and Councils faced the fact that their relief budgets could not possible meet the demands and requested some national declaration, that would stimulate the appropriations of local public funds. The Association took this position, however, with reluctance and only when it became inevitable. The community chest had built its prestige and reason for being upon the assumption of responsibility for all community needs. However, the effort of the Association of Community Chests and Councils and the local chests to carry the load had a deterrent effect upon city officials. The failure of many city governments to act during the early portion of the depression may have been due to a sense of freedom from responsibility fostered by the very existence of the community chest.

In summary, despite the general suffering of the American people, public action to meet the emergency needs was not evident for some time, especially since public home relief had abandoned so many localities. Public officials made some effort to encourage employment. For example, a few committees were organized by state and federal personnel to encourage the expansion of employment opportunities, but they were advisory in nature, and, for the most part, they confined themselves to continued encouragement of local enterprise (Trattner, 1999). Other than certain municipal and state public works projects, no public action of consequence was taken until September 1931—almost two years after the crash. Under the direction of New York Governor Franklin D. Roosevelt, the state legislature acted to provide unemployment relief to jobless citizens of the state.

THE POLITICAL ARENA

As the nation experienced economic decline, Hoover maintained unquestioning faith in the American notion of self-help by considering relief more of a moral issue than an economic concern. From his perspective, private charity should address the needs of the poor as opposed to people receiving relief assistance from the federal government.

A variety of ideas about the role and operation of government supported Hoover's opposition to federal aid. Specifically, Hoover's administration concluded that federal relief could:

- Derail the natural economic recovery process that relies on work
- Commit the government beyond the scope of current revenues
- Inhibit charitable giving and private agency support for poor people
- Limit the responsiveness to local needs
- Enhance the development of politicized bureaucracies
- Undermine free enterprise and the entrepreneurial spirit
- Jeopardize local responsibility and states' rights.

In December 1930, Hoover demonstrated his attitude toward public relief when he approved a congressional appropriation of $45 million to assist Arkansas farmers with feed for stricken livestock (Trattner, 1999). However, a year later, when House Speaker John Garner and Senator Robert F. Wagner of New York sponsored a measure for a $2.6 billion federal public works program, Hoover vetoed the measure, declaring that "never before in the nation's entire history has anyone made so dangerous a suggestion" (Trattner, 1999, p. 278).

Hoover continued to treat the depression as a fleeting condition and as a problem to be managed by private charities. It was not until the summer of 1932, after almost all private social work agencies, the governors of industrial states, and other prominent persons had taken up the call for federal relief that Hoover approved a relief bill. The bill permitted the Reconstruction Finance Corporation (RFC), created earlier to make federal loans to businesses, to lend up to $300 million to the states for unemployment relief (McJimsey, 1987).

In sharp contrast to Hoover's reluctant actions were the bold measures of New York Governor Franklin D. Roosevelt in providing relief for unemployed people. Less traditional than Hoover, Roosevelt sensed that the problems associated with unemployment, such as crime, family suffering, and sickness, were mounting. In response, Roosevelt called a special session of the New York legislature in August. During the session Roosevelt requested that the state's lawmakers allocate funds to assist local authorities with unemployment relief. The resulting legislation was the State Unemployment Relief Act—better known as the Wicks Act, the nation's first program to provide unemployment relief to its needy citizens.

Enacted on September 23, 1931, the Wicks Act provided funds to localities throughout the state, on a matching basis, for work and for home relief under the direction of a new, independent agency, the Temporary Emergency Relief Administration (TERA) (Trattner, 1999; McJimsey, 1987). The act was a hallmark in social welfare policy. Specifically, it supported the public recognition for adequate public relief and challenged the notion that such assistance created dependency. The sheer number of unemployed people altered the environment for social work practice. Rather than work on individual cases, social workers were forced to consider the welfare of many people. Furthermore, the TERA recruited trained social workers for government service from private agencies, thus strengthening the connection between private charity and public welfare.

By the end of 1931, 24 states had followed New York's example of providing assistance for unemployment people through new state agencies that administered funds. The TERA, conceived of as a temporary intervention, served as a prototype for future federal practices. It also highlighted the significant contribution of Harry Hopkins, an energetic young social worker and the executive director of the program.

Harry Hopkins, a graduate of Grinnell College, began his professional career as a social worker at the Association for Improving the Condition of the Poor. He was assigned to study unemployment in New York City to discover why relief applications had increased dramatically. After conducting research on the subject, Hopkins concluded that the principal cause of unemployment had little to do with moral deficits and, rather, with a decrease in the availability of jobs exacerbated by an influx of unskilled workers migrating to New York City in search of work. He recommended creating local, state, and national labor exchanges (employment offices) to classify people for jobs and to refer unemployable people to settlement houses.

When Roosevelt was nominated for the presidency by the Democratic National Convention, many poor people expressed contempt for the government; and they considered the system responsible for their dismal situations but unresponsive to their plight. The election of Franklin D. Roosevelt as the 32nd president of the United States gave citizens a sense of hope for the future. Roosevelt was considered by many an excellent governor of New York. Although he favored small government, local responsibility, and balanced budgets, Roosevelt was more concerned about the unemployed and other needy people. Consequently, during his governorship, New York became the most progressive state in nation by initiating legislative action to reduce distress and prevent further economic disaster.

President Roosevelt's administration operated on principles similar to those who had guided his actions as governor. For example, Roosevelt held that:

- Society had a responsibility for the well-being of all citizens.
- The economic system rather than individual deficits such as idleness caused uncertain financial conditions.
- Marketplace cycles caused unemployment.
- Public assistance was charity but an issue of social justice.
- Americans had a right to a minimum standard of living.
- Liberty and security were interconnected elements of democracy (Axinn & Levin, 1992; McJimsey, 1987; Trattner, 1999)

Within this framework, Roosevelt revitalized the economy in a slow, methodical fashion. His actions succeeded in restoring the public's confidence in the nation's basic institutions, therefore preventing further catastrophe.

It was mid-May 1933 before President Roosevelt called Harry Hopkins to invite him to Washington to organize federal unemployment relief. Within a few days of Hopkins' arrival in Washington, D.C., Congress passed the Federal Emergency Relief Act (FERA), a tradition-shattering statute that opened up an era of federal aid. The FERA produced significant consequences for social welfare by (a) providing $500 million of federal funds as grants-in-aid to the states for emergency unemployment relief and (b) assuming federal responsibility for the relief of a large number of citizens.

Roosevelt offered Hopkins, the director of the FERA, two pieces of advice: give the unemployed quick and adequate relief, and ignore the politicians. Hopkins responded by firing telegrams to state governors, informing them of their opportunities for aid and telling them that they could simply send him a telegram and wait until later to file a formal application. An important measure of the FERA was that all federal grants were to be handled by public agencies. Thus, state bodies were prohibited from allocating federal funds to private agencies, a critical point in regard to the use of the subsidy system and the subsequent abuses that occurred. Another distinguishing feature of the FERA was its stipulation that each local relief administrator employ social workers. Thus, social work practice became an integral part of every county and township across the nation. Social work became more closely aligned with social welfare policy whereby policy specified social work services.

In many ways, Ellen Sullivan Woodward was as significant to the FERA as was Harry Hopkins; unfortunately her name is often forgotten as a program administrator under President Roosevelt. Woodward went to Washington in 1933 to become director of women's work under the FERA, and many of her programs continued under the Civil Works Administration (CWA). Closely connected to Eleanor Roosevelt, who recognized the plight of poor women, Woodward was an astute Mississippi politician with the assignment of (a) coordinating into nationwide projects the state relief programs that had 50,000 women already working and (b) designing new programs for women who wanted to work (Swain, 1983).

Woodward began the massive employment effort for women by appointing Dr. Chloe Owings, a social work professor and director of the University of Minnesota Social Hygiene Bureau, as her assistant. The two women, along with an all-woman staff of consultants, technical advisees, and public relations specialists, formed the Women's Division of the FERA. From December 1933 to 1935, the Women's Division delineated 23 work activities for registered nurses, 28 for unemployed librarians, and numerous other employment placements for professional women (Swain, 1983). Untrained women became involved in mattress making, library work that included Braille translations, and home economics positions such as housekeeping aides, canning, and school lunch room and matron services.

The women projects were not permitted to compete with private industry or impinge upon other projects of the FERA. Mass projects such as those for men in the construction trades were not considered appropriate for women. Public opinion had to be reshaped to accept the fact that women were often the heads of households. However, Woodward wrote optimistically of the work opportunities for women, and she reported that 53% of both men and women throughout the country who were certified for work were assigned to projects (Woodward, 1937).

The backbone of the women's division was the sewing rooms. The mechanized sewing rooms were located near factories that might offer permanent jobs. Tasks ranged from detailed handwork to the completion of an entire garment. In February 1936, there were 294,532 women employed in 9,000 sewing units, at an average of 40.5 cents an hour. Woodward defended the sewing projects against opponents who called them "female ditch digging," because she knew that many of the unskilled women could not be on other projects (Woodward, 1937).

The sentiment among some groups was that the FERA and its Women's Division largely ignored the economic conditions of minority groups. In the case of the Women's Division, white-collar workers who were African American voiced concerns over placements to menial or physical projects and expressed frustration over limited opportunities for employment in the all–African American projects. Alfred Edgar Smith, whose assignment was to monitor African American affairs, submitted annual reports to Woodward on the status of African American women workers. He cited the relegation to manual labor of women released from other projects, half-time employment in some Southern states, and wage classification scales that resulted in pay levels for African American women below the average for white women (Weaver, 1936).

Mary McClead Bethune, director of Minority Affairs in the National Youth Administration, and in consultation Mrs. Roosevelt, requested that the Women's Division conduct a White House Conference to address the employment needs of minority women. Women administrative heads of government agencies and leaders from the Council of Negro Women were invited to participate in the national conference, one of the first of its kind. Prior to the event, Woodward wrote Mrs. Roosevelt that they could anticipate considerable insistence from the Council leaders to add to its staff an outstanding African American woman in an advisory capacity (Swain, 1983). At the conference Woodward held the position that the Women's Division maintained a good record with regard to work opportunities for minority women. Prejudice, according to Woodward, could not be "solved in one generation, especially through the efforts of a government organization not designed primarily to cope with such a problem" (Woodward, 1938, p. 4).

An evaluation of the FERA indicates that it was one of the largest public relief programs in the world, eventually touching some 20 million lives and expanding some $4 billion. Its policies were uniform across the nation; it was implemented and functioned effectively with little waste or corruption. Critics of the program argued that the FERA lured people away from private employment and even encouraged them to refuse jobs when they were available. Certainly more Americans believed that relief was not a sign of failure or disgrace.

PEOPLE'S ART MOVEMENT

The Federal Emergency Relief Act (FERA) was not the only outcome of President Roosevelt's departure from tradition. Reforms in the 1930s also stimulated major changes in art that can be called a "People's Art Movement." It encompassed the massive collection of socially conscious art created during this period for government commissions for professional as well as for other purposes. The movement marked the first time in American history that creations of art were significantly influenced by the social, economic, and political climate of the epoch. Artistic pursuits, such as those by Ben Shahn, William Gropper, and Harry Gotlieb, reflected the lives of ordinary people and depicted the hardship of life for many of the working class.

The impetus for the movement began after World War I and reflected the growing support for Marxist ideals. Other factors that contributed to the movement were the current forms of art patronage and the growing social protests depicted through magazine illustrations and cartoons (Weinstein, 1967).

The political, cultural, and aesthetic elements of the 1920s gained momentum in the early 1930s, as the nation's economic conditions continued to worsen. In the backdrop of civil war in Spain and the rise of fascism in Asia and Europe, Roosevelt initiated the New Deal government. The most important programs for artists were the Works Progress Administration (WPA), which later became the Works Projects Administration, and the Fine Arts Section ("the section") of the Treasury Department (Braufman, 1997). These programs hired thousands of artists to produce thousands of murals, posters, prints, and photography for public buildings. Government-sponsored exhibitions and community art schools were regularly scheduled or established across the nation.

Many of the artistic creations illustrated representational styles and themes that portrayed the work ethic to appeal to people who visited post offices, hospitals, and government sites where the art was placed. These choices were strongly influenced by the Mexican mural masters Diego Rivera, Jose Clemente Orozoco, and David Alfaro Siquieros, all of whom worked in the United States during the period under discussion.

In addition, the artists' new status as wage earners provided strength and encouragement to the movement. No longer were artists creating alone; they mingled with workers to document life in the factory and the field. In their determination to teach "the people," members of the newly formed American Artists Union contracted other trade unions to solicit ideas for subject matter; they received clear directives for realistic art reflecting working conditions, antiwar, antilynching subjects, and the exploitation of women (Egbert & Persons, 1952, p. 643). Artists began incorporating these social issues in their noncommissioned artwork, and even artists not employed in relief projects began reflecting social concerns in their work.

The People's Art Movement provided a powerful social commentary on the American society. For example, Shahn's *New Jersey Homesteads* (1937) reflects the plight of the immigrants and underscores the "have nots" in American society. Ribak's (1937) *Hooverville on East 10th Street* captured one of the hundreds of villages that sprang up throughout the United States during the depression; it was named for the president who appeared to ignore the plight of the poor people. Both paintings depict the substandard and makeshift housing some people were forced to inhabit during the depression.

The racial inequality against African Americans and immigrants that permeated both North and South was vividly documented by the People's Art Movement. Lynchings were portrayed by William Gropper's (1937) *Hunt* and Boris Gorelick's (1936) *Lynching;* however, the efforts of African Americans to organize and to lobby for equality and antilynching laws often failed. Isaac Soyer's *The Laundress* (1935) portrays the work of women during the period. The image is one of isolation, monotony, and drudgery.

As the nation's economy began to improve and government work projects were disbanded, the People's Art Movement lost momentum. By the 1940s, many of the artists became disillusioned with radical politics or were ready to move on to other subject matters.

FEDERAL WORKS PROGRAMS

The pace of the New Deal was established by Franklin D. Roosevelt who recognized the prevailing despair of the nation and "lashed out against profiteers and the selfish among the monied class" (Fishel, 1964–65, p. 111). This quotation is similar to many of Roosevelt's statements, in that he described conditions and goals in terms that the average citizen understood. The general public responded favorably to Roosevelt's personal charm and persuasiveness; his picture hung in living rooms, and he was the namesake for many children.

It is important to note, however, that Roosevelt had his shortcomings. In particular, he moved slowly on issues of civil rights, especially for African Americans. Although Roosevelt sympathized with the plight of African Americans, his compassion was tempered by the political considerations he had to face. In 1933, he did request that Harold Ickes appoint an administrator to be responsible for the fair treatment of African Americans. Ickes recruited Clark Foreman, a young white man from Georgia, for the position; and Foreman brought his assistant, a young African American man, Robert C. Weaver. Together, they called attention to the special needs of minorities.

Eleanor Roosevelt, often considered to be the New Deal's conscience, made it her business to influence the president on equality for all. Throughout her travels across the nation, she took opportunities to visit diverse neighborhoods or poor people such as those of Appalachia. Her influence on the president was profound. She supported the federal antilynching bill and negotiated permission for Marian Anderson to use the Lincoln Memorial when the Daughters of the Revolution prohibited Anderson's performance in Constitution Hall.

The progress of many federal relief measures was marked by racial discrimination. Specifically, the Civilian Conservation Corp (CCC) not only restricted the enrollment of African Americans to 10% of the total but also in many instances placed African Americans in segregated areas. African American tenant farmers and sharecroppers suffered greatly from government-induced crop reductions under the provisions of the Agricultural Adjustment Act. The work of the National Recovery Administration (NRA) resulted in the loss of jobs when small businesses closed to such a degree that African Americans referred to the measures that had created the new federal agency as the "Negro Removal Act."

In any event, President Roosevelt plunged the federal government into the business of relief. The Civilian Conservation Corps (CCC) employed thousands of young men in reforestation projects and flood and fire control. Millions of citizens found work through the Public Works Administration (PWA), which was created to stimulate depressed industries, especially construction. The National Youth Administration (NYA) provided part-time jobs for high-school and college students. Such work enabled students to earn and save an adequate amount of money to complete their education. As mentioned previously, artists, musicians, and scholars found work opportunities through the Works Progress Administration (WPA, later known as the Works Projects Administration). Finally, numerous social welfare policies were enacted in support of workers, including:

- The Wagner National Labor Relations Act, which recognized the right of unions to organize
- The Farm Security Administration, which provided a variety of support to small farmers and migratory workers
- The Wagner-Steagall Housing Act, which established the U.S. Housing Authority to provide low-interest loans to local officials to build public housing

The federal works programs and social welfare policies of the New Deal demonstrated Roosevelt's willingness to mobilize the resources of the nation to battle hard times and to assist those in need through no fault of their own. Remember that the programs and policies were designed to support the American system of economy rather than to cause far-reaching changes. In no way did the works programs compete with or jeopardize the private sector and profit or free market trade. In keeping with the capitalist economy, partial unemployment was considered desirable to maintain the salary structure whereby it was difficult, if not impossible, to shift from one income class to another, higher bracket.

Even with their shortcomings, the New Deal initiatives were a departure from social welfare as usual. Most Americans considered the work relief as appropriate because benefits were earned rather than given. The far-reaching impact of the programs provided the majority of Americans with a sense of the needs of poor people and also some form of assistance.

Perhaps the best of the New Deal welfare measures was the Civil Works Administration (CWA), which was created by an executive order of the president on November 9, 1933. The new program was intended to remedy the defects of the FERA work programs, to meet the critical unemployment needs of the winter, and to promote recovery through the injection of purchasing power into the economic system within a short period of time.

Half of the workers to be employed in the CWA were taken over from emergency work relief rolls. The other half were to be people who needed jobs, and they were to be asked for no proof of need. They were not to be investigated or submitted to a "means test." Furthermore, the program offered a "regular" schedule of work hours and paid "going" wages, which averaged 2 1/2 times the FERA benefits (Brown, 1940). As a result, no New Deal creation was received with more enthusiasm than the CWA. The major criticism of the program came from social workers who were disturbed that the CWA was under the administration of engineers who were unsympathetic to the social work profession.

The high point of the CWA was in January 1934 when 4,260,000 workers were employed in the program. Approximately one half of the projects workers were without particular qualifications except the need for the job and fitness to do the work to which they were assigned. At the end of the program, in March 1934, only those workers who were eligible for relief were supposed to be transferred to the FERA work relief program. However, the speed with which the CWA was liquidated made it impossible for the social service system to investigate adequately and determine eligibility of all workers who applied for transfer. The result was that thousands of people were included in the new relief rolls who were never subjected to means testing. The FERA itself was phased out a year and a half later, again placing the unemployed at the mercy of the states and localities, neither of which had the financial resources to care adequately for them (see Table 7.1).

The CWA brought to a head some social worker discontent with Roosevelt and the New Deal. Seeking fundamental changes in society—a planned socialist economy—members of a group led by Mary van Kleeck of the Russell Sage Foundation and Harry Lurie, head of the Council of Jewish Federations and Welfare Funds, were dissatisfied with both the aims and the accomplishments of the New Deal, as well as with their colleagues who supported it. Known as the "Rank-and Filers," the group began in a few private social service agencies before the depression and grew in number as a result of adverse working conditions and low relief standards. In 1935, there were 21 of these organized groups, most of them located in large local relief organizations. The socialist group opposed the administration for (a) abruptly terminating CWA; (b) racism in project assignments and work opportunities; and (c) its emphasis on work relief, among a number of other things (Brown, 1940; Trattner, 1999). The lack of national health care and the decision to end the FERA also troubled them.

TABLE 7.1

AVERAGE MONTHLY RELIEF BENEFITS PER FAMILY MAY 1933 THROUGH MAY 1935

	Amount of Benefits				Amount of Benefits		
	Total United States	Principal Cities	Remainder of the Country		Total United States	Principal Cities	Remainder of the Country
1933				**1935**			
May	$15.59	$21.23	$11.48	January	30.43	38.97	24.39
July	15.07	19.86	10.83	February	28.08	35.76	22.64
September	17.17	21.93	12.64	March	28.73	36.91	23.06
October	19.18	24.60	14.27	April	28.96	36.91	23.06
November	18.31	23.74	13.54	May	29.34	36.76	23.64
December	16.88	21.46	12.42				
1934							
January	$16.71	$21.46	$12.95				
February	16.57	24.22	11.84				
March	17.93	24.83	13.14				
April	20.98	26.68	16.28				
May	23.90	30.80	18.53				
June	23.28	29.92	18.14				
July	24.05	31.51	18.59				
August	25.83	34.20	19.96				
September	24.10	31.42	18.93				
October	26.24	33.67	20.78				
November	28.31	35.74	22.94				
December	28.37	35.95	22.94				

Source: *FERA Monthly Report*, June 1935, p. 31.

Note. Average monthly relief benefits are computed by dividing the total amount of relief (both direct relief and Emergency Work Relief Program earnings) extended to all relief families under the general relief program by the total number of such families who received aid at any time in the course of the month. Since this family total includes those who received relief during only a part of the month, as well as those who received only supplementary aid, the resulting averages always understate to some extent the amounts actually paid to families who were entirely dependent on public agencies for subsistence throughout the month. From *Public Relief, 1929–1939* (p. 466), by J. C. Brown, 1940, New York: Henry Holt and Company.

THE EMERGING WELFARE STATE
FROM A STRENGTHS PERSPECTIVE

The potential of the strengths perspective in social policy is in its usefulness in designing policy that addresses the immediate needs of people and their communities. The purpose of policy development from a strengths perspective ensures that environmental resources are available for people to achieve their goals. The economic uncertainty of the depression provides an example of how common need was perceived and how environmental resources were allocated by policymakers at all levels of government.

Figure 7.1 depicts the essential themes of the New Deal work programs. One prevailing theme is that New Dealers sought to make work relief the selected method of relief by poor people. Unemployed people were subjected to means testing to prove their unmet common needs and state of destitution. Throughout the 1930s, social workers continued to be agents through whom relief was administered. They were called upon to study every aspect of a family's life (Kurtz, 1933). Further, direct relief was given in kind, thus shifting control and decision making from the poor to people in power. Viewed as charity, direct relief carried with it a stigma derived from traditional assumptions that workless people were personally responsible for their misfortunes and incapable of managing their own affairs. Finally, the New Dealers, through the work programs, told unemployed people where, how, when, and for what salary they were to work. The perspectives of working people were not sought; they had no input into the definition of problems or the design of goals.

Based on the themes of the New Deal, the assumption was made that the environment was to blame for the economic misfortune of millions of American citizens. The implication was that if the work and business environments changed, the lives of people would improve. Missing from the formula of relief was the political nature of the depression and the New Deal. Could the New Deal have done more to initiate change not only in the availability of work but also in the kinds and manner of work? Historians contend that the political obstacles that existed independent of the New Deal accounted for its economic conservatism and inhibited major structural changes in the American political arena or economic system. They emphasize that the electorate never gave Roosevelt a mandate to transform America. Further, with the passing of time, conservative opposition to the New Deal programs and policies grew in intensity and influence, forcing New Dealers to seek political expedients that precluded radical innovations (Bremer, 1975, pp. 644–650).

Unlike the strengths perspective of social policy development, the work projects permitted little personal planning or negotiating of goals and objectives. Rather, reliance was placed on the traditional approach of work to alleviate

FIGURE 7.1

Essential Themes of the New Deal Work Programs

economic difficulties as well as physical and mental problems. Work placements did not compete with private business or take business from private contractors involved with government contracts in the production, distribution, or sale of goods and services normally provided by private employers. Consequently, the government prohibited government interference with the ongoing capitalistic economy. In fact, the New Deal was committed to maintaining incentives to guide relief recipients back to private enterprise, and inferior earnings served as a most effective incentive (Bremer, 1975).

The New Dealers' determination to maintain noncompetitive relief jobs and incomes led them to impose maximums on monthly earnings. This policy limited the number of hours a person could work at a prevailing wage, thereby ensuring that a person could not earn as much as his/her counterpart in the private industry. These restrictions placed barriers on the economic security of common people and minimized the notion of guaranteed work and jobs as a right afforded every American regardless of need. In other words, at no time did the New Deal assume the task of reconceptualizing work or the economic environment of work. The root causes of unemployment and poverty were ignored so that systematic change was not a possibility.

Instead of guaranteeing a "right to work" through employment opportunities, education, and training on a regular basis in spite of the economic climate, New Dealers designed an unemployment insurance system to prevent unemployed, able-bodied citizens temporary relief at the public expense. The stigma of public dependency continued with work relief even when the relief aid was earned. New Dealers appeared to fear, as did President Roosevelt, encouraging dependency by creating an expectation among able-bodied people that the federal government would always provide jobs (Bremer, 1975). Work relief was a divergence from the American tradition; it was more charity than permanent employment.

The emphasis of the strengths approach on searching the environment for opportunities and resources that reallocated resources for people to meet their needs was largely missed during the New Deal. In no way were working people connected to policy formulation or a consensus process that contained their view of reality. Although economy recovery and security were restored to the nation, family roles, racism, sexism, classism, and traditional work went unchallenged, as did the basic economic system of private property.

SUMMARY

The Great Depression and the New Deal had a profound effect on social welfare policies, social workers, and the lives of ordinary citizens. The work relief programs brought the federal government into the business of providing aid to needy people and linking with private agencies. However, none of the programs marked a shift from the traditional problem-centered approach to policy development.

Social work assumed a leading role in the New Deal. Harry Hopkins, Frances Perkins, Molly Dewson (leader of the Women's Division of the Democratic National Committee), Katherine Lenroot, Martha Eliot (of the U.S. Children's Bureau), and Ellen Woodward (of the FERA Women's Division) went to Washington, D.C., and gained power, as well as prestige, for their work in social policy and administration. Social workers were central figures in park and recreational programs, community development, and agricultural resettlement (Trattner, 1999). No longer associated with emergency needs, social work stepped forward as a profession that addressed not only the needs of individuals and families but also national issues, including work and social reform.

REFERENCES

Abramovitz, M. (1996). Regulating the lives of women. Boston, MA: South End Press.

American Association of Social Workers. (1938). Survey of Current Relief Situation, Box 19 (p. 18), *Social Welfare History Archives,* University of Minnesota.

Axinn, J., & Levin, H. (1992). *Social welfare: A history of American response to need.* New York: Longman.

Braufman, S. B. (1997, February). When artists became workers: The People's Art movement of the '30 & '40s. *American Art Review, IX* (1), 96–103.

Bremer, W. W. (1975, December). Along the "American way": The New Deal's work relief programs for the unemployed. *The Journal of American History, 62* (3), 636–652.

Brown, J. C. (1946). *Public relief, 1929–1939.* New York: Henry Holt and Company.

Calkins, C. (1930). *Some folks won't work.* New York: Henry Holt and Company.

Colcord, J. C. (1930, November). Facing the coming winter. *Survey Midmonthly,* 29–35.

Egbert, D. D., & Persons, S. (1952). *Socialism and American life* (Vol. 1, p. 643). Princeton, NJ: Princeton Press.

Fishel, L. H. (1964–65, Winter). The Negro in the New Deal. *Wisconsin Magazine of History,* 111–126.

Hayes, E. P. (1936). *Activities of the president's emergency committee for unemployment, 1930–1931.* Concord, NH: The Rumford Press.

Hopkins, H. L. (1933). *Spending to save.* New York: W. W. Norton & Co.

Kimberly, C. M. (1975, Summer). The depression in Maryland: The failure of voluntaryism. *Maryland Historical Magazine, 70* (2), 189–202.

Kurtz, R. H. (1933, August). Two months of the New Deal in federal relief. *Survey, LXIX,* 286, 289.

Le Sueur, M. (1982). Women are hungry. In E. Hedges (Ed.), *Ripening: Selected work, 1927–1980.* Old Westbury, NY: The Feminist Press. (Original work published 1927).

McJimsey, G. (1987). *Harry Hopkins: Ally for the poor and defender of democracy.* Cambridge, MA: Harvard University Press.

McMillen, A. W. (1935). *Some statistical comparisons of public and private family social work.* Proceedings of the National Conference of Social Work, San Francisco, CA.

Patterson, J. T. (1981). America's struggle against poverty 1900–1980. Cambridge, MA: Harvard University Press.

Sterner, R. (1943). *The Negro's share.* New York: Harper and Brothers.

Swain, M. H. (1983). 'The Forgotten Woman': Ellen S. Woodward and Women's Relief in the New Deal. *Prologue* is (Winter 1983): 201–14.

Trattner, W. I. (1999). *From poor to welfare state.* New York: The Free Press.

Weaver, R. C. (1936, September 8). Memorandum on Ellen S. Woodward. Works Progress Administration, GSS 236.2, RG 69, NA.

Weinstein, J. (1967). *The decline of socialism in America, 1912–1925.* New York: Praeger.

Wolters, R. (1970). *Negroes and the Great Depression.* Westport, CT: Greenwood.

Woodward, E. S. (1937, January 13). Memorandum on sewing projects to Harry Hopkins. Works Progress Administration, GSS 237, RG 69, NA.

Woodward, E. S. (1938). Memorandum Eleanor Roosevelt. Works Progress Administration, GSS 230, RG 69, NA.

Works Progress Administration. (1936). *Urban Workers on Relief* (pp. 50–52). Washington, DC: Author.

THE SOCIAL SECURITY ACT: THE FOUNDATION OF SOCIAL WELFARE

This chapter discusses the impact of the Social Security Act on the federal government's role in the welfare system and on the development of the social work profession. The driving force behind the act was Franklin D. Roosevelt, U.S. president from 1933 to 1945. From the beginning of his terms as president, Roosevelt sensed America's despair and committed himself and his administration to a brighter future. Aware of the misery of the unemployed and underprivileged, he later likened the depression to a war emergency and warned that he was prepared to mobilize the resources of the federal government to fight it (Roosevelt, 1938).

ROOSEVELT AND THE RELIEF EFFORT

Roosevelt began a long process of establishing an almost personal relationship with Americans through speeches and informal fireside chats. His voice exuded a warmth and optimism that brought him close to his listeners. The general public's response to Roosevelt's magnetism was evident when many people hung his picture in their living rooms or named their children after him. Even though polio weakened Roosevelt's legs, he managed to keep his disability from the public by always standing when he spoke. His son and others were at his side, secretly supporting him. More of a symbol than an activist in his own right. Roosevelt's actions were prompted by the enormity of the decisions he was forced to make and by political considerations (Fishel, 1964–1965).

The Roosevelt administration focused on the business of relief. Table 8.1 summarizes the important events and initiation dates of the permanent program of federal grants to the states for categorical assistance. As the table indicates, on June 8, 1934, President Roosevelt delivered a special message to Congress. His message on the need for safeguards against the hazards of life was followed by the creation of the Committee on Economic Security, charged with the responsibility of designing a social security program that could be submitted to Congress for action.

The committee was headed by Secretary of Labor Frances Perkins and included Harry Hopkins, Edwin E. Witte, an economist from the University of Wisconsin, and Wilbur J. Cohen, one of Witte's students. On January 15, 1935, after considerable deliberation and policy considerations, the committee provided Roosevelt with social security recommendations, which the president then transmitted to Congress. The recommendations primarily addressed unemployment compensation, old age insurance, old age assistance, and assistance to dependent children. In terms of people who were not employed in work programs, the committee stated:

> As for the genuine unemployables—or near unemployables—we believe the sound policy is to return the responsibility for their care and guidance to the states. . . . We suggest that the Federal government shall assume primary responsibility for providing work for those able and willing to work; also that it aid States in giving pensions to the dependent aged and the families without breadwinners. . . . With the federal Government carrying so much of the burden for

<table>
<tr><td>TABLE
8.1</td><td>SIGNIFICANT EVENTS AND DATES RELATED
TO THE SOCIAL SECURITY ACT</td></tr>
</table>

President Roosevelt's First Message to Congress on Social Security	June 8, 1934
Committee on Economic Security created by Executive Order No. 6757	June 29, 1934
President's Message to Congress on Work Relief	January 4, 1935
Report of Committee on Economic Security submitted to president	January 15, 1935
Report of committee transmitted to Congress by president	January 17, 1935
Social Security Bill (Economic Security Act) introduced in Congress	January 17, 1935
Emergency Relief Appropriation Bill introduced in Congress	January 23, 1935
Emergency Relief Appropriation Act of 1935, appropriating $4,880,000,000 approved by the president	April 8, 1935
Social Security Act approved by the president (no appropriation made by Congress)	August 14, 1935
Social Security Board began operating	October 1, 1935
Federal Emergency Relief Administration final grants to states made	November–December, 1935
First appropriation made by Congress for purposes of Social Security Act (Public 440, 74th Congress)	February 11, 1936
First Federal grants made to states by Social Security Board for public assistance	February 11, 1936

(Brown, 1940, p. 302)

pure employment, the State and local governments, we believe should resume responsibility for relief. . . .

To prevent such a step from resulting in less humane and less intelligent treatment of unfortunate fellow citizens, we strongly recommend that the States substitute for their ancient, out-moded poor laws, modernized public assistance laws, and replace their traditional poor-law administrations by unified and efficient State and local public welfare departments, such as existed in some States and for which there is a nucleus in all states in the Federal emergency relief organizations. . . . (Economic Security Act: Hearings Before the Committee on Finance, 1935, p. 1141).

The Advisory Committee further recommended that the Federal Government should replace the poor law system of relief with a permanent Public Welfare Department in the federal government that would grant funds for public assistance and coordinate federal, state, and local public welfare activities.

In opposition to the Advisory Committee recommendation for categorical assistance, Dorothy Kahn of the American Association of Social Workers stated:

> We believe that the social hazards referred to in this bill, aggravated by the depression, affect families in a variety of ways, and that unified programs of general assistance are required to provide for the needs of great numbers of families who do not fall in the particular classifications or categories like those mentioned in title I and II of the bill. These family situations, however, represent individual problems and are in constant change. Measures for dealing with them must, therefore, be unified and must be general enough so each person is not shifted from one jurisdiction to another when a change in category occurs. (Economic Security Act: Hearings Before the Committee on Finance, 1935, p. 649)

President Roosevelt responded to the Advisory Committee's recommendation and all testimony associated with the report with words of gratitude and asked that prompt federal action be taken on the bill. During the next seven months, the measure, with its numerous and complicated provisions, was given hearings in committees of both houses of Congress. The bill, passed in Congress by a vote of 371 to 33 in the House and 77 to 6 in the Senate, became law on August 14, 1935.

THE SOCIAL SECURITY ACT

The Social Security Act was approved on August 15, 1935. It was the major piece of legislation that emerged from the depression and the New Deal, and with its passage came the demise of the Emergency Relief Appropriation Act of 1935 that provided for continuing relief as authorized under the Federal Emergency Relief Act of 1933 (Trattner, 1999). The period of transition between the passage of the Social Security Act and the liquidation of the FERA at the end of 1935 was marked by general confusion in public relief. The chaos resulted in inadequate general relief or relief that was entirely lacking in state after state, the transition states assuming the primary responsibility for direct relief and categorical assistance. The federal government carried the major costs of work relief for a large number of the employable people who were in need, and surplus food was distributed to the states by the Federal Surplus Commodities Corporation (Brown, 1940).

As finally adopted, the Social Security Act (please refer to Appendix 8–A) was an omnibus measure that brought two lines of defense aimed at preventing destitution: contributory social insurance and public assistance, Comprising 11 titles, the Social Security Act provided for three types of federal assistance: insurance, assistance to people in need, and health services. More specifically, it provided for old-age insurance (or pension) and public assistance for the aged; unemployment insurance (or compensation) for the jobless; public assistance to

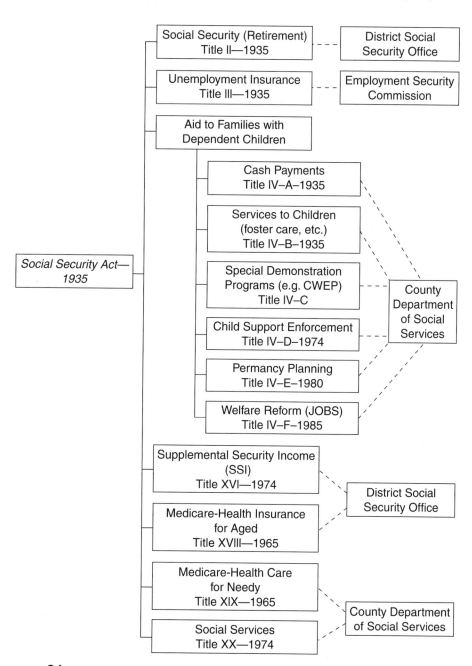

Federal Legislation · Program · Local Agency

Social Security (Retirement)
Title II—1935

District Social
Security Office

Unemployment Insurance
Title III—1935

Employment Security
Commission

Aid to Families with
Dependent Children

Cash Payments
Title IV–A–1935

Services to Children
(foster care, etc.)
Title IV–B–1935

Special Demonstration
Programs (e.g. CWEP)
Title IV–C

Child Support Enforcement
Title IV–D–1974

Permancy Planning
Title IV–E–1980

Welfare Reform (JOBS)
Title IV–F–1985

Social Security Act—
1935

County
Department
of Social
Services

Supplemental Security Income
(SSI)
Title XVI—1974

Medicare-Health Insurance
for Aged
Title XVIII—1965

District Social
Security Office

Medicare-Health Care
for Needy
Title XIX—1965

Social Services
Title XX—1974

County Department
of Social Services

FIGURE **8.1**

Programs Under the Social Security Act

Source: Conference on Poverty, *Community Social Program Inventory.* Chapel Hill, N.C.,
September 1994. In Dobelstein, A.W. (1997). Social Welfare Policy & Analysis. Chicago, Nelson-Hall
Publishers, p. 229.

dependent children in single-parent families, to crippled children, and to the blind; and federal monies for state and local public health works.

The act created a national system of old-age insurance (OAI) in which most employers were compelled to participate. According to the act, a state plan for old age assistance had to include the following:

1. provide that it shall be in effect in all political subdivisions of the state, and if administered by them, be mandatory upon them;
2. provide for participation by the state;
3. either provide for the establishment or designation of a single state agency to administer the plan, or provide for the establishment or designation of a single state agency to supervise the administration of the plan. . . . (Social Security Board, 1937).

Under the plan, workers at age 65 would receive retirement benefits financed by taxes on their wages and on their employers' payrolls; the benefits would reflect earnings and contributions. Consequently, only workers with a steady employment record were eligible for benefits.

The act also established a federal system of unemployment insurance for which states were responsible. The law required that employers contribute a specified percentage of their payroll to the federal treasury for insurance purposes. It also stipulated that 90% of that levy would be returned to those states that established their own unemployment insurance plans in accordance with standards approved by a federal Social Security Board created to administer the program (Trattner, 1999). Within two years, every state had established an unemployment insurance system that met the requirements fixed by the board.

The Social Security Act had a significant impact on family welfare and the role of family members. For women, the addition to old-age insurance of dependents' benefits in 1939 reinforced their role as wives and homemakers (Axinn & Levin, 1992). Although the number of women in the labor force increased, the act neglected to include many traditionally female jobs. Further, it penalized women for interrupted employment histories, and provided little compensated pay discrimination. Consequently, women workers have found it more advantageous to draw benefits as dependents rather than on their own labor force participation (Axinn & Levin, 1992).

From the beginning the Social Security Act rewarded stable marriages by connecting marital status to benefits. To receive dependent's benefits, a woman had to be married for at least five years, and living with the eligible worker at the time of application (Abramovitz, 1996, p. 261). A widow was required to be living with her husband at the time of his death to receive benefits. Divorced women lost spousal allowances, and a widow who remarried forfeited her survivor benefits. These rules protected the program from abuse by those who saw marriage as a means to increase benefits.

It is important to note that the provisions of the Social Security Act were not novel. Based more on the insurance principle than on the public assistance model, the act continued the American tradition of providing "welfare" only to the truly needy. It reflected the influences of past and present federal and state statues, including the Sheppard-Towner and Federal Emergency Relief Acts as well as numerous state widows' aid and old-age pension laws.

PRINCIPLE CRITICISMS OF THE SOCIAL SECURITY ACT

The enactment of the Social Security Act was followed with a great deal of criticism from all sides. Secretary of Labor Frances Perkins, the first woman to hold a cabinet position, supported the measure as a major and much needed step toward developing the nation's sense of long-term financial security. In contrast, the U.S. Chamber of Commerce and the National Association of Manufacturers contended that the measure was too extreme and too radical a departure from core American concepts such as self-help and individual responsibility.

Many voiced the opinion that the Social Security Act did not go far enough in its program initiatives. In actuality, the Social Security Act involved a compromise act reflecting the political and economic forces of the time. It was recognized as a measure to return equilibrium to the nation and to maintain the status quo in a changing world. From a conservative perspective, it was considered racist and sexist and trapped people in a life of poverty.

The social insurance aspects of the act were financed through individual contributions; thus, it not only tied benefits to lifelong employment, but it was a regressive measure. Specifically, the act made low-income workers pay for assistance programs available to poor people by placing a greater tax burden on low-income earners than on higher ones. Since employers were taxed for old-age insurance and unemployment benefits, the program costs were placed on the consumer first through higher prices and subsequently through a lower standard of living.

The Social Security Act defined benefits short in duration and minimal in scope. People with lifelong needs such as those with mental illnesses or with permanent disabilities were categorically excluded from benefits. Furthermore, provisions of the act neglected housewives and temporary workers including migrant workers.

The omission of health insurance was the most serious criticism of the Social Security Act. Although the need for it was apparent, health insurance was not covered under the act. The Committee on Economic Security did discuss the topic of health insurance, and committee members recognized the relationship between access to preventive services, medical treatment, and financial security. They documented the need for a national health program to President Roosevelt, but the medical profession was formidable in its opposition. In a compromise measure, health care was eliminated from the Social

Security Act with the understanding that a separate national health insurance proposal would be introduced in Congress shortly after passage of the first measure (Trattner, 1999, pp. 290–293).

Social security did not automatically become a functioning institution. The act required collection of 1% of the first $3000 of each employer's earnings, and that amount was to be matched by 1% from his employer (Berkowitz, 1983). Although the described provisions were in January 1937, the actual payments were not scheduled to begin until 1940. Consequently, people's money was collected for five years before benefits were received.

On May 24, 1937, a landmark in American history occurred when the Social Security Act was upheld by the U.S. Supreme Court in two separate decisions: Steward Machine Co. v. Davis (301 U.S. 548) and Helvering v. Davis (301 U.S. 619) (Axinn & Levin, 1992; Trattner, 1999). These legal decisions were followed by the 1939 Social Security Amendments that effected substantial and comprehensive changes in the original act. The most significant changes were those addressing the old-age insurance program that was expanded to include survivors. Other amendments related to the federal-state systems of unemployment insurance and public assistance. Also, included in the amendments were increased amounts authorized for federal grants to the states for maternal and child health, crippled children, child welfare, vocational rehabilitation, and public health. An excerpt from the Fourth Annual Report of the Social Security Board (1939, pp. 166–184) describes the impact the amendments had on aid to dependent children:

> Federal participation in the program for aid to dependent children is increased by one-third to one-half of the costs incurred for administration and assistance under the approved State plans, not including amounts by which monthly payments exceed $18 for one dependent child and $12 for each additional child aided in the same home. The age limit for children toward whose payments federal funds are used is raised from 18 to 22 years if the State agency finds that these changes will enable the State to provide monthly payments for many additional children. . . .

By extending coverage to widows, older wives, and surviving children, the cost for social security provisions increased to the point that the program became technically bankrupt (Karger & Stoesz, 1998). In response to the fiscal crisis, the federal government assumed financial responsibility for the program provisions and by doing so assumed responsibility for the welfare of Americans covered by the Social Security Act.

SOCIAL WORK AND THE SOCIAL SECURITY ACT

The Great Depression and the New Deal had a significant impact on the profession of social work. In the early 1930s, there were approximately

30,000 employed social workers; this number doubled by the end of the decade. The demand for qualified social workers was constant. Consequently, many people employed as investigators or supervisors in the emerging welfare system bureaucracies had little training or experiences in social work. Further, it was not uncommon for recent college graduates or people who had partially completed college graduate requirements to be recruited for social work positions in local social service agencies.

The supply of trained social workers tended to vary considerably in different sections of the country. Generally speaking, the northeastern states, parts of the Midwest, and the Pacific coast had an adequate supply of social workers because of the location of training schools and institutes of social work (Brown, 1940). Social service agencies located in other sections of the country recruited staff from across the country to fill many or all the key positions. States that needed more social workers depended upon private agencies and permanent public welfare departments to meet staffing needs, but even then they were forced to employ people who were not social workers.

In rural communities, social service agencies employed local people who had little previous training or experience; they were called social workers or caseworkers because of their job responsibilities. The Federal Emergency Relief Administration report on "Social Workers in Rural Problem Area Counties, Summer of 1934" stated that in the 64 rural counties in 23 states included in the study, 91.5% of the 324 visitors and 68% of the 37 supervisors were untrained and inexperienced; that is, they "had never attended a school of social work, had never had a course in case work, and had never had a paid social work position outside the emergency relief administration of a rural county" (FERA Research Bulletin, 1935).

The unprecedented demand for social workers created by the Federal Emergency Relief Administration and the New Deal programs placed demands on training schools, especially on their curricula and resources for field experience. The American Association of Schools of Social Work provided training programs on methods in taking applications, making investigations, and administering relief. Supervised field experiences were limited due to the lack of qualified instructors in comparison to the students flocking to take social work courses. The increase in social work stimulated the organization of undergraduate curricula, the inception of new schools of social work, and also increased the attendance at accredited schools.

Given the surge in the number of social work positions across all levels of government and the interest in social work education, the profession of social work gained considerable prestige in American life during the depression and the New Deal. Social workers such as Harry Hopkins, Frances Perkins, Molly Dewson (of the Women's Division of the Democratic National Committee), Aubrey Williams (director of NYA), Kathryn Lenora and Martha Eliot (of the U.S. Children's Bureau), Jane Hooey (of the Social Security Administration),

Ellen Woodward (of the FERA and WPA), and numerous others were on the inside, in high positions, shaping policy and making all sorts of basic designs (Axinn & Levin, 1992; Trattner, 1999; Brown, 1940).

Social workers, perhaps as never before, became aware of the nature and depth of poverty in both urban and rural communities. The depression promoted a resurgence of interest in issues related to social justice and reform including segregation, housing, and education. The experiences of the 1930s provided undisputed proof that economic forces were at the root of the problems with which social work dealt. Consequently by the end of the decade, the scope of social work extended beyond an emergency profession to an obligatory part of federal and state governments and an essential element of the modern industrial society.

THE NEW DEAL FROM A STRENGTHS PERSPECTIVE

The strengths perspective in social policy focuses on the power of people in shaping policies that will be effective interventions. During the depression and the New Deal era, the conditions faced by ordinary people and the resourcefulness of these people was documented through the work of Walker Evans, a documentary photographer of social conscience.

Evans began working for the Farm Security Administration late in 1935. The agency had begun on its legendary photographic survey of rural America, and Evans saw his role as a "roving social historian" (Fonvielle, 1993). Evans photographed a wide range of subjects, invariably executed in a series: a sequence of views of Pennsylvania mining towns, sequences illustrating the effects of soil erosion, a sequence depicting African American neighborhoods in various southern cities. Throughout his photographs, Evans demonstrated a natural respect for people and their work. Always avoiding outright emotional appeal, Walker's art conjured a level of serious moral reflection and concern.

From a strengths perspective, the value of Walker's photography is that it showed poverty as an exclusion from educational, political, and economic opportunities rather than as the result of individual characteristics. In his subject matter, Evans presented people in their environment to suggest that structural barriers limited people's ability to be self-sufficient.

The notion of common needs and structural barriers to meeting them is further illustrated by the excerpt from Tillie Olsen's (1961), *I Stand Here Ironing*, a short story depicting life during the depression. Born in Nebraska, Olsen came of age during the Great Depression. Committed to social and political activism, Olsen helped organize meatpacking workers in Omaha and Kansas City. In the following excerpt, Olsen describes a young mother during the

Great Depression who is faced with difficult decisions concerning employment and the need for childcare:

> She was a beautiful baby. She blew shining bubbles of sound. She loved motion, loved light, loved color and music and textures. She would lie on the floor in her blue overalls patting the surface so hard in ecstasy her hands and feet would blur. She was a miracle to me, but when she was eight months old I had to leave her daytimes with the woman downstairs to whom she was no longer a miracle at all for I worked or looked for work and for Emily's father, who "could no longer endure" (he wrote in his good-bye note) "sharing want with us."
>
> I was nineteen. It was pre-relief, pre-WPA world of the depression. I would start running as soon as I got off the streetcar, running up the stairs, the place smelling sour, and awake or asleep to startle awake, when she saw me she would break into clogged weeping that could not be comforted, a weeping I can hear yet. (p. 447)

From the strengths perspective, did the Social Security Act identify and support individual and community resources that could be used to create opportunities for inclusion or to provide clear-cut alternatives that bypassed the predominant economic system (Chapin, 1995)? Table 8.2 examines the Social Security Act in terms of its response and barriers to common needs. A review of the table indicates five themes that were in conflict with a strengths perspective of policy development:

1. The Social Security Act reinforced the concept of work derived from values inherent in a capitalistic ethos and incorporated practices of private market system including insurance. The act, as exemplified by the omission of health care provisions, accepted capitalism and the proclivity to innovate within the confines of the capitalistic order.
2. In keeping with traditional relief practices, means testing and investigations were used to determine eligibility for public assistance. It was often the social worker who was called upon to study the financial status and intimate details of families in need. Indeed, aspects of eligibility determination delayed assistance until destitution was apparently painful.
3. Despite the increase of women and minority groups in the workforce, the act provided such groups few benefits. Further, the system paid benefits on the basis of past earnings and contributions, not on current needs. Moreover, the benefits were minimal, and they did not insure against poverty.
4. The system of social insurance did not redistribute income or challenge the prevailing social structure. The system of financing was regressive so that relatively speaking, poor people paid the benefits for poor people.
5. The act ignored structural barriers such as access to adequate housing, healthcare, employment, and education, to meeting human needs.

TABLE 8.2 THE SOCIAL SECURITY ACT (SSA) FROM A STRENGTHS PERSPECTIVE

Issue	SSA Response	Barrier to Need
Framework of the Act	• Reflected acceptance and reinforcement of traditional cultural norms	• Bore a stigma derived from assumptions related to public assistance
	• Political and economic concerns were to maintain status quo	• The "American Way" to achieve social insurance and public assistance was through work
System of Financing	• Largely financed through individual contributions	• Regressive in that low-wage earners paid proportionately more than high-wage earners
Benefits	• No provisions for employment traditionally held by women	• Neglected to recognize women's work
	• No provisions for seasonal or migrant workers	• Reinforced occupational integrity and status
	• Benefits tied to stable long-term employment	• Penalized interrupted employment history
Benefit Levels	• The states were responsible for setting levels	• Process insured disparities
Income Distribution	• Did nothing about fundamental social and economic problems	• Compensated inadequately for life-long pay discrimination
"Non-deserving" Poor	• States and localities developed programs without federal aid	• Bore a stigma of individual deficit and pathology
	• General inattention to provisions	• Eligibility investigations intervened in the lives of people
	• Recipients were subject to means testing	• Highlighted the role of social workers as supervisors in the lives of people
Old-Age Insurance	• Recognized flaws in the private enterprise system	• 1939 Amendments reinforced women's role as wives and homemakers
	• Joint employee—employer contributory scheme	
	• Assumed viability of the market system	
Dependent Children	• Limited attention given to children	• Children considered sole responsibility of parents
	• Aid was defined as money payments to a dependent child(ren) and not to include caregivers	
Unemployment	• Benefits limited to a relatively short period of time	• Provided no training or education
Permanent Disability	• No provision for coverage	• Individuals supported by families and charity
Health Care	• No provisions for coverage	• Coverage dependent on private pay and insurance

The emphasis on the themes suggests that the Social Security Act had the potential to search the environment for opportunities and resources to connect commonly shared human needs to policy development imaginatively. Although the act did not achieve all that it could, it did give birth to America's welfare state and to the notion that destitution (at least in theory) was no longer regarded as a question of individual weakness.

SUMMARY

The Great Depression of the 1930s had a significant impact on the way the nation thought about social need. The economic crisis demonstrated all too clearly that people could be unemployed and in need through no fault of their own. It was this realization that led to the notion of an at-risk individual in the system. In response, a national system of social security was introduced to thwart both national and individual economic disasters. For the first time, Americans as a whole accepted the idea that a large number of people had a right to public funded benefits, or at least that the failure to provide such benefits was socially and economically shortsighted.

The Social Security Act defined new responsibilities in the field of public welfare. Its passage initiated a relationship based on federal aid to the states on a permanent basis, thus ending three centuries of the poor law with the principle of local responsibility. For the first time in American history, the needs of selected groups were addressed through a permanent line item in the federal budget. Furthermore, entitlement became associated with social policy whereby the federal government assumed responsibility for the welfare specified citizens.

For social work, the Social Security Act ushered in a period of professionalization. The 1930s began with social workers as social reformers, and the decade ended with the profession considering social work methodology and education. Social workers were challenged with concerns related to individuals, families, and communities in the context of federal and state programs. More than ever before, the profession was involved with social insurance programs and social services that were to become a permanent part of the American welfare state.

REFERENCES

Abramovitz, M. (1996). Regulating the lives of women. Boston, MA: South End Press.

Axinn, J. & Levin, H. (1992). *Social welfare: A history of the American response to need.* New York: Longman.

Berkowitz, E. D. (1983, Fall). The first social security crisis. *Prologue 15*, 133–149.

Brown, J. C. (1940). *Public relief 1929–1939.* New York: Henry Holt and Company.

Chapin, R. K. (1995, July). Social policy development: The strengths perspective. *Social Work, 40* (5), 506–514.

Dobelstein, A. W. (1997). Social Welfare Policy & Analysis. Chicago: Nelson-Hall, Publishers.

Federal Emergency Relief Administration Research Bulletin (1935, February 15), Division of Research Statistics and Finance, C-17. Washington, DC: Government Printing Office. Author.

Fishel, L. H. (1964–1965). The Negro in the New Deal. *Wisconsin Magazine of History, 48*, 111–126.

Fonvielle, L. (1993). *Walker Evans: Masters of Photography.* New York: Aperture Foundation.

Fourth Annual Report of the Social Security Board, Supplementary Data. (1939, July 1–October 31), pp. 166–184.

Economic Security Act: Hearings before the Committee on Finance, U.S. Senate, 74th Cong., S. 1130, (1939) 649, 1141.

Karger, H. J. & Stoesz, D. (1998). *American social welfare policy: A pluralist approach.* New York: Longman.

Olsen, T. (1961). I stand here ironing. In B. Soloman (Ed.), *The haves and have nots* (446–455). New York: Signet Classic.

Roosevelt, F. D. (1938). *The public papers of Franklin D. Roosevelt.* New York: Harper & Row II: 11, 12, 13.

Social Security Board (1937). Report on the Committee of Economic Security. Part IV, Chapter 13. Washington, DC: Government Printing Office. Author.

Trattner, W. I. (1999). *From poor law to welfare state: A history of social welfare in America.* New York: The Free Press.

APPENDIX 8–A

THE SOCIAL SECURITY ACT

Approved, August 14, 1935

[PUBLIC–NO. 271–74TH CONGRESS]

[II. R. 7260]

AN ACT

To provide for the general welfare by establishing a system of Federal old-age benefits, and by enabling the several States to make more adequate provision for aged persons, blind persons, dependent and crippled children, maternal and child welfare, public health, and the administration of their unemployment compensation laws; to establish a Social Security Board; to raise revenue; and for other purposes.

Be it enacted by the Senate and House of Representatives of the United States of America in Congress assembled,

TITLE I—GRANTS TO STATES FOR OLD-AGE ASSISTANCE

APPROPRIATION

SECTION 1. For the purpose of enabling each State to furnish financial assistance, as far as practicable under the conditions in such State, to aged needy individuals, there is hereby authorized to be appropriated for the fiscal year ending June 30, 1936, the sum of $49,750,000, and there is hereby authorized to be appropriated for each fiscal year thereafter a sum sufficient to carry out the purposes of this title. The sums made available under this section shall be used for making payments to States which have submitted, and had approved by the Social Security Board established by Title VII (hereinafter referred to as the "Board"), State plans for old-age assistance.

STATE OLD-AGE ASSISTANCE PLANS

SEC. 2 (a) A State plan for old-age assistance must (1) provide that it shall be in effect in all political subdivisions of the State, and, if administered by them, be mandatory upon them; (2) provide for financial participation by the State; (3) either provide for the establishment or designation of a single State agency to administer the plan, or provide for the establishment or designation of a single State agency to supervise the administration of the plan; (4) provide for granting to any individual, whose claim for old-age assistance is denied, an opportunity for a fair hearing before such State agency; (5) provide such methods of administration (other than those relating to selection, tenure of office, and compensation of personnel) as are found by the Board to be necessary for the efficient operation of the plan; (6) provide that the State agency will make such reports, in such form and containing such information, as the Board may from time to time find necessary to assure the correctness and verification of such reports; and (7) provide that, if the State or any of its political subdivisions collects from the estate of any recipient of old-age assistance any amount with respect to old-age assistance furnished him under the plan, one-half of the net amount so collected shall be promptly paid to the United States. Any payment so made shall be deposited in the Treasury to the credit of the appropriation for the purposes of this title.

(b) The Board shall approve any plan which fulfills the conditions specified in subsection (a), except that it shall not approve any plan which imposes, as a condition of eligibility for old-age assistance under the plan-

(1) An age requirement of more than sixty-five years, except that the plan may impose, effective until January 1, 1940, an age requirement of as much as seventy years; or

(2) Any residence requirement which excludes any resident of the State who has resided therein five years during the nine years immediately preceding the application for old-age assistance and has resided therein continuously for one year immediately preceding the application; or

(3) Any citizenship requirement which excludes any citizen of the United States.

PAYMENT TO STATES

SEC. 3. (a) From the sums appropriated therefore, the Secretary of the Treasury shall pay to each State which has an approved plan for old-age assistance, for each quarter, beginning with the quarter commencing July 1, 1935, (1) an amount, which shall be used exclusively as old-age assistance, equal to one-half of the total of the sums expended during such quarter an old-age assistance under the State plan with respect to each individual who at the time of such expenditure is sixty-five years of age or older and is not an inmate of a public institution, not counting so much of such expenditure with respect to any individual for any month as exceeds $30 and (2) 5 per centum of such amount, which shall be used for paying the costs of administering the State plan or for old-age assistance, or both, and for no other purpose: *Provided,* That the State plan, in order to be approved by the Board, need not provide for financial participation before July 1, 1937 by the State, in the case of any State which the Board, upon application by the State and after reasonable notice and opportunity for hearing to the State, finds is prevented by its constitution from providing such financial participation. . . .

DEFINITION

Sec. 6. When used in this title the term "old-age assistance" means money payments to aged individuals. . . .

TITLE II—FEDERAL OLD-AGE BENEFITS

OLD-AGE RESERVE ACCOUNT

Section 201. (a) There is hereby created an account in the Treasury of the United States to be known as the "Old-Age Reserve Account" hereinafter in this title called the "Account." There is hereby authorized to be appropriated to the Account for each fiscal year, beginning with the fiscal year ending June 30, 1937, an amount sufficient as an annual premium to provide for the payments required under this title, such amount to be determined on a reserve basis in accordance with accepted actuarial principles, and based upon such tables of mortality as the Secretary of the Treasury shall from time to time adopt, and upon an interest rate of 3 per centum per annum compounded annually. The Secretary of the Treasury shall submit annually to the Bureau of the Budget an estimate of the appropriations to be made to the Account. . . .

OLD-AGE BENEFIT PAYMENTS

Sec. 202. (a) Every qualified individual (as defined in section 210) shall be entitled to receive, with respect to the period beginning on the date he attains the age of sixty-five, or on January 1, 1942, whichever is the later, and ending on the date of his death, an old-age benefit (payable as nearly as practicable in equal monthly installments) as follows:
(1) If the total wages (as defined in section 210) determined by the Board to have been paid to him, with respect to employment (as defined in section 210) after December 31, 1936, and before he attained the age of sixty-five, were not more than $3,000, the old-age benefit shall be at a monthly rate of one-half of 1 per centum of such total wages; (2) If such total wages were more than $3,000, the old-age benefit shall be at a monthly rate equal to the sum of the following:
(A) One-half of 1 per centum of $3,000; plus
(B) One-twelfth of 1 per centum of the amount by which such total wages exceeded $3,000 and did not exceed $45,000; plus
(C) One-twenty-fourth of 1 per centum of the amount by which such total wages exceeded $45,000.
(b) In no case shall the monthly rate computed under subsection (a) exceed $85.
(c) If the Board finds at any time that more or less than the correct amount has theretofore been paid to any individual under this section, then, under regulations made by the Board, proper adjustments shall be made in connection with subsequent payments under this section to the same individual.

(d) Whenever the Board finds that any qualified individual has received wages with respect to regular employment after he attained the age of sixty-five, the old-age benefit payable to such individual shall be reduced, for each calendar month in any part of which such regular employment occurred, by an amount equal to one month's benefit. Such reduction shall be made, under regulations prescribed by the Board, by deductions from one or more payments of old-age benefit to such individual.

PAYMENTS UPON DEATH

SEC. 203. (a) If any individual dies before attaining the age of sixty-five, there shall be paid to his estate an amount equal to 3 1/2 per centum of the total wages determined by the Board to have been paid to him, with respect to employment after December 31, 1936.

(b) If the Board finds that the correct amount of the old-age benefit payable to a qualified individual during his life under section 202 was less than 3 1/2 per centum of the total wages by which such old-age benefit was measurable, then there shall be paid to his estate a sum equal to the amount, if any, by which such 3 1/2 per centum exceeds the amount (whether more or less than the correct amount) paid to him during his life as old-age benefit.

(c) If the Board finds that the total amount paid to a qualified individual under an old-age benefit during his life was less than the correct amount to which he was entitled under section 202, and that the correct amount of such old-age benefit was 3 1/2 per centum or more of the total wages by which such old-age benefit was measurable, then there shall be paid to his estate a sum equal to the amount, if any, by which the correct amount of the old-age benefit exceeds the amount which was so paid to him during his life.

PAYMENTS TO AGED INDIVIDUALS NOT QUALIFIED FOR BENEFITS

SEC. 204. (a) There shall be paid in a lump sum to any individual who, upon attaining the age of sixty-five, is not a qualified individual, an amount equal to 3 1/2 per centum of the total wages determined by the Board to have been paid to him, with respect to employment after December 31, 1936, and before he attained the age of sixty-five.

(b) After any individual becomes entitled to any payment under subsection (a), no other payment shall be made under this title in any manner measured by wages paid to him, except that any part of any payment under subsection (a) which is not paid to him before his death shall be paid to his estate. . . .

OVERPAYMENTS DURING LIFE

SEC. 206. If the Board finds that the total amount paid to a qualified individual under an old-age benefit during his life was more than the correct amount to which he was entitled under section 202, and was 3 1/2 per centum or more of the total wages by which such old-age benefit was measurable, then upon his death there shall be repaid to the United States by his estate the amount, if any, by which such total amount paid to him during his life exceeds whichever of the following is the greater: (1) Such 3 1/2 per centum, or (2) the correct amount to which he was entitled under section 202. . . .

DEFINITIONS

SEC. 210. When used in this title—

(a) The term "wages" means all remuneration for employment, including the cash value of all remuneration paid in any medium other than cash; except that such term shall not include that part of the remuneration which, after remuneration equal to $3,000 has been paid to an individual by an employer with respect to employment during any calendar year, is paid to such individual by such employer with respect to employment during such calendar year.

(b) The term "employment" means any service, of whatever nature, performed within the United States by an employee for his employer, except—

(1) Agricultural labor;

(2) Domestic service in a private home;

(3) Casual labor not in the course of the employer's trade or business;

(4) Service performed as an officer or member of the crew of a vessel documented under the laws of the United States or of any foreign country;

(5) Service performed in the employ of the United States Government or of an instrumentality of the United States;

(6) Service performed in the employ of a State, a political subdivision thereof, or an instrumentality of one or more States or political subdivisions;

(7) Services performed in the employ of a corporation, community chest, fund, or foundation, organized and operated exclusively for religious, charitable, scientific, literary, or educational purposes, or for the prevention of cruelty to children or animals, no part of the net earnings of which insures to the benefit of any private shareholder or individual.

(c) The term "qualified individual" means any individual with respect to whom it appears to the satisfaction of the Board that—

(1) He is at least sixty-five years of age; and

(2) The total amount of wages paid to him, with respect to employment after December 31, 1936, and before he attained the age of sixty-five, was not less than $2,000; and

(3) Wages were paid to him, with respect to employment on some five days after December 31, 1936, and before he attained the age of sixty-five, each day being in a different calendar year.

TITLE III—GRANTS TO STATES FOR UNEMPLOYMENT COMPENSATION ADMINISTRATION

APPROPRIATION

SECTION 301. For the purpose of assisting the States in the administration of their unemployment compensation laws, there is hereby authorized to be appropriated, for the fiscal year ending June 30, 1936, the sum of $4,000,000, and for each fiscal year thereafter the sum of $49,000,000, to be used as hereinafter provided.

PAYMENTS TO STATES

SEC. 302. (a) The Board shall from time to time certify to the Secretary of the Treasury for payment to each State which has an unemployment compensation law approved by the Board under Title IX, such amounts as the Board determines to be necessary for the proper administration of such law during the fiscal year in which such payment is to be made. The board's determination shall be based on (1) the population of the State; (2) an estimate of the number of persons covered by the State law and of the cost of proper administration of such law; and (3) such other factors as the Board finds relevant. The Board shall not certify for payment under this section in any fiscal year a total amount in excess of the amount appropriated therefore for such fiscal year.

(b) Out of the sums appropriated therefore, the Secretary of the Treasury shall, upon receiving a certification under subsection (a), pay, through the Division of Disbursement of the Treasury Department and prior to audit or settlement by the General Accounting Office, to the State agency charged with the administration of such law the amount so certified.

PROVISIONS OF STATE LAWS

SEC. 303. (a) The Board shall make no certification for payment to any State unless it finds that the law of such State, approved by the Board under Title IX, includes provisions for-

(1) Such methods of administration (other than those relating to selection, tenure of office, and compensation of personnel) as are found by the Board to be reasonably calculated to insure full payment of unemployment compensation when due; and

(2) Payment of unemployment compensation solely through public employment offices in the State or such other agencies as the Board may approve; and

(3) Opportunity for a fair hearing, before an impartial tribunal, for all individuals whose claims for unemployment compensation are denied; and

(4) The payment of all money received in the unemployment fund of such State, immediately upon such receipt, to the Secretary of the Treasury to the credit of the Unemployment Trust Fund established by section 904; and

(5) Expenditure of all money requisitioned by the State agency from the Unemployment Trust Fund, in the payment of unemployment compensation, exclusive of expenses of administration; and

(6) The making of such reports, in such form and containing such information, as the Board may from time to time require, and compliance with such provisions as the Board may from time to time find necessary to assure the correctness and verification of such reports; and

(7) Making available upon request to any agency of the United States charged with the administration of public works or assistance through public employment, the name, address, ordinary occupation and employment status of each recipient of unemployment compensation, and a statement of such recipient's rights to further compensation under such law.

(b) Whenever the Board, after reasonable notice and opportunity for hearing to the State agency charged with the administration of the State law, finds that in the administration of the law there is-

(1) a denial, in a substantial number of cases, of unemployment compensation to individuals entitled thereto under such law; or

(2) a failure to comply substantially with any provision specified in subsection (a); the Board shall notify such State agency that further payments will not be made to the State until the Board is satisfied that there is no longer any such denial or failure to comply. Until it is so satisfied, it shall make no further certification to the Secretary of the Treasury with respect to such State.

TITLE IV—GRANTS TO STATES FOR AID TO DEPENDENT CHILDREN

APPROPRIATION

SECTION 401. For the purpose of enabling each State to furnish financial assistance, as far as practicable under the conditions in such State, to needy dependent children, there is hereby authorized to be appropriated for the fiscal year ending June 30, 1936, the sum of $24,750,000, and there is hereby authorized to be appropriated for each fiscal year thereafter a sum sufficient to carry out the purposes of this title. The sums made available under this section shall be used for making payments to States which have submitted, and had approved by the Board, State plans for aid to dependent children.

STATE PLANS FOR AID TO DEPENDENT CHILDREN

SEC. 402. (a) A State plan for aid to dependent children must (1) provide that it shall be in effect in all political subdivisions of the State, and, if administered by them, be mandatory upon them; (2) provide for financial participation by the State; (3) either provide for the establishment or designation of a single State agency to administer the plan, or provide for the establishment or designation of a single State agency to supervise the administration of the plan; (4) provide for granting to any individual, whose claim with respect to aid to a dependent child is denied, an opportunity for a fair hearing before such State agency; (5) provide such methods of administration (other than those relating to selection, tenure of office, and compensation of personnel) as are found by the Board to be necessary for the efficient operation of the plan; and (6) provide that the State agency will make such reports, in such form and containing such information, as the Board may from time to time require, and comply with such provisions as the Board may from time to time find necessary to assure the correctness and verification of such reports.

(b) The Board shall approve any plan which fulfills the conditions specified in subsection (a), except that it shall not approve any plan which imposes as a condition of eligibility for aid to dependent children, a residence requirement which denies aid with respect to any child residing in the State (1) who has resided in the State for one year immediately preceding the application for such aid, or (2) who was born within the State within one year immediately preceding the application, if its mother has resided in the State for one year immediately preceding the birth.

PAYMENT TO STATES

SEC. 403. (a) From the sums appropriated therefore, the Secretary of the Treasury shall pay to each State which has an approved plan for aid to dependent children, for each quarter, beginning with the quarter commencing July 1, 1935, an amount, which shall be used exclusively for carrying out the State plan, equal to one-third of the total of the sums expended during such quarter under such plan, not counting so much of such expenditure with respect to any dependent child for any month as exceeds $18, or if there is more than one dependent child in the same home, as exceeds $18 for any month with respect to one such dependent child and $12 for such month with respect to each of the other dependent children. . . .

DEFINITIONS

SEC. 406. When used in this title—

(a) The term "dependent child" means a child under the age of sixteen who has been deprived of parental support or care by reason of the death, continued absence from the home, or physical or mental incapacity of a parent, and who is living with his father, mother, grandfather, grandmother, brother, sister, stepfather, stepmother, stepbrother, stepsister, uncle, or aunt, in a place of residence maintained by one or more of such relatives as his or their own home;

(b) The term "aid to dependent children" means money payments with respect to a dependent child or dependent children.

TITLE V—GRANTS TO STATES FOR MATERNAL AND CHILD WELFARE

Part 1—Maternal and Child Health Services

APPROPRIATION

SECTION 501. For the purpose of enabling each State to extend and improve, as far as practicable under the conditions in such State, services for promoting the health of mothers and children, especially in rural areas and in areas suffering from severe economic distress, there is hereby authorized to be appropriated for each fiscal year, beginning with the fiscal year ending June 30, 1936, the sum of $3,800,000. The sums made available under this section shall be used for making payments to States which have submitted, and had approved by the Chief of the Children's Bureau, State plans for such services.

ALLOTMENTS TO STATES

SEC. 502. (a) Out of the sums appropriated pursuant to section 501 for each fiscal year the Secretary of Labor shall allot to each State $20,000, and such part of $1,800,000 as he finds that the number of live births in such State bore to the total number of live births in the United States, in the latest calendar year for which the Bureau of the Census has available statistics.

(b) Out of the sums appropriated pursuant to section 501 for each fiscal year the Secretary of Labor shall allot to the States $980,000 in addition to the allotments made under subsection (a), according to the financial need of each State for assistance in carrying out its State plan, as determined by him after taking into consideration the number of live births in such State.

(c) The amount of any allotment to a State under subsection (a) for any fiscal year remaining unpaid to such State at the end of such fiscal year shall be available for payment to such State under section 504 until the end of the second succeeding fiscal year. No payment to a State under section 504 shall be made out of its allotment for any fiscal year until its allotment for the preceding fiscal year has been exhausted or has ceased to be available.

APPROVAL OF STATE PLANS

SEC. 503. (a) A State plan for maternal and child-health services must (1) provide for financial participation by the State; (2) provide for the administration of the plan by the State health agency or the supervision of the administration of the plan by the State health agency; (3) provide such methods of administration (other than those relating to selection, tenure of office, and compensation of personnel) as are necessary for the efficient operation of the plan; (4) provide that the State health agency will make such reports, in such form and containing such information, as the Secretary of Labor may from time to time find necessary to assure the correctness and verification of such reports; (5) provide for the extension and improvement of local maternal and child-health services administered by local child-health units; (6) provide for cooperation with medical, nursing, and welfare groups and organization; and (7) provide for the development of demonstration services in needy areas and among groups in special need.

(b) The Chief of the Children's Bureau shall approve any plan which fulfills the conditions specified in subsection (a) and shall thereupon notify the Secretary of Labor and the Sate health agency of his approval. . . . .

Part 2—Services for Crippled Children

APPROPRIATION

SEC. 511. For the purpose of enabling each State to extend and improve (especially in rural areas and in areas suffering from severe economic distress), as far as practicable under the conditions in such State, services for locating crippled children, and for providing medical, surgical, corrective, and other services and care, and facilities for diagnosis, hospitalization, and aftercare, for children who are crippled or who are suffering from conditions which lead to crippling, there is hereby authorized to be appropriated for each fiscal year, beginning with the fiscal year ending June 30, 1936, the sum of $2,850,000. The sums made available under this section shall be used for making payments to States which have submitted, and had approved by the Chief of the Children's Bureau, State plans for such services.

ALLOTMENTS TO STATES

SEC. 512. (a) Out of the sums appropriated pursuant to section 511 for each fiscal year the Secretary of Labor shall allot to each Sate $20,000, and the remainder to the States according to the need of each State as determined by him after taking into consideration the number of crippled children in such State in need of the services referred to in section 511 and the cost of furnishing such services to them.

(b) The amount of any allotment to a State under subsection (a) for any fiscal year remaining unpaid to such State at the end of such fiscal year shall be available for payment to such State under section 514 until the end of the second succeeding fiscal year. No payment to a State under section 514 shall be made out of its allotment for any fiscal year until its allotment for the preceding fiscal year has been exhausted or has ceased to be available.

APPROVAL OF STATE PLANS

SEC. 513. (a) A State plan for services for crippled children must (1) provide for financial participation by the State; (2) provide for the administration of the plan by a State agency or the supervision of the administration of the plan by a State agency; (3) provide such methods of administration (other than those relating to selection, tenure of office, and compensation of personnel) as are necessary for the efficient operation of the plan; (4) provide that the State agency will make such reports, in such form and containing such information, as the Secretary of Labor may from time to time require, and comply with such provisions as he may from time to time find necessary to assure the correctness and verification of such reports; (5) provide for carrying out the purposes specified in section 511; and (6) provide for cooperation with medical, health, nursing, and welfare groups and organizations and with any agency in such State charged with administering State laws providing for vocational rehabilitation of physically handicapped children.

(b) The Chief of the Children's Bureau shall approve any plan which fulfills the conditions specified in subsection (a) and shall thereupon notify the Secretary of Labor and the State health agency of his approval. . . .

Part 3—Child-Welfare Services

SEC. 521. (a) For the purpose of enabling the United States, through the Children's Bureau, to cooperate with State public-welfare agencies in establishing, extending, and strengthening, especially in predominantly rural areas, public-welfare services (hereinafter in this section referred to as "child-welfare services") for the protection and care of homeless, dependent, and neglected children, and children in danger of becoming delinquent, there is hereby authorized to be appropriated for each fiscal year, beginning with the fiscal year ending June 30, 1936, the sum of $1,500,000. Such amount shall be allotted by the Secretary of Labor for use by cooperating State public-welfare agencies on the basis of plans developed jointly by the State agency and the Children's Bureau, to each State, $10,000, and the remainder to each State on the basis of such plans, not to exceed such part of the remainder as the rural population of such State bears to the total rural population of the United States. The amount so allotted shall be expended for payment of part of the cost of district, county or other local child-welfare services in areas predominately rural, and for developing State services for the encouragement and assistance of adequate methods of community child-welfare organization in areas predominately rural and other areas of special need. The amount of any allotment to a State under this section for any fiscal year remaining unpaid to such State at the end of such fiscal year shall be available for payment to such State under this section until the end of the second succeeding fiscal year. No payment to a State under this section shall be made out of its allotment for any fiscal year until its allotment for the preceding fiscal year has been exhausted or has ceased to be available. . . .

Part 4—Vocational Rehabilitation

SEC. 531. (a) In order to enable the United States to cooperate with the States and Hawaii in extending and strengthening their programs of vocational rehabilitation of the physically disabled, and to continue to carry out the provisions and purposes of the Act entitled "An Act to provide for the promotion of vocational rehabilitation of persons disabled in industry or otherwise and their return to civil employment," approved June 2, 1920, as amended (U.S.C., title 29, ch. 4; U.S.C. Supp. VII, title 29, secs. 31, 32, 34, 35, 37, 39 and 40), there is hereby authorized to be appropriated for the fiscal years ending June 30, 1936, and June 30, 1937, the sum of $841,000 for each fiscal year in addition to the amount of the existing authorization, and for each fiscal year thereafter the sum of $1,938,000. Of the sums appropriated pursuant to such authorization for each fiscal year, $5,000 shall be apportioned to the Territory of Hawaii and the remainder shall be apportioned among the several States in the manner provided in such Act of June 2, 1920, unamended. . . .

Part 5—Administration

SEC. 541. (a) There is hereby authorized to be appropriated for the fiscal year ending June 30, 1936, the sum of $425,000, for all necessary expenses of the Children's Bureau in administering the provisions of this title, except section 531.

(b) The Children's Bureau shall make such studies and investigations as will promote the efficient administration of this title, except section 531.

(c) The Secretary of Labor shall include in his annual report to Congress a full account of the administration of this title, except section 531. . . .

TITLE X—GRANTS TO STATES FOR AID TO THE BLIND

APPROPRIATION

SECTION 1001. For the purpose of enabling each State to furnish financial assistance, as far as practicable under the conditions in such State, to needy individuals who are blind, there is hereby authorized to be appropriated for the fiscal year ending June 30, 1936, the sum of $3,000,000, and there is hereby authorized to be appropriated for each fiscal year thereafter a sum sufficient to carry out the purposes of this title. The sums made available under this section shall be used for making payments to States which have submitted, and had approved by the Social Security Board, State plans for aid to the blind.

STATE PLANS FOR AID TO THE BLIND

SEC. 1002. (a) A State plan for aid to the blind must (1) provide that it shall be in effect in all political subdivisions of the State, and if administered by them, be mandatory upon them; (2) provide for financial participation by the State; (3) either provide for the establishment or designation of a single State agency to administer the plan, or provide for the establishment or designation of a single State agency to supervise the administration of the plan; (4) provide for granting to any individual, whose claim for aid is denied, an opportunity for a fair hearing before such State agency; (5) provide such methods of administration (other than those relating to selection, tenure of office, and compensation of personnel) as are found by the Board to be necessary for the efficient operation of the plan; (6) provide that the State agency will make such reports, in such form and containing such information, as the Board may from time to time require, and comply with such provisions as the Board may from time to time find necessary to assure the correctness and verification of such reports; and (7) provide that no aid will be furnished any individual under the plan with respect to which he is receiving old-age assistance under the State plan approved under section 2 of this Act.

(b) The Board shall approve any plan which fulfills the conditions specified in subsection (a), except that is shall not approve any plan which imposes, as a condition of eligibility for aid to the blind under the plan—

(1) Any residence requirement which excludes any resident of the State who has resided therein five years during the nine years immediately preceding the application for aid and has resided therein continuously for one year immediately preceding the application; or

(2) Any citizenship requirement which excludes any citizen of the United States.

PAYMENT TO STATES

SEC. 1003. (a) From the sums appropriated therefore, the Secretary of the Treasury shall pay to each State which has an approved plan for aid to the blind, for each quarter, beginning with the quarter commencing July 1, 1935, (1) an amount, which shall be used exclusively as aid to the blind, equal to one-half of the total of the sums expended during such quarter as aid to the blind under the State plan with respect to each individual who is blind and is not an inmate of a public institution, not counting so much of such expenditure with respect to any individual for any month as exceeds $30, and (2) 5 per centum of such amount, which shall be used for paying the costs of administering the State plan or for aid to the blind, or both, and for no other purpose. . . .

SHORT TITLE

SEC. 1105. This Act may be cited as the "Social Security Act." Approved, August 14, 1935.

THE GREAT SOCIETY: A SOCIAL WELFARE LEGACY

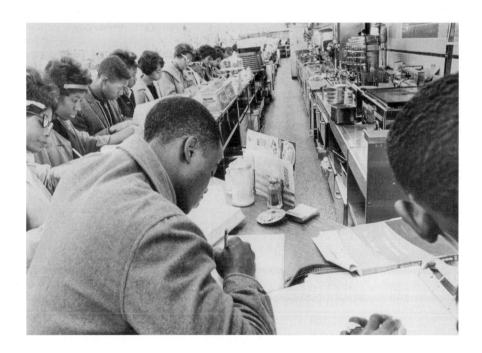

Even though Franklin Roosevelt's dream was that there would be a new reform era after the end of World War II, due to strong conservative forces, social reform did not begin taking place until the political climate changed in the 1960s. This political era, beginning with President Kennedy and continuing with Johnson, demonstrated compassion for the poor with many programs put in place that provided assistance and relief. Like those of administrations preceding and following, however, the policies were filtered through the lens of predominately white, middle-class men. While these men were well intended, their lenses were not clearly focused on what the real needs of women, racial groups, and gay and lesbians were.

This chapter reviews the political economy of the 1960s as it explores the policies and events of the post–World War II era that led up to the reforms of the time and takes the reader through the major events of the civil rights movement.

OCCURRENCES AND RESISTANCE LEADING UP TO SOCIAL REFORM OF THE 1960s

Affluence Masks Continuing Poverty

During the Truman presidency, most Americans were not interested in social reform. For the first time since the Great Depression of 1929, they were enjoying a newfound affluence and were oblivious to the needs of impoverished people in urban and rural areas. With a widespread belief in mass prosperity, concern with poverty was remote and nearly antiquarian during the war and postwar years. This widespread view of prosperity, although inaccurate, was, in part, responsible for the decline of social reform during the period. Almost everyone owned a television and a car, didn't they? So why engage in reform (Trattner, 1999)? Mainstream Americans were even less aware of the needs of African Americans, who continued to live in poverty under the Jim Crow laws (Jansson, 1997).

Jim Crow Laws

Jim Crowism was the antithesis of middle American affluence. Jim Crow legislation deprived African Americans of their basic civil rights, asserting that individuals, though not states, could legally discriminate against black Americans. Not only did the laws limit areas in which African Americans could live, in both southern and northern towns, they also encompassed the segregation of housing, facilities, education, medical treatment, and burial plot; and they stayed in place for almost a century after the Civil War (Day, 1989; Jansson, 1997).

School segregation proved increasingly harmful for black children, with psychologists arguing that it instilled feelings of inferiority among the children. This prompted the National Association for the Advancement of Colored People (NAACP) in 1952 to consolidate a series of cases under the name of the first case—*Brown v. Board of Education of Topeka*—challenging the very existence of the separate-but-equal doctrine in education (Martin, Roberts, Mintz, McMurry, & Jones 1993). It was not until May 1954 that the Supreme Court acted on the case, declaring that "separate educational facilities are inherently unequal," consequently violating the 14th Amendment's guarantee of "equal protection of the laws." The *Brown* decision was probably the most important civil rights ruling of the century and helped bring an end to Jim Crow laws (Levine, 1996). The discussion of *Brown v. Board of Education* continues later in this chapter.

Even though the rigid Jim Crow laws did not exist in the North, the situation was not much better. Informally, blacks were excluded from the better schools and neighborhoods as well as jobs (Martin et al., 1993). These laws stayed in place for almost a century after the Civil War.

So deluded was mainstream America in its illusion of affluence that well-known and highly regarded economist John Kenneth Galbraith wrote a book entitled *The Affluent Society,* which was on the best-seller list in the late 1950s. Galbraith stated that America had essentially solved the problems of scarcity and poverty. He did not say, however, that there was absolutely no poverty in America, just that there was some and that it was a disgrace in such an affluent society. While stressing affluence, he described poverty as a uniquely minority problem, mostly confined to Appalachia and a few other depressed areas (Trattner, 1999). There are other schools of thought to be considered about this view of poverty.

Frances Piven and Richard Cloward (1971), in their profound book *Regulating the Poor,* hold the view that relief giving is secondary to meeting need. They see relief in the broader context of how it serves the larger economic and political order. They suggest that relief is given or withheld depending on the problems of regulation in the larger society with which government must contend. In other words, their analysis would argue that, during times of affluence and stability in the country, relief would be withdrawn. An example of the flip side would be the outpouring of relief payments in the 1960s with the argument that it was a political response to civil disorder. Furthermore, Piven and Cloward would contend that the relief was not necessarily the result of the urban migration or the increase in poverty of the times but, rather, a response to urban violence and an attempt to quell the growing demands of masses of poor blacks.

The more direct, productive way of responding to poverty would have been to deal with racial discrimination and structural unemployment head on rather than using money to pacify the poor. In any event, "the staggering increase in the number of people applying for and receiving public assistance and the enormous growth of welfare expenditures during these years helped make the problem a major topic of public concern rather than merely a marginal affair" (Trattner, 1999, p. 315).

Other drawbacks to social reform existed—for example, the nation's disdain of poverty in general and the white population's animosity toward African Americans. A large influx of African Americans was looking for work during World War II in the war industry. In Detroit and other northern urban centers, this influx angered whites and intermittent race riots broke out. An editorial in the *Detroit News,* June 23, 1943, stated: "We must keep in mind the kind of people we have to deal with in this connection. They are half-baked, half-edu-cated—white and colored alike" (Mitchell, 1970, p. 169). Hershel Richey attended Indiana University and worked for the U.S. Post Office for 30 years, becoming president of the National Alliance of Postal Employees. In an oral history of Detroit's African American community, Richey tells of mov-ing to Detroit:

> I am an American, too—despite the fact that my skin is dark, despite the fact that my forefathers were slaves who came over in chains sweltering in the stifling, musty hold of some ship. . . . I have tried to create and adjust my life. . . . I have read of many great men of my race. . . . But I also know of many great men and of many great deeds unsung and unrecorded. . . . I remember a rav-ing, fanatical mob, not in the South, but in Michigan, the heart of the American war industry, abetted by biased policemen, trying to prevent Negroes from mov-ing into homes built for them, homes which were to house them while they labored to produce materials for the protection of all American mankind. (Moon, 1994, p. 234)

Southern and northern legislators joined forces at the end of the war and blocked civil rights legislation along with the Fair Employment Practices Commission (discussed further in a subsequent section), which intended to assure black Americans equal opportunity to obtain defense plant jobs. This was also the time of the cold war and McCarthyism, both dampening the cli-mate for social reform. The cold warriors were obsessed with the subversion of government and society by Communists and demanded the dismissal of civil servants and the prosecution of ordinary citizens with leftist or radical leanings. Joseph McCarthy submitted many citizens to public interrogation and was eventually discredited and censured by the Senate, but the whole process left the public with suspicions of social reformers (Jansson, 1997).

Even Hollywood got drawn into the ugliness of McCarthyism and the cold war. In 1947, many witnesses, mostly script writers, were subpoenaed to appear for hearings in Washington before the House UnAmerican Activities Committee (HUAC). Most went to jail for their refusal to answer the com-mittee's questions about their personal political beliefs and, consequently, were blacklisted by the studios. A six-part personal history of the Hollywood blacklist was written, depicting one of the bleakest periods for the First Amendment in American history; *Blacklisted* tells the story of Gordon Kahn's 15 years of persecution and the fears that followed him, his family, and thou-sands of other Americans for having the wrong political ideas (www.weisbroth. com/blacklisted 1999).

Some of the movies of the times were: *Big Jim McClain* (1952), starring John Wayne who plays a two-fisted HUAC investigator pursing Communists in Hawaii; *I Married a Communist* (1950), in which the male lead plays a prewar radical blackmailed into working for the Reds; *My Son John* (1952), which portrays a typical American couple who discover that their oedipal son is a party member; *Pickup on South Street* (1953), which portrays a patriotic New York pickpocket who stumbles across a spy ring; and *Dr. Strangelove* (1963), starring George C. Scott, which is about a deranged cold warrior in command of an American Air Force base who unleashes a preemptive nuclear strike against the Soviet Union and the U.S. president is forced to contact his Soviet opposite number on the Moscow hot line and discuss ways of averting imminent Armageddon.

McCarthyism is also spoken of by Arthur Michael Carter III in Moon's (1994) African American's oral history. Carter—a former teacher, dean of Wayne County Community College, Wayne County commissioner, and superintendent of Detroit Public Schools—highlights some political aspects of the 1940s:

> I also remember the national convention of the Progressive Party. The Progressive Party was a party which was viewed as a party to the left of central political philosophy in the United States. Erma Henderson, my godmother, supported Henry Wallace of the Progressive Party, for president in 1948. I can also remember the rumors about our phones being tapped as we moved from the '40s after the convention, into what I later learned was the Senator Joe McCarthy era. McCarthy was a U.S. Senator who ruined the lives of thousands of citizens by accusing them of being members of the Communist party. I remember discussions around the issue of our family phone being tapped because of family support for Henry Wallace. (Moon, pp. 262–263)

Small Gains for Black Americans On the up side during this era, there were some positive outcomes for black Americans after World War II. As a response against Nazi racism and anti-Communism (the Soviets used American racism as a propaganda weapon), white Americans questioned their racial practices. It was during this time period that noted anthropologists began disproving racist theories that blacks were innately inferior, leading to a new attitude toward race relations. This new attitude began to appear in school textbooks and in professional and liberal publications. Liberal white organizations began to form coalitions with black–led civil rights groups to fight prejudice and discrimination with two labor federations, the Blacks of Labor (AFL) and the Congress of Industrial Organizations (CIO), as important components. African Americans, working with Mexican American organizations in the West and Puerto Rican groups in the Northeast, were part of the Leadership Conference on Civil Rights in 1948 that brought liberal organizations together to lobby in Washington, D.C. (Levine, 1996).

Meanwhile, African Americans gathered momentum in advancing their interests and many significantly improved their economic status during the prosperous 1940s and 1950s (Levine, 1996). In the 1940s, southern blacks began to migrate to the North to follow the jobs. World War II accelerated the process of industrialization and mechanization, making small marginal farmers obsolete, and millions fled the southern rural communities in search of factory jobs. This migration continued well into the 1970s, and, as history shows, racism and discrimination followed (Axinn & Levin, 1997). Even with the hardships encountered by discrimination, white-collar jobs increased for blacks and their income jumped from 41% of white income in 1939 to 51% in 1947 and to 57% in 1952, enabling almost a third of them to own their own homes. The National Association for the Advancement of Colored People (NAACP) membership soared, which led to expanded activities; and the efforts of the United Negro College Foundation helped increase the number of blacks in college, giving them a much broader base for their future leadership (Levine, 1996).

American blacks gained many advantages under the New Deal and attained many more prominent political positions. Threatened with a march on Washington, President Roosevelt issued, on June 25, 1941, Executive Order 8802 barring discrimination in the employment of workers in defense industries or government. A Fair Employment Practices Committee (FEPC) soon followed, and the politics of the Fair Deal were even more pro–black than those of the New Deal. Although Roosevelt created social welfare programs that helped many black Americans, he remained silent on civil rights matters. Harry Truman found himself in a different political situation and, despite some views to the contrary, he was committed to civil rights, with his greatest monuments in this area being the report "To Secure These Rights," which strongly denounced the denial of civil rights to some Americans and called for a positive program to strengthen civil rights. The program included the elimination of segregation based on race, color, creed, or national origin. Additionally, his revolutionary Executive Order 9981 decreed an end to racial discrimination in the military (Franklin & Moss, 1994; Levine, 1996; Wilhoit, 1973).

Another boon for the era was the Servicemen's Readjustment Act of 1944, called the GI Bill, which made access to college education more readily available for the middle/working-class veterans. The GI Bill was part of the bigger postwar social legislative package that centered on the welfare needs of soldiers and veterans. The Bill was part of the rehabilitation idea that the country owes an obligation to its veterans to restore to them the civilian status and opportunities they would have enjoyed had there not been a war. Not only did the Bill provide stipends to support veterans and their families while they went to school for vocational or higher education, it also averted a depression by upgrading the quality and earning power of the American workforce for a generation (Axinn & Levin, 1997; Day, 1999).

Racial tensions and discrimination were further eased in the six years following the riots of 1943 by the formation of human relations commissions in

30 cities. Black and white churches worked with other organizations, helping to nearly eradicate lynchings by the early 1950s. In 1944, in Atlanta, the biracial Southern Regional Council was formed, which was made up of clergy and professionals. The biracial group cautiously promoted the slow elimination of Jim Crow laws. In 1953, a week-long black boycott of the bus system in Baton Rouge, Louisiana, ended the system of segregated seating that forced blacks to ride at the back of the bus (Levine, 1996); and poverty and discrimination continued in America.

So it was ironic that as white animosity grew toward the blacks that were migrating from the South, black political power grew. The 1940s migration greatly added to the numbers of blacks who—now out of the South—could vote. White politicians in the North and West were paying greater heed to the expanding black electorate (Levine, 1996).

Despite more favorable conditions in the 1940s and 1950s for African Americans, white resistance toward social reform did not lessen nor did racism decline, especially not in the South. In fact, the two conditions remained parallel for some time. As the resistance to social reform continued, it was met with alarm by many people; scholars, reporters, politicians, and social workers were among those who spoke out urging folks to take a stand and reinvolve themselves in social action. Some paid attention to the plea, and neither welfare expansion nor welfare reform completely disappeared in the 1950s. Many public programs increased their benefits, and some were broadened (Trattner, 1999); and poverty and discrimination continued.

A historian growing up in North Carolina recalled that race relations in the South in the mid-1950s were much as they had been in the 1890s. He stated:

> [B]lacks who had to enter our house, for whatever reason, came in the back door. Unless employed as domestic servants, blacks conducted business with my father or mother on the back porch or, on rare occasions, in the kitchen. Blacks never entered our dining or living area . . . except as domestics. . . . When a black person approached a doorway at the same time as a white adult, the black stepped back and sometimes even held the door open for the white to enter. The message I received from hundreds of such signals was always the same, I was white; I was different; I was superior. It was not a message with which an adolescent boy was apt to quarrel. (Martin et al., 1993, p. 951)

From a book of oral histories by unidentified common people, an unknown historian from North Carolina speaks on discrimination:

> There's discrimination all right. There'll be discrimination as long as we live. I don't really think the demonstrations did any good. There'll always be somebody that'll look down on us as Negroes, and we're not supposed to make what the white make or live where the white live or do things what the white does. . . . The only thing to do is just pray that they'll stop, and see they're hurtin' nobody but themselves. (Faulkner, Heisel, Holbrook, & Geismar, 1982, p. 59)

An unknown historian from Virginia wrote:

> And she [white friend] would ask me, "Willie, what difference is it in white and in colored?" "Well," I told her, "I don't think that there is no difference—there is no difference in God's sight. If there was, then we would die and you all would live. But we all have to die. To God it don't make no difference." (p. 75)

Other Racial Groups

Civil rights before President Kennedy saw the formation of the Southern Christian Leadership Conference in Atlanta, a nonviolent group led by Dr. Martin Luther King Jr., and the Congress of Racial Equality (CORE). The CORE, a Black Muslim religious group that was militant in nature, advocated separatism and was lead by the charismatic Malcolm X. These pre-Kennedy times also saw television bring an immediacy to civil rights. For the first time, people far removed from such problems were able to view the paradox of freedom denied in a free country, while police brutalized the innocent (Day, 1999). "For some, this was the end of innocence and belief in the American system. Civil rights was no longer 'somewhere and someone else': It was a national awareness and shame" (Day, 1999, p. 322).

Other protests began among Native Americans, Hispanics, white women, women of color, and welfare activists who included men and women across the lines. At first, most protests were modeled on King's nonviolent example. The Mexican Americans, and/or Hispanics, and Native Americans had long been mired in poverty (Day, 1999; Trattner, 1999).

In 1949, to rid itself of the "Indian problem," Congress began to turn Native American programs over to state governments. The process of "termination" began in 1953, which ended federal supervision of the tribes and freed Native Americans from government wardship. *Termination* meant, ostensibly, that Native Americans were given the same privileges and responsibilities as other citizens but with no transitional period. Many necessary support programs were abandoned; and, without the programs to help them through the transition stage, they suffered great personal and financial losses. The Native Americans in Wisconsin, for example, were billed for property taxes that they were unable to pay. This meant they lost sanitation services, police and fire protection, and highway maintenance. With such a small tax base, they were unable to support adequate schools and health services in their community and many lost their homes and life savings. Not all tribes were treated so harshly; however, from the Native American perspective, termination was another kind of oppression. In spite of groups like the National Congress of American Indians, founded in 1944, working vigorously against termination, several dozen groups were terminated between 1954 and 1960. President Kennedy did end termination; nonetheless, it had become a rallying point for activism. Despite other efforts of protest groups (the National Indian Youth Council), the economic status of Native Americans grew increasingly worse. By 1960, unemployment had risen to 38% compared to 5% of all males in the United States (Day, 1999).

Mexican Americans, persons of Mexican ancestry, were also disadvantaged, with 4 million still gathered in various barrios thought the Southwest and the West. Mexican Americans were hampered by lack of job skills, inadequate schooling, language problems, and discrimination. They were now being spurred to action by black activism in their search for increased racial and ethnic pride (Trattner, 1999).

Hispanics in the United States have traditionally been agricultural workers. In the general unrest after World War II, with Hispanic Americans' average annual income at $2,600 (1956), they began to organize for political action (Day, 1989). "Excluded from labor unions, Hispanic agricultural workers were continually denied economic advancement until Cesar Chavez organized the National Farm Workers Association" (p. 323). There were some victories; but, in 1965, there was police harassment and brutality in California, and the Texas Rangers were brought in to enforce the growers' demands in Texas, resulting in strikers and their leaders being imprisoned. The most militant group was the Alianza Federal de Mercedes formed in 1963 by Reies Tijerina who took his grievances concerning old Mexican land grants to the New Mexico government at Santa Fe. Tijerina's group was later arrested and tried for civil disobedience (Day, 1989).

Gays and Lesbians

The 1950s, with their conservative social and political nature, were not a good time to be different in the United States, especially in the arena of gender roles and sexual expression. Senate hearings on homosexuals and other "sex perverts" who held positions in the government made it an unlikely time for the publication of *The Homosexual in America: A Subjective Approach.* Writing under a pseudonym, the author argued that homosexuals were an oppressed minority analogous to racial and religious groups. The American Civil Liberties Union (ACLU) turned its back on gays and lesbians during this time in history, too. Some local chapters of the ACLU were more supportive, but it was not until after several U.S. Supreme Court rulings affirmed sexual privacy in marriage that the national board of directors made changes in policy (Rayside, 1998).

The isolation for gays and lesbians was complete. Discovery of homosexuality in the military and other government jobs guaranteed dismissal. It was also a time when the American Psychiatric Association formed the official opinion that homosexuality was an illness. Despite the risk of homosexuals organizing, the 1950s saw the birth of the first sustained homophile organizations in the United States. The Mattachine and the Daughters of Bilitis were two of the largest organizations, both based in California. Chapters spread across the country by the late 1960s, and other groups began to organize. The groundwork was laid for a political and cultural movement (Rayside, 1998). This is discussed further in Chapter 10.

Poverty, the Disabled, and Public Assistance

Huge strides were taken between the years 1890 to 1940 to provide adequately for impoverished and handicapped citizens, but the nation still had a long way to go. In the late 19th century, public assistance was the responsibility of the localities and was mostly confined to institutional care for the young, the old, and the physically or mentally debilitated. While the states accepted the obligation of caring for the mentally ill and delinquents, almost no preventive work was being undertaken. The public health movement was just being talked about, and the mental health movement had not emerged. Nothing existed resembling a partnership of federal, state, and local governments aimed at a national system of social welfare delivery. Primarily because of the passage of the Social Security Act and its 1939 amendments, by 1940 the situation had greatly changed (Trattner, 1999).

The 1939 amendments, along with other legislation, propelled states and the federal government to link in their public assistance to the aged, the blind, and crippled and dependent children in the expansion of public health programs. Soon to follow would be mental health programs. The administration of unemployment compensation was also included at this time, as well as a national system of old-age and survivors' insurance and other programs to include low-cost housing, public works, and agricultural resettlement (Trattner, 1999).

Further amendments of the Social Security Act in 1950 provided caretaker grants to mothers of dependent children and added a new category of public assistance—Aid to the Permanently and Totally Disabled (APTD). The amendment to mother's aid resulted in a name change from ADC to AFDC, Aid to Families with Dependent Children. Other changes included the addition of Disability Insurance (DI); other previously omitted groups—for example, farm workers and the self-employed—were included and the AFDC program added a social welfare component extending child welfare from rural to urban areas. The new welfare programs that were included were the Servicemen's Readjustment Act (G.I. Bill of Rights, 1944); the National Mental Health Act; The National School Lunch Program; the Full Employment Act (1946); the Housing Act (1949); and, in 1954, the School Milk Program and the Vocational Rehabilitation Act (Trattner, 1999)—and poverty continued to grow, along with racism and discrimination.

Women and Children While gains are acknowledged, the pervasive mood of complacency nationally, resulting from the illusion of affluence, tended to lead away from reform to broader governmental goals like containing Communism, balancing the budget, and cutting taxes. As a means of achieving some of these goals, there was a push to get the needy off the welfare rolls, which were actually increasing despite claims to the contrary. By the middle of the 1950s, recipients of AFDC outnumbered all others receiving government assistance. Unlike the earlier welfare rolls of dependent white children and widowed mothers, those receiving the bulk of the aid were single black women with illegitimate children (Trattner, 1999). An up side to those growing numbers receiving AFDC was the indication that people of color and poor white women were challenging their exclusion and insisting on their citizenship rights by claiming assistance (Gordon, 1998).

The claiming of welfare was a part of the civil rights movement. Even though today the mistaken assumption exists that being on welfare is a sign of dependency and despair, for many women that is not the case. On the contrary, "going to the welfare office was a step towards citizenship with government but also a statement of citizenship, not only the first entrance into a relationship with the government but also a statement of self-esteem" (Gordon, 1998, p. 8). The claiming of welfare, including the 1960s welfare rights movement, was also a woman's movement. It was a strategy for upward mobility, especially for one's children. It meant keeping the children out of the fields—where so many black children labored—and in school (Gordon, 1998).

Factors in the Rise of the Welfare Roles The economy worsened, and the demand for labor receded. While the urbanization of the new migrants represented upward mobility, they suffered greatly from the recession as they were the first fired and the last hired. Consequently, marriage and family patterns changed, with divorce, marital separation, and out-of-wedlock births increasing the numbers of single mothers. Also, a new standard of medical care was put in place. Over time, most Americans began to have higher medical standards. Children were no longer expected to die from influenza or scarlet fever or tuberculosis. Just as today, those left out in the cold without medical coverage were those not covered by an employer. This lack of medical care had the effect of trapping single parents in AFDC because they would lose their medical coverage for their children if they left the rolls (Gordon, 1998).

The stigma attached to welfare grew along with the numbers. The shame associated with AFDC was created, in part, by the design of the program, along with the conservative pressure against ever giving *single* mothers enough money to move out of poverty. Constant searches for moral or financial cheating spread suspicion on all AFDC recipients, which was magnified by the race, sex, and marital status of recipients. With the stigma, a downward spiral emerged making recipients politically weak. They lacked political clout, and programs exclusively for the poor could not gather the support necessary to keep up with inflation. The downward spiral drove the programs into more impoverished states, which, in turn, increased the stigma (Gordon, 1998).

In response to the growing number of blacks welfare recipients, the states began instituting punitive administrative policies crafted to reduce their numbers and to deter new applications. By the late 1950s, states were strictly enforcing residency requirements so that the migrant blacks would not receive assistance; and all sorts of new eligibility investigations were initiated (Trattner, 1999).

Much of our knowledge of households comes from government reports with race tallied in separate tables. Therefore, cautions must apply to interracial comparisons. Those figures need to be placed in the larger context. If there is too great of an emphasis placed on race, it can divert attention from forces that have been reshaping the entire society. This is apparent when we look at figures tracing rates and ratios for families headed by women over the last four decades. In 1950, 17.2% were black and 5.3% were white; in 1960, 24.4% were black and 7.3% white; in 1970, 34.5% black and 9.6% white; in 1980, 45.9% black, 13.2% white; and, in 1993, 58.4% black, 18.7% white. The numbers by themselves, however, convey only part of the picture. If we just look at the numbers, we see that black families headed by women has always been higher, but an equally pervasive pattern emerges when black percentages are transformed into multiples of the white figures. By doing this, it turns out that the biracial ratio has remained remarkably stable throughout the 40-year period: The black multiple for 1950 is 3.2; for 1960, it is 3.3; for 1970, it is 3.6; for 1980, it is 3.5; and, for 1993, it is 3.1 (Table 9.1). By placing the figures into proper perspective, it is possible that what we have seen is not so much racial differences as concurrent adaptations to common cultural trends (Hacker, 1995)—and poverty and discrimination continued in America.

On the whole, these are relatively recent changes. In 1950, only 17% of black households were headed by women, which is fewer than today's white rate. What we see, within living memory, is that homes with two parents present have always been very much the black norm. "This makes it difficult to describe the matrifocal families that preponderate today as being a 'legacy' of slavery" (Hacker, 1995, p. 75). Once black were freed, they sought the durable unions they had been denied in slavery. For most of the century following the Civil War, black families remained remarkably stable, despite low incomes and uncertain employment. Nonetheless, the rates for female-headed households always exceeded those of other races. Looking at figures as recent as the 1950s, however, we see that such families were exceptions and not the rule. It is safe to say then that the more recent increases in homes headed by single parents cannot be attributed to a plantation past. There have been other developments at work that cut across racial lines (Hacker, 1995). These developments are covered more in later chapters.

TABLE 9.1	HOUSEHOLDS HEADED BY WOMEN: 1950–1993		
Year	Black	White	Black Multiple
1950	17.2%	5.3%	3.2
1960	24.4%	7.3%	3.3
1970	34.5%	9.6%	3.6
1980	45.9%	13.2%	3.5
1993	58.4%	18.7%	3.1

Note. Figures focus on families that have no husband present and with children under the age of 18. Hispanic families are omitted after 1960. Adapted with permission from *Two Nations: Black and White, Separate, Hostile, Unequal*, by A. Hacker, 1995, New York: Ballantine Books.

Other Areas of Unrest Facing Social Reform

As we have seen from history, conservative politics during the presidencies of Truman and Eisenhower, and all that that represented, dogged social reform for well over a decade. With dismay, liberals watched the dismantling of many major social programs from the New Deal during World War II. For example, the Works Progress Administration (WPA), the Public Works Administration (PWA), the Civilian Conservation Corps (CCC), and the National Youth Administration (NYA) were all gone by 1943 (Day, 1999). These programs were part of the precedent-breaking Federal Emergency Relief Act, which, for the first time, established a system of federal relief. These agencies were established under the direction of a social worker in New York—Harry Hopkins—and had set about tackling the problem of aid for the unemployed (Blum, Catton, Morgan, Schlesinger, Stampp, & Woodward, 1968).

During McCarthyism, the Internal Security Act (McCarran Act) was passed in Congress, which established six concentration camps to house political prisoners. Imprisonment was allowed without trial for anyone suspected of treason. Thousand of teachers, social workers, newspapermen, screenwriters, and government workers were found guilty of nothing more than organizing unions, attending a radical meeting, or supporting liberal causes. Scores lost their jobs for refusing to cooperate with investigatory committees. This pressure caused the labor movement to pull back from radical action, and many renounced social programs; while, at the same time, libraries removed controversial books, and teaching communism or socialism was barred (Jansson, 1997).

From 1945 to 1970, Americans saw war becoming the basis for economic prosperity, with the federal government spending 69% of its total budget on defense ($1 trillion). The Kennedy-Johnson era saw a dramatic increase in the defense budget with the Korean War, 1950–1953, and the Vietnam War that plagued President Johnson in the 1960s. At the end of the 1960s, 10% of all jobs were tied to the defense budget. Tension was mounting as we saw young people's lives traded for monetary profit, while we invaded foreign countries in the name of economic prosperity. It was this tension, leading to people asking why, that lead to the eruption of the social revolution of the 1960s (Day, 1999).

The Kennedy Years

Kennedy's presidential win in 1960 looked like the sign of a new era of liberalism. In truth, despite his liberal oratories and expressed concern about poverty, Kennedy straddled the political fence until forced to take a stand. Political tug-of-wars occurred. His Democratic Party lost power in the South among Dixiecrats opposing social programs that benefited people of color and among white urban workers, who had traditionally been Democrats, because of Roosevelt's social insurance programs. Tension arose between black urban Democrats and white erstwhile Democrats as they competed for the same jobs. The risk of helping black urban poor proved too great a task for Kennedy because he was unwilling to alienate the white urban workers and the southern aristocracy (Day, 1999). Moreover, Kennedy, coming from a wealthy Boston family and having attended private schools, had a limited understanding of poverty and racism. While a congressman and senator in the postwar era, he had rarely assumed leadership roles on domestic issues. He was ambivalent in his orientation to social reform because his wealthy, businessman father had had a conflicted relationship with Roosevelt. Kennedy regarded New Deal reforms as outmoded in an affluent era, believing that problems of poverty involved intergenerational pockets of poverty in inner cities and rural areas (Jansson, 1997).

Not until he was forced to look at the facts that his own investigators brought to him, in the summer of 1963, did he get off the political fence. It was no longer possible to ignore the fact that poverty was widespread and that people of color were being systematically discriminated against in all facets of American life (Day, 1999). From a televised address, June 1, 1963, Kennedy said:

> This nation was founded by men of many nations and backgrounds. It was founded on the principle that all men are created equal, and that the rights of every man are diminished when the rights of one man are threatened. (Sorensen, 1988, p. 192)

From a special message to the Congress on Civil Rights and Job Opportunities, June 19, 1963, he said:

> That is a daily insult which has no place in a country proud of its heritage—the heritage of the melting pot, of equal rights, of one nation and one people. No one has been barred on account of his race from fighting or dying for America—there

are no 'white' or 'colored' signs on the foxholes or graveyards of battle. . . . For these reasons, I am today proposing, as part of the Civil Rights Act of 1963, a provision to guarantee all citizens equal access to the services and facilities of hotels, restaurants, places of amusement, and retail establishments. . . . (pp. 199–201)

Kennedy had campaigned on a promise to get the country "moving again" toward new frontiers and was highly critical of the 1950s and the neglect of social problems. In his inaugural address of 1961, Kennedy asked the nation to bear the burden in the struggle against the common enemies of man: tyranny, poverty, disease, and war. He challenged the nation to extend the hand of hope to the poor and the depressed. His pleas resonated among many citizens, especially the young people, and helped to revive faith in social action and reform (Axinn & Levin, 1997; Trattner, 1999).

Kennedy was much more open to black appeals for justice than President Eisenhower had been. The Kennedy campaign reached out to blacks in a number of ways; for example, when Martin Luther King Jr. was jailed in Atlanta as a result of civil rights demonstrations, Kennedy telephoned his wife to express his concern. His brother Robert Kennedy had a role in getting King released from jail the day after his arrest. President Kennedy also expressed his support for the sit-ins and promised to issue an executive order against discrimination in housing built with federal assistance (Levine, 1996).

Kennedy won his presidency by a narrow margin, with the black votes playing an important part in his winning coalition. Nonetheless, because his margin was so narrow, Kennedy owed debts to many interests and had to be careful not to offend any of them. It took heavy pressure from the civil rights movement before Kennedy took strong steps against racial discrimination (Levine, 1996).

As the country moved into the 1960s, the mood of the nation began to change. The optimism of the postwar years had started to slide, and, in 1964, President Johnson declared a war on poverty. This was a rather sudden turn of events resulting from a variety of factors. There were a series of recessions, unemployment rates rose, and citizens began to awaken to the fact that poverty was indeed more widespread than they had realized (Axinn & Levin, 1997).

During this time, the popular art of the nation began to change form. Two examples are pop art and the paintings of Norman Rockwell. *Pop art* reflected the times with an expression of society that put less emphasis on breeding, formal education, and wealth than it did on presentation. Size was an important feature, with repetition and magnification the standard. The imagery is direct and simple, omitting details, but little is left to the imagination. Pop art was a celebration of reality, dismissing pretension. It was used for commercial advertising and reflected the mirth and joy of the time (Rublowsky, 1965).

Norman Rockwell, a commercial artist, painted for commercial gain. His work, which tells single-frame stories in human details without the use of words, depicts 20th-century American culture. For example, one of his works depicts Ruby Bridges, an African American who, at age six, in November,

1960, walked into an all-white elementary school in New Orleans to integrate it. She was escorted by 75 federal marshals as she bravely withstood jeers and curses of segregationists.*

Despite the upswing in the nation's mood, mainstream America clung to its notion of an affluent society. Kenneth Galbraith went so far as to imply that poverty was not systemic. He identified what he called "case" poverty brought on by personal deficits such as ill health, lack of education, or even racial or sexual discrimination. This was opposed to what he called "insular" poverty that supposedly rose from structural unemployment and differential unemployment rates. No matter which definition one used, the problem was seen as employability rather than as poverty per se (Axinn & Levin, 1997).

Counter to Galbraith's claim of affluence, Michael Harrington, one of the liberal scholars and intellects of the time claimed otherwise. In his provocative book *The Other America: Poverty in the United States* (1977), he tells of two nations: one a culture of affluence, enjoying the highest standard of life in the world, the other a culture of poverty. The country is caught in a paradox, says Harrington. Because the country's poverty

> is not so deadly, because so many are enjoying a decent standard of life, there is indifference and blindness to the plight of the poor. . . . At precisely that moment in history where for the first time a people have the material ability to end poverty, they lack the will to do so. They cannot see; they cannot act. The consciences of the well-off are the victims of affluence; the lives of the poor are the victims of a physical and spiritual misery. (p. 167)

The response to poverty slowly emerged with a programmatic emphasis on employment. The focus was on opening up employment opportunities and the upgrading of labor market skills of the poor (Axinn & Levin, 1997):

THE WAR ON POVERTY

The Economic Opportunity Act of 1964

88th Congress—2nd Session, Document No. 86

AN ACT

To mobilize the human and financial resources of the

Nation to combat poverty

in the United States

Be it enacted by the Senate and the House of Representatives of the United States of American in Congress assembled. That this Act may be cited as the "Economic Opportunity Act of 1964."

---

*Ruby Bridges was honored with the Presidential Citizens Medal for her activist work by President Clinton in a ceremony at the White House in January 2001. She currently runs the nonprofit Ruby Bridges Foundation, visiting schools across the country to share her story with young people, promoting racial reconciliation.

FINDINGS AND DECLARATION OF PURPOSE

SEC. 2. Although the economic well-being and prosperity of the United States have progressed to a level surpassing any achieved in world history, and although these widely shared benefits are widely shared throughout the Nation, poverty continues to be the lot of a substantial number of our people. The United States can achieve its full economic and social potential as a nation only if every individual has the opportunity to contribute to the full extent of life's capabilities and to participate in the workings of our society. It is, therefore, the policy of the United States to eliminate the paradox of poverty in the midst of plenty in this Nation by opening to everyone the opportunity for education and training, the opportunity to work, and the opportunity to live in decency and dignity. It is the purpose of this Act to strengthen, supplement, and coordinate efforts in furtherance of that policy. (Axinn & Levin, 1997, pp. 256–257)

It was during this time that social revolution erupted. Students rioted against their schools as people of color staged demonstrations demanding equality. Welfare and economic rights became intertwined with civil rights in a new ideological struggle for human rights. Pragmatic politicians expanded civil rights by developing new social programs. Presidents Kennedy and Johnson joined in claiming that our nation had the power to create a great society (Day, 1999).

President Johnson spoke to the graduating class of the University of Michigan announcing his dramatic blueprint for the Great Society:

. . . The Great Society rests on abundance and liberty for all. It demands an end to poverty and racial injustice, to which we are totally committed in our time. But that is just the beginning. The Great Society is a place where every child can find knowledge to enrich his mind and to enlarge his talents. . . . It is a place where the city of man serves not only the needs of the body and the demands of commerce but the desire for beauty and the hunger for community. . . . It is a place where men are more concerned with the quality of their goals than the quantity of their goods. But most of all, the Great Society is not a safe harbor, a resting place, a final objective, a finished work. It is a challenge constantly renewed, beckoning us toward a destiny where the meaning of our lives matches the marvelous products of our labor. (Torricelli & Carroll, 1999, p. 256)

Significant Legislation of the Time   Even though many of the programs and legislation that sprung up during the Kennedy-Johnson era did not survive, many were of national significance. In the spring of 1961, Kennedy created the President's Committee on Juvenile Delinquency and Youth Crime, leading to the passage of the Juvenile Delinquency and Youth Offenses Control Act. The Act helped fund and operate projects for the prevention and treatment of delinquency in inner-city neighborhoods, including Mobilization for Youth. Two years later, Congress enacted the Mental Retardation Facilities and Community Mental Health Centers Act, providing funds for research, training, and the construction and staffing of community mental health centers throughout the United States (Trattner, 1999).

Of significance, too, were the 1962 Public Welfare Amendments to the Social Security Act. More familiarly known as the Social Service Amendments, these measures increased federal support to the states for the provision by local welfare departments of casework job training, job placement, and other soft services to public assistance recipients. Unfortunately, because most of the measures did not deal with the social, economic, and demographic forces that were responsible for the increase in the welfare rolls and for the continuation of poverty, they failed (Trattner, 1999). The answer to the question of why there are poor among us lies in our understanding of the power construct: who has the power, why they have it, and how they keep it. People are not poor because they lack resources or adequate services; they are poor because they lack the power to control their lives. Poverty is a structural aspect of a capitalistic society, and many people are conditioned by the institutions to conform to being poor. That conditioning, in part, stems from structural barriers such as chronic unemployment, a lack of access to quality education and health care, and dependency on governmental assistance programs (Chisom & Washington, 1997). This discussion on poverty and race provides the backdrop for a strengths analysis at the end of the chapter of some of the programs stemming from the war on poverty and the civil rights movement.

In his commencement address at Howard University, June 4, 1965, President Johnson proclaimed:

> You do not take a person who for years has been hobbled by chains and liberate him, bring him up to the starting line of a race and then say, "You are free to compete with the others," and still justly believe that you have been completely fair. Thus it is not enough just to open the gates of opportunity. All our citizens must have the ability to walk through those gates. This is the next and the more profound stage of the battle for civil rights. We seek not just freedom but opportunity. We seek not just legal equity but human ability, not just equality as a right and a theory but equality as a fact and equality as a result. (Hampton & Fayer, 1990, p. 621)

Popular at the time was the Economic Opportunity Act (EOA), or the antipoverty bill, which established the Office of Economic Opportunity (OEO), calling for the creation of Volunteers in Service to America (VISTA), a domestic peace corps; a Job Corps for school dropouts; a Neighborhood Youth Corps for jobless teenagers; Community Action Programs (CAPs) designed to empower the poor by securing their participation in the creation and operation of community actions agencies (CAAs) to combat poverty in their communities; and several other programs to fight poverty (Trattner, 1999).

Perhaps the most important, albeit controversial, the CAPs were defined as those that promised progress toward the elimination of poverty, provided for maximum feasible participation of the residents of the geographic areas of group members covered, and were conducted by public or private nonprofit community action organizations. The initial popularity stemmed from the CAPs' ability to fund projects administered by public and voluntary agencies freed from the administrative control of city halls and united funds. Popular programs emerged—for example, an Upward Bound program to encourage bright children who lived in the Projects to go to college; Operation Head Start, a project to give preschool training to children; and special programs of grants and loans to low-income rural families and migrant workers (Axinn & Levin, 1997). Head Start has continued to assist preschool children for the last 3½ decades.

Other programs that came into existence during this period have gone on to have lasting effects. Among them is Title XVIII, the medicare amendments to the Social Security Act, approved by President Johnson on July 30, 1965. Another program that also aided the older adults was the Older Americans Act. Among other things, this Act subsidized a variety of programs and services for older adults at the state level, including those who were homebound, and established a national network of Area Agencies on Aging (AAA). The AAA served as a foundation on which other programs and services could be built and still exists today (Trattner, 1999).

The great optimism and hope for The New Frontier and The Great Society and the call for the "unconditional war on poverty" declared by Johnson fell with a resounding thud on the nation. The Public Welfare Amendments of 1962 and the EOA fell short of ending poverty. The welfare crisis continued as programs fell to the wayside. Such optimistic and hopeful measures as the Elementary and Secondary Education Act of 1965, the Higher Education Act of the same year, and the 1966 Demonstration (Model) Cities and Metropolitan Development Act did not last long enough to get off the relief rolls and onto the tax rolls (Trattner, 1999).

The poem "The Grate Society" by George Bowering gives one viewpoint of the time:

> The Pentagon's
> Anti-personnel bombs
> Are made in
> Equal-opportunity factories
> Fragments for the war on poverty.

(McGovern & Snyder, 1969)

The burst of idealism lasted less than a decade. The internal political stresses of the war on poverty along with the disastrous and expensive war in Vietnam led to a renewed backlash of conservatism undermining the 1960s inspired movements. All too soon, welfare cutbacks and civil repression returned (Day, 1999). Lest we get ahead of ourselves, let us examine what took place during the civil rights movement and how it shaped future events.

Civil Rights

To place the civil rights movement into perspective, we need to explore its status before the Kennedy era. In 1948, Southern Democrats led by Strom Thurmond were successful at challenging the Democratic Party's support of civil rights when they defeated Truman's bill to reestablish the Fair Employment Practices Commission, which eliminated segregation in public transportation and outlawed poll taxes. The hostility toward civil rights prevailed throughout the Eisenhower administration, even though a federal antilynching law was passed in 1951. In both the North and the South, segregation was deeply ingrained and fostered economic and political oppression. What this translated into was that the nonwhite median income in 1947 was 51% that of white families. In 1952, it was 60% that of whites, decreasing by 1962 to 56% (Day, 1999). While the income disparity between the races is shocking, black American history casts it in a more positive light in that income for blacks Americans had risen significantly from a low of 41% of white income in 1939 to 51% in 1947 (Levin, 1996). Unemployment figures were bleak. In 1952, 5.4% of African Americans were unemployed, compared to 3.1% of their white counterparts; in 1960, 10.2% versus 4.9%; and in 1964, African American workers had 11% unemployment versus 4.6% white unemployment. Unemployment for African Americans generally remained double that of white unemployment even through the poverty programs of the late 1960s (Day, 1999).

The NAACP adopted a policy of taking grievances to court, which increased the legal rights of people of color. Among those who battled against segregation were Thurgood Marshall, Walter White, and William Hastie. In three important cases in the 1950s, the Court struck down segregation in schools and dining cars, stating that equal rights were more than physical facilities. The 1954 case of *Brown v. Topeka Board of Education* ruled that separate educational facilities were inherently unequal, overturning the separate-but-equal doctrine of *Plessy v. Ferguson* (Day, 1999). The *Brown v. Board of Education* decision said that states and localities could no longer maintain school systems that separated pupils by their race. The Court's reasoning was that the schools set aside for blacks would always be inferior and would send the message to black children that whites did not want them in their schools. Moreover, even if separate schools for blacks were well-financed and academically sound, the problem would not be solved. The justices concluded that isolation would generate feelings of inferiority as to their status in the community and that it may affect their "hearts and minds in a way unlikely ever to be undone" (Hacker, 1995, p. 166).

The overturn of *Plessy v. Ferguson* revitalized the white backlash with vigilante groups, including the Ku Klux Klan and White Citizen's councils. When elected police and justice officials refused to reinforce the federal rulings, blacks realized that legal victories were not enough. The resistance of Governor Orval Faubus to the young people trying to enter Central High School in Little Rock provoked President Eisenhower to send federal troops to enforce the ruling. Ten years after the *Brown* decision, only about 2% of segregated schools had been integrated, and, just as alarming, 15 years later, 80% of blacks youth were still in separated facilities (Day, 1999).

Modest, Incremental Changes

Other small inroads against bias occurred during this time. Important symbolic victories came with the integration of professional sports. Progress at state and local levels occurred with 33 cities forming human relations commissions to ease racial tensions and discrimination in the six years following the riots of 1943. Black and white churches—primarily their women's auxiliaries—worked with other organizations to eradicate lynchings. With the formation of the biracial Southern Regional Council, made up of clergy and professionals, Jim Crow was eventually eliminated. Segregated seating on buses had ended in the North in 1946 with a Supreme Court ruling as a result of *Morgan v. Virginia* (Levine, 1996).

In the 1940s and 1950s, Black schoolteachers demanded and won equal pay in some southern cities, some voluntary integration occurred in more than 40 private colleges, and blacks were admitted to parks, museums, and public libraries. Other changes included the banning of the white primary system that excluded blacks from voting in Democratic primaries and the elimination of the poll tax in several upper southern states. Consequently, in 1952, the number of black registered voters was one million, or 20%, up 5% from 1940. The increase in black voters resulted in a handful of blacks being elected to city council and some being appointed to minor local positions. New trials were granted for southern blacks because of the exclusion of blacks from juries; for the first time in decades, blacks began to appear on juries in some parts of the South. By 1955, laws had been passed in six southern states to restrict the Ku Klux Klan (Levine, 1996). However, racism does not obey the law and the Klan rode largely unfettered.

Many northern and western states and localities came under attack for discrimination; and, between 1945 and 1953, 12 of 30 cities passed fair employment laws. This was, in large part, due to pressure from black and Jewish groups as well as some Protestant and Catholic organizations. By 1949, 18 states had banned segregation on buses and in restaurants, hotels, educational institutions, parks, libraries, and places of amusement. With the increase in the black electorate outside of the South, two new blacks joined William Dawsom of Chicago in the House of Representatives: Adam Clayton Powell Jr. from Harlem in 1944 and Charles C. Diggs Jr. from Detroit in 1954. Both were Democrats. In the late 1940s, the Red Cross stopped their practice of labeling its blood by race and many medical, legal, and other professional associations opened their doors to blacks (Levine, 1996).

As significant as postwar progress was, it barely scratched the surface of racial discrimination. The black middle class grew, but most remained poor. Despite some gains, the vast majority of blacks in the South still could not vote due mostly to intimidation and discriminatory use of literacy tests. The mid-1950s saw barely a dent in segregation and other forms of discrimination in the Lower South. Segregation in the North was in decline mostly because the resources did not exist to carry out strong enforcement programs to ban employment discrimination. More bad news was that few states and cities took action against housing discrimination. Leadership from the federal government, in part, was needed to wage war against racial bias and its consequences (Levine, 1996).

In the meantime, with the entrance of Martin Luther King Jr.'s nonviolence tactics onto the scene, young people in the South became increasingly active in demonstrations and sit-ins. After the Montgomery boycott, King helped to organize the Southern Christian Leadership Conference, which became the central organizing body for passive resistance (Day, 1999).

Sit-Ins

Civil rights history was made on February 1, 1960, when four black students from North Carolina Agricultural and Technical College, a black school, sat down at a whites-only counter in Greensboro. They remained until closing time without receiving service, and this simple demand eventually sparked a direct action movement against discrimination. The civil rights struggle went from the courthouse to the street, and American race relations were revolutionized (Levine, 1996).

Sit-in movements led by black college students spread quickly, reaching seven southern states by the end of February. Students organized, independent of the established civil rights movement, forming the Student Nonviolent Coordinating Committee (SNCC). Their philosophy was based on the principles of racial equality, integration, and nonviolence and were joined by the northern-based CORE. Martin Luther King Jr.'s SCLC assisted them financially, and the NAACP Legal Defense Fund provided the newly organized SNCC with legal assistance. At the same time, the NAACP lobbied Congress for civil rights legislation (Levine, 1996).

The sit-ins spread to all the southern states and a few northern ones within 18 months. The goal was to confront just about any kind of segregated facility, including theaters, churches, swimming pools, retail stores of all types, shopping centers, and drive-in movies. The demonstrators often became targets of white violence; but, with the support of economic boycotts, they managed to desegregate their sites (Levine, 1996).

The civil rights efforts went from sit-ins to other forms of direct action. The Supreme Court in *Boynton v. Virginia* (1960) extended earlier rulings against segregation in interstate transportation. This declared that the ban on Jim Crow applied to stations and terminals, as well as vehicles; and, in 1961, the Congress of Racial Equality (CORE) made the ruling a reality by launching a series of "freedom rides." There was much publicity, and the freedom riders became an unwelcome distraction from foreign policy matters for the Kennedy administration. The persistence of the efforts led Robert Kennedy, the U.S. attorney general, to ask the Interstate Commerce Commission to begin carrying out the Court's 1960 ruling against segregated facilities in interstate transportation. Subsequently, the Justice Department had all Jim Crow bus terminal signs taken down, ending interstate transportation segregation by the end of 1962 (Levine, 1996). Some lyrics from one of the freedom riders of 1961 going from Alabama to Mississippi follow:

> I'm taking a ride on the Greyhound bus line,
> I'm a-riding the front seat to Jackson this time.
> Hallelujah, I'm a-travelin',
> Hallelujah, aint it fine?
> Hallelujah, I'm a travelin',
> Down Freedom's main line.

> (Hampton & Fayer, 1990, p. 93)

With the federalization of the Mississippi National Guard to see that James Meredith was admitted safely to the University of Mississippi at Oxford after his acceptance, the pressure continued to grow in the civil rights movement. Finally, in November 1962, the president carried out his campaign promise to issue an executive order banning discrimination in the sale or rental of federally financed housing. However, because the order did not include privately financed housing, it covered less than 20% of all residents (Levine, 1996).

Martin Luther King Jr.

By the early 1960s, Martin Luther King Jr. was the generally acknowledged leader of the nonviolent civil rights movement. On April 3, 1963, King took his campaign to Birmingham, Alabama, with participants demanding desegregation and equal employment opportunity through marches, rallies, sit-ins, and boycotts. King was arrested; from jail, we wrote his famous "Letter From a Birmingham Jail" in response to criticism for his methods and for creating tension between the races. He wrote:

> We who engage in nonviolent direct action are not the creators of tension. We merely bring to the surface the hidden tension that is already alive. We bring it out in the open, where it can be seen and dealt with. . . . Injustice must be exposed . . . to the light of human conscience and the air of national opinion before it can be cured. (Quoted in Levine, 1996, p. 187)

Two hundred thousand blacks, whites, and other people of color showed up in Washington, D.C., for a demonstration that culminated with a historic speech by Martin Luther King Jr. in a march for jobs and freedom and an interracial display of solidarity (Axinn & Levin, 1996). The rally was the largest held in the nation's capital to that time, and King's address became one of the most famous orations in American history. With the theme of "I have a dream," King eloquently described his vision of a prejudice-free nation ending with the cry, "Free at last! Free at last! Thank God almighty, we are free at last!" (Levine, 1996). In the August 28, 1963 address, King said:

> . . . I say to you today, my friends, so even though we face the difficulties of today and tomorrow, I still have a dream. It is a dream deeply rooted in the American meaning of its creed, "We hold these truths to be self-evident, that all men are created equal." I have a dream that one day on the red hills of Georgia sons of former slaves and the sons of former slave owners will be able to sit down together at the table of brotherhood. I have a dream that one day even the state of Mississippi, a state sweltering with the heat of injustice, sweltering with the heat of oppression, will be transformed into an oasis of freedom and justice. I have a dream that my four little children will one day live in a nation where they will not be judged by the color of their skin, but the content of their character. . . . (Hampton & Fayer, 1990, p. 167)

A New York policeman, William H. Johnson Jr., who provided security for the march, said, ". . . But Dr. King brought to life the hope that someday we could walk together hand in hand, that despite all this, one day we could smooth out our differences. It was a matter of being inspired and moved. It was an awfully sentimental and spiritual experience for me" (Hampton & Fayer, 1990, p. 168).

President Kennedy responded to the march:

> One cannot help but be impressed with the deep fervor and the quiet dignity that characterize the thousands who have gathered in the nation's capital from across the country to demonstrate their faith and confidence in our democratic form of government. . . . The cause of twenty million Negroes has been advanced by the program conducted so appropriately before the nation's shrine to the Great Emancipator, but even more significant is the contribution to all mankind. (Sorensen, 1988, p. 202).

Obstacles Emerge

The mid-1960s brought a growing number of black Americans who began to reject the goal of nonviolence and integration. Angry black leaders denounced white Americans, including liberals, as incurable racists with no intention of accepting blacks as equals. The stance was for black Americans to work together to build their self-pride, their own economy, and their own communities. Some of the new black voices argued that blacks must use any means necessary, "including violence, to defeat racism" (Levine, 1996, p. 195).

In mid-1966, Stokely Carmichael, who lost his bid for the leadership of SNCC, questioned the value of white alliances and rejected nonviolence. He began using the slogan "black power," and soon "black power" advocates described themselves as "black nationalists." Some "black power" supporters advocated violence; others did not, but most rejected integration, thus rejecting the civil rights coalition of blacks and white liberals (Levine, 1996). Also in 1966, Malcolm X, described by his followers as "Our Black Shining Prince," (Hampton & Fayer, 1990, p. 243) founded the Black Panther 10-point party program:

> . . . to bring about an immediate end to police brutality and murder of black people, power to determine the destiny of black communities, the need for full employment, financial restitution for slavery and black suffering, decent housing, education that reflected black history and the black experience, exemption for black men from military service, release of all blacks held in prison, a demand for black juries for black defendants, and a demand for land, bread, housing, education, and the formation of a black colony in which only black colonial subjects would be allowed to participate to determine the will of the black people as their "national destiny." (p. 350)

Civil rights leaders attacked "black power" and "black nationalism." Morally, they condemned them for rejecting the idea of a common humanity. Politically, they argued that "black separatism" would never work because black Americans lacked the necessary resources to establish a separate economy. Blacks lost political allies as a result of white backlash. The bulk of the backlash came in the mid- to late 1960s in a reaction to "black power" rhetoric and the ghetto riots and included white moderates and liberals as well as conservatives (Levine, 1996).

In September 1966, Congress responded with the Senate defeating a fair housing bill that would have allowed the secretary of housing and urban development to order the end of discriminatory practices after an investigation. Congress also imposed new restrictions on the use of antipoverty funds, and, in November, Republicans gained 47 seats in the House and 3 in the Senate. Most of the defeated Democrats were liberals who had supported the civil rights agenda. Ronald Reagan was elected governor in California, seemingly as a reward for opposing the Civil Rights Act of 1964, and his severe condemnation of the Watts riot in 1965 (Levine, 1996).

STRENGTHS PERSPECTIVE

It is a given that there needs to be careful problem definition for effective social policy. As we have learned so far, the missing component typically has been the factoring in of the strengths and resources of the people and the environment in the formulating process of policy making (Chapin, 1995). That missing component will be used to explain why, in part, many of the reform programs of the 1960s failed to meet their objectives. While we can never underestimate the power of politics, in terms of the directions of social policy, there are other factors that can make or break their effectiveness in correcting the problems for which they are designed.

In the process of defining the social problem, a labeling process occurs. As part of that process, a societal predisposition creates a social construction of reality that fits the needs of the people in power to transform people into problems (Chapin, 1995) and programs into failures. For example, poverty can be conceptualized as a pathological condition needing a cure, and "families who have systematically been denied access to employment, education, and health care become 'the underclass' " (p. 506).

Most people would agree that poverty is a social ill; however, the pathological spin placed on it during the war on poverty tended to blame the victim. Referring to our earlier discussion of why people are poor, we know that it is because they lack power, not resources. Resources and services are necessary, certainly; but, without the power to control their lives, resources and services become bandages that keep people downtrodden. We now review some of the policies that were signed into law during the Great Society era.

The Equal Employment Opportunity Act

As the number of poor were counted, the special plight of the so-called minority population became dramatically clear. For black Americans, the risk of poverty was three times greater than for white Americans. One of the major factors was discriminatory employment practices. The civil rights movement continued to bring to light the dire consequences of social, political, and economic discrimination and what the consequences of this discrimination were for unemployment and relief rolls. Included in the Civil Rights Act of 1964 was a section prohibiting racial, sexual, or ethnic discrimination in employment (Axinn & Levin, 1997). President Johnson issued Executive Order 11246 in September 1965 stating:

> . . . to promote the full realization of equal employment opportunity through a positive, continuing program in each executive department and agency. . . [and] will take affirmative action to ensure that applicants are employed and that employees are treated during employment, without regard to their race, creed, color, or national origin. (Hampton & Fayer, p. 621)

Under the Equal Employment Opportunity Act, Johnson promised to eliminate discrimination in employment, but this promise was not aggressively implemented. The Department of Labor was not given a significant role in monitoring federal contracts for discrimination. Under Title VII, the Equal

Employment Opportunity Commission (EEOC) was established for this purpose but not empowered to initiate suits until 1972 (Jansson, 1997).

The Office of Equal Opportunity

The Equal Opportunity Act (EOA), or the antipoverty bill, was passed, establishing the Office of Economic Opportunity (OEO). The OEO ran most of the antipoverty programs of the time. While there was valuable assistance given to poor blacks and other poor people, not enough funding was provided to make a great difference for those most in need. The OEO spent an average of only $70 a year on each poor person, and the funding quickly faced cutbacks largely because of the escalating cost of the Vietnam War (Levine, 1996).

The EOA was badly conceived and never fully understood by many of its commanders. The Act lacked hard-core political support and, like other programs before it, failed because, in part, it was designed not to change society but to change its victims. The new approach that was promised to end poverty was, in fact, an old approach, which sought the cause of poverty within the individual with the strategy of helping individuals to change themselves so they could function in an apparently well-functioning economy. So, what we had was not a war on poverty but a minor skirmish. It was a war declared but never fought. Much of the appropriated money was squandered or caught in bureaucratic red tape, delaying tactics, and political imbroglios (Axinn & Levin, 1997; Trattner, 1999).

In the meantime, with the civil rights legislation and the antipoverty programs at work, Martin Luther King Jr. took the civil rights cause to the North; and, as he did, he came to realize that poverty was more difficult to fight than Jim Crow practices. He quickly saw that most of the Chicago demonstrators could not afford the houses in the neighborhood that they marched on, regardless of racial barriers. It was clear that it would take a national commitment of many billions of dollars to confront poverty. Some of King's followers did not believe that this sort of federal commitment could be won by demonstrations that had brought down Jim Crow in the South. Bayard Rustin, one of the many black leaders, believed that the elimination of poverty could only be attained through the political system with the African American voting power, along with forging coalitions with the labor movement and other allies (Levine, 1996).

King became disillusioned while working in Chicago in 1966. He was struck in the head by a rock and later commented, "I've been in many demonstrations all across the South, but I can say that I have never seen—even in Mississippi and Alabama—mobs as hostile and hate-filled as I've seen in Chicago" (quoted in Levine, 1996, p. 205). The lack of success he had in Chicago and the cutbacks in federal programs for the poor in 1966 and 1967 led King to wonder whether America would be able to render economic justice to blacks (Levine, 1996).

Policy Themes

So we see, again and again, the overriding theme of poverty and its prominence in the American society. "Year after year, the poverty groups were identified as children, the aged, large families, and families headed by women. A double risk was suffered by rural families and men and women of color. However, urban and rural poverty were equally devastating. Surprisingly, work—even full-time work—was no guarantee against ". . . poverty. . . . The 'working poor' became identified as a poverty group" (Axinn & Levin, 1997). The other theme that emerged in this era is what we call "rebound." People, most notably the disenfranchised and those who advocated for them, rebounded from despair to hope and back to despair. Like the Great Depression and the resulting New Deal programs established to assist the poor and the needy, the Great Society programmatically came to the aid of the poor; and, like the New Deal, the conservative faction, in part, dismantled them.

What were some of the specific reasons the programs were dismantled? Despite the national attention paid to poverty and the need for its elimination and the many programs brought about through social policy for its elimination, why did it persist? Ryan (1971/76, p. 6) refers to a generic process of blaming the victim that is applied to almost every American problem. For example, "The 'multi problem' poor, it is claimed, suffer the psychological effects of impoverishment, the 'culture of poverty,' and the deviant value system of the lower classes; consequently, though unwittingly, they cause their own troubles." From this viewpoint, the obvious fact that poverty is primarily an absence of money can be overlooked or set aside (Ryan, 1971/76).

As we look to connect policy to practice, along with highlighting human needs rather than social problems, let us talk about what is normal and see if we can tease out how labeling occurs. Who defines what is normal in terms of human behavior in our society? If we look to scientific knowledge for the meaning, we see human behavior as something that can be measured, tested, and objectively verified. Social workers, however, tell us that human behavior is dynamic rather than static with interplay between events and the meanings we attach to them. For example, the lack of an adequate education or job training typically results in low-paying jobs or chronic unemployment. The lack of adequate day care can prevent a mother from showing up at work. The fear of not having medical coverage (Medicaid) for her children could prevent her from seeking paid work. The meaning of reality for the individual is shaped and negotiated as a social process. It is from scientific knowledge, then, that problems are deemed identifiable, measurable entities susceptible to being investigated and solved. More to the point, however, is that it is unrealistic to set a standard for normalcy when dealing with human behavior. It is this measurement of a standard set for normal behavior that assigns labels and creates the problems. Social workers are then commissioned to deal with the problem—people who do not fit the norm, the homeless, the poor, the mentally ill, the disabled, the learning impaired, the sick, and so on (Weick, 1992).

Certainly, the people we have mentioned are in need of assistance, so let us look at how strengths-based policies and programs would look. First, we consider what typically goes into the planning of policy and what the actual policy consequences are in terms of services and programs. We use the example of social welfare policies and their effects on black Americans. In the planning stage, the tendency is to look at the people who will be served rather than the system(s) that serves them. A commonly held belief of poor people is that they are lazy, not motivated to change, or that they have too many babies. Policies are then constructed from these types of labels or stereotypes rather than addressing the systemic changes that are necessary for self-empowerment in order to really help lift people out of poverty.

As is the case in direct practice so often, policymakers know very little about their African American constituents for whom they are formulating policies. They do not see the importance of learning about their culture and history. The importance of knowing the history helps foster sensitivity to the plight of black Americans, which in turn gives them a sense of historical continuity that can help them build productively on what has been learned from the past (Carlton-LaNey, 1999).

For strengths-based policy, we begin by looking at the strengths and resources of the communities as well as the environment:

Strengths

- *The ability to pull together for mutual help and support.* Because African Americans have been overwhelmingly excluded from full participation in the social system, they have developed a dogged determination to take care of their own (Carlton-LaNey, 1999).
- *The ability to challenge the system.* There is an on-going struggle to dispel myths and to establish powerful social institutions along with strong role models for their people (Carlton-LaNey, 1999).
- *Race pride.* A historical legacy, race pride, race consciousness, and racial uplift have become part of many African American communities. This is taught and mentored, bringing with it a sense of self-empowerment (Carlton-LaNey, 1999) and leads to
- *Group solidarity.*

Resources

- Strong family ties
- Community collectives
- Churches
- Neighborhood-based agencies
- Schools

By being aware of these strengths and resources and factoring them into the early planning stages of social policy, the implementation of programs and services could take on a more comprehensive and appropriate meaning as we look at common human need. This information could be used to shape some systemic changes that could better serve the community.

Policy needs to address the poor quality of many urban public schools, the severe lack of jobs, and the discriminatory practices of many police officers if social and economic justice is to prevail. The aim of social policy should be the elimination of pessimism and feelings of powerlessness and hopelessness that have resulted as consequences of generational deprivation and bias that culminates in the destruction of the individual, families, and society at large (Allen-Meares & Burman, 1995). Factoring in existing strengths and resources and focusing on what works—what is right—rather than what is wrong could make a big difference in actual change.

Another factor in the process of establishing strengths-based policy is collaboration with community, literally using the community as the major informant of how to best meet its needs. This approach would allow practice to benefit from policy—a policy that would be based on the true needs and the establishment of services and programs to best meet those needs. One of the end results from this strengths-based approach would be programs and services that would send healthy people back to their respective communities with the tools necessary to apply what they have learned, through self-empowerment, to live and work in the community collectively, to be interdependent with each other and not so reliant upon outside resources for their survival. We build on these concepts in following chapters.

Some of the programs that came out of this era held the promise of strength-based policies. For example, by its very design, Community Action Programs were to lead to self-empowerment by securing the participation of the community in the creation and operation of community action agencies. Two more successful programs of the times that held strengths-based concepts were Head Start and the Older American's Act, both still fully functioning today.

SUMMARY

The 1960s and the political era of the Great Society under Presidents Kennedy and Johnson were full of hope and dynamic energy. Reform legislation and programs abounded, and the War on Poverty broadened the scope and dimension of social welfare programs and services. The civil rights movement reached its peak during this era, progress was made in eradicating poverty and discrimination, and there was good reason for despair to turn to hope of better things to come.

While the modern era of the civil rights movement was short-lived, a number of doors were opened during that brief period that created new opportunities for people of color—opportunities in education, jobs, housing, and policies. Thousands were able to walk through those doors, many of which were soon slammed shut. The efforts of the movement did, however, significantly increase the size of the minority middle class who represented a new and potentially powerful leadership for the future. Among them were educators, communicators, business people, social scientists, and political leaders. The presence of this new generation of highly skilled people is being felt today (Barndt, 1991).

With strengths-based social policies, the long-term goal is to guide people toward self-empowerment, which would lead people to having greater control over their environment and the resources that can improve the quality of their lives. When whites work toward creating strengths-based social policies that affect people of color, it is critically important that they remain accountable to the communities of color and get feedback from them as they push forward any agenda that has implications for all (Chisom & Washington, 1997).

REFERENCES

Allen-Meares, P., & Burman, S. (1995). The endangerment of African American men: An appeal for social action. *Social Work, 40,* 268–274.

Axinn, J., & Levin, H. (1997). *Social welfare: A history of the American response to need* (4th ed.). New York: Longman.

Barndt, J. (1991). *Dismantling racism: The continuing challenge to white America.* Minneapolis, MN: Augsburg Fortress.

Blum, J. M., Catton, B., Morgan, E. S., Schlesinger, A. M. Jr., Stampp, K. M., & Woodward, C. V. (1968). *The national experience: A history of the United States since 1865, part two* (2nd ed.). New York: Harcourt, Brace & World.

Carlton-LaNey, I. (1999). African American social work pioneers' response to need. *Social Work, 44,* 311–321.

Chapin, R. K. (1995). Social policy development: The strengths perspective. *Social Work, 40,* 506–514.

Chisom, R., & Washington, M. (1997). *Undoing racism: A philosophy of international social change.* (2nd ed.). New Orleans: The People's Institute Press.

Day, P. J. (1989). *A new history of social welfare.* Englewood Cliffs, NJ: Prentice Hall.

Day, P. J. (1999). *A new history of social welfare* (3rd ed.). Boston, MA: Allyn & Bacon.

Faulkner, A. O., Heisel, M. A., Holbrook, W., & Geismar, S. (1982). *When I was comin' up*. Hamden, CT: Archon Books.

Franklin, J. H., & Moss, A. A. (1994). *From slavery to freedom: A history of African Americans* (7th ed.). New York: McGraw-Hill.

Galbraith, J. K. (1984). *The affluent socity* (4th ed.), A Mentor Book. New York.

Gordon, L. (1998). How welfare became a dirty word. *New Global Development: Journal of International & Comparative Social Welfare, XIV*, 1–14.

Hacker, A. (1995). *Two nations: Black and white, separate, hostile, unequal* (2nd ed.). New York: Ballantine Books.

Hampton, H., & Fayer, S. (with Flynn, S). (1990). *Voices of freedom: An oral history of the civil rights movement from the 1950s through the 1980s*. New York: Bantam Books.

Harrington, M. (1977). *The Other America: Poverty in the United States*. New York, NY: Penguin Books.

Jansson, B. S. (1997). *The reluctant welfare state* (3rd ed.). Pacific Grove, CA: Brooks/Cole.

Levine, M. L. (1996). *African Americans and civil rights: From 1619 to the present*. Phoenix, AZ: The Oryx Press.

Martin, J. K., Roberts, R., Mintz, S., McMurry, L. O., & Jones, J. H. (1993). *America and its people: Volume two from 1865* (2nd ed.). New York: HarperCollins.

McGovern, R., & Snyder, R. (Eds.). (1969). *60 on the 60s: A decade's history in verse*. Ashland, OH: Ashland Poetry Press.

Mitchell, J. P. (Ed.). (1970). *Race riots in black and white*. Englewood Cliffs, NJ: Prentice-Hall.

Moon, E. L. (1994). *Untold tales, unsung heroes: An oral history of Detroit's African American community, 1918–1967*. Detroit, MI: Wayne State University Press.

Piven, F. F., & Cloward, R. A. (1971). *Regulating the poor: The function of public welfare*. New York: Vintage Books.

Rayside, D. (1998). *On the fringe: Gays and lesbians in politics*. London: Cornell University Press.

Ryan, W. (1971/76). *Blaming the victim*. Vintage Books: New York.

Rublowsky, J. (1965). *Pop art*. New York: Basic Books.

Sorensen, T. C. (1988). *Let the work go forth: The speeches, statements, and writings of John F. Kennedy*. New York: Delacorte Press.

Torricelli, R., & Carroll, A. (1999). *In our own words: Extraordinary speeches of the American century*. New York: Kodansha International.

Trattner, W. I. (1999). *From poor law to welfare state: A history of social welfare in America* (6th ed.). New York: The Free Press.

Weick, A. (1992). Building on a strengths perspective for social work. In D. Saleebey (Ed.) *The strengths perspective in social work*. 18, 26. New York: Longman.

Wilhoit, F. M. (1973). *The politics of massive resistance*. New York: George Braziller.

www.weisbroth.com/blacklisted/abouttheshow.htm, 1999.

A TURN TO THE RIGHT

The nation took a turn to the right, politically, with the presidential election of Republican Richard Nixon (1968–1974) and remained there for 24 years under the conservative leadership of Presidents Gerald Ford (1974–1976), Jimmy Carter (1977–1980), Ronald Reagan (1981–1988), and George Bush (1989–1992). This chapter focuses on the time period leading us into the

Reagan-Bush years and addresses the political struggles over issues posed by poverty as well as other social concerns. There is a little spillover into the Reagan-Bush years, but their administration is the focus of Chapter 11. Social work's role in organizing and representing women, racial minorities, and gays and lesbians is discussed in the context of welfare policy and is woven into the text throughout this chapter where appropriate.

A NATION IN TRANSITION

After four decades of activity, the yearning for social change and increased federal involvement in social welfare faded, resulting in the transition of a new arch conservative era. Increasing numbers of Americans had grown tired of decades of social turmoil and became resentful of the attention directed toward minorities and the poor. They felt that the middle-class values of thrift, hard work, and self-reliance had been assaulted, that the "welfare mess" continued in spite of federal social programs funneling billions of dollars into the inner cities to help the poor and unemployed, and that this had come about at the expense of "hard-working citizens" and of local and state governments. In their opinion, it was time for change and Richard Nixon seemed to be the person who mirrored the mood of those unhappy middle-class Americans (Day, 1999). What history tells, however, is that the very same groups that were poor in the 1950s and 1960s remained poor in the 1970s—blacks, Spanish-speaking people, the unemployed and the underemployed, the citizens of depressed regions, the aging, and Native Americans, the poorest of all (Harrington, 1977). Harrington (p. x) goes on to say:

> . . . [E]ven though the society has failed to redeem the pledges of the Sixties it has taken to celebrating paper triumphs over poverty. Thus in August of 1969 the Department of Commerce announced the happy news that the number of poverty-stricken had dropped from 39 million to 25 million in a matter of nine years. The only problem . . . is that the numbers prettied up the reality. This was a sign that, in the Seventies, America might be going back to the established procedures of the Eisenhower years, deluding itself with happy reports on the state of the nation. It was another ominous portent that one of Richard Nixon's top domestic advisers, Arthur Burns, said in the summer of 1969 that poverty is only an "intellectual concept" defined by "artificial statistics." That is precisely the kind of callous thinking that made the poor invisible in the first place. . . .

As a country, we have given witness to how we try to keep our poor invisible.

To understand the cruel prospects for poverty in the 1970s, it is necessary to go behind the optimism of the time with its juggling of the social books, which is easily done since this society, in one of its typical ironies, has spared no expense in recording its injustices (Harrington, 1977). Harrington (p. xi) goes on to challenge us, as a society, "to examine the official figures critically and to glimpse the human faces and the tragic tendencies that are hidden in them. Only then can we know how much still needs to be done." That examination is one of the goals of this book.

THE CONSERVATIVE ERA

Nixon was strongly attached to traditional values and the conservative approach. Other forces behind Nixon's elections were the growing unpopularity of Johnson's Vietnam policies and the divisions within the Democratic Party over the war and other matters (Trattner, 1999). After Nixon's election, which was fueled by a white backlash, particularly in the South, there were increasingly severe recessions that racked the economy during the 1970s, with the one of 1975 equal to the Great Depression, albeit softened by the Roosevelt social programs. An even more severe economic crisis occurred in 1981–82. Until 1975, unemployment averaged 5.4%, then jumped to 8.5%, returning to 5.8% in 1979. Employment trends saw manufacturing declining to 25% of all employment, with 17% of employment being in service occupations and the government employing 18% of all workers. During the 1970s, the gross national product grew from $982 billion to $2,369 billion, but, because of inflation, real median family income grew a mere 5%. The mid-1980s saw an overall unemployment rate of 7.8%, with twice that for African Americans (Day, 1999).

Nixon and the conservative Congress began their domestic reform by first dismantling the Office of Equal Opportunity (OEO) and next responding to cries for law and order (one of his campaign promises). They poured funds into law enforcement with part of the push being for law and order against civil dissidents. The surveillance and harassment of militant and radical communities and student groups were stepped up by Nixon's counterintelligence program, and, by the time of his reelection in 1972, most civil and human rights movements had ended, with the exception of the women's movement, which remained strong (Day, 1999).

The Conservative Influence on Civil Rights

Not only the economic trends posed problems for the civil rights movement. With the rapid expansion of the American economy from the end of World War II, other countries such as Japan and Germany began seriously to challenge American domination of world markets. At the same time (around 1970), America became less competitive because of a slowdown in productivity growth, which lead to a slowdown in the expansion of the economy, meaning fewer new jobs were being created. Furthermore, the average income of Americans stopped increasing, which meant that the economic pie no longer seemed to be enlarging. Many whites began to worry that a bigger slice for black Americans would mean a smaller piece for them. This further lead to more reluctance to support equal employment opportunities. These factors, along with government budgets becoming tighter, saw public spending to aid the poor decrease (Levine, 1996).

Nixon's surveillance and harassment of militant and radical communities helped to create controversies over how to enforce the civil rights laws of the 1960s, which often put black and white Americans on opposite sides of the fence. By 1970, most whites were probably accepting the principle of a color-blind policy under which everyone, regardless of race, would have an equal chance to vote and get a good education, a decent job, and more. However, under pressure from the NAACP Legal Defense and Educational Fund, along with other rights groups, various federal agencies and the federal courts began going beyond the color-blind approach and began requiring positive steps to eliminate the consequences of past discrimination. For example, employers guilty of past discrimination had to do more than simply stop discriminating; they had to raise the proportion of blacks in their workforce. Similarly, colleges now had to take positive steps to attract black students to their campuses. This type of approach, used in most areas of civil rights enforcement, was known as *affirmative action.* The effects of affirmative action and employment policies are discussed later in the chapter. The argument was that, after 300 years of oppression, whites could not fairly expect black Americans to compete on an equal basis; blacks needed, and were owed, special consideration. Furthermore, it was argued that a color-blind approach would allow whites to continue discriminating while claiming not to, because in many cases it would be impossible to prove intent (Levine, 1996).

Affirmative action was opposed by many whites and some blacks who believed that American society should be based on the principle of equal rights for individuals, regardless of the racial, religious, ethnic, or other group to which they might belong. Its critics maintained that affirmative action established the principle that members of certain groups had more rights than members of other groups and that represented reverse discrimination. In other words, just as whites had been given special rights in the past, now blacks were being given special rights. This controversy over affirmative action, along with the end of America's postwar economic boom, pulled white voters farther to the political right (Levine, 1996).

The Transition of the Civil Rights Movement   As the nation moved from the liberal sixties into the conservative seventies, we see from history that the struggle for civil rights for black Americans was the real force behind the civil rights movement. Indeed, the victories of blacks and their allies sparked the formation of new rights movements. This placed advocates of black equality in competition with new causes for public support, and one of the most important was the women's movement. With full knowledge that American society had systematically assaulted the dignity of black men for centuries, most black women were reluctant to become involved in the women's movement (Levine, 1996).

The reality was that many white women did not have a full understanding of the African American woman's unique place at this time in history; nor did the social work profession. In discussing the different experiences of black women in relation to feminism, Joseph (1980), an African American social worker, noted:

> . . . [L]imitations exist in social work if the paucity of literature can be taken as a gauge of practice in the field. The two main journals, *Social Casework* (in 1970) and *Social Work* (in 1972), both attempted to deal with the black experience and ethnicity, but little or no reference was made to the Black woman. A few years and some occasional articles later, in close proximity, both journals printed articles on feminism and social work. Again no reference was made to the Black woman, although in its special issue on women, *Social Work,* in an editorial, "Is It Sex, Race, or Class?" referred to the issue of racism but discounted its impact, stating the overriding problem as one of inequality based on sex. This perspective is defended as the editorial goes to some lengths to identify possible sources of conflict between the movements, as if objective competition for energies and resources were a real factor. It then reinforces the notion of separate agendas for minority women by calling for compromises to "avoid conflict." The opportunity was missed to stress sources of commonality as women, to acknowledge and build upon the historical linkages between the movements, and to stress the necessity not for compromise but for collaboration on the overall objective of a liberated people. (pp. 95–96)

It was at this time that many of the white liberal women and men who had been supporters of civil rights turned their focus more on their own concerns as well as other rights movements such as Hispanics, Native Americans, homosexuals, older adults, and the disabled. Also gaining popularity in the 1970s was the environmental movement (Levine, 1996).

These civil rights groups made important changes in tactics and organization in the 1970s. The groups saw the emergence of relatively radical leadership from about 1965 to 1969. By the mid-1970s, the first wave of these civil rights groups had died out, but some regrouped over time. At this time, it became clear to the groups that they faced dauntingly complicated problems in obtaining legislative and legal advances for their groups—problems that could not easily be addressed by direct action. They needed work on a number of fronts simultaneously to obtain things like expert legal advice, to surmount honest differences within their groups about how best to proceed, and to develop staying power as complex legal initiatives were processed and litigated (Jansson, 1997). In this chapter, we focus on the activities of Native Americans, Asian Americans, Hispanics, gays and lesbians, and women in general.

Native Americans

Native Americans, while making some gains in health status, continued to be a beleaguered minority during the 1970s. While there was an attempt to encourage Native Americans to leave their reservations for urban areas during the 1960s and 1970s, most returned to reservations after finding poverty and discrimination in the cities. By 1980, however, half of all Native Americans lived in metropolitan areas (Day, 1989).

The improved health of Native Americans is credited to the advent of the Indian Health Service in 1955. Substantial improvements in mortality rates and life expectancy were achieved between 1955 and 1971; yet, when compared to other groups' mortality rates, including infant mortality, that of Native Americans remained quite poor. The American Indian Policy Review Commission was formed in 1973 to investigate the conditions of Native Americans and reported the status of Native Americans in stark terms:

> From the standpoint of personal well-being, the Indian of America ranks at the bottom of virtually every social statistical indicator . . . the highest infant mortality rate, the lowest longevity rate, the lowest level of educational attainment, the lowest per capita income, and the poorest housing and transportation in the land. (Day, 1989, p. 368)

Because of or in spite of these social conditions, the Native American family suffered from a revised version of forced assimilation as social workers often placed Native American children in white child care settings, based on the assertion that Native American homes were not proper places for children to be raised (Day, 1989).

Out of these conditions and in the spirit of the times, Native American protest groups formed to assert their rights. The most famous of these groups, the American Indian Movement (AIM), staged protests at Alcatraz in 1969, by then an unoccupied prison island, and in 1973 at Wounded Knee on Pine Ridge Reservation. In the former instance, AIM was trying to exercise its claimed treaty rights to unused federal lands. The protestors were removed in 1971. At Wounded Knee, they were armed and protesting the domination of the tribal government by whites. This action ended in violence as federal civilian and military forces took control of the reservation. Two Native Americans were killed and two federal officials wounded. Other actions in the 1970s, both through protests and in the courts, led to some recognition of Native Americans' rights to land and resources, but such actions often led to congressional attempts to reverse any gains made. By 1973, over $300 million in land claims were awarded to Native Americans, but that represented less than 4% of the total claims made (Day, 1989).

The Reagan years brought more hard times for Native Americans. Unemployment increased from 40% to 80% on reservations. In some tribes, family income for four was no more than $900 per year. Cuts to federal social programs had a devastating effect on Native Americans living in the worst poverty conditions (Day, 1989).

There is a moving poem entitled *Not Vanishing* that summarizes the history and suffering of Native Americans, but also articulates the strength won through survival. It is also a play on the words "Wounded Knee." The author, Chrystos, is a political activist, speaker, artist, and writer. Her tireless momentum is directed at better understanding the issues of colonialism, genocide, class, and gender and how they affect the lives of women and Native people (Gillan & Gillan, 1994).

Chrystos tells of women in her joints, locked in because they refuse to talk to the police. She vividly tells of her blood engorged with those arrested and shot. The anger reaches her tendons, stretching them, making them brittle. Her swollen hands hold the marrow of her people not allowed to hunt, move, nor to be. She tells of the scars on her knees where the children have been torn from their families, bludgeoned into government schools, of pins in her bones where you can see her people being held prisoners of a long war. Her passion is palpable as she describes, "My knee is so badly wounded no one will look at it; The pus of the past oozes from every pore," and she says even with a wounded knee, she is still walking (Chrystos, 1988, pp. 303–304).

In a later commentary on this poem, a critic discusses its meaning in terms of community, "Community is founded on a history of pain, realized by the speaker in her own body's ills and in her memory, and confirmed by difference: 'In my marrow are hungry faces/who live on land the whites don't want'" (Fast, 1999, 59).

The accompanying photograph further portrays the dignity and pride of a people under siege in their own country.

Japanese Americans and Other Asian American Minorities

Japanese Americans have largely found economic success. Of the 591,000 Japanese Americans in the United States in 1970, only 7.5% were below the poverty level, median family income exceeded the national average, and their educational attainment was greater than any other ethnic group. The Japanese American community asserted in the federal courts its civil rights claims relating to its forced interment during World War II (Day, 1999) and received reparations in 1999.

Immigration changed the face of Asian Americans during the 1970s. More than 1.5 million Asian immigrants arrived in the United States during this time. By 1980, the Chinese had overtaken the Japanese as the most populous Asian group in the country. Vietnamese immigrants made up a substantial portion of the Asian influx in the 1970s, and many of them faced harassment from white groups as they settled around the Gulf of Mexico to pursue their livelihoods as fishermen. Despite a strong economic and cultural presence in the United States, there was evidence of racial violence directed against Asian Americans during the recessions of the 1980s (Day, 1999). The following excerpts are from oral histories of first to fourth generation Asian Americans (Lee, 1991):

> Charles Ryu is a Korean American and minister for the Korean Methodist Church and Institute in New York. He says of his experiences in coming to America at the age of seventeen, ". . . coming to America shattered my self-image tremendously, I had to rebuild it. And the rebuilding process, which is still going on, is something good. . . . But my naive idealism was shattered. Anything and everything American does promise a lot of idealism: If you try hard, you will make it, it's up to you. If you don't make it, there's something wrong with you, which is not true. . . ." (p. 53)
>
> Kenny Lai sneaked out of the People's Republic of China at age twenty-three, and later (1978) immigrated to the United States. He says, "The worst thing about this country is the sense of racial differences between people. I still don't feel that this is my country even though I am a U.S. Citizen. White people ultimately think they are superior to you, and you are a level beneath them. It's not a very obvious thing, but I certainly feel it among my neighbors. . . ." (p. 72)

Hispanics/Latinos

The three main Hispanic subgroups in the United States are Mexican Americans, Puerto Ricans, and Cuban Americans. There were about 4.5 million Mexican Americans in the United States in 1970, with most of them located in the American Southwest; and 25% of them lived below the poverty level. Mexican Americans encountered educational problems throughout the 1970s, many resulting from language differences. Weak bilingual programs persisted despite provisions for them in the Elementary and Secondary Education Act of 1968 and court rulings mandating them. In 1979, more than half of Mexican American children did not complete high school. Despite a strong economic and cultural presence in the United States, there was evidence of racial violence directed against Asian Americans during the recessions of the 1980s (Day, 1999).

Mexican Americans face substantial problems because of concerns over illegal immigration. Ironically, U.S. agricultural growers supported illegal immigration to meet their labor demands. Over 4 million undocumented workers came to the United States between 1920 and 1980; and, while many returned to Mexico, others stayed to avoid the poverty of their home country. Undocumented workers end up receiving low wages, poor health care, inadequate food, and substandard shelter (Day, 1999). The following excerpts are from oral histories of Mexican immigrants to the United States (Davis, 1990):

> Elena Rodriquez is a hairstylist from Guadalajara, Mexico, and says, ". . . This is what I have always liked about the United States. The rich and poor all have the same rights. In the United States everyone is equal, everyone." (p. 239)
>
> Ana De Haro, the son of Mexican-born parents, is a disc jockey in El Paso, Texas, and says of his experience growing up in San Antonio, "I knew early in life that being Mexican was different. I was proud of it, but there were many times in my life that people wanted me to be ashamed. . . . [W]hen I was growing up there in the early sixties there was a lot of prejudice." (p. 348)
>
> Maria Aguirre, a pediatrician in Redlands, California, says, ". . . I was brought up with the notion that it was much better to be white. It was much better. Just, you're a better person if you're white. I didn't feel sorry for myself, but I longed to be white. I just felt that they were better people, they couldn't possibly do anything wrong. This was from education, but also from my family." (p. 395)

Jimmy Santiago Baca, born in Santa Fe, New Mexico, a poet and an author, wrote a poem in 1979 that is a Mexican-American statement on the conflict between Mexican immigrants and the Anglo society, and the lack of justice provided to Mexicans. It is entitled, "So Mexicans Are Taking Jobs from Americans" (Baca, 1979).

He begins, tongue in cheek, saying, "O Yes? Do they come on horses with rifles, and say, *Ese,* gringo, gimmee your job?" In the same tone, he asks if the gringo takes off his ring and drops it, along with his wallet, into a blanket and walks away. He further inquires as to whether Mexicans sneak into town at night and take away jobs, hold you at knife point, mug you. With anguish, Baca demands to know where the hell these fighters are, he has searched and cannot find them. He exclaims that he hears the rifles of white farmers in the night shooting people with black and brown skin whose ribs jut out. He sees starving children and poor people marching for what little work there is. He sees small white farmers who sell to clean-suited farmers who live in New York and have never been on a farm, have never known the look of a hoof nor smelled a woman's body bent the long day in fields. He sees it, he hears only a few people

getting all the money, while the rest count pennies to buy bread and butter. Beneath the green sea of money, millions fight to live, searching the depths of their dreams, trying to cross poverty. He ends by proclaiming that instead of saying the Mexicans are taking our jobs, we should be saying that we are not giving the children a chance to live. (Bacca, 1979, pp. 115–116).

The accompanying painting shows immigrants under the hot sun bent, laboring in the fields for their day's wages.

Puerto Ricans have faced great economic hardship as the poorest of the people of color, except for Native Americans. In 1980, the median income of Puerto Ricans was one half the national average. Another sign of the oppressive treatment of Puerto Ricans comes from sterilization data. A sterilization rate of 30% to 35% existed in Puerto Rico as the government tried to control population and welfare costs (Day, 1999).

Most Cuban Americans living in the United States in the 1970s had fled in response to Fidel Castro coming into power. This group consisted largely of professionals and persons of financial means who tended to be conservative in their political beliefs. In 1980, a second wave of Cuban immigrants came who were poorer and less educated. They had greater problems in adjusting to life in the United States as work was more difficult to find and they came into conflict with Miami's low-wage earners from Miami's African American community (Day, 1999).

Gays and Lesbians

Homosexual rights, or Gay Liberation, were actively pursued in the 1960s and 1970s. The most prominent event that propelled homosexuals into actively pursuing civil rights was the Stonewall riot. New York police raided a gay bar and the gay men resisted. During this time, the Gay Activist Alliance, the Lambda Defense and Educational Fund, and the National Gay Task Force were formed. These groups play varying, though sometimes overlapping, roles in the gay community. The Alliance is a community organizing and protest group; Lambda protects and pursues the legal interests of gays; and the Task Force is a lobbying and networking group (Day, 1999).

When young gay and lesbian radicals flocked to join the Gay Liberation Front, they brought with them a rich set of insights from their prior involvement in other activist groups; for example, from the black civil rights movement came an awareness of the inequities of American life, and from the women's movement came a consciousness of sexism and the profoundly important idea that the personal is political. They organized the first gay pride march in New York City in 1970 (Duberman, 1993).

The New York Times published a lengthy article entitled "Growth of Overt Homosexuality in City Provokes Wide Concern" in 1963. The piece was a marker in ending public silence, even though it was weighted toward a traditional, negative point of view. The early 1960s saw a sharp increase in the amount of public discussion and representation of homosexuality. Lesbian pulp novels and male pornography became plentiful—only after the Supreme Court decision cleared physique magazines of obscenity charges. Best-selling fiction and popular films, such as James Baldwin's *Another Country; The L-Shaped Room;* and *Lilith, Darling* continued to emphasize negative images. However, at least peripherally, some sympathetic portraits of gays and lesbians were offered. The new frankness about homosexuality went along with a much larger cultural upheaval; for example, the conformity and deference to authority of the fifties gave way under the hammer blows of the black civil rights struggle, and the Vietnam War was escalating (Duberman, 1993).

These events were followed by "The Hope Speech" in 1978 by Harvey Milk. Milk was elected to the San Francisco Board of Supervisors in 1977 and was tragically assassinated not long after by Dan White, a former policeman and political opponent (who later killed himself). The speech is presented here:

> In 1977, gay people had their rights taken away from them in Miami. . . . Unless you have dialogue, unless you open the walls of dialogue, you can never reach to change people's opinion. In those two weeks, more good and bad was said, but *more* about the word homosexual and gay was written than probably in the history of mankind. Once you have dialogue starting, you know you break down the prejudice. (Blasius & Phelan, 1997, p. 451)

While blacks were always visible during slavery, Jim Crow, and the civil rights movement, gays were like ghosts who suddenly materialized, marching on the steps of government buildings. Another organization that emerged during this time was the Gay & Lesbian Alliance Against Defamation (GLAAD). After being named director, Donna Red Wing expressed a profoundly wise understanding of the religious right:

> . . . [I]n their "fear" . . . [they] continue to attempt to oppress such minorities as homosexuals. . . . When we look at the members of the religious right, we see people who want things to be the way they were before, people looking back to a time and a place that made sense to them. They're afraid of affirmative action, they're afraid of diversity, they're afraid of things changing, and you juxtapose all of those changes with a bad economy and you get people looking for somebody to blame. . . . I wish I could point to the religious right and say that they are evil people. They're not. They're regular folks and they're afraid and in that fear they're looking for someone to blame. It's that simple. (Deitcher, 1995, p. 129)

Gay rights were largely dismissed during the Reagan era as political groups on the right, such as the Moral Majority, opposed support for homosexuals. Even a devastating disease like AIDS did not move these groups or the government to action on behalf of homosexuals. Only when heterosexuals began to be infected in adequate numbers did the government step up measures to deal with the epidemic (Day, 1999).

Goodman (1980) states that social workers have not done enough in their work with the gay and lesbian community. In speaking of the turbulent times during the unrest against homosexuals in the 1970s, she states:

> The social work profession has always defined its basic role as mediator and defender of the oppressed—the poor, the racially abused—and as protector against the exploitation of children, workers, and women. This ideal is nonexistent where gay people are concerned. This seems particularly strange since it would seem that many of the founders of the profession and the leaders in the field today are gay. This lack of history makes the work related to gay issues extremely difficult. . . .
>
> In order to rectify this situation of neglect, social work needs to reevaluate its present concepts of family, sexuality, and women. These reevaluations have to be made in the light of how people really feel, and love, and live, not by some academic, middle-class Judeo-Christian value system that states what people should do or be. Some of the leaders in social work who have made extensive contributions to society did not publicly make statements about their lesbian lifestyle. This failure has continued to maintain the myths about lesbians and homosexuals in general. (pp. 172–173)

Goodman goes on to cite a paper delivered by Blanche Cook at the Berkshire Conference on the History of Women:

> As I think about Anita Bryant's campaign to "Save Our Children from Homosexuality," my thoughts turn to Lillian Wald, who insisted that every NYC public

school should have a trained nurse in residence and who established free lunch programs for the city's school children. My thoughts turn to Jane Addams who [wrote] an essay called, "Women, War, and Babies." (p. 173)

In the essay, Addams referred to women as the custodians of the life who will no longer consent to its reckless destruction. She commented that social workers are charged with the future of childhood, and so forth (Goodman, 1980).

Goodman reminds the reader that Lillian Wald and Jane Addams campaigned for the creation of the United States Children's Bureau, which set up programs throughout the United States to care for battered wives and battered children; it crusaded against child labor and for humane child care. Goodman ponders whether Anita Bryant would demand that we save our children from Jane Addams if she knew that Addams lived and slept with a woman (1980).

The National Association of Social Workers (NASW) did take a position on homosexuality during the late 1970s:

> Along with the American Psychiatric Association and the American Psychological Association, the profession of social work has finally taken a public position on homosexuality. On May 22, 1977, at the delegate assembly of the National Association of Social Workers in Portland, Oregon, . . . the assembly passed a public policy statement on gay issues and gay rights. This historic document includes a section which states that NASW's position in a custody action between legal parents is that the sexual orientation of either parent shall not be a factor in determining custody. The policy position also called for the establishment of a National Task Force on Gay Issues to begin implementing recommendations embodied in the statement [further stating that] . . .
>
> The profession of social work is uniquely suited to assist American society in understanding the relationship between environmental conditions and human functioning. The burden of the eradication of homophobia—the fear of homosexuality—cannot be placed on the homosexual minority. . . . The ultimate responsibility for the eradication of discriminatory practices which impinge on the lives of the homosexual minority falls on the social work profession, together with other groups in the society. (Goodman, 1980, pp. 175–176)

Two years later, in spite of these policy changes, little if anything had changed in the attitudes of professionals toward gays, lesbians, and lesbian mothers (Goodman, 1980). See Appendix 10–A for a critique of the NASW policy statement of the first meeting proposed by the National Task Force on Gay Issues.

Women and Civil Rights in the 1970s

The struggle for women's civil rights in the 1970s was focused on two issues: the Equal Rights Amendment (ERA) and reproductive rights. The Equal Rights Amendment was introduced in almost every Congress since 1923, so it signifies an enduring effort to achieve equality under the law for women. The version passed by the Congress in 1972 was direct and simple in its construction:

> Section 1: Equality of rights under the law shall not be denied or abridged by the United States or by any State on account of sex.
> Section 2: The Congress shall have the power to enforce, by appropriate legislation, the provisions of this article.
> Section 3: The amendment shall take effect two years after the date of ratification. (Davis, 1994, p. 4)

While the amendment was clear on its face and 21 states quickly ratified it, vigorous opposition developed from the political right. The National Organization of Women (NOW) was the major organized voice for passage of the ERA, but groups such as the Moral Majority and conservative leaders such as Phyllis Schlafly, who led a group called STOP-ERA, led opposition to the amendment in the states (Day, 1999). Opposition forces played on the fear that society would be unrecognizably altered, envisioning an America where "women and men shared the same public restrooms and prisons, pregnant women and mothers were forced to go to war, and homosexuals could marry and adopt children" (Davis, 1994). The ERA never won the approval of 38 states as required to become part of the U.S. Constitution.

While battling for the ERA, women worked on incremental changes in the law and won important gains. Title IX of the Education Amendments of 1972, the Equal Credit Opportunity Act of 1975, and the Pregnancy Discrimination Act of 1978 attacked discrimination against women in the areas of higher education, credit opportunities, and in the workplace. While women faced the same conservative backlash as other groups in the 1980s, they continued to maintain significant political power as evident in voting patterns, officeholding, and social activism (Davis, 1994; Wambach & Harrison, 1992).

Reproductive rights, or issues concerned with abortion and birth control, were a major battleground in the 1970s, and the abortion issue remains controversial. The Supreme Court decision that remains the focus of attention for both opponents and proponents was decided during this time. *Roe v. Wade*, issued in 1973, legalized abortion, but Congress acted to restrict this right following the Court's decision. Since 1981, Medicaid funds for an abortion have been restricted to situations in which the woman's life is endangered, a requirement that limits access of poor women to an abortion. Subsequent Supreme Court decisions have modified *Roe v. Wade* to allow for the prohibition of abortions in publicly financed facilities even when private funds are used to pay for the procedure and to uphold regulations that prohibit clinics receiving Public Health Service Act (Title X) funds from providing abortion information to pregnant women (Davis, 1994).

Assertive attempts to expand women's rights were represented in feminist art of the period, and such art helps to illustrate how women were coming to a different understanding of their roles in society. A collaborative art project called *Womanhouse* took over an actual house and installed scenes from the life of the housewife. The artists' work made clever social statements about women's evolving position in society. The *Linen Closet* represents a woman stepping out from the confining expectations of a patriarchal society into a life of possibility (Raven, 1994).

> Womanhouse literally brought to life the ideas fad viewpoints first articulated in Betty Friedan's 1963 *The Feminine Mystique* and soon to be developed in *Ms.* magazine, which was founded in 1972. The emphasis in these first feminist ideas and viewpoints concerning menstruation, sexuality, marriage, and promiscuity, pregnancy and postpartum depression, psychic breakdown and suicide in middle-class suburban homes was one of frustration and despair. This kind of bold looking at issues created apprehensive tension in the audience for Womanhouse, provoking argument as well as revealing terrible pain. (Raven, 1994, p. 55)

Another poignant piece from the Womanhouse project is *Menstruation Bathroom* by Judy Chicago, which presents the taboo of women's blood and, by implication, puberty as the moment of shame when signs of womanhood appear, having to hide it behind a locked bathroom door (Raven, 1994). Chicago commented on this painting:

> Under a shelf full of all the paraphernalia with which this culture "cleans up" menstruation was a garbage can filled with the unmistakable marks of our animality. One could not walk into the room, but rather, one peered in through a thin veil of gauze, which made the room a sanctum. (Raven, 1994, p. 55)

The convergence of race and gender and the changes both were undergoing during this period can be found in the work of Betye Saar. She took an image of stereotyped oppression, Aunt Jemima, and transformed her into a woman empowered to take charge of her life. Her painting entitled *Liberation of Aunt Jemima,* in which a cookie-jar Aunt Jemima holds both broom and guns, and, while she continues to smile, a Black Power salute is forcefully centered before her image. In this portrait, the black woman will not be confined to roles that history has placed upon her (Lopez & Roth, 1994, p. 146).

Many women artists used their art as a political function. At the height of the civil rights movement and the beginning of Black Power, between 1963 and 1967, Faith Ringgold came up with her series, American People, focusing on images of hostile whites and uneasy attempts in integration. *The Flag Is Bleeding* tells a story of struggle (Lopez & Roth, 1994, p. 142).

The artistic representations demonstrate the changed consciousness of women in the 1970s, but the mixed results in the attempts to expand equal rights and reproductive rights indicate that women's place in society is still not settled. Davis (1994) suggests that the strong feelings over these issues "are about more than keeping women out of the army or protecting unborn fetuses. It is about continuing to exclude women from equal participation in society" (p. 11), and, hence, there is still a need for a woman's agenda in social work.

The social work profession has been slow to develop practice strategies or curriculum initiatives that reflect women's life experiences in spite of the fact that women comprise the majority of both service providers and recipients of social services (Hooyman, 1994). Hooyman (p. 313) notes that "it was not surprising that not until 1980 was a woman, Maryann Mahaffey, elected president of the National Association of Social Workers." See Appendix 10–B for a critique of the NASW's and the Council of Social Work Education's (CSWE's) stance on women's status in the conservative era.

GAINS AND LOSSES IN SOCIAL POLICY

Nixon turned out to be a leader full of paradox. He lambasted the Great Society, "big spenders," on an ongoing basis, claiming that liberals, especially federal civil servants, were undermining conservative programs and that social workers coddled the poor. His promise, after his landslide re-election victory in 1972, was to cut back many of the welfare programs enacted by his predecessors, as many of his supporters called for reductions in government services and expenditures. In 1973, American troops were withdrawn from Vietnam, with Nixon announcing that none of the "saved" defense funds would be diverted to domestic social programs, as many earlier had hoped (Trattner, 1999).

In spite of all of his conservatism and harsh rhetoric, Nixon went on to support, and in some cases even initiated, many important social policy measures. He approved passage of a slew of costly measures designed to help needy people, albeit "deserving" needy people, or the permanently disabled, older adults, and the working poor while at the same time placing many anti-welfare conservatives in office and frequently impounding funds appropriated by Congress for various social programs. Among the programs he signed into law were the Rehabilitation Act of 1973, providing physically disabled persons protection from discrimination; and legislation establishing the Earned Income Tax, or a negative income tax of sorts, that provided families with dependent children who earned $4000 a year or less a refundable tax credit of 10 percent of their earnings up to $400, to be administered through the Internal Revenue Service as part of the annual tax collection process. This was the first time in American history that the tax system was used as a mechanism to provide resources to the needy, expanding in the future and thus ameliorating, somewhat, the regressive nature of the Social Security tax. In addition, the Comprehensive Employment and Training Act, or CETA, served to subsidize hundreds of thousands of public service jobs in both public and private non-profit agencies for the unemployed, without a means test, and, thus, was reminiscent of the best of the public works programs of the 1930s; the Social Service Amendments of 1974, or Title XX, allocated $2.5 billion annually to the states to be used by them with broad latitude for programs they saw as best to meet the needs of their welfare recipients on a fee-for-service basis; and there were others as well. This marked the first time the federal government funded, or at least subsidized, "social services" for people above the poverty line, with the exception of older adults. Further changes and improvements were made in the Food Stamp Program, as well as additional increases in Social Security—11% in 1974—and, perhaps most important, the indexing of Social Security and SSI—that is, the decision to make an automatic "cost-of-living adjustment" (COLA) in such benefits, which would increase them annually whenever the rate of inflation rose by 3% or more (Trattner, 1999).

Most political commentators and analysts agreed that, whatever his motives, whether political opportunism—an attempt to broaden the base of the Republican Party in the face of pressure from a Democratic Congress and an increasingly powerful group of needy citizens or whatever—Nixon enacted the greatest extensions of the modern welfare system under a conservative presidency, dwarfing in size and scope the initiatives of Kennedy's New Frontier and Johnson's Great Society. The spending for various poverty programs nearly doubled during Nixon's years in the White House than that of the Kennedy-Johnson administration. Upon closer scrutiny, it was suggested that perhaps the nature of Nixon's welfare reforms obscured their reality. For example, inasmuch as his predecessors had sought new measures, many of Nixon's measures were procedural and administrative changes in established programs, like increasing and indexing Social Security benefits and federalizing food stamps and aid to older adults, the blind, and the disabled (SSI). Also, many of Nixon's programs relied on local officials and used private market mechanisms to achieve their ends, such as revenue sharing and CETA, thus giving a conservative appearance, whereas the Kennedy-Johnson measures usually utilized the services of federal bureaucrats and professional social workers (Trattner, 1999).

In August of 1974, when faced with almost certain removal from office through impeachment, Nixon resigned from the presidency. "After two years of lies and evasions, President Nixon recognized the end had arrived. 'You soldiers have the best way of dealing with a situation like this,' the president told his chief of staff, General Alexander Haig. 'You just leave a man alone in a room with a loaded pistol' " (Torricelli & Carroll, 1999). Just after 9:00 p.m. on August 8, 1974, the president addressed the nation. He said:

> I am not a quitter, but as President, I must put the interests of America first. America needs a full-time President and a full-time Congress, particularly at this time with problems we face at home and abroad. (Torricelli & Carroll, 1999, p. 316)

The next morning, he bade farewell to his staff:

> . . .[T]he record should show that this is one of those spontaneous things . . . always arrange[d] whenever the president comes in to speak. . . . But on our

part, believe me, it is spontaneous. You are here to say good-bye to us, and we don't have a good word for it in English. The best is *au revoir;* We'll see you again. . . . I ask all of you . . . to serve our next president as you have served me and previous presidents . . . with devotion and dedication, because this office . . . can only be as great as the men and women who work for and with the president. . . . This house isn't the biggest . . . but this is the best house . . . [it] has a great heart, and that heart comes from those who serve. (pp. 316–317)

The Watergate scandal, in which Nixon was heavily involved, brought sharp questions by both liberals and conservatives alike as to the ability of elected officials to govern fairly and to control the course of events, especially in a humane and rational way, and urged that government involvement in social programs be curtailed, thus moving the nation away from the expansive path of the recent past (Trattner, 1999).

The first to succeed Nixon was Gerald Ford, his vice president, who took the oath of office in August 1974. Ford was thought to be a moderate, but in reality he was even more conservative than his predecessor. He expressed no concern, whatsoever, for the needy; nor did he mention welfare reform as one of his or the nation's legislative priorities while in the White House (Trattner, 1999).

Ford identified inflation, which he called Public Enemy Number 1, and the ailing economy as his top priorities, taking a conservative approach to the matters. His obsession with inflation actually made conditions bad or worse for many Americans as he tried to fight inflation with unemployment, pushing joblessness to 9% by the spring of 1975, the highest since 1941. At the same time, the gross national product had fallen more sharply than at any other time since the collapse of the economy in 1929. As the inflation rate remained high, it created a condition termed *stagflation,* which continued to baffle the experts and plague the nation. Poverty figures reflected the situation; not only did they cease to decline, but the number of poverty-stricken citizens in the nation increased significantly once again. In early 1975, the number of poor in America was close to 25 million, about the same as 6 years earlier. By the end of the year, some 2.5 million citizens dropped below the official poverty level—the largest increase in a single year since the federal government began keeping such figures in 1959. This was due primarily to long-term unemployment, spiraling inflation, and a decline in purchasing. The figure continued to rise each year so that by 1980 the total number of people below the poverty level would be greater than in 1969. While some white, male-headed families were included in these numbers, the distribution of poverty remained, as always, structured by race, ethnicity, sex, family situation, and employment status, being lowest for whites, higher for Hispanics, and highest for black Americans; higher for women than for men (with exception of African American men); higher for single-parent as opposed to two-parent families; and so on (Trattner, 1999).

Next in line to succeed Nixon was Democrat Jimmy Carter, elected in 1976. He and Ford maintained a holding pattern on conservatism. However, Carter tried to move the nation toward social progress with a new welfare reform bill that was to guarantee annual income, inflation reduction, and more jobs. Carter's civil rights stance was reflected in his federal appointments. He appointed 298 federal judges with 23% being minorities and 15% women, with many having records of sympathy toward civil rights and equal opportunity (Day, 1999). Among his African American appointments were Patricia Harris to secretary of housing and urban development, former Congressman Andrew Young to U.S. ambassador to the United Nations, Walter McCree as general in the Justice Department, Drew Days III to assistant attorney general for civil rights, Clifford Alexander Jr. as secretary of the army, and Ernest Green as assistant secretary of labor. John Lewis became associate director of Volunteers for Action, and Louis Martin joined the White House staff as a special assistant to the president (Levine, 1996).

Carter did not always please the African American community, largely because he had to please an increasingly conservative white community. He was neither against nor wholly for affirmative action quotas. Politically, had he supported quotas, many more whites would have left the Democratic Party. While there were black Americans who resented the forced resignation of Andrew Young in August 1979 for an unauthorized meeting he had with representatives of the Palestine Liberation Organization, most acknowledged that Carter strengthened civil rights enforcement agencies, attempted to upgrade fair housing legislation, and vetoed an antiquing proposal (Levine, 1996).

Even though President Ford failed to tackle welfare reform, both Presidents Nixon and Carter did propose basic guaranteed annual income plans to provide a minimum income through benefits and tax credits. While Nixon's plan only provided for families with children, Carter's plan would have set an income floor for all Americans. The plans were both securely tied to work for the able-bodied, with provisions made for those who could not work. Social insurance benefits were incrementally expanded under both (Day, 1999). Carter was more interested in balancing the budget than in promoting new spending programs for the poor. School lunch programs and financial aid to black students were cut to bring federal spending down. Carter also gave only mild support to full employment and health care bills introduced by liberal Democrats in Congress (Levine, 1996).

THE SOCIAL WORK PROFESSION TAKES A STAND

The social work profession took a stance on political and social action about the time the War on Poverty programs became increasingly bureaucratized.

The focus of social work practice and social work education turned toward management and administrative theories and techniques, while losing sight of advocacy and reform goals. Competition for funds increased as federal monies decreased, with skills in grant writing, planning, and financial accountability taking on more importance (Haynes & Mickelson, 2000).

As the shift was away from social action, the Council on Social Work Education put out a report (1970–71) entitled "Social Work Education in a Period of Change." The executive director Arnulf Pins made the following comments:

> Our nation, along with the rest of the world, is facing major social problems. Large segments of our population suffer from neglect, physical and mental illness, poverty, discrimination, and racism. Government leaders, citizen groups, and all professions must give immediate attention to the solution of these social and human problems. Social work has a unique role and opportunity. Consequently, social work education has a special responsibility and challenge for it must prepare social work personnel with the commitment, knowledge, and skills needed: (1) to recognize and call attention to social needs, human injustices, and dysfunctional systems for service delivery; (2) to plan and bring about needed changes; and (3) to provide and administer social services in a more humane and effective way. (Haynes & Mickelson, 2000, p. 13)

THE TRANSITION OF THE FAMILY

During this time of conservative dominance in the United States, the composition of the American family was also changing. The nation had seen the family structure change dramatically since the passage of the Social Security Act in 1935 when the typical nuclear family in white, middle-class America consisted of a mother who was a homemaker, a father who went to work, and perhaps three children. The expectation was that the one (male) wage earner would earn a family wage and that the marriage would remain in effect for life. In 1990, by contrast, the average household was no longer a two-parent home with several children. Less than 30% of American households and 38% of families fit the description. There were two parents with one wage earner and one person home with the children in only about 13% of families. There were larger numbers of single persons, unmarried people having children, divorces, and desertions. Divorce rates rose, and marriage was not as popular. The number of female-headed households rose sharply, with the most rapid increase in the 1970s. Families headed by single women (or grandmothers) increased in the 1980s but at a slower rate. By 1990, 51% of all black children under age 18, 27% of Hispanic children, and 16% of white children were living with only one parent. The proportion of families that were headed by females had doubled in 20 years, up by 75% among black Americans and by 106% among whites, with the children being supported by their mothers (Axinn & Levin, 1997).

In the 20 years from 1970 to 1990, the average size of the U.S. household decreased about 21%, but this drop was not equally distributed as there were more people who never married, more families that had no children, and more families that had just one child. In 1990, half of all American families had no child-rearing responsibilities, while some families had three, four, or five children, meaning that 80% of children were supported by only 30% of the population. There was a racial dimension in the unequal distribution, with the birthrate significantly higher in the black community than in the white, which meant that the population least able to afford the responsibility of raising children bore a disproportionate share of it (Axinn & Levin, 1997).

The leadership of the Council on Social Work Education also took a stand on family issues, testifying in the early 1970s before the Senate Finance Committee. The testimony highlighted the deficiencies in existing family assistance plans and sought the inclusion of funds for labor power development in a proposed companion social services bill (Haynes & Mickelson, 2000).

Facts and Fiction About the Black Family

We learned in Chapter 9 that black female-headed households always exceed those of other races; and, when we interpret the figures accurately, we find that the biracial ratio has remained stable for a 40-year period (see Table 10.1 on p. 228). We know too that such families have been exceptions and not the rule over the years.

Parents and Children   At first glance, the statistics are startling. Over two thirds of black babies are now born outside of wedlock with over half of black families being headed by women. The majority of black children live with their mothers, and over half of those mothers have never been married. In the early 1990s, over half of all single black women had children. Among these women, less than half of the ones in their mid- to late thirties had intact marriages. These figures range from three to five times greater than their white counterparts and are markedly higher than those recorded for blacks a generation ago (Hacker, 1995).

We must avoid the temptation to rush to judgment and must guard against generalizations that oversimplify the facts. How people live and reproduce are most often sensitive subjects. There are many complex reasons for the higher figures among African Americans, and they are delved into throughout the remaining chapters. Keep in mind that there are no generic "black families" just as there are no white family norms. Black Americans account for more than 10 million households and represent young adults in condominiums to suburban couples with two children and a swimming pool. There are no specific domestic arrangements that are typical for one race or the other. We can, however, point to trends and tendencies as long as it is understood that they refer to developments within a varied universe (Hacker, 1995).

| TABLE 10.1 | FERTILITY RATES: 1940–1992 (PER 1,000 WOMEN AGED 15 TO 44) | | |

Years	Black Women	White Women	Black Multiple
1940	102.4	77.1	1.33
1950	137.3	102.3	1.34
1960	153.5	113.2	1.36
1970	115.4	84.1	1.37
1980	90.7	62.4	1.45
1992	85.5	60.2	1.42

Note. From *Two Nations: Black and White, Separate, Hostile, Unequal,* by A. Hacker, 1995, New York: Ballantine Books. Adapted with permission.

Increasingly common in America and the rest of the world, over the past generation, are single-parent households, which in most cases means homes headed by the mother. Concern has been raised that this arrangement now accounts for over half of black families. As always, there are extraneous factors that must be considered here—for example, the loss of many male breadwinners.* This occurrence has done much to perpetuate poverty with more homes now lacking the man's earnings, causing them to fall below the level of subsistence. Some observers also perceive an erosion of potential controls, especially over teenagers, which were once maintained by fathers in the home (Hacker, 1995).

Even though slavery and legal servitude ended well over a century ago, as a society, we cannot discount the fact that it still exerts a force. This assertion

---

*Increasingly, we are a nation strained by racism, hostility, and hatred, with our communities and neighborhoods overcome by violence, fear, and apathy. Many African American men are caught up in this violence. Our society is experiencing the adverse consequences of this cycle, including major injury and death, which will continue to affect the future of African American men and their families for generations to come. There are relatively higher victimization rates of violent crimes being reported for individuals who are African American, male, poor, young, or single. African American men have an unusually high likelihood of being murdered, with homicide being the leading cause of death of black men between ages 15 and 34; and, since 1960, the suicide rate for African American men between 15 and 24 tripled. In 1992, of the 23,760 homicide victims reported, 50% were black and 48% white. This is vastly disproportionate considering that African Americans are only 11% of the population. Ninety percent of those arrested for homicide were men, 55% black. In 1990 black Americans were 35.7% of the prison population, compared with 50% for white people. While these figures are startling, they do not examine the structural forces that engender crime, for example, inadequate education and job training, unemployment and underemployment, and the inequitable distribution of wealth and power (Allen-Meares & Burman, 1995; also see Blake & Darling, 1994).

is made with caution; however, it holds a place in history. Hacker (1995) goes on to tell us that:

> We know that in the slave system, adult pairings were denied legal standing, since owners did not want their chattels committed to lifetime covenants. Slaves were always subject to sale, which meant wives and husbands, parents, and children could be wrenched apart. . . . [W]omen had to endure assaults by white men, including bearing their offspring. Such circumstances might not seem a forerunner for enduring marriages. (p. 75)

[For an exquisite, powerful account of how a slavery past influences the African American families of today, see Pinderhughes, 1982 & 1997.]

Other developments are at work here that cut across racial lines. For example, Hacker (1995) refers to the "liberation of men" who apparently feel freer now than in the past to leave their wives and children and often start over with younger companions. Often, departing fathers either pay no child support or remit less than the agreed-upon amounts. The other development he calls "the right to reproduce," the choice of single women to reproduce and start families of their own.

Women have always been free to bear a child, in theory, but in the past if a girl became pregnant she usually got married before the child came. If she did not, social censure set in and, in some states, birth certificates were stamped "ILLEGITIMATE." Today, reproduction is seen as a personal right and a girl/woman cannot be ordered to have an abortion, nor to place her child up for adoption (Hacker, 1995). See Figure 10.1 for figures by race of a first birth for women ages 15 to 34.

More single women than ever before are deciding they want to be mothers, and over 90% of those carrying the pregnancy to term opt to take the infant home and raise it themselves. Possibly the clearest racial parallel is seen in the basic natal measure, fertility rates, which represent the number of annual births per 1000 women from age 15 to 44, the most common childbearing years. Due to the desire of black women to have larger families, coupled with less sustained use of birth control, they tend to have more children. Again, though, racial differences can conceal common causes as shown in Table 10.1.

The figures show that for the past half century, fertility indexes for white and black women have moved up and down with considerable consistency. Both went up during the baby boom (1950–1960); and, more significantly, we see that when they wish, black women can and do have fewer children. In 1940, their fertility rate was actually lower than the one recorded for white women 20 years later. Also, black women have been reducing their childbearing even further in recent years (Hacker, 1995).

The facts and figures suggest that much of the sexual behavior of black Americans may be defined less as "racial" than as within the national mainstream. The fact is, it would have been surprising had black men and women remained untouched by such forceful trends.

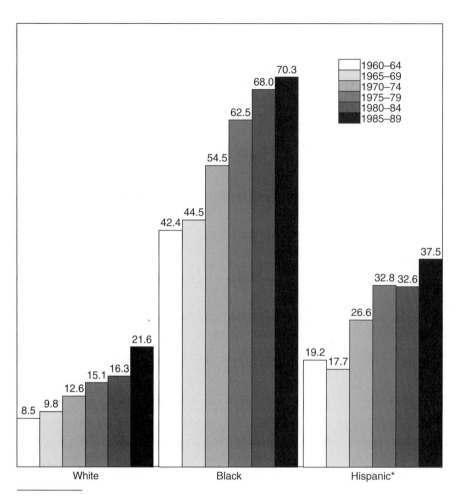

*May be of any race.

Premarital Births Increase

Because of the growing percentage of women deciding not to marry before their first birth, the number of premarital births is on the rise. In the 1985–89 period, there were about 2.2 million premarital births compared to about 700,000 premarital births for the 1960–64 period. Premarital births have been more common among black women than among whites or persons of Hispanic origin (who may be of any race) since at least the early 1960s. However, the percentage of white women age 15 to 34 with their first birth occurring premaritally more than doubled between the 1960–64 period and the 1985–89 period, from 9% to 22%. The proportion also doubled for Hispanics from 19% to 38%. The proportion for blacks increased from 42% to 70%.

FIGURE **10.1**

Women 15 to 34 Years with a First Birth—Percent with First Birth Occurring Before First Marriage, by Race and Hispanic Origin: 1960–64 to 1985–89
Note: From the U.S. Bureau of the Census, Current Population Reports, pp. 23–181, Households, Families, and Children: A 30-Year Perspective. Washington, DC: U.S. Government Printing Office.

Regarding African American households, Hacker (1995) explains:

> Even given their ties to national trends, households headed by women and births outside of wedlock have become basic facts of life within much of black America. Most matrifocal families still adhere to the "nuclear" model of a mother on her own raising one or more children. Among black households, however, other configurations have begun to emerge. The fastest-growing group consists of three generations residing in a single household. One common arrangement consists of a mother, one or more of whose adolescent daughters has come home from the hospital with her own child. Thus the original family headed by the mother, who has become a grandmother, now includes a "subfamily" headed by the daughter. (p. 78)

Making Ends Meet   Many households headed by single mothers get by on close to subsistence level. For example, in 1992, half such households had incomes of less than $14,000. This is where the feminization of poverty takes its greatest toll. The figures show that 57.2% of black single mothers, compared to 39.1% of their white counterparts, are trying to clothe and feed their children on incomes below the poverty threshold. White women usually fare better because they tend to have more education and to be older when they find they must manage on their own. It should be noted that at the same time approximately half of all black single mothers are fully self-supporting and many on welfare do off-the-books work to supplement their stipends (Hacker, 1995).

Joseph (1980) argues that social science has inaccurately portrayed the black family as pathological, adding to the existing fiction, while ignoring the larger context in which they live in an oppressive society:

> Given the relative powerlessness of social workers, is there a process they could help generate which would in fact lend itself to the mobilization of Black women to understand and involve themselves more directly in their struggle for change? This is an absolutely different tack for social workers—teaching themselves, freeing themselves of the myth [i.e, fiction] of Black family pathology, which must be continually challenged in all its subtleties and resisted if we are to be responsive to the needs of Black women. As social workers it would be refreshing to forgo the myth of objectivity and to argue instead that the inability to be objective about poverty, racism, disease, genocide, and all the problems that face Black women is a strength and a stimulus to work for change, particularly in the area of social policy. (p. 98)

Out-of-Wedlock Births   There has been an increase in out-of-wedlock births for black Americans, and it is often taken as evidence that they are evolving a separate sexual culture. Again, race-based explanations need to be placed into perspective. There is ample evidence that many white women are making essentially the same decisions and often for similar reasons. Still, racial differences can be found. Black teenagers are more likely than their white counterparts to begin sexual activity earlier and are less apt to use contraception, which accounts for their higher pregnancy rates. Black teens are also more apt than white girls to carry their pregnancies to completion. Another perspective that needs to be considered is that teenagers the world over are pubescent earlier and are increasingly independent as well as being exposed to similar erotic influences (Hacker, 1995). Nonetheless, in America, we continue to grapple with the phenomenon of children having children, even as the statistics drop.

As we look at the mixed racial composition of society at this time, the political implications of this demographic are grave; it became harder to obtain money for programs for the support of women and children as this was seen as a less universal need than it was in the past. Mounting concern with family policy throughout the period led President Nixon to call a White House Conference on Families. However, the debate hit a snag about the acceptability of alternative family forms and mores, making it difficult to devise an acceptable conference agenda and making a shambles of its implementation.

Carter's 1980 Conference on Families was no more successful. President Reagan had concerns about the trends in family structure and sponsored a study calling for government encouragement of "traditional family values and behavior," which failed to make any programmatic proposals. President Bush rounded out the consensus about the need for governmental family policy at national or state level by stating that he supported the idea of parental leave but declined government intervention into companies' compliance for such benefits (Axinn & Levin, 1997).

DISTRIBUTION OF POVERTY AND INCOME

The Social Security Administration first took a count of poverty in 1959, finding 39.5 million poor. That number declined to 31.9 million in 1988, showing a reduction in the poverty rate from 22.4% of the population to 13.1%. The count is based solely on the receipt of money income, which, in part, explains the decline. With the rapid growth of in-kind programs such as food stamps, housing subsidies, and medical care payments, real income of the lowest income group has increased, further reducing the number of poor. A quick glance could fool the casual observer into thinking that the goal, stated by President Johnson in 1964, of eliminating income poverty had been virtually achieved (before the onset of the 1974–75 recession). The argument would be that the expansion of noncash transfers and the suspected underreporting lowered the poverty (Axinn & Levin, 1997).

If we take a close and honest look at the history of this country, however, we see that poverty has always existed and indeed seems to get worse no matter how figures are interpreted, or misinterpreted. The War on Poverty led to a dramatic decrease in the late 1960s, and during the 1970s the poverty rate remained stable at about 11 to 12%, but it increased in the 1980s. During the

TABLE 10.2	COMPOSITION OF POVERTY POPULATION (PERCENT OF POVERTY POPULATION)			
Years	White	Black	Other Races	Hispanic Origin*
1959	72.1	25.1	2.8	NA
1966	67.7	31.1	1.2	NA
1975	68.7	29.2	2.1	11.6
1985	69.1	27.0	3.9	15.8

*Hispanic origin may be of any race; therefore, numbers add to more than 100%.
Note. From U.S. Ways and Means, 1998, p 1306.

Reagan recession of 1982–1983, it rose to 15.2% and, by 1990, 33.6 million people were counted poor—32% more than in 1970. Furthermore, the distribution of poverty was far from random. Conversely, it was structured by race, ethnicity, sex, family situation, age, and employment status. The official poverty rate for whites was about 11% in 1990; for Hispanics, 25%; for African Americans, 30%; and for Native Americans, 31%. Households where the head worked full-time had a rate of 4% with the rate for nonworking households at 25% (Axinn & Levin, 1997).

Table 10.2 shows that the composition of the poverty population prior to 1990 is overwhelmingly white. In addition, Hispanics and other non-black races have come to represent a greater portion of persons living in poverty, while the proportion of blacks has deceased over the last 30 years. The disparity between the black and white population is explained further in the next section.

THE RACIAL INCOME GAP

Black Americans have figured disproportionately among the nation's poor since their first arrival and continued after they started receiving wages. Differences in incomes, of course, can have explanations separate from race. The argument goes, a lot of white people are poor, and there are a number of blacks who are very rich. While this argument has some truth, after other factors have been accounted for, race still seems to play a role in people's financial affairs. The important thing that needs to be considered is how being black or white affects economic opportunities and outcomes (Hacker, 1995).

Discussions of income and earnings are strongly dependent on statistics. Equity cannot be measured with precision, but numerical disparities represent real facts about the races. The census asks a national sample of Americans each year to estimate their total incomes during the previous year. Table 10.3 provides some of the results from the 1992 survey, reported first as median incomes and then by how much blacks received for every $1000 going to whites.

The listings include every type of income for families and for all men and women from pensions and welfare payments to disability benefits and capital gains. For employed men and women, the figures reflect only the earnings of individuals who held full-time jobs throughout the year. For black families as a group and for black men, the relative incomes are embarrassingly low, particularly when compared with those for the earnings of black women (Hacker, 1995).

Table 10.4 shows us what unemployment rates looked like between 1976 and 1990. These figures help us to put income, or the lack thereof, into better perspective for that time period. We see when comparing unemployment

---

TABLE 10.3 — **INCOMES AND EARNINGS: MEDIANS**

	Whites	Blacks	Ratio*
Families	$38,909	$21,161	$544
All men	21,645	12,754	589
All women	11,036	8,857	803
Employed men	31,012	22,369	721
Employed women	21,659	19,819	915

*Income of blacks per $1000 for whites. Earnings for year-round full-time workers as of 1992.
Note. From *Two Nations: Black and White, Separate, Hostile, Unequal,* by A. Hacker, 1995, New York: Ballantine Books. Adapted with permission.

TABLE 10.4 — **UNEMPLOYMENT RATES BY RACE**

Year	White	Black	Black and Other
1976	7.0	14.0	13.1
1980	6.3	14.3	13.1
1985	6.2	15.1	13.7
1990	4.8	11.4	10.1

Note. From U.S. Ways and Means, 1998, p. 1237.

rates of whites to minority populations over time the persistent disparity between the groups. For this time period, the annual unemployment rate of blacks is at least double that of whites. The unemployment rate of blacks combined with other groups (includes American Samoans, Native Americans, Asians, and Hispanics) is nearly always at least double that of whites for each year during this same time period (U.S. Ways and Means, 1998, p. 1237).

In 1992, personal income received by everyone living within the country added up to a grand total of $4.1 trillion. Black Americans made up 12.1% of the tabulated population but ended up with only 7.3% of the monetary pie. Some 134 million gainfully employed persons accounted for earnings totaling $3 trillion of the income total. Of that employment force, black workers comprised 10.2% but received only 8.1% of all earnings. The conditions causing these gaps are discussed subsequently (Hacker, 1995).

In white households, there is the probability of both a husband and wife present, raising the likelihood of multiple incomes. During this time period, 59% of white families have two or more earners, whereas only 47% of black families do. Among married couples, a smaller percentage of white wives work: 58.6% are in the labor force, compared with 64.7% of married black women. With the earnings of black men tending to be lower, fewer of their families can afford the luxury of full-time housewives. With working white wives, they are more likely to take part-time jobs, and their paychecks tend to be supplemental. With black families, the husbands' and wives' earnings are often of equal value. Furthermore, with more black families headed by single women, it takes a higher proportion of their households to make do with only one income. In addition, when black single mothers work, and the majority do, it is generally at a job that pays relatively low wages (Hacker, 1995).

According to Hacker (1995), the question arises as to whether income ratios would change if black families had the same mixture of single parents and married couples as white households. If this were to happen, then many more African American homes would have someone bringing in a man's earnings, which would mean that the median income for black families would increase from $21,161 to $29,919 and the ratio would rise from $544 to $769. Even so, this still leaves some distance from parity because, even though it would help, black men still make considerably less than white men. Furthermore, even given more men residing in African American households, similar to white households, some of the men would be unemployed or removed from the labor force for other reasons (see footnote, p. 228), thus only closing about half of the income gap (Hacker, 1995).

What we know is that, on the whole, increased education tends to bring in higher incomes. Exceptions can always be found; however, for most people most of the time, staying in school does pay off. For both white and African American men and women, incomes tend to ascend with added years of schooling. However, even when black men reach the same educational level as white men, their incomes still stay several steps behind. For example, African American men with bachelor's degrees earn only $764 for each $1000 going to white men with equivalent degrees. An even grimmer statistic is that the racial ratio for a black man having completed college is actually lower than if he only had finished high school. For example, with a graduate degree, he would earn only $870 compared with his white counterpart's $1000, less than for black men having never completed college. What this means for African American men is that the advice to remain in school appears only valid insofar as it moves them ahead of others of their own race with little evidence that it would improve their positions in relation to whites (Hacker, 1995).

There is more equity among women largely because it is a fact that few women of either race rise far in the earnings hierarchy. African American women earned, in 1992, $966 for each $1000 of their white counterpart. While comparing status of black women is a good thing, achieving equality is easier with an underpaid cohort. Remaining is the larger question of why black men are denied even the limited equity that black women enjoy. The suspicion arises that perhaps some of the racial earnings spread among men stems from the fact that African American men are given fewer opportunities to rise to better-paying positions (Hacker, 1995). We explore some of those employment opportunities.

FAIR EMPLOYMENT POLICIES

It was in the 1960s when most white Americans finally accepted the principle that employers should not consider race when hiring, promoting, or firing. As stated earlier, it would seem that hiring and promoting African Americans was more likely to come at the expense of whites. It was at this time that affirmative action became a tool of fair employment policy. Companies guilty of intentional discrimination not only had to take a color-blind approach, but they also—if color-blind policies failed to significantly change the employee racial mix—had to give black Americans priority in hiring and promotions. This came at a time when jobs were becoming harder to find; thus, affirmative action became more controversial in the equal employment field than in any other area of civil rights (Levine, 1996).

Affirmative action is not new. It began under President Franklin D. Roosevelt in 1941 when he signed an executive order ordering defense plants to demonstrate how they would open jobs to black workers. A Fair Employment Practices Committee was established by Roosevelt to ensure that his ruling would be enforced. This committee was continued under Presidents Truman and Eisenhower, and later Congress expanded its authority and renamed it the

Equal Employment Opportunity Commission. The administration under Kennedy coined the actual phrase *affirmative action* in a ruling directing firms with federal contracts to take "positive steps" to have a racially representative workforce. The Civil Rights Act of 1964, passed by a bipartisan majority, created Title VII, banning employment discrimination that might be based on race, religion, sex, or national origin. President Johnson signed it into law in 1965, illustrating the thinking that led to racial preferences. In the same year, he issued an executive order that banned all federal contractors and subcontractors, including unions, from practicing employment discrimination. The Labor Department supervised this policy by establishing an Office of Federal Contract Compliance Programs (OFCCP). The OFCCP began issuing affirmative action guidelines in 1968 that required contractors to submit specific goals and timetables for hiring black Americans. It started to require federal contractors to hire specific numbers of African Americans during the early 1970s for their workforces based on the proportion of blacks in the local workforce. There were significant but limited results with this approach. Because the OFCCP was not adequately staffed to review the actions of most contractors, most cases had to rely on voluntary compliance (Levine, 1996).

New rules were announced in 1982 by Ray Donovan, President Reagan's secretary of labor, in an attempt to limit the OFCCP's authority. As it stood, the OFCCP supervised all contractors with more than 50 employees and federal contracts worth $50,000. Donovan's plan raised it to greater than 250 employees and $1 million in contracts. This plan would have freed 75% of all federal contractors from the OFCCP's affirmative action demands. These new rules never fell into place because of pressure placed on Donovan from civil rights organizations, women's groups, and businesses that had built their employment policies around the existing rules. The president did cut the OFCCP's budget and slashed its staff by 52%, reductions from which it never fully recovered (Levine, 1996).

The Civil Rights Act of 1964 established a five-member Equal Employment Opportunity Commission (EEOC) to prevent employment discrimination by private employers in general. In the beginning, the EEOC was authorized only to persuade businesses to stop discriminating. In the case of failed negotiations, the agency turned the matter over to the Justice Department. President Nixon opposed a plan by liberals to permit the EEOC to issue cease-and-desist orders against discrimination, but a compromise was reached. It resulted in the Equal Employment Opportunity Act of 1972 giving the EEOC the right to take employers to court, as well as declaring that the Civil Rights Act of 1964 applied to private employers as much as to government agencies and to private companies doing government work. This new power brought about successful lawsuits against AT&T, Household Finance, United States Steel, other companies, and some unions to force them to adopt affirmative action plans (Levine, 1996).

Meanwhile, the legal basis for affirmative action was strengthened by the Supreme Court's decision, *Griggs v. Duke Power Company* (1971), issuing its first interpretation of Title VII. The case involved hiring practices, stating that in the past Duke had discriminated against black Americans by reserving certain jobs for whites. The company had dropped the policy by the time of the *Griggs* case, but it required job applicants to have a high school education and to pass a general intelligence test. These requirements were unrelated to the skills needed for the jobs, and even though they seemed to be race-neutral, they had a disparate impact on blacks, meaning there were a higher number of black applicants disqualified than white. The Court ruled against Duke's job requirements with the justices stating that at workplaces with a record of past discrimination, job requirements violated equal employment opportunity when they maintained the results of past discrimination so that blacks continued to be underrepresented in the workforce and when they were related to the skills needed for the job. It did not matter that there was no intent to discriminate; it was the results of the requirements that counted. This meant that employers who had once discriminated would have to take affirmative action measures until the racial balance of their workforce matched the proportion of blacks in the local workforces, if successfully used (Levine, 1996).

There were two other significant rulings: one, *United Steelworkers v. Weber* (1979), applied strict affirmative action plans requiring a quota system in companies for training, hiring, and promoting blacks; and *Teamsters v. United States* (1977) set limits to affirmative action. In the latter, the government sought to apply affirmative action to union seniority systems, which was basically a "first hired, last fired" rule for layoffs to protect employees who had worked the longest at a particular place (Levine, 1996).

While the OFCCP and the EEOC were the major federal fair employment agencies, 16 others existed during the 1970s, which resulted in inefficiency in the enforcement of fair employment practices. In 1978, the Congress, under President Carter, tried to improve enforcement with a plan that concentrated power in the EEOC, transferring responsibility for discrimination in federal employment to the EEOC from the Office of Personnel Management, which had been ineffective (Levine, 1996). The courts began to seesaw on the issues of affirmative action throughout the 1980s; and, by 1989, as the composition of the Supreme Court changed, with conservatives achieving a majority, the Court backed away from its support of affirmative action (Axinn & Levin, 1997).

Fair Employment Policies for African Americans

It is difficult to say what the effects of affirmative action policies have been. It cannot be said for sure how many white Americans have been displaced or bypassed because preferences were given to black Americans. During the time period between 1974 and 1980, a carefully controlled survey focused on some 68,000 firms that had government contracts and were required by executive order to emphasize minority hiring. It was shown within this group of companies that the employment of black men rose by 6.5% and that of black women by 11%. Racial ratios, however, can change for various reasons. For example, there are more black telephone operators not because of quotas but because fewer white people are applying for those jobs. On the other hand, between the years 1970 and 1993, there was a growing black representation in a number of positions that many people regard as desirable, such as police officers, electricians, bank tellers, health officials, pharmacists, and athletes, in that order (Hacker, 1995).

Black employment rose several times over in all six of these fields, while the black workforce as a whole grew by only 60% during this period. It remains a matter of speculation as to whether these increases can be attributed to affirmative recruitment or preferential hiring. There is reason to believe that traditionally white-dominated professions such as police officers and electricians would not have made much of an effort to hire more black men and women if they had not been subjected to some kind of pressure or sanction (Hacker, 1995).

One thing is certain: if a country wants to vouchsafe that it has overcome discrimination and prejudice, there needs to be visible evidence. Alexander Hamilton said, over 200 years ago, that the promise of America was to allow every individual to "find his proper element and call into activity the whole vigor of his nature" (Hacker, 1995, p. 127). The requirement would not be for membership of all professions to mirror the population precisely, as not everyone will want to go into every field or speciality. However, no group chooses to have most of its members remain below the norm in pay and prestige. Affirmative action is not about eliminating gaps between the well-off and the poor, but it seeks to redistribute status and rewards with more concern for racial equity (Hacker, 1995).

Almost from the beginning of affirmative action policies, there has been talk of reverse discrimination with many whites resenting policies that would allow others to move ahead of them. If whites do "lose out" to blacks, they are generally more the blue-collar workers or persons at lower administrative levels, whose skills are not greatly in demand. In fact, evidence shows that white women have benefited more from the workforce changes due to affirmative action than have black men, and black women have gained more than black men (Hacker, 1995).

Perhaps some changes in racial ratios can be ascribed to affirmative action, but the programs themselves were never intended to create new jobs. They focus rather on the allocation of jobs that already exist. If employment is to expand, the determinate is more dependent on a flourishing economy, plus new kinds of positions the society is willing to pay for—for example, prison guards and nursing home attendants. No matter what the controversies surrounding affirmative action, it needs to be stressed that fewer blacks have steady jobs of any kind and their unemployment rates have been growing progressively worse relative to those recorded for whites (Hacker, 1995). [For an extensive and compelling discussion of equity in employment and educational achievement for African Americans, see Hacker (1995).]

The social work profession has inadequately addressed oppression over the years. This inadequacy is glaring because of the strong links between oppression and the injustices that lead to the conditions that cause people to seek help from social services and social workers. The Council on Social Work Education (CSWE) did not include the study of oppression and injustice in its curricula before 1983 (Gil, 1994). See Appendix 10–C for a critique of CSWE's Curriculum Policy Statement from 1982 to 1992.

THE STRENGTHS PERSPECTIVE: A TWO-WAY LOOK AT SOCIAL POLICY

The following scenario helps to illustrate several points pertaining to the intricacies of developing social policy, how it could affect out-of-wedlock teenagers, and how it influences practice:

> Well-meaning, white, middle-class women working with unwed mothers had sought consultation on how to better work with their clientele. The clients were poor, black teenagers overwhelmed with their circumstances. The typical client had dropped out of high school as one result of her pregnancy; she lived in a substandard slum tenement apartment on the third floor on the typically stingy budget of a welfare recipient. She was faced with the dauntless tasks of learning how to be a mother, how to manage a household on a budget far below the poverty line, how to control rats and cockroaches in her apartment, how to live all alone with an infant without relief of any kind, and how to negotiate with her overworked welfare worker. The first consultation session was spent discussing the strange sexual mores of the lower class black girls, how to motivate them to get educated, employed, and off welfare. The women were dedicated to helping the young black teens adjust to their impossible life circumstances rather than changing those circumstances. (Ryan, 1979, p. 89)

First, how might policy be developed from a problem definition? The problem is that there is a high percentage rate of black teenage pregnancies. The policy will address two areas: (a) how best to provide services, and (b) how to decrease the high pregnancy rate among teens. As social policy would dictate, there is a social responsibility to help clients deemed worthy of assistance. As we know, values shape policy. We have gotten a sense from the service providers on how values can influence policy indirectly; next is an example of how values can shape it directly. An underlying question of policymakers might be, were the teens responsible for their position in society? Are they really "deserving" or just looking for a handout? In other words, when is policy addressing service assistance and when is it concerned with maintenance of the person(s) in need? Using these questions, based on the problem definition, a policy to deliver services might look something like this: An agency would be established, with limited funding, to provide services to help the teens complete their education and get a job. Of course, there is nothing wrong with this type of policy, and the actual delivery of services would be more humane and inclusive than what is spelled out here.* Nonetheless, there are definite limitations; for example, the concern seems to be how to save government dollars rather than how to address human need.

Let us look at the same scenario from a strengths-based definition: how to empower black teenagers so that they can get the nurturing and guidance necessary to lead a productive life while parenting their child(ren) and how to help decrease the high rate of teen pregnancy. Yes, a problem does exist and it must be addressed, but we will also want to give equal attention to the strengths of the people we will be serving and their environments. The strengths perspective assumes the position that policies need to be designed to help empower clients and to preserve their freedom, capacity and dignity. To begin with, we would need to ensure that clients' voices are heard and understood by policymakers, as well as including them in the actual policymaking, focusing on strengths rather than deficits (Chapin, 1995). We start by crafting nurturing services that would not foster dependence but would, more realistically, strive toward the humanness of interdependency. The focus would be on common human needs and how services could be provided to meet those needs, the assumption being that basic needs must first be met, thus allowing the person to utilize opportunities for independence (Towle, 1945/1987).

In reflecting on the concept of empowerment, Edith Lewis, a social worker, relates it to her own experience:

> The empowerment perspective rings true to my own experience and development. During my childhood on Chicago's South Side, no one asked African American families what they needed; we were told what we needed. When as a girl of 15 I told my high school counselor that I wanted to be a social worker, she told

---

*The federal division of the Adolescent Health Services and Pregnancy Prevention Act of 1978 implemented an interactive model of support by the Office of Adolescent Pregnancy Programs (OAPP). While only a subset of eligible pregnant and parenting adolescents receives the services needed, there are a number of comprehensive programs available around the country. The goals of the programs typically are successful completion of school, a decrease in the incidence of rapid succession births, and economic self-sufficiency for the teen and her baby. The programs vary, but some of the services provided are prenatal education, covering human sexuality and family planning; risks of teenage pregnancy; adoption; prevention of birth defects and low birth weights; fetal development; physical and psychological aspects of pregnancy; and childbirth education and preparation (Brindis, 1993).

me, "You're a smart colored girl; learn to type," and then made it impossible for me to take the college preparatory classes offered by the school. I wondered why she thought she knew what was best for me. . . . [Later] at 22, when I had earned enough money and release time from my job to be able to return to college full-time and the admissions officer said to me, "You're not college material," I wondered why he thought he knew more about my capacity than the instructors who had worked with me and encouraged me to complete my degree. When I received my undergraduate degree from that institution, *summa cum laude,* I went back to that admissions officer and showed him the credential.

Having been surrounded all of my life by children and adults who have thought through the options available to them and made informed decisions based on those options, I don't wonder whether people know what is really best for them. Instead, as a social worker, I wonder how options not open to them might be opened and how their confidence might be expanded through building their capacity to exercise those options. (Gutiérrez & Lewis, 1999, pp. 4–5)

By focusing on human needs as the basic criteria, the teenage parents (and other teens) do not have to be described as deficient to justify receiving services. There are some immediate things that could help lead to self-empowerment; at the fore is providing assistance to the staff to gain a better understanding of their clients' needs and circumstances. Enlightenment regarding the actuality of the girls' environment and the conditions under which they live would enable the staff to work more effectively with them to meet the basic goals of the program, completing their education and getting a job. Some of the more immediate issues that could be dealt with are the pressing problems of how to cope with neglectful slum landlords and the penurious welfare department and developing a preventive program centering on sex education and contraceptive services (Ryan, 1979).

Several decades after the pioneering of African American social work, Barbara Solomon, in 1976, wrote her groundbreaking book championing the ideology of empowerment to help black Americans fight against a hostile social environment that held them down. Like the pioneer African Americans before her, Solomon was responding to community needs that were not being met by the predominantly white social service system. Both focused on community practice with a macro- and micro-orientation.

Solomon (1976) wrote her book for social workers in training and in practice who were seeking more effective strategies for helping clients in black communities achieve personal and collective goals. Solomon explains:

[The book] was experimental . . . designed as action research involving students, field instructors, agency staff, and others in an intensive search for the concepts and principles regarding problem solving in black communities which had apparently escaped us too often in the past. . . . The significance of powerlessness in the etiology of problems faced by individuals, families, and groups in black communities became a persistent theme in almost every issue raised in the course. It emerged in the consideration of the hard-working, low-earning parents with high aspirations for a teen-age son whose poor grades, truancy, gang membership, and contempt for authority were tearing them apart. . . . In these and many other problem situations, the underlying and overweening motif was unerringly the stamp of powerlessness to exercise the kind of interpersonal influence needed to achieve the cherished objective. (pp. 2–5)

Once again, we see how social policies direct social work practice (see Figure 10.2).

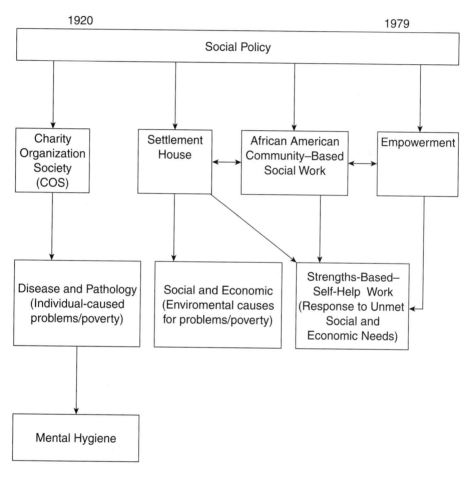

FIGURE 10.2

Social Policy

When social policies and programs emphasize individual pathologies and deficits, they ignore structural barriers that many people face in getting ahead—poor educational preparation, lack of decent jobs, inadequate day care and health care, and poverty. When we continue to look at the individualistic nature of problems such as AIDS, pregnant teenagers, and truant children, we fail to examine the institutional nature of the social problems, especially the endemic, insidious repercussions of institutionalized racism, and may fail to see the potential of a community to address its problems when given the resources to assert itself.

SUMMARY

Full-fledged conservative movements against what was considered excess of reform were manifested in the form of a backlash against feminism, affirmative action, social spending, and taxes. This put the advocates for women, gay men and lesbians, and people of color on the defensive (Jansson, 1997). Jansson criticizes historians for sometimes characterizing historical eras as liberal or conservative. He saw the 1970s as a peculiar mixture of both, with major policy reforms happening, but in the context of a nation with an emerging conservative movement that ended up viewing Richard Nixon as too liberal. Conservatives were not disappointed by the results of the 1980 presidential election (Jansson, 1997).

The door slammed shut on the gains of the more liberal social welfare era of the sixties, and on the other side was a wave of conservative politics that would continue to guide our country for two more decades. It would be too dramatic of a statement to say that the liberal progressive gains of the time got shut behind that door, but we can say that the configuration of the welfare state was drastically changed.

REFERENCES

Allen-Meares, P., & Burman, S. (1995). The endangerment of African American men: An appeal for social work action. *Social Work, 40*(2), 268–274.

Axinn, J., & Levin, H. (1997). *Social welfare: A history of the American response to need* (4th ed.). New York: Longman.

Baca, J. S. (1979). *Immigrants in Our Own Land*. Baton Rouge: Louisiana State University Press.

Blake, W. M., & Darling, C. A. (1994). The dilemmas of the African American male. *Journal of Black Studies, 24*(4), 402–415.

Blasius, M., & Phelan, S. (Eds.). (1997). *We are everywhere: A historical sourcebook of gay and lesbian politics.* New York: Routledge.

Brindis, C. (1993). Antecedents and consequences: The need for diverse strategies in adolescent pregnancy prevention. In A. Lawson & D. L. Rhode (Eds.), *The politics of pregnancy: Adolescent sexuality and public policy* (pp. 257–283). New Haven, CT: Yale University Press.

Chapin, R. K. (1995). Social policy development: The strengths perspective. *Social Work, 40,* 506–514.

Chrystos. (1988). *Not Vanishing.* Vancouver, Canada: Press Gang Publishers.

Davis, L. V. (1994). Why we still need a woman's agenda for social work. In L. V. Davis (Ed.), *Building on women's strengths: A social work agenda for the twenty-first century* (pp. 1–25). New York: The Haworth Press.

Davis, M. P. (1990). *Mexican voices American Dreams: An oral history of Mexican immigration to the United States.* New York: Henry Holt and Co.

Day, P. J. (1989). *A new history of social welfare.* Englewood Cliffs, NJ: Prentice Hall.

Day, P. J. (1999). *A new history of social welfare* (3rd ed.). Boston, MA: Allyn & Bacon.

Deitcher, D. (Ed.). (1995). *The question of equality: Lesbian and gay policies in America since Stonewall.* New York: Scribner.

Duberman, M. (1993). *Stonewall.* New York: Dutton.

Fast, R. R. (1999). *The heart as a drum: Continuance and resistance in American Indian poetry.* Ann Arbor, MI: University of Michigan Press

Gil, D. (1994). Confronting social injustice and oppression. In F. G. Reamer (Ed.), *The foundations of social work knowledge* (pp. 231–263). New York: Columbia University Press.

Gillan, M. M., & Gillan, J. (1994). *Unsettling America: An anthology of contemporary multicultural poetry.* New York: Penguin.

Goodman, B. (1980). Some mothers are lesbians. In E. Norman & A. Mancuso (Eds.), *Women's issues and social work practice* (pp. 153–180). Itasca, IL: F. E. Peacock.

Gutiérrez, L. M., & Lewis, E. A. (1999). *Empowering women of color.* New York: Columbia University Press.

Hacker, A. (1995). *Two nations: Black and white, separate, hostile, unequal.* New York: Ballantine Books.

Harrington, M. (1977). *The other America: Poverty in the United States.* New York: Penguin Books.

Haynes, K. S., & Mickelson, J. S. (2000). *Affecting change: Social workers in the political arena* (4th ed.). Boston: Allyn & Bacon.

Hooyman, N. R. (1994). Diversity and populations at risk: Women. In F. G. Reamer (Ed.), *The foundations of social work knowledge* (pp. 309–345). New York: Columbia University Press.

Jansson, B. S. (1997). *The reluctant welfare state* (3rd ed.). Pacific Grove, CA: Brooks/Cole.

Joseph, B. (1980). Ain't I a woman. In E. Norman & A. Mancuso (Eds.), *Women's issues and social work practice* (pp. 91–111). Itasca, IL: F. E. Peacock.

Lee, J. F. J. (1991). *Asian American experiences in the United States: Oral histories of first to fourth generation Americans from China, the Philippines, Japan, India, the Pacific Islands, Vietnam and Cambodia.* Jefferson, NC: McFarland & Company, Inc.

Levine, M. L. (1996). *African Americans and civil rights: From 1619 to the present.* Phoenix, AZ: The Oryx Press.

Lopez, Y. M., & Roth, M. (1994). Social protest: Racism and sexism. In N. Broude & M. D. Garrard (Eds.), *The power of feminist art: The American movement of the 1970s, history and impact* (pp. 140–157). New York: Harry N. Abrams.

Pinderhughes, E. (1982). Black genealogy: Self liberator and therapeutic tool. *Smith College Studies in Social Work, LII* (2), 93–106.

Pinderhughes, E. (1997). The interaction of difference and power as a basic framework for understanding work with African Americans: Family theory, empowerment and educational approaches. *College Studies in Social Work, 67*(3), 323–345.

Raven, A. (1994). Womanhouse. In N. Broude & M. D. Garrard (Eds.), *The power of feminist art: The American movement of the 1970s, history and impact* (pp. 48–65). New York: Harry N. Abrams.

Ryan, W. (1971/76). *Blaming the victim.* Vintage Books: New York.

Solomon, B. B. (1976) *Black empowerment: Social work in oppressed communities.* New York: Columbia University

Torricelli, R. [Senator] & Carroll, A. (1999). *In our own words: Extraordinary Speeches of the American Century.* New York: Kodansha International.

Towle, C. (1945/1987). *Common human needs.* Sliver Spring, MD: National Association of Social Workers.

Trattner, W. I. (1999). *From poor law to welfare state: A history of social welfare in America* (6th ed.). New York: The Free Press.

U. S. Bureau of the Census (1992). *Households, families, and children: A 30-year perspective* (Current Population Reports, P23–181). Washington, DC: U.S. Government Printing Office.

U.S. Ways and Means Committee. (1998). *Green Book.* Washington, DC: U.S. Government Printing Office.

Wambach, K. G., & Harrison, D. F. (1992). Social work practice with women. In D. F. Harrison, J. S. Wodarski, & B. A. Thyer (Eds.), *Cultural diversity and social work practice* (pp. 157–180). Springfield, IL: Charles C. Thomas.

APPENDIX 10–A

The following was reported in the June 1979 *NASW News,* cited in Goodman (1980, pp. 175–177).

Nearly a decade of struggle by gay social workers for professional recognition and support culminated in the first association-sponsored meeting of NASW's Task Force on Gay Issues, held 5–7 May at national headquarters in Washington, D.C.

The meeting, termed "highly productive" by NASW Program Director Shirley D. LeBlanc, resulted in the formulation of specific goals and activities designed to alleviate problems such as gay social workers' need for support from the professional organization and the inability of any social workers to meet gay clients' needs because of the lack of appropriate knowledge and skills. Task force members included an open community meeting on their agenda and also met with the executive directors of the Council on Social Work Education (CSWE) and the National Commission for the International Year of the Child.

The goals established by the task force are:

- to help create a professional environment conducive to the professional and personal growth of gay social workers;
- to promote high quality social work services for gay clients;
- to achieve full recognition within NASW for the oppressed status of gay people;
- to review all existing NASW structures, publications, and policies to ensure that they reflect NASW's policy statement on gay issues;
- to aid the formation of gay issues task forces and committees in all NASW chapters;
- to organize a nationwide network of gay social workers to serve as regional resource persons for consultation, in-service education programs, and research of local needs and problems such as those cited in the policy statement;
- to encourage gay social workers and students to openly declare their sexuality professionally and work for full implementation of the policy statement, and to use NASW's available resources and advocacy mechanisms to counter discrimination;
- to assure that NASW responds to both progressive and discriminatory types of legislation and media presentations that affect the health and welfare of gay practitioners and clients; and
- to create and participate in coalitions with any organizations or groups, particularly the proposed CSWE gay issues task force, to pursue issues of mutual interest.

APPENDIX 10–B

Women's Status in Social Work, 1973–1992

In 1973, NASW targeted social conditions and populations at risk, with women as the lowest priority among these populations. In the same year, CSWE's *Report From the Committee on Objectives and Strategies*, presented at the Delegate Assembly, began to implement regulations regarding curriculum content on women. In response to the women's movement and pressure to consider women's viewpoints on social problems, the CSWE Board in 1977 adopted the standard on women, which was codified as 1234B. In 1982, CSWE issued its *Curriculum Policy Statement for Master's Degree and Baccalaureate*

Degrees in Social Work Education. Standard 7.3 mandated that social work curricula must provide content on the "experiences, needs and responses of special populations and people who have been subjected to institutionalized forms of oppression." Standard 7.5 spoke specifically to women: "The program shall make specific, continuous efforts to assure enrichment of the educational experience it offers by including women in all categories of persons related to the program and by incorporating content on women's issues into the curriculum" (CSWE, 1991). The 1992 curriculum policy statement includes women under populations at risk as follows: "The curriculum must provide content about people of color, women, and gay and lesbian persons." In addition, structural factors that affect women as clients, educators, and students are recognized by "such content must emphasize the impact of discrimination, economic deprivation, and oppression upon these groups (CSWE)" (Hooyman, 1994, p. 310).

APPENDIX 10–C

CSWE's Curriculum Policy Statement, 1982–1992

The 1982 Curriculum Policy Statement is the first one that referred specifically to the promotion of "social and economic justice" (4.1) and noted that "social workers hold that people should have equal access to resources, services, and opportunities" (5.1). Under the heading "Special Populations," the statement noted that "the profession has also been concerned about the consequences of oppression" (7.3) and that "curricula must give explicit attention to the patterns and consequences of discrimination and oppression" (7.4). . . . .

A 1992 revision of the CSWE Curriculum Policy Statement is clearer than the 1982 statement concerning oppression and injustice and stresses the responsibility of schools of social work to teach about social justice and about approaches to overcome oppression. . . . .

Social policies and social services have hardly been affected in recent decades by the progressive Curriculum Policy Statements concerning oppression and social injustice. Rather, recent "reforms" of these policies and services reflect ultra-conservative ideologies, which do not even aim to ameliorate oppression and unjust conditions, as "liberal" policies tend to do.

As for recent social work practice, it helps people to adapt as best as they can to existing unjust conditions rather than to support efforts to change during these conditions in accordance with human rights standards and people's needs. Practice, as well as policies and services, thus appears to move in opposite directions from social work education standards, a glaring contradiction that causes severe ethical dilemmas for the profession (Gil, 1994, pp. 258–259).

SOCIAL WORK IN THE WAKE OF CONSERVATISM

The conservative political faction had taken a firm grip on the nation by the time Ronald Reagan was elected in 1980. Nixon had begun the dismantling of social services, and the brunt of the increasing restrictions placed on services was felt most by the poor and women, children, and people of color. Ford and Carter followed Nixon's lead despite the dim hope that Carter, a democrat, might bring back a more liberal philosophy. This chapter will focus on the impact of these cuts, what policies made their way into the conservative wake, and other significant events to the period such as Americans with Disabilities Act, the war on drugs, and the Los Angeles race riots. The impact of the nation's conservative mood is discussed from two positions, that of the people who were most affected, and that of the social work profession. The Americans with Disabilities Act will be analyzed from a strengths perspective.

THE REAGAN ADMINISTRATION

Reagan won an overwhelming victory, not only capturing the White House but controlling the Senate. The outcome of the election represented less a right-wing realignment than a dissatisfaction with Carter's leadership. People were concerned about the increasing unemployment and skyrocketing inflation in the nation's economy (Trattner, 1999). Reagan's election and reelection had the overt backing of both the Far Right and Moral Majority with a mandate to enforce certain ideological beliefs, for example, the Christianization of American politics, the return to marriage and family norms, the breakup of social programs, and the continued retreat from civil rights (Day, 1999).

Reagan shares the spotlight in U.S. history with Franklin Roosevelt for having the most impact on social welfare. However, they will be remembered for very different reasons: Roosevelt for building a stronger social welfare state and Reagan for attempting to dismantle it. Even after being put to the stringent, conservative test and after Reagan's attempts to destroy it, the welfare state was so strong that it withstood the onslaught. Roosevelt understood that the conservatives, by definition, posed a potential danger to the survival of the welfare state (Jansson, 1997). Conservatives believe that, "freedom is fundamental; they value the freedom to retain personal wealth and to conduct enterprises with minimal public regulation. Conservatives are optimistic that unfettered capitalism will produce prosperity if government does not place excessive regulations upon it" (Jansson, 1997, p. 4). Reagan embraced the philosophy of conservatism during his presidency and adopted policies and legislation clearly rooted in this philosophy as well.

The Reagan administration intended to arrive at a balanced budget by abolishing social programs and protecting military expenditures. Reagan's plan was to cut social programs for everyone except those who proved to really need it. This was to be accomplished by allowing individuals receiving social insurance to continue to do so, but public assistance programs would be cut drastically to encourage individuals to return to work (Day, 1999).

Reagan imposed conservative, traditional values on policy development permeated with three morality-based issues: first, the sanctity of the nuclear family, with the maintenance of its traditional male/female roles; second, the moral value of income-producing labor at any wage; and third, but less precise, a superpatriotism and religious belief in the God-ordained future of America. None of these issues takes into account the real intricacies underlying poverty such as that two adults working may not be able to support a family or that industry is taken out of the United States and brought to countries where wages are cheaper, leaving many Americans unemployed (Day, 1999).

Reagan introduced the idea of supply-side economics, which proposed reductions in social programs so that tax dollars could be reinvested in the private sector to capitalize on economic growth (Karger & Stoesz, 1998). Prior to the Reagan Era, the United States had historically adopted the philosophy of Keynesian economics, which emphasized government spending and changes in interest rates to offset recession and inflation (Jansson, 1997). The theory of supply-side economics is that if large corporations are afforded tax cuts, jobs will be produced because the corporations will have more money to create additional jobs. This theory also has a basic belief that wealthy individuals, because of these tax cuts, will begin to donate more money to charities, thus alleviating the necessity for the federal government to be involved in social welfare. It was this supply-side economics, along with ground already lost in three previous decades, that contributed to the continuing decline of the U.S. social welfare (Haynes & Holmes, 1994).

Policies and Issues

The policies developed during the Reagan administration were a direct reflection of his ideology and his desire to return to more traditional values in America. New Federalism was the basic ideology underlying most of the administrations social welfare policies. This ideology comprised two parts, one being reprivatization whereas charities and churches would take over care of the poor on a local "neighborly" basis, and the other being that state governments would assume all costs for Aid to Families of Dependent Children (AFDC), Supplemental Security Income (SSI), and food stamps; the federal government taking full responsibility for Medicaid (Day, 1999).

Economist Ronald Lekachman expressed his view of Reagan's economic and social policies:

> Ronald Reagan must be the nicest president who ever destroyed a union, tried to cut school lunch milk rations from six to four ounces, and compelled families in

need of public help to first dispose of household goods in excess of $1,000. This amiable gentleman's administration has been engaged in a massive redistribution of wealth and power for which the closest precedent is Franklin Roosevelt's New Deal, with the trifling difference that FDR sought to alleviate poverty and Ronald Reagan enthusiastically enriches further the already obscenely rich. (Haynes & Holmes, 1994, p. 95–96)

The Siege on Social Welfare

Omnibus Budget Reconciliation   The Omnibus Budget Reconciliation Act (OBRA) was passed in 1981 to reduce funding to social programs. These budget cuts resulted in a 11.7% reduction in AFDC funding, with stiffer eligibility requirements, along with a 19% reduction in food stamp funding. In 1984 the poverty rate rose to 15.3%, higher than any year since the early 1960. Under OBRA, the federal government decided on a Social Service block grant to all states for social welfare programs. This grant would relieve the federal government of its obligation to match funds and also end most federal regulations providing for services to the poor. This move had sweeping ramifications in that the block grant consolidated more than 90 categorical programs into four blocks, reducing federal funding for each 20 to 25%. With the states no longer required to match funds, this meant, in most cases, a real reduction of 50% from the programs (Day, 1999; Haynes & Holmes, 1994).

Such cuts had real consequences in the lives of the poor. The Reagan policy rhetoric advocating self-sufficiency sounded hollow to those who lacked resources even before the budget cuts were executed. Peterson Zah, chairman of the Navaho tribe, indicated that self-reliance was fine in theory but pointed out the fatal flaw of Reagan's belief that private enterprise could fill any gaps in public funding reductions, " 'We don't have the people Reagan is calling on—private sector development, business people—to pick up the slack' " (Forbes, 1983, p. 34). The reality on the reservation was that federal funds to the Navaho tribe were cut about 30% and unemployment rose from 50% to 80% (Forbes, 1983).

The cuts in social spending were nowhere more apparent than in the streets of America during the 1980s. The National Coalition for the Homeless maintained that there were more homeless people in the 1980s than at any time since the Great Depression of the 1930s, and it cited the Reagan budget cuts in subsidized housing (78% cut from 1980 to the mid-80s) as a key cause. As well, the cuts in AFDC left poor women with children in a desperate position as they made choices between housing, food, and clothing. The median rent for a one-bedroom apartment in Los Angeles in the 1980s was $491 while the monthly AFDC payment for a mother with one child was $448. As the director of a program for homeless families said, "So these women face a choice. They can buy food and diapers, or they can pay the rent. Some months they decide to eat" (Stengel, 1986, p. 28).

With deteriorating social support, people who never expected to be without a home found themselves living in shelters. Where previously the homeless were seen as hopeless alcoholics, drug addicts, or deinstitutionalized mentally ill persons, the face of the homeless changed. The National Coalition for the Homeless reported that "families with children [were] the fastest-growing segment of the nation's homeless" (Stengel, 1986, p. 27). Included within the growing population were the working poor. In 1985 *The Washington Post* reported that suburban shelters were becoming overcrowded, citing a situation where persons "often working at service jobs for the minimum wage of $3.50 an hour . . . they may be hit by a run of bad luck, or their housing situation may simply collapse under the strain of skyrocketing rents" (Wickenden, 1985, p. 20).

In spite of the evidence that the poor and working poor were being pushed over the edge and into the streets, President Reagan, in responding to a question about the effects of his social policies on the poor, said, "What we have found in this country—and maybe we're more aware of it now—is one problem that we've had, even in the best of times, and that is the people who are sleeping on the grates, the homeless who are homeless, you might say, by choice" (Wickenden, 1985, p. 24). That would have been news to the 24-year-old college student living in a New York City shelter after losing his job and forced to leave an apartment after a dispute with a roommate: "When I first got to the shelter . . . I wondered what I had gotten into. I had never been in anything like this—the odor, the dirt, people all over the floor. Then I realized I had no choice" (Stengel, 1986, p. 27). It also would have been news in the more typical case of a 43-year-old housewife with few job skills from Anaheim, California, who found herself in a shelter after her 19-year marriage crumbled in divorce. She lost her four-bedroom house and lived in a car with her three children for eight months before shelter workers found her, "My life simply fell apart . . . I lost everything. Why, I even had a microwave oven" (Stengel, 1986, p. 27).

While the homeless were clearly visible indicators of the budget cuts, they were widespread enough to affect every human need. A report on the impact of the cuts on Greensboro, North Carolina, puts them into perspective. In that medium-size city, public health services were substantially curtailed when chronic disease and cancer prevention and screening visits were cut in half; fewer indigent patients received outpatient services; fewer prenatal visits were provided; treatment services for dental problems, victims of child abuse, and speech and hearing problems were eliminated; and services for treatment of "children enrolled for seizures, heart defects, visual problems, and orthopedic or crippling conditions were reduced by 25–30%" (Wineburg, Spakes, & Finn, 1983, p. 491).

Inpatient mental health services were cut by about 50% and an adolescent care program was eliminated. These cuts led to more institutionalizations of patients, which was "not a treatment necessity but a budgetary requirement" (Wineburg, Spakes, & Finn, 1983, p. 491). In mental retardation services, residential care and sheltered workshop funding was cut. In nutritional services, public funding for the mobile meals program for the older adults was eliminated and the cost of public school lunches was increased. The eligibility scale for free and reduced lunches was also modified, resulting in a reduction in the number of students receiving free or reduced price lunches. Some parents had difficulty paying the higher-priced reduced fee lunches and school officials reported that many children "are bringing bag lunches; some are going without" (Wineburg, Spakes, & Finn, 1983, p. 492). Income support programs (AFDC, food stamps, disability income, Medicaid) were also cut back, but in at least AFDC and food stamps, the poor economy led to an increased number of persons receiving these benefits.

The breadth and depth of the cuts left persons in Greensboro frustrated as they tried to find services or, worse, found themselves without services that they previously received:

> One such person is a 27-year-old man who is four feet, eight inches tall who has a spinal deformity. Having received disability income for the last nine years, he was able to be self-sufficient in his own apartment and led a fairly independent life. However, a re-evaluation of his disability resulted in his being declared eligible to work. The case was appealed but his checks stopped coming. Although he sought work, with a 10% unemployment rate and severe restrictions on the type of work he might be able to do, no one would hire him. He lost his apartment; his grooming slipped; he became depressed and suffered from a loss of self-esteem. As he put it, "The government says I'm not worth supporting and the employers say I'm not worth hiring." What is left for people in such situations? (Wineburg, Spakes, & Finn, 1983, p. 493)

Once again the Reagan policy of public funding reductions combined with the hope that the private sector would fill the gap in services proved lacking in this man's case. More generally, Wineburg, Spakes, and, Finn (1983) asserted that private agencies could not meet the need for services in Greensboro due to understaffing, difficulties in fund-raising due to a recession and increased competition among agencies, and loss of their own federal funding. At the same time, the Greensboro community proved that policy does drive practice by organizing itself to provide new services in troubled times, including a food bank, housing rehabilitation program, and a community soup kitchen. See Figure 11.1. In addition, human service agencies worked to better coordinate services, promote their work through the media, and to hold political candidate

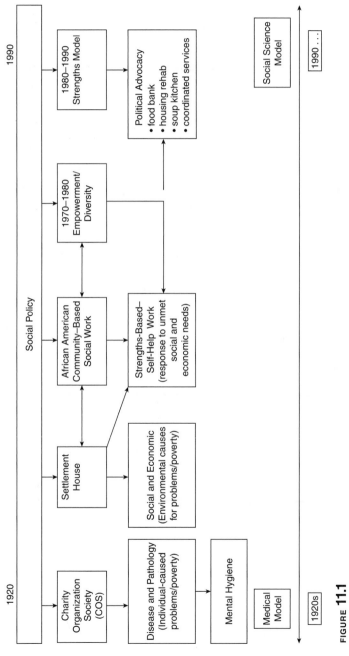

FIGURE 11.1

Once again we see how policy, or the lack thereof, drives practice. With the reduction of public funding, and the private agencies unable to meet the needs for service, the Greensboro community provided new services for the unmet human needs of the people; a strengths-based approach.

forums on human service issues. Perhaps, at least partially, as a consequence of such political action, the district congressman who supported Reagan's cuts was voted out of office by more than 10,000 votes (Wineburg, Spakes, & Finn, 1983). Some would argue that the move to patch the service needs with soup kitchens and food banks was to buy into the Reagan administration's drive to return to a charity model of social welfare. The political advocacy approach to cause social change was needed much more (see Haynes & Mickelson, 1992).

Indeed, the political advocacy approach depicted in Figure 11.1 is an excellent example of strengths-based practice. The community leaders went from a problem-centered approach to a strengths-centered approach by taking a political problem (Reagan's policy of public funding reductions) and transforming it into a community-based advocacy effort, thereby highlighting common, human need, not the social problem. The planners were able to broaden the knowledge base to include the views and realities of those experiencing the brunt of the social problem and to use community resources to provide a clear-cut alternative that would bypass the predominant system, turning to that which works better for the community (Chapin, 1995).

A study of the impact of the Omnibus Budget Reconciliation Act (OBRA) of 1981 and the impact of its welfare eligibility restrictions on New Jersey families also indicated that the Reagan presumption that self-sufficiency could be gained by simply forcing people off government assistance was flawed. It should be noted that 100 of the 129 welfare recipients in this study were working prior to termination of benefits. While measuring the quality of life (using such issues as food, shelter, clothing, health, and child care as indicators) of these former welfare recipients who lost eligibility due to OBRA requirements, it was found that a third of them were working at jobs that paid less than the legal minimum wage; 59% found child care payments more burdensome; more than half fell below the federal poverty threshold for families; excluding food stamps from the calculation, 87% of the family's total income was spent on food and housing; 40% of the families reported times of not having enough to eat; 54% of families were late paying their rent or mortgage; 51% were late paying utilities; 78% of the respondents did not obtain some type of medical care (including dental and purchase of medications) for themselves or their children due to the expense, and in most cases this was for a condition for which care had been received prior to termination of benefits; about half of the deferred medical cases involved severe problems; more than half of the families were in greater debt; and 65% of the families reported that their lives had changed for the worse since OBRA. Hispanic and African American families were more disadvantaged than white families. Because most of the families in this study were headed by persons working before and after termination of benefits, the stereotype of the undeserving welfare mother was deflated, and the underlying reasons for persistent poverty were revealed. As the authors state, "The . . . study suggests that structural, rather than motivational, factors are the major impediments to the economic self-sufficiency of families" (Wolock, Geismar, Lagay, & Raiffe, 1985/1986, p. 95).

In September 1981, *The Washington Post* and *The New York Times* referred to one particular provision of the Reagan cuts: searching homes. From *The Post*, we learn that the provision caught little attention at first. However, two months later it came to public attention and the welfare experts expressed alarm that it could force the state to send out inspectors to assess personal items such as used clothing, old furniture, and pots and pans. To eliminate such a possibility the word "home" was defined to include all items essential to everyday life and not just the structure in which a family lives. The Secretary of Health and Human Service, Schweiker, said, "I just didn't feel we should be forcing people who are on the AFDC rolls to sell their furniture and equipment; that makes no sense at all" (Mintz 1981, p. 1).

The Times reported:

> . . . The courts have said that Government agents need a search warrant to enter a home if they are seeking evidence of a crime. Where there is no criminal investigation, the Supreme Court has said that caseworkers may visit a home to establish a family's eligibility for welfare as long as the visit is announced in advance and meets certain tests of "reasonableness" "The cost to count personal property and household goods far exceeds the projected savings," said a spokesman for the National Council of State Public Welfare Administrators, a nonprofit organization of state officials. Federal officials said . . . that the proposed rules would reduce cheating . . . [and] that the new rules would carry out the will of Congress, which . . . wanted poor families to consider liquidating personal assets before resorting to public assistance. (Pear, 1981, p. 1)

The following year, *The Christian Science Monitor* reported:

> Five months after its inception, the federal "workfare" program is the focus of intense debate. The stance taken by supporters is summed by Robert Carleson, special assistant to the president for policy development Workfare [as] "an idea whose time has come," a program that gives the taxpayer a return on the "welfare dollar." Mothers should be happy to "work for their welfare checks." Opponents vehemently disagree. Boston welfare rights activist Sherrill Twine, a single mother who has worked her way off Massachusetts welfare rolls, calls workfare "a worknapping" of women at minimum wages. The government calls all the shots in a program that provides neither training nor jobs that get women off AFDC. (Overbea, 1982, p. 6)

And two years later, *The San Diego Union-Tribune* reported:

> People removed from the welfare rolls in 1981 generally have increased their work efforts and their earnings, but did not earn enough to make up for the loss of welfare and food-stamps benefits in the last three years, the General Accounting Office said yesterday. Thus, many of the people removed from the welfare rolls were living in poverty . . . the law [OBRA] had achieved two of its main purposes, to save money and to reduce welfare caseloads. It also confirmed the administration's

contention that people would not quit jobs to regain eligibility for welfare. But the study also documented significant hardships among the people cut from the rolls [and many] had been denied medical or dental care because they could not pay for it . . . they ran out of food . . . and could not pay monthly rent. . . . The study was done at the request of the House Ways and Means Committee. Rep. Charles B. Range, D-NY said the study indicated that "low-income individuals are willing to work, but have been make poorer by Mr. Reagan's administration policies. . . ." Dr. Robert Jr. Rubin, an assistant Secretary of Health and Human Services, said the national statistics in the report were accurate, but he denied that people had suffered hardships as a result of losing welfare benefits. With a few isolated exceptions, people are no worse off than they had been before the cuts took effect in October 1981. (Wires; From News Services, p. 1)

Gramm-Rudman-Hollings   In 1986, the Gramm-Rudman-Hollings bill (GRH) was supposed to help eliminate the federal debt by offering across-the-board budget cuts if Congress and the president were unable to decide on how to balance the budget. As a result, the budget was cut by $11.7 million, affecting important health and maintenance programs (Day, 1999).

Some of the many other social welfare components that were affected were AFDC, child welfare, day care, physical and mental health, and housing. Some of the repercussions of the new rules were that it became unlikely that a family with a parent working at a low-paying job would receive a supplementary benefit, nor were the children of AFDC recipients not expected to graduate high school or vocational training by age 19 eligible for benefits. Pregnant women without children had to be six months along before they were eligible for benefits, and a limit was placed on how much child care costs for working mothers could be referred from benefit checks (Karger & Stoesz, 1998).

Reagan interrupted an almost 80-year tradition when he canceled the White House Conference on Children in 1981, and made the largest cuts ever to the funding of federal programs for childcare services. This happened despite the finding of a 1982 survey by the Census Bureau revealing that the most frequently acknowledged problem of single mothers with regards to securing employment was finding a day care program that they could trust and afford (Karger & Stoesz, 1998).

Health, mental health services, and housing took hits as well. Medicaid came under attack with a reduction in the amount of money allowed to states, along with changes in governing rules that resulted in fewer services. The block grants, which replaced the federal funding, eliminated direct funding to Community Mental Health Centers. Low cost housing assistance (HUD) was slashed by 60% between 1981 ($31 billion) and 1985 ($10 billion) (Karger & Stoesz, 1998).

Family Support Act of 1988   The Family Support Act (FSA) was designed to provide education and job training programs for AFDC recipients; however, the effort lacked any real substance. The assumption of the bill was that the economy would be able to produce large numbers of jobs that paid well. Punitive measures for noncompliance were included, and it did not tackle the important issue of the absence of a federal AFDC benefit standard (Haynes & Holmes, 1994). The message from the administration was clear: The federal government should not be involved in the social welfare system.

The punitive elements of the Family Support Act tended to attack that which it claimed to support: the family. Patterned after workfare programs operating in several states, the FSA included such provisions as allowing states to reduce benefits to parents whose children were at least three years old if they were not working or otherwise enrolled in a training or educational program. While such provisions sounded good in theory and were thought to encourage self-sufficiency, a lack of job opportunities and social supports, such as adequate child care, led to failure and a greater burden on struggling mothers. In New York City in 1990, the phone lines to request child care assistance were almost continuously busy for the three weeks at the beginning of the school year as families searched for placements. Even if they were able to speak to a person at the agency, the city could only provide support to one out of five children (Udesky, 1990).

In addition to its lack of resources to provide care, the bureaucracy's concern for the children of welfare was not always evident. One woman living in the Bronx was sanctioned for turning down a job assignment for fear that her children, who suffered from severe asthma, would suffer. The children attended a school that required the mother to take the children to the hospital if they suffered an attack. The New York City welfare office was requiring her to clean an abandoned building with no phone as part of her work requirement. " 'I feared for their lives, . . . If an ambulance doesn't get there in time, my child could die' " (Udesky, 1990, p. 303). Such practice decisions by welfare officials were supported by an internal policy document that told caseworkers "not to allow exemptions for 'the numerous difficulties that are often associated with poverty,' such as general worries about children" (Udesky, 1990, p. 303).

With the new "morality" brought to light during the Reagan era, its dynamics became seriously intertwined with the political economy of oppression. Women were expected to "keep their place" and the problems of institutional sexism was held in check with them earning only 60% of men's wages for the same work.

Women's "Work" A startling trend, beginning in the 1950s, in women's employment was the on-going reality of the low salaries they worked for. Evidence appeared in the late 1980s showing that 77% of all employed women worked in low pay occupations and industries, with the prediction that the trend would extend into the twenty first century° (National Commission on Working Women, 1986; Perkins, 1993a). Women in lower paying jobs are typically considered working class; are defined as semi-skilled and unskilled, and hold traditional, sex segregated, low paying jobs that have become referred to as pink-collar, for example, bookkeepers, beautician, secretary, nursing aide, clerical, food preparation and services, retail sales, housekeeping, and child-care workers. This pink-collar working domain is particularly staffed by African American women, over half of whom are employed in clerical and service occupations (Perkins, 1993a). By 1970, more than 50% of all women from ages 35 to 54 held jobs outside the home. Although a major shift in women's occupations occurred between 1940 and 1981 from service jobs to white-collar occupations, women remain overrepresented in low paying occupations and in industries where they receive virtually no on-the-job training (see Perkins, 1991).

For women as well as men, earnings are crucial for personal and family support. A major reason for the increase in women's employment over the last four decades has been the growing number of female-headed households. The differences, however, are significant with regard to earnings and occupations. Women's salaries are substantially less than men's salaries. Women have earned an average of $.64 for every $1.00 earned by men since 1950. This gap closed slightly (about 10%) in the 1980s, not due to salary increases for women, but due to the decline in men's salaries.†In 1984 women working full time had median annual earnings of $14,780, about $8,438 less than the median for employed men (Perkins, 1993a).

The role of the employer in promoting job segregation is manifested in hiring, placement, and promotion decisions. Organizational characteristics, for example structured mobility ladders, connote discrimination. There are two types of employment discrimination. The first is job discrimination by employers, a major catalyst for job segregation by sex and race. The second is the practice of allowing workers with equal productivity to earn different wages. Occupational mobility, on-the-job-training, and union membership are additional areas where discrimination exists for women (Perkins, 1993a).

°Between 1985 and 1995 occupational differences between women and men declined, but at a slower rate than during the 1970s and 1980s. For example in 1995 women accounted for 43% of managerial and related employment, nearly double their share in 1975 (22%). The employment in professional occupations for women also rose from 45% to 53% over this period. While women and men were almost equally represented among managers and professionals in 1995, gender differences were still pronounced. Women continued to hold four out of five administrative support jobs and were heavily represented in services occupations (Wootton, 1997).

†This gap between women's and men's salaries has closed slightly through 1995. One source (U.S. Women's Bureau, 1997) put the percentage for women's salaries at 75.5% in 1995, while the U.S. Bureau of Census (1997) placed the percentage at 71%, with women's full-time median annual earnings at $22,497 and men's at $31,496.

The predominate reason for women's low earnings is job segregation by sex. Job segregation is an accepted and basic feature of the world of work. Female-dominated occupations characteristically have shorter career ladders, meaning women often "max-out" on employment ladders within a few years. Women in traditionally male-identified occupations are often assigned jobs that offer fewer opportunities for promotion, for example, personnel administration rather than sales. Structured mobility ladders, both at the entry level and within the employment structure, perpetuate job segregation by sex and, consequently, produce discrimination in the workplace. Women receive less on-the-job training than men or are given jobs with shorter training periods, leading to higher rates of turnover (Perkins, 1993a, 1993b).

African American women have a narrower sex-wage different than white women due to the interaction of race and sex discrimination in hiring and promotion. Discrimination can cause wage differentials among equally skilled occupations, and wage differentials by race may be maintained through occupational segregation rather than by overt wage discrimination. The discrimination coefficient differs among occupations because of status considerations; employers prefer to hire whites over blacks (Perkins, 1993a).

An examination of the work histories among black and white male and female adults in the 1980s found black women's work histories to be less continuous than those of black and white males. Black women worked fewer years after leaving school, worked fewer years full time, had more frequent and longer work interruptions with shorter tenure in a single job. African American women's work histories were less continuous than men's but more continuous than white women. Also, the incidence of physical disability is higher among older working-class black women. Disability limits labor force participation and is an important predicate of work and retirement patterns and benefits (Gibson, 1983, 1987; Perkins, 1993a).

Low level occupations, discontinuous work histories, physical disabilities, discrimination, and early retirement contribute to depreciation of the working-class black woman's earning power. Working-class black women accumulate less human capital through work experience, (although their participation in the labor market over many years is greater than white women's years), and they are unable to fully participate in human capital investment. Human capital appreciation also reflects the investment of time and money in schooling and job training, neither of which are available to many black women participating in the labor force (Perkins, 1993b).

Vulnerable Groups

Any person or groups of people in need of public assistance were affected and rendered even more vulnerable with the constant threat of the safety net slipping out from under them. The way our welfare system is designed, certain groups will always be poor, such as single women with children, African Americans, Latinos, persons with disabilities, and those in unskilled jobs (Jansson, 1994).

Virginia Woolf, an English novelist, critic, and ardent feminist, writes about the need for inferior beings in any society. The following passage is from her critically acclaimed, nonfiction work, *A Room of One's Own* (1929) with her arguments being oblique, not polemical, and still relevant. She speaks of women, but her words can easily be used as an analogy for any group of people marginalized in our society and is still applicable today.

> Life for both sexes . . . is arduous, difficult, a perpetual struggle. It calls for gigantic courage and strength. More than anything, perhaps, creatures of illusion as we are, it calls for confidence in oneself. Without confidence we are as babes in the cradle. And how can we generate this imponderable quality, which is yet so invaluable, most quickly? By thinking that other people are inferior to oneself. By feeling that one has some innate superiority—it may be wealth, or rank, a straight nose, or the portrait of a grandfather by Romney—over other people. Hence the enormous importance to a patriarch who has to conquer, who has to rule, of feeling that great numbers of people, half the human race indeed, are by nature inferior to himself. . . . Women lived all these centuries as looking glasses possessing the magic and delicious power of reflecting the figure of man at twice its natural size. Without that power probably the earth would still be swamp and jungle. The glories of all our wars would be unknown. . . . Whatever may be their use in civilized societies, mirrors are essential to all violent and heroic action. That is why Napoleon and Mussolini both insist so emphatically upon the inferiority of women, for if they were not inferior, they would cease to enlarge. That serves to explain in part the necessity that women so often are to men. . . . (Sancier, 1992, p. 346)

These values and attitudes, which were probably somewhat unconscious, were apparent in the policies and legislation developed by the Reagan administration. Any legislation tainted by these unconscious beliefs held by men, or people in power, will never touch or address the needs of *all* Americans—most notably, the "common" man and woman. With regards to women, since they make up such a large majority of individuals receiving public assistance, most of them do not fit the image held in the minds of the country's leaders of what a woman's role is. This is why policies developed by men in power, the vast majority of whom are white, middle-to-upper class, do little to address the true needs of those individuals the policies are supposed to help. This assessment of policymakers adds credence to what has been said in previous chapters about the importance of individuals having input into policy decisions. Those affected by policies or legislation having input, so as to paint a more accurate picture of what their circumstances and needs really are, is crucial. Under Reagan's administration, policies were not designed to offer real choices, rather they offered the governmentally accepted choices, typical of a problem-oriented analysis of need.

THE BUSH ADMINISTRATION

Bush was a conservative and came from a wealthy family. He ran his campaign on the shirttails of Reagan ideology. Bush actually declared a mandate to continue with the policies established by Reagan, holding the line of domestic spending, avoiding a tax increase, and maintaining a strong national defense. Bush's election campaign was supported by the same traditional movement that supported Reagan—religious fundamentalists and conservative populists (Karger & Stoesz, 1990; Trattner, 1999).

His views differed very little from Reagan's with regard to the federal government's need for social spending. The difference between the two administrations was Bush's power to implement policies to reflect this view. During Bush's presidency, the Democrats had more control in Congress. This allowed for more social spending during his term. Bush, like Reagan, believed that social welfare could be best addressed by promoting individual involvement. This was done with his "kinder and gentler" rhetoric that advanced the notion that volunteers, those "thousand points of light," could help achieve his domestic agenda. Hence, be continued to emphasize both privatization and volunteerism, showing little ideological or philosophical redirection during his presidency (Haynes & Holmes, 1994).

Where Bush did differ was in his opinion of supply-side economics, referring to it as "voodoo economics." He was as zealous as Reagan about the necessity of continued increased military spending and agreed that taxes should not be raised. Without the support of a Republican Congress, the budget stalemate continued incurring huge deficits; however, social spending rose at a much higher rate than in the Reagan administration (Jansson, 1997).

Outside the domestic arena, there was a considerable lessening in the tensions surrounding the Cold War, with the Soviet Union and other Eastern European states becoming more independent. Many social reformers felt this should have allowed for a decrease in military spending and an increase in social spending. Bush, however, was being pressured by the conservatives to remain true to his promise of no new taxes. This dispute was negotiated in the budget summit of 1990 ending with everyone getting something, but with very little change to the federal budget. With pressure to reduce the deficit, Bush did back off his promise and agreed to some new taxes with the ratio of military and domestic spending in the budget preserved. The overall budget, however, was to be reduced incrementally in coming years by putting a cap on the aggregate social spending and military spending (Jansson, 1997).

Civil Rights Under Reagan-Bush

Reagan, unlike Ford and Carter, seemed to believe that racial discrimination had nearly disappeared. He went broader and deeper with attacks on civil rights enforcement than did his predecessors. Along with sharp reductions in the number of civil rights enforcement personnel, the Department of Justice filed far fewer antidiscrimination suits, and in the mid-1980s Reagan's assistant attorney general for civil rights, William Bradford Reynolds, unsuccessfully tired to persuade the Supreme Court to outlaw affirmative action. His appointments also reflected his aggressive opposition to the views of civil rights advocates. The U.S. Civil Rights Commission (CRC) had no enforcement authority; however, they issued reports critical of the president's policies. As a retaliation, Reagan attempted to pack the CRC with members whose views mirrored his own. He fired the CRC chairman in 1981 and replaced him with Clarence Pendleton, a conservative black Republican. Despite a Congressional battle in 1982, Reagan succeeded in creating a conservative majority on the CRC (Levine, 1996).

Reagan selected a black man, William Bell, to head the Equal Employment Opportunity Commission (EEOC) in 1981 despite Bell's having no qualifications for the post. The appointment spared an outcry from civil rights supporters, and the following year the president replaced Bell with Clarence Thomas, another black conservative. Samuel Pierce, a black Republican, was selected to the cabinet as head of the Department of Housing and Urban Development (HUD), and when Reagan reversed Carter administration efforts to enforce fair housing policy, Pierce make no objection (Levine, 1996).

Even though Vice President George Bush claimed he was campaigning for "a kinder, gentler America," other aspects of his campaign contradicted that promise, and ultimately his record as president did little to improve his standing among African Americans. For example, in his campaign speeches, Bush often featured the case of Willie Horton, an African American convict who had raped a white woman while on a parole granted by Michael Dukakis, Bush's opponent. By his frequent mention of this incident, Bush played on some whites' centuries-old fears of black men's sexuality and violence (Levine, 1996). Bush was, however, applauded on one decision: his appointment of Colin Powell in 1989 as the first black chairman of the military's Joint Chiefs of Staff. But his other black nominees were much more controversial; for example, William Lucas, a Republican from Michigan, whom Bush nominated for assistant attorney general for civil rights. Lucas had neither a civil rights background nor any courtroom experience, and his nomination was rejected. Bush went on to nominate Clarence Thomas to succeed the retiring Thurgood Marshall on the Supreme Court, a selection widely opposed by liberals. On matters of civil rights policy, this president followed the Reagan pattern (Levine, 1996).

Other Events of the Time

Here we will highlight a few of the other significant events that characterized this time period. The Americans with Disabilities Act (ADA), the war against drugs, and race riots.

The Americans with Disabilities Act   One of the more productive developments to emerge from the conservative era was the Americans with Disabilities Act. Boosted by the Rehabilitation Act of 1973, persons with disabilities evolved and mobilized behind the establishment of independent living centers. Federal funding was received through a national network of local organizations, which enabled them to provide an array of outreach, educational, and advocacy services, with the intent of freeing persons from dependence on medical institutions (Jansson, 1997). At the end of this chapter, there is an analysis of the ADA from a strengths perspective. See Appendix 11–A for the complete Americans with Disabilities Act.

War Against Drugs   Beginning from the late 1960s onward, the increase in drug use rose sharply throughout all segments of American society. The inner cities, however, were struck the hardest as drugs provided an escape from despair. This was especially true after crack, a cheap form of cocaine, appeared on the streets in the early 1980s, with addiction reaching epidemic proportions. Attached to this epidemic came violence produced by proliferating drug markets and dealers in urban communities. These events were major factors in the passage by Congress of the Anti-Drug Abuse Act of 1988. This move was hailed by many African American leaders who felt it was long overdue and a necessary response to the problems of their beleaguered communities. A drug czar, or director, was appointed to oversee and coordinate the actions of more than 30 federal agencies involved in the fight against drugs. President Bush choose William J. Bennett, who had served as secretary of education under Reagan, to lead the efforts (Franklin & Moss, 1994; Levine, 1996).

   Bennett held the post for one and a half years, expending considerable energy to find new approaches to solving the drug problem, with little immediate effect. He used the post to launch attacks against liberal intellectuals, academics, and journalists for what he termed their "morally scandalous positions" advocating either tolerance of drug use or legalization. He left the post claiming that America had gained ground in its war against drugs, but critics argued that he and the Bush administration had failed to produce an effective strategy to confront the problem and that drug trafficking and the violence associated with it had soared to even higher levels. None of his successors to the post had his ability to capture public attention and made even less impact on these worsening problems (Franklin & Moss, 1994).

Other devastating outcomes from this severe drug problem were the birth of a growing number of black babies being born addicted to crack, and the rise in acquired immunodeficiency syndrome (AIDS) from users sharing needles. Through 1992, 30% of those who died from AIDS were African Americans. Further, unemployed youth formed armed gangs who participated in the highly profitable drug trade. A greater number of youth died from drug overdoses or in the gang shootouts that plagued the inner cities. In the ghettos, crime in general increased with the black prison population almost tripling from 1978 to 1991; the number of white inmates only doubled (Levine, 1996).

Race Riots   The despair in most inner cities promoted anger and violence. Major race riots broke out around the country. In August 1980 a riot broke out in the black section of Miami, leaving 16 dead and hundreds injured. One year later, another riot broke out in the Crown Heights section of Brooklyn after a Hasidic Jewish driver ran over and killed a seven-year-old black boy. Investigators claimed it was an accident, but there were nights of violence afterward with a Hasid being killed at random by a black mob. It was at this time that rap music emerged from the inner cities, often expressing rage against women, Jews, whites in general, and homosexuals. Frequently the lyrics described violent acts against the targets of rage, especially women (Levine, 1996).

In the 1970s a Bronx disc jockey, Afrika Bambaataa is credited with being one of the pivotal forces in the development of the music that picked up the label of "rap." An ex-gang member and self-taught student of the black culture, Bambaataa came to believe that the arts could be used to combat the rampant street violence in his community. He founded the Youth Organization of Adlai Stevenson High School (later renamed Zula Nation), bringing together large numbers of youth who shared his interest in the street arts. The artistic expression of these youth that prepared the way for the inner-city youth art movement of the 1970s. Their activities included break dancing, disc jockeying, rapping, and graffiti drawing. Bambaataa pointed out, " I had them to battle against each other in a nonviolent way, like rapper against rapper rather than knife against knife" (Southern, 1997, p. 599). He is credited with applying the term "hip-hop" to the South Bronx street culture after he heard a rapper at a party chanting, "Hip-hop, you don't stop/that makes your body rock" and after he started using the term, it caught on. Youths in black communities across the nation were "partying" to this new kind of dance music by the mid-1970s (Southern, 1997, p. 599).

With the spread of rap through inner-city neighborhoods, Sugar Hill Records, a small, black, New York label, released the first rap single in 1979, titled "Rapper's Delight," which quickly sold over 500,000 copies. Rap groups were very visible in the music scene by 1982, with touring and recording activities. Early rap produced what is often cited as the first rap album (CD) by Flash and the Furious Five with a social message appropriately titled "The

Message" which "gave a harsh and graphic picture of life in the nation's black slums" (Southern, 1997, p. 600).

It's like a jungle sometimes, it makes me wonder
How I keep from going under
It's like a jungle sometimes, it makes me wonder
How I keep from going under

Broken glass everywhere
People pissing on the stairs
You know they just don't care
I can't take the smell, can't take the noise
Got no money to move out, I guess I got no choice

Rats in the front room, roaches in the back
Junkies in the alley with a baseball bat
I tried to get away but I couldn't get far
'Cause the man with the tow truck repossessed my car

Don't push me 'cause I'm close to the edge
I'm trying not to lose my head
Ah huh huh huh huh
It's like a jungle sometimes, it makes me wonder
How I keep from going under

Standing on the front stoop, hanging out the window
Watching all the cars go by, roaring as the breezes blow
Crazy lady, living in a bag
Eating outta garbage pails, used to be a fag hag
Says she danced the tango, skip the light fandango
Was zircon princess seemed to lost her senses
Down at the peep show, watching all the creeps so
She could tell the story to the girls back home
She went to the city and got social security
She had to get a pension, she couldn't make it on her own

Don't push me 'cause I'm close to the edge
I'm trying not to lose my head
Ah huh huh huh huh
It's like a jungle sometimes, it makes me wonder
How I keep from going under
Huh ah huh huh huh
It's like a jungle sometimes, it makes me wonder
How I keep from going under

My brother's doing bad, stole my mother's TV
Says she watches too much, it's just not healthy
"All My Children" in the daytime, "Dallas" at night
Can't even see the game or the Sugar Ray fight
The bill collectors, they ring my phone
And scare my wife when I'm not home
Got a bum education, double-digit inflation

Can't train to the job, there's a strike at the station
Neon King Kong, standing on my back
Can't stop to turn around, broke my sacroiliac
A mid-range migraine, cancered membrane
Sometimes I think I'm going insane
I swear, I might hijack a plane

Don't push me 'cause I'm close to the edge
I'm trying not to lose my head
It's like a jungle sometimes, it makes me wonder
How I keep from going under

My son said, "Daddy, I don't want to go to school
'Cause the teacher's a jerk, he must think I'm a fool
And all the kids smoke reefer, I think it'd be cheaper
If I just got a job, learned to be a street sweeper
Dance to the beat, shuffle my feet
Wear a shirt and tie and run with the creeps
'Cause it's all about money, ain't a damn thing funny
You got to have a con in this land of milk and honey"

They pushed that girl in front of the train
Took her to the doctor, sewed her arm on again
Stabbed that man right in his heart
Gave him a transplant for a brand new start
I can't walk through the park 'cause it's crazy after dark
Keep my hand on my gun
'Cause they got me on the run
I feel like a outlaw
Broke my last glass jaw
Hear them say, "You want some more?"
Livin' on a seesaw

Don't push me 'cause I'm close to the edge
I'm trying not to lose my head
Say what?
It's like a jungle sometimes, it makes me wonder
How I keep from going under

A child is born with no state of mind
Blind to the ways of mankind
God is smiling on you but he's frowning too
Because only God knows what you go through
You grow in the ghetto, living second rate
And your eyes will sing a song of deep hate
The place that you play and where you stay
Looks like one great big alleyway
You'll admire all the number book-takers
Thugs, pimps, and pushers and the big money makers
Driving big cars, spending twenties and tens
And you wanna grow up to be just like them, huh

Smugglers, scramblers, burglars, gamblers
Pickpockets, peddlers, even panhandlers
You say, "I'm cool, huh, I'm no fool"
But then you wind up dropping out of high school
Now you're unemployed, all nonvoid
Walking 'round like you're Pretty Boy Floyd
Turned stick-up kid but look what you done did
Got sent up for a eight-year bid
Now your manhood is took and you're a Maytag
Spend the next two years as a undercover fag
Being used and abused to serve like hell
'Til one day you was found hung dead in the cell
It was plain to see that your life was lost
You was cold and your body swung back and forth
But now your eyes sing the sad sad song
Of how ya lived so fast and died so young

So don't push me 'cause I'm close to the edge
I'm trying not to lose my head
Ah huh huh huh huh
It's like a jungle sometimes, it makes me wonder
How I keep from going under

(*Dialogue*)
Yo, Mel, you see that girl man?
Yeah, man
Cowboy
Yo! That sound like Cowboy, man
That's cool
Yo! What's up money?
Yo!
Hey, where's Creole and Rahiem at, man?
They upstairs cooling out
So, what's up for tonight y'all?
Yo! We could go down to Fever, man
Let's go check out June Bug, man
Hey yo! You know that girl Betty?
Yeah, man
Her moms got robbed, man
What?
Not again?
She got hurt real bad
When this happen? When this happen?
(*Tires squeal*)
Everybody freeze! Don't nobody move nothing, y'all know what this is
Get 'em up!
What?
Get 'em up!
Man, we down with Grandmaster Flash and the Furious Five
What's that? A gang?
No!

Look, shut up! I don't want to hear your mouth
'Scuse me, Officer, Officer, what's the problem?
You the problem, you the problem
You ain't got to push me, man
Get in the car! Get in the car! Get in the godda—
Get in the car! (Morley, 1992, pp. 150–154)

"The Message" was considered a sequel to Stevie Wonder's 1971 rock hit, "Living for the City," with the former advancing the vocal innovations of early rap and combining them with the sociopolitical ambitions of the black rockers, popular a decade earlier. "Both were cautionary tales of getting caught up in the temptations of big-city life. Both end with a fade-out confrontation between homeboys and cops" (Morley, 1992, p. xxiii).

By the mid-1980s rap evolved from dance music to become fragmented into subsets that reflected the social class of the rappers. For example, rappers living in inner-city Los Angeles were perceived as being uneducated but streeetwise and obsessed with violence, drugs, sex, gangs, and guns. It was their rap that acquired the label "gangsta rap" (for gangster rap). High school graduates and college students living in middle-class neighborhood in New York were called "black Bohemians" because their rap interests lie in the classics, the arts, poetry, and the sciences (Southern, 1997).

The following lyrics give an example of the misogynist tone demeaning women. These artists often refer to their partners as "bitches" and "whores" as they take pride in describing their abuse of power in sexual situation. The first few verses of a 1992 song by Snoop Doggy Dogg . . . "before you hit on a bitch you have to find a contraceptive/you never know she could be learning her man/ . . . /and at the same time burning her man/ . . ." (Krohn & Suazo, 1995, p. xx). [This lyric is very mild compared to most.]

Los Angeles Race Riots   It was the Los Angeles ghetto riots that unleashed the most vivid expression of black anger and despair. In March 1991 Rodney King, an African American, was arrested after a high-speed chase by white Los Angeles policemen who severely beat him after alleging that he resisted arrest and threatened the officers. A man on a balcony recorded the event, shocking many Americans, black and white, and millions of others around the world as it was played back on television (Franklin & Moss, 1994). A Glasgow new release appeared in *The Herald*, entitled, "The Ugly Side of American Life." The text read, in part, "President Bush last night ordered the Army into riot-torn Los Angeles to restore order. . . . Thousands of troops patrolled the city like a war zone, with fixed bayonets . . ." (Davidson, 1992, p. 1). Minor rioting and protests spread to cities across the country with fear enveloping urban homes "during America's worst social unrest since the 1960s" (Davidson, 1992, p. 1).

Closer to home, *The Washington Post* ran a column with the headline, "POP RECORDINGS: The Rage and the Rhythm of West Cost Rappers." The report is about the aftermath of the Los Angeles riots in April, 1991 and refers to the police beating victim Rodney King who asked, "Can we all get along?" Through new releases from several prominent West Coast rappers, came an unsettling answer. The lyrics from their albums reveal the despair and diffuse rage that continues to simmer in black communities (Briggs, 1992). With his album *Predator,* Ice Cube wrote, "Everything you wanted to know about the riots was on the records before the riots. . . ." His third solo album, No. 1 on the Billboard charts, was a counterattack to the LAPD's assault on King and south-central LA's residents, as well as an indictment of the American social system. . . . "Ice Cube wishes to acknowledge white America's continued commitment to the silence and oppression of black men . . . and America's cops for their systematic and brutal killings of brothers . . ." (Briggs, 1992, p. G10).

To the shock of many, the police officers were acquitted in April 1992 by a suburban jury with no black members. The verdict ignited an enormous riot in Los Angeles's south-central ghetto with buildings set ablaze, stores were looted, and whites who were driving by were dragged from their vehicles and beaten. At the end of the violence, a few days later, there were 38 dead, near 4,000 placed under arrest, and approximately 3,700 buildings burnt to ruins (Levine, 1996).

There was a brief period of time after the Los Angeles riots when President Bush and other leaders spoke generally about the need to help inner-city communities and whites who were polled agreed. However, this was an era when whites were insecure about their own economic future, strongly opposing higher taxes, and sympathy for the ghettos faded quickly (Levine, 1996).

From *The Los Angeles Times* Nuestro Tiempo section came the headline: VOICES FROM THE COMMUNITY. The events surrounding the rioting in Los Angeles elicited a variety of responses. These are a few of their comments:

- Police brutality was a major issue that framed our (Chicano) movement. Yet here we are in 1992, and the issue continues to be the same. . . . How are we going to fight for equality in the communities that have remained quiet?
- Gloria Romero, member of the L.A. Police Commission's Hispanic Advisory Council "I lost everything. Nothing was saved—nothing, nothing, nothing."
- Arturo Ybarra, president of Watts/Century Latino Organization, "In particular, the (King) trial affected the Central American community because of the issue of police impunity. It's incredible to see it in a country where democracy is supposed to work. . . . I can see it in El Salvador, but not here."
- Radolfo Acuna, historian, Cal State Northridge Chicano Studies program, "No one should mistake our lack of action to say we are not equally as angry, equally as upset about the Rodney King verdict. . . . We have to turn our anger into positive energy."

- Cesar Chavez, founder of United Farmworkers Union, "A part of me would like to see our (Latino) Community as nothing but law-abiding people. That's the goal we expect from everyone. But we are talking about a human phenomenon (looting and violence), and I guess the reality is that we are all human."
- Raul Yzaguirre, National Council of La Raza president, "The hardest part is rebuilding the spirit of the city—what holds us together as Angelenos. It's the rebuilding of trust. . . . It's connecting communities that have never been connected. . . . At the table in the business community, Koreans, Latinos and Blacks and others have to interconnect." (Di Rado, 1992, p. 5)

There were different views on what happened in Los Angeles. It was called an uprising, a rebellion, an act of resistance to injustice and oppression by some. By others, it was seen as a spontaneous outburst, an expression of pent-up anger and rage. Still others wondered how massive looting could be endowed with political motives (Hacker, 1995). Hacker states that all those factors were at work, going on to explain that

> Los Angeles' South-Central section is part of inner-city America, in which millions of black men, women and children know a poverty and a despair unmatched elsewhere in the advanced world. Seen as subordinate citizens, they know they are scorned by mainstream society, and few see hope for a change in their fortunes. Indeed, there had been similar rioting in Los Angeles and elsewhere a quarter of a century earlier. Yet despite exhortations to action and political promises, the festering conditions remained in place. To burn down the shops you will need the next day may not seem to make sense. But one cannot always expect civil protests from people who have been rebuffed and betrayed by the American dream. (p. 238–239)

Hacker (1995) goes on to ask the question, "is anyone responsible for the fact that a growing group of Americans, the majority of them black, feel imprisoned from birth behind forty-foot walls?" He contends that they know they are regarded as superfluous and that society has no use for them. That belief, knowing there is not a way out, leads to desperation and despair. The Kerner Commission answers the question, in part when using the term "ghetto" to explain similar outbursts of a generation earlier:

> What white Americans have never fully understood—but what the Negro can never forget—is that white society is deeply implicated in the ghetto. White institutions created it, white institutions maintain it, and white society condones it. (Hacker, 1995, p. 240)

It was not just the underclass who expressed black anger at this in history. There was a growing middle class with many members feeling that their hopes were being thwarted, a good example being black managers working in corporate America. The number of black men holding management position in the corporate world between 1982 and 1992 increased by more than 20%. As we have learned, historically, there was even more employment discrimination for black women. From the period between 1982 and 1992, however, their presence in corporate management grew by about 65%. Yet frustration by both the men and women grew, with complaints that they had "black jobs," for example, jobs that mainly involved improving the company's racial image. There were also complaints that large numbers of black managers had no "sign off power," or decision-making power. There was the glass ceiling, which was based on unofficial, or invisibly, discriminatory practices that limited how far people of color could rise within the corporate world. By the mid-1990s, almost all the members of the inner circle were still white men with very few blacks reaching top level management (Levine, 1996).

There were other forms of discrimination facing middle-class blacks. Housing for example, remained widely segregated, forcing blacks who could afford first-rate homes to often settle for second-rate dwellings. Many were able to have the promise of good incomes fulfilled, but they could not always live as well as their white counterparts. They were still subject to racial harassment, such as being more likely than whites of any class to being stopped by police as crime suspects. There were violent white racist groups that emerged in the 1980s, including youth gangs known as skinheads, who assaulted black lawyers and corporate mangers as well as black underclass. There was the frequent reminder for the middle-class black that no matter how high they rose in status, their blackness still reflected inferiority in the eyes of many whites (Levine, 1996).

Latino Art, Murals, and Strengths

While most literature on Latinos is generally focused on socioeconomic challenges, not enough attention has been paid to indicators of community health. For example, "Latinos consistently have a disproportionate number of families in poverty, high rates of school dropout; alcohol, tobacco, and other drug abuse; and HIV/AIDS, to list just four social problems" (Delgado & Barton, 1998, p. 346). Latinos generally reside in inner cities, and social workers, as well as other mental health providers, tend to identify social indicators related to urban despair—billboards selling alcohol and tobacco, large numbers of bars and liquor establishments, vacant lots, boarded-up buildings, and abandoned cars. Social workers, and others, need a better understanding of the social-political importance of murals in Latino communities from an asset (strengths) perspective (Delgado & Barton, 1998). "Murals . . . are newspapers on walls and a wealth of information is contained in them. They can be valuable to educators, politicians, sociologists, political scientists [social workers, etc.]" (Delgado & Barton, 1998, p. 346). One well-known mural entitled, "We Are Not a Minority," was painted in 1978. It is an example of Chicano art, which differs from purely Mexican and Latino art. Chicano art has affinities with Pop Art, which draws similarities to comic strips and illustrations from popular magazines (Lucie-Smith, 1994).

Diego Rivera, a famous muralist, summed up the importance of murals quite well, "Mural painting must help in [a person's] struggle to become a human being, and for that purpose it must live wherever it can; no place is bad for it, so long as it is there permitted to fulfill its primary functions of nutrition and enlightenment" (Delgado & Barton, 1998, p. 346).

SOCIAL WORK AND OPPRESSED/MINORITY GROUPS 1980–1992

While oppressed groups were struggling with the effects of squeezed social spending, the profession of social work was discussing how to respond to these groups. In 1982, the National Association of Social Work (NASW) held a national conference titled "Color in a White Society," which resulted in an article by the same name being published in a special issue of *Social Work*. At the conference, panel members who discussed "Building on the Strengths of Minority Groups," "stressed that social workers have an ethical obligation to work for system change rather than focus solely on individual change" (Sancier, 1982a, p. 3). Social work and civil rights groups were exhorted to return to grass-roots political activism, become politically informed, and closely monitor the courts, especially federal judicial appointments, to help insure that minority rights were not trampled (Hopps, 1982a).

Minority Children in the System

The relationship between the profession and minorities can be seen to some degree through the child welfare system, in which the consequences of the move to private therapeutic settings are evident. While the profession moved to private practice and away from the public service, the presence of social work in the child welfare system decreased. According to a 1987 national survey, social work training was not usually required for entry-level child welfare positions; in addition, an earlier study found that "only 25% of public agency child welfare social workers have any formal training in social work—16% at the bachelor's degree level and 9% at the master's degree level" (Hogan & Siu, 1988, p. 496). This was at a time when minorities were overrepresented in the system. In 1980, the ratio of white/minority children in out-of-home placement was 58% to 42%. Black children were the most overrepresented. Hispanic children were also overrepresented, and "service providers were more likely to recommend increased protective services for Hispanic children and to treat them as behaviorally disturbed (Olsen, quoted in Hogan & Siu, 1988, p. 495).

Problems related to Native American children, also overrepresented in the system, were recognized by the passage of the Indian Child Welfare Act, which was intended "to stabilize Native American families through the regulation of placement procedures and the establishment of American Indian social services" (Hogan & Siu, 1988, p. 495). This was not without controversy in social work circles as arguments about giving too much control to tribes over child welfare decisions emerged. In response to such concerns, a Native American social worker argued that social work had ignored its historic commitment to supporting and strengthening family life when Native American families were involved. Citing congressional testimony, she stated that "the manner in which American Indian children were repeatedly removed from their families approximated kidnapping" (Blanchard & Barsh, 1980, p. 353), and that the Indian Child Welfare Act provided a chance for the social work profession to reexamine its practice with American Indian families and to allow American Indians to preserve their culture. Blandard and Barsh (1980) also indicate that at about the time of the passage of the act, one out of four Native American children was in out-of-home placement, with 85% of those living in non-Indian homes away from their tribal community.

In response to the problems of minority children in the system, the social work profession was urged to pursue the training of culturally competent workers, to include "child welfare knowledge into social work education along with a renewed emphasis on practice in the public sector, . . . [and] advocacy to halt declassification of child welfare workers in the public sector" (Hogan & Siu, 1988, p. 497). In other words, the profession was being asked to revisit part of its core mission of service to the oppressed and disenfranchised, especially in the context of minority groups that it had increasingly abandoned as it moved to serve the concerns of middle-class whites.

A review of social work articles about Asian Americans, African Americans, Hispanic Americans, and Native Americans published in the 1980s concluded that "the literature portrays the social work profession as naïve and superficial in its antiracist practice" (McMahon & Allen-Meares, 1992, p. 537). The authors of the study cited four reasons for this conclusion:

> First, much of the surveyed social work literature is naïve because it decontextualizes minority clients, intellectually removing them from the racist context in which they live. This color-blind approach treats all clients the same without regard to their specific needs (Dominelli, 1988). Second, despite its emphasis on ethnic-sensitive practice, one of the main remedies proposed for the racism minorities suffer focuses, according to the literature, on mere change in the awareness of social workers. This attitude reveals a racist attitude in some of the surveyed literature because it views minorities' oppression as normal and natural. . . . Third, even though social workers know of the institutional causes of poverty and racism, the heavy emphasis in the literature on solely individual intervention can only help minority clients to adapt or resign themselves to their oppression. Last, and this is an inference drawn from the other reasons given, the way in which the literature articulates practice maintains a status quo that adversely affects minorities. (McMahon & Allen-Meares, 1992, p. 537)

Again, the profession's focus on the individual kept it from dealing more fully with the problems of oppressed minorities during a time when the need for social action was evident. McMahon and Allen-Meares (1992) stated flatly that "there needs to be a change in the focus of the profession. Minority populations are increasing in America and so, too, are the problems that beset them. . . . People can feel empowered in a social worker's office but racist laws, practices, and conditions can just as easily disempower them" (p. 537).

Gays and Lesbians in the System

Social work's dual struggle to serve the individual and act on a more macrolevel can be seen in the rhetorical support for gays and lesbians during the 1980s. Nancy Humphries (NASW president, 1979–1981) cited three reasons for social workers to be knowledgeable about and sensitive to gay and lesbian issues: (a) gays and lesbians are becoming a larger part of the client base of the profession; (b) many social workers are themselves gay and lesbian; and (c) "perhaps most importantly, gay and lesbian people represent an oppressed population, the protection of whose rights, as those of all oppressed populations, should be of primary concern to the profession of social work" (Hidalgo, Peterson, & Woodman, 1985, p. 167). Professional support for the gay community was also found as the gay community faced its greatest health crisis: AIDS. The National Association of Social Workers adopted an AIDS Policy Statement in 1984:

> Acquired Immune Deficiency Syndrome (AIDS) presents a public health crisis to the nation. Much can be done by social workers and other helping professionals to foster knowledge, heighten the awareness of and response to it by various institutions, marshall social resources, and otherwise mediate and assist those individuals and their loved ones who are affected by AIDS. Because of the complex biopsychosocial issues presented by AIDS, social workers, with their special knowledge, skills and sensitivity, are uniquely capable of responding to this crisis by pursuing action in each of the following areas: (1) research, (2) public education and dissemination of information, (3) psychological and social supports, (4) community development, (5) civil rights, and (6) professional accountability. (Hidalgo, Peterson, & Woodman, 1985, p. 163)

Within the educational realm, the Council on Social Work Education issued supportive statements during this time. The 1982 Council on Social Work Education Curriculum Policy Statement (CPS) stated that content on lesbian and gay persons was foundation knowledge, but it was not required content. The 1992 CPS required inclusion of lesbian and gay content in the standard on populations-at-risk. In the absence of such a requirement, little was done. A 1983 study of California schools of social work found that the way homosexuality was most often mentioned in the classroom was when a student raised a question. When efforts were made to include gay and lesbian issues in the curriculum, most schools limited them to providing bibliographies on homosexuality (Newman, 1994).

Despite statements and policies of support within the social work profession, action is often lacking. In explaining the profession's tepid response to gays and lesbians, Newman (1994) refers to literature that cites homophobia and heterosexism within the social work professional community, a dominant attitude of rejecting homosexuality within minority cultures, and the idea that "if one group gets resources, it is at the expense of another; or if gays and lesbians are included in the social work curriculum, it will leave less room for minorities of color or women, or content on research methods" (p. 351). Rather than seeking ways to promote interdependence that would empower all groups, within the profession, much like within the larger society, individualistic or discrete group interests were seen to be waging a competition fueled by fear and ignorance.

A STRENGTHS PERSPECTIVE

Out of the civil rights initiatives of the 1980s came the Americans with Disabilities Act (ADA) of 1990, which serves as an excellent example of policy designed to build on clients' strengths, enhancing community resources (see Appendix 11–A). The voices of the people greatly influenced the legislation designed to help them. The Civil Rights Act mandates equal opportunity for people with disabilities in employment, public accommodation, transportation, state and local government services, and telecommunication (Croser, cited in Chapin, 1995). "The problem definition underlying this legislation was reformulated so that the emphasis is no longer on the deficits of the individual. Instead, disabilities are viewed as the gap between a person's capability and the environment's demands" (Chapin, 1995, p. 511).

The strengths and potential contributions of people with disabilities are recognized by the ADA. Reasonable accommodations are spelled out in the legislation on how to make it possible for people with disabilities to participate in the workplace and the community in a manner that empowers rather than stigmatizes them. Supports that enable the individual are emphasized in the act so individuals can achieve inclusion rather than just services, thus achieving the desired outcome of inclusion in the community (Chapin, 1995).

This act is in contrast to earlier programs for people with disabilities that were based on the policy assumption that disabilities necessarily preclude employment and participation in the community. These assumptions are also reflected in income and medical assistance programs serving people with disabilities today. Policy analysts are aware of this contrast and are working to modify policies of the earlier programs to support the capacities and strengths of the people they serve rather than presume incapacities that do not exist (Chapin, 1995).

Chapin (1995) suggests that "the strengths approach may also help point social workers toward interventions that can influence the normative-affective factors and the logical-empirical factors that shape policy" (p. 511). She addresses the evidence presented by Etzioni that choices are made on the basis of emotional involvement and value commitments, which he terms "normative-affective" factors, and is used instead of basing choices primarily on logical-empirical considerations. The goal for social workers is to bring people who are the targets of the intended policy into the problem definition and policymaking process, causing positive emotional involvement and producing decisions more supportive of the needs of the people. An example would be, "after state policymakers spent two days simply talking with residents and observing interactions in an assisted-living facility for people with developmental disabilities, support for funds for more community-integrated programming increased" (Chapin, 1995, p. 511).

See Appendix 11-B for a poem written by someone who is deaf.

On the tenth anniversary of ADA, it was noted in *The Chicago Tribune:*

> Thirty-three-year-old Brian Dusza, sitting in his wheelchair as he overlooked Wrigley Field, spent time reflecting on the wide range of benefits resulting from the Americans with Disabilities Act and how the law profoundly touched almost every factet of his life. Dusaz sees the law as the vehicle to independence and opportunity for handicapped people. These benefits included something as simple as curb cuts, allowing his wheelchair to traverse city sidewalks, to the fact that he could now make a living as a records specialist in a suburban Chicago police department. He says, "Not everyone recognized the tremendous changes that came about because of ADA . . . there's no denying the difference it's made in my own life and for people bringing equality to people with disabilities." Brian was born with spina bifida. (Smallwood, 2000, p. A-1)

When it is agreed upon by agency administrators that achieving specific client outcomes should be the basis for evaluation and when they commit themselves to meeting intended standards, there may be a shift in normative commitments that are more positive for clients. For social workers who approach policymaking from a strengths perspective, there are interventions designed to influence both normative-affective and logical-empirical factors that will shape policymakers' decisions (Chapin, 1995).

If the strengths approach in policy formulation is effective, it will influence policy practice that ultimately brings about positive changes for clients. This type of policy practice is essential and affects social workers in whatever setting they choose to work: legislatively, interorganizationally, or within their own agencies. With the strengths approach, there can be a new understanding conceptualized about the relationship between those who are helped and those doing the helping where practitioners ceases to view themselves as experts who bring solutions to the unwashed. The helper and helpee need to become collaborators. This collaboration needs to be with traditional client groups as well as with all key players in the policymaking arena. The pivotal component here is the expansion of the role of people receiving the help. In order for this to work, the policy practitioner needs to work to develop policies and practices that undergirds this expansion such as outreach and training efforts that are designed to help oppressed groups to speak for themselves (Chapin, 1995).

SUMMARY

The Reagan and Bush presidencies comprised the first major era of conservatism since the 1950s. Rhetoric that flamed racial animosities and social tension was skillfully used to help Reagan and Bush cultivate the white voters. Reagan's counterrevolution against the social welfare programs of the 1960s and 1970s substantially reduced domestic spending and the policy roles of the federal government while increasing military spending. Most remarkable was that Reagan did not cut all social programs, but rather put the focus primarily on those used by low-income Americans (Jansson, 1997).

Homelessness became a way of life for many people, not just from the ranks of the poor but also from some lower- and middle-class people for whom the nation's shaky safety net failed. Racial tensions mounted resulting in major riots in urban cities throughout the country. Poor people were in pain, physically, emotionally, and spiritually and the youth began crying out the only way they know how, short of violence: rap music.

REFERENCES

Blanchard, E. L., & Barsh, R. L. (1980). What is best for tribal children? A response to Fischler. *Social Work, 25,* 350–357.

Briggs, J. (1992, November 29). Pop recordings: The rage and the rhythm of west coast rappers. *The Washington Post,* p. G10.

Chapin, R. K. (1995). Social policy development: The strengths perspective. *Social Work, 40*(4), 506–514.

Corbet, J. (1996). *Bad-mouthing: The language of special needs.* Washington, DC: The Falmer Press.

Davidson, R. (1992, May 2). President orders in the Army. Bush puts bayonet patrols on streets. The ugly side of American life. *The Herald* (Glasgow), p. 1.

Day, P. J. (1989). *A new history of social welfare.* Englewood Cliffs, NJ: Prentice Hall.

Day, P. J. (1999). *A new history of social welfare* (3rd Edition), Needham Heights, MA: Allyn & Bacon.

Delgado, M., & Barton, K. (1998). Murals in Latino communities: Social indicators of community strengths. *Social Work, 43*(4) 346–356.

Di Rando, A. (1992, May 21). Voices from the community. *The Los Angeles Times,* p. 5.

Franklin, J. H. & Moss, A. A. (1994). *From slavery to freedom: A history of African Americans.* (7th ed.) New York: McGraw-Hill.

Gibson, R. C. (1983). *Work and retirement [of] aging black women: A race and sex comparison.* Unpublished manuscript. Ann Arbor: The University of Michigan, The Institute of Gerontology.

Gibson, R. C. (1987). Reconceptualizing retirement for Black Americans. *The Gerontologist, 27*(6) 691–698.

Hacker, A. (1995). *Two nations: Black and white, separate, hostile, unequal.* New York: Ballatine Books.

Haynes, K. S., & Holmes, D. A. (1994). *Invitation to social work.* White Plains, New York: Longman.

Haynes, K. S., & Mickelson, J. S. (1992). Social work and the Reagan era: Challenges to the profession. *Journal of Sociology & Social Welfare, 19,* 169–183.

Hidalgo, H., Peterson, T. L., & Woodman, N. J. (Eds.). (1985). *Lesbian and gay issues: A resource manual for social workers.* Silver Spring, MD: National Association of Social Workers.

Hogan, P. T., & Siu, S. (1988). Minority children and the child welfare system: An historical perspective. *Social Work, 33,* 493–498.

Hopps, J. G. (1982a). Oppression based on color. *Social Work, 27,* 3–5.

Jansson, B. S. (1994). *Social policy: From theory to policy practice.* (2nd ed.). Belmont, CA: Brooks/Cole.

Jansson, B. S. (1997). *The reluctant welfare state.* (3rd ed.) Pacific Grove, CA: Brooks/Cole.

Karger, H. J. & Stoesz, D. (1998). *American social welfare policy.* New York: Addison Welsey Longman.

Krohn, F. B., & Suazo, F. L. (1995). Contemporary urban music: Controversial messages in hip-hop and rap lyrics. *A Review of General Semantics, 52,* 139–155.

Levine, M. L. (1996). *African Americans and civil rights: From 1619 to the present.* Phoenix, AZ: The Oryx Press.

Lucie-Smith, E. (1994). *Race, sex, and gender in contemporary art.* New York: Harry N. Abrams, Inc.

McMahon, A., & Allen-Meares, P. (1992). Is social work racist? A content analysis of recent literature. *Social Work, 37,* 533–539.

Mintz, M. (1981, September 5). Tightened welfare rules approved: Controversial rules on welfare are approved by administration; $1,000 limit on personal property. *The Washington Post,* p. A1.

Morley, J. (1992). Rap music as American history. In L.A. Stanley (Ed.), *Rap: The lyrics* (pp. xv–xxxi), New York: Penguin Books.

National Commission on Working Women (1986, Spring/Summer). *Women at Work, 3,* 2.

Newman, B. S. (1994). Diversity and populations at risk: Gays and lesbians. In F. G. Reamer (Ed.), *The foundations of social work knowledge* (pp. 346–392). New York: Columbia University Press.

Overbea, L. (1982, January 26). Reagan-era welfare: Washington gives push to self-help. *The Christian Science Monitor,* p. 6

Pear, R. (1981, September 4). U.S. welfare plan to require check on family assets. *The New York Times,* p. A1.

Perkins, K. (1991). Blue-collar and retirement. *Social Work Research and Abstracts: Abstracts of Dissertations, 27*(3) (University Microfilms, University of Pennsylvania, No. 91–23424).

Perkins, K. (1993a). Working-class women and retirement. *Journal of Gerontological Social Work, 20*(1) pp. 129–146.

Perkins, K. (1993b). Recycling poverty: From the workplace to retirement. *Journal of Women and Aging, 5*(1) 5–23.

Sancier, B. (1982a). Minority issues—report from a panel. *Practice Digest,* 5 (3), 3, 19.

Sancier, B. (Ed.). (1982b). Building on the strengths of minority groups. *Practice Digest,* 5 (3).

Schneir, M. (1992). *Feminism: The essential historical writings.* New York: Vintage Books.

Smallwood, L. (2000, July 25). Disabilities Act turns 10 with torch-relay fanfare. *The Times Picayune,* p. A–21.

Southern, E. (1997). *The music of black Americans.* (3rd ed.) New York: W.W. Norton.

Stengel, R. (1986, November 24). Down and out and dispossessed; many of the new homeless include families and the young. *Time, 128,* 27–28.

Trattner, W. I. (1999). *From poor law to welfare state: A history of social welfare in American.* (5th ed.) New York: The Free Press

Udesky, L. (1990, September 24). Welfare reform and its victims. *The Nation, 251,* 302–306.

U.S. Bureau of Census. (1997). *Statistical Abstract of the United States.* Washington, DC: Government Printing Office.

U.S. Women's Bureau. (1997). The wage gap between women and men [on line]. Available: *htpp://www.dol.gov/dol/wb/public/programs/1w&occ.htm.* (Retrieved June 26, 2000).

Wickenden, D. (1985, March 18). Abandoned Americans: What Ronald Reagan could learn from Charles Dickens. *The New Republic, 192,* 19–25.

Wineburg, R. J., Spakes, P., & Finn, J. (1983). Budget cuts and human services: One community's experience. *Social Casework: The Journal of Contemporary Social Work, 64,* 489–496.

Wires; from news services. (1984, March 31). *The San Diego Union-Tribune,* p. A1.

Wolock, I., Geismar, L., Lagay, B., & Raiffe, P. (1985–1986). Forced exit from welfare: The impact of federal cutbacks on public assistance families. *Journal of Social Service Research, 9,* 71–96.

Wootton, B. (1997). Gender differences in occupational employment. *Monthly Labor Review, 120* (4), 15–24.

APPENDIX 11–A

Introduction

This is a compilation of the laws which affect the United States Architectural and Transportation Barriers Compliance Board (Access Board). Over the years, all of the Access Board's activities have had a single goal: to enable persons with disabilities to live and work in society. If persons with disabilities are to be able to live and work alongside their peers without disabilities, then the built environment must be designed and constructed to accommodate the needs of everyone.

This publication contains three laws. The first is the **Architectural Barriers Act of 1968 (ABA),** as amended, which mandates that buildings or other facilities financed with certain Federal funds are accessible to persons with disabilities. The second law in this publication is **Section 502 of the Rehabilitation Act of 1973,** as amended, which establishes and sets out the functions of the Access Board. Finally, this document includes the section of the **Americans with Disabilities Act of 1990 (ADA),** which significantly expanded the role of the Access Board. Under the ADA, the Access Board is responsible for developing accessibility guidelines for entities covered by the Act and for providing technical assistance to individuals and organizations on the removal of architectural, transportation, and communication barriers.

These three laws form the basis for building an accessible environment for all people. The Access Board remains committed to achieving this goal, as reflected in the agency's mission statement: "Enhance the quality of life by ensuring accessibility and broadening public awareness that access makes economic and practical sense for all."

May 1994

Architectural Barriers Act of 1968, as amended

42 U.S.C. § 4151 et seq.

§ 4151.   Definitions

As used in this chapter, the term "building" means any building or facility (other than (A) a privately owned residential structure not leased by the Government for subsidized housing programs and (B) any building or facility on a military installation designed and constructed primarily for use by able bodied military personnel) the intended use for which either will require that such building or facility be accessible to the public, or may result in the employment or residence therein of physically handicapped persons, which building or facility is—

(1) to be constructed or altered by or on behalf of the United States;

(2) to be leased in whole or in part by the United States after August 12, 1968;

(3) to be financed in whole or in part by a grant or a loan made by the United States after August 12, 1968, if such building or facility is subject to standards for design, construction, or alteration issued under authority of the law authorizing such grant or loan; or

(4) to be constructed under authority of the National Capital Transportation Act of 1960, the National Capital Transportation Act of 1965, or title III of the Washington Metropolitan Area Transit Regulation Compact.

§ 4152.   Standards for design, construction, and alteration of buildings; Secretary of Health and Human Services

The Administrator of General Services, in consultation with Secretary of Health and Human Services, shall prescribe standards for the design, construction, and alteration of buildings (other than residential structures subject to this chapter and buildings, structures, and facilities of the Department of Defense and of the United States Postal Service subject to this chapter) to insure whenever possible that physically handicapped persons will have ready access to, and use of, such buildings.

§ 4153.   Standards for design, construction, and alteration of buildings; Secretary of Housing and Urban Development

The Secretary of Housing and Urban Development, in consultation with the Secretary of Health and Human Services, shall prescribe standards for the design, construction, and alteration of buildings which are residential structures subject to this chapter to insure whenever possible that physically handicapped persons will have ready access to, and use of, such buildings.

§ 4154.   Standards for design, construction, and alteration of buildings; Secretary of Defense

The Secretary of Defense, in consultation with the Secretary of Health and Human Services, shall prescribe standards for the design, construction, and alteration of buildings, structures, and facilities of the Department of Defense subject to this chapter to insure whenever possible that physically handicapped persons will have access to, and use of, such buildings.

§ 4154a.   Standards for design, construction, and alteration of buildings; United States Postal Service

The United States Postal Service, in consultation with the Secretary of Health and Human Services, shall prescribe such standards for the design, construction, and alteration of its buildings to insure whenever possible that physically handicapped persons will have ready access to, and use of, such buildings.

§ 4155. Effective date of standards

Every building designed, constructed, or altered after the effective date of a standard issued under this chapter which is applicable to such building, shall be designed, constructed, or altered in accordance with such standard.

§ 4156. Waiver and modification of standards

The Administrator of General Services, with respect to standards issued under section 4152 of this title, and the United States Postal Service with respect to standards issued under section 4154a of this title, and the Secretary of Housing and Urban Development, with respect to standards issued under section 4153 of this title, and the Secretary of Defense with respect to standards issued under section 4154 of this title,

(1) is authorized to modify or waive any such standard, on a case-by-case basis, upon application made by the head of the department, agency, or instrumentality of the United States concerned, and upon a determination by the Administrator or Secretary, as the case may be, that such modification or waiver is clearly necessary, and

(2) shall establish a system of continuing surveys and investigations to insure compliance with such standards.

§ 4157. Reports to Congress and congressional committees

(a) The Administrator of General Services shall report to Congress during the first week of January of each year on his activities and those of other departments, agencies, and instrumentalities of the Federal Government under this chapter during the preceding fiscal year including, but not limited to, standards issued, revised, amended, or repealed under this chapter and all case-by-case modifications, and waivers of such standards during such year.

(b) The Architectural and Transportation Barriers Compliance Board established by section 792 of Title 29 shall report to the Public Works and Transportation Committee of the House of Representatives and the Public Works Committee of the Senate during the first week of January of each year on its activities and actions to insure compliance with the standards prescribed under this chapter.

Section 502 of the Rehabilitation Act of 1073, as amended
29 U.S.C. § 792

§ 792. **Architectural and Transportation Barriers Compliance Board**

(a) **Establishment; membership; Chairperson; vice-chairperson; term of office; Termination of membership; reappointment; compensation and travel expenses; by laws; quorum requirements**

(1) There is established within the Federal Government the Architectural and Transportation Barriers Compliance Board (hereinafter referred to as the "Access Board") which shall be composed as follows:

  (A) Thirteen members shall be appointed by the President from among members of the general public of whom at least a majority shall be individuals with disabilities.

  (B) The remaining members shall be the heads of each of the following departments or agencies (or their designees whose positions are executive level IV or higher):

  (i) Department of Health and Human Services.
  (ii) Department of Transportation.
  (iii) Department of Housing and Urban Development.
  (iv) Department of Labor.
  (v) Department of Interior.
  (vi) Department of Defense.
  (vii) Department of Justice.
  (viii) General Services Administration.
  (ix) Department of Veterans Affairs.
  (x) United States Postal Service.
  (xi) Department of Education.
  (xii) Department of Commerce.

The Chairperson and vice-chairperson of the Access Board shall be elected by majority vote of the members of the Access Board to serve for a term of one year. When the chairperson is a member of the general public, the vice-chairperson shall be a Federal official; and when the chairperson is a Federal official, the vice-chairperson shall be a member of the general public. Upon the expiration of the term as chairperson of a member who is a Federal official, the subsequent chairperson shall be a member of the general public; and vice versa.

(2)(A)   (i) The term of office of each appointed member of the Access Board shall be 4 years, except as provided in clause (ii). Each year, the terms of office of at least three appointed members of the board shall expire.

(ii)(I) One member appointed for a term beginning December 4, 1992 shall serve for a term of 3 years.

(II) One member appointed for a term beginning December 4, 1993 shall serve for a term of 2 years.

(III) One member appointed for a term beginning December 4, 1994 shall serve for a term of 1 year.

(IV) Members appointed for terms beginning before December 4, 1992 shall serve for terms of 3 years.

(B) A member whose term has expired may continue to serve until a successor has been appointed.

(C) A member appointed to fill a vacancy shall serve for the remainder of the term to which that member's predecessor was appointed.

(3) If any appointed member of the Access Board becomes a Federal employee, such member may continue as a member of the Access Board for not longer than a sixty-day period beginning on the date the member becomes a Federal employee.

(4) No individual appointed under paragraph (1)(A) of this subsection who has served as a member of the Access Board may be reappointed to the Access Board more than once unless such individual has not served on the Access Board for a period of two years prior to the effective date of such individual's appointment.

(5)(A) Members of the Access Board who are not regular full-time employees of the United States shall, while serving on the business of the Access Board, be entitled to receive compensation at rates fixed by the President, but not to exceed the daily equivalent of the rate of pay for level IV of the Executive Schedule under section 5315 of Title 5, including travel time, for each day they are engaged in the performance of their duties as members of the Access Board; and shall be entitled to reimbursement for travel, subsistence, and other necessary expenses incurred by them in carrying out their duties under this section.

(B) Members of the Access Board who are employed by the Federal Government shall serve without compensation, but shall be reimbursed, subsistence, and other necessary expenses incurred by them in carrying out their duties under this section.

(6)(A) The Access Board shall establish such bylaws and other rules as may be appropriate to enable the Access Board to carry out its functions under this chapter.

(B)The bylaws shall include quorum requirements. The quorum requirements shall provide that (I) a proxy may not be counted for purposes of establishing a quorum, and (ii) not less than half the members required for a quorum shall be members of the general public appointed under paragraph (1)(A).

(b) Functions

It shall be the function of the Access Board to—

(1) ensure compliance with the standards prescribed pursuant to the Act entitled "An Act to ensure the certain buildings financed with Federal funds are so designed and constructed as to be accessible to the physically handicapped," approved August 12, 1968 (commonly known as the Architectural Barriers Act of 1968; (42 U.S.C. 4151 et seq.) (Including the application of such Act to the United States Postal Service), including enforcing all standards under such Act, and ensuring that all waivers and modifications to the standards are based on findings of fact and are not inconsistent with the provisions of the section;

(2) develop advisory guidelines for, and provide appropriate technical assistance to, individuals or entities with rights or duties under regulations prescribed pursuant to this subchapter or titles II and III of the Americans with Disabilities Act of 1990 (42 U.S.C. 12131 et seq. And 12181 et seq. With respect to overcoming architectural, transportation, and communication barrier;

(3) establish and maintain minimum guidelines and requirements for the standards issued pursuant to the Act commonly known as the Architectural Barriers Act of 1968 (42 U.S.C.A. 4151 et seq.) and titles II and III of the Americans with Disabilities Act of 1990 (42 U.S.C.A 12131 et seq. And 12181 et seq.);

(4) promote accessibility throughout all segments of society;

(5) investigate and examine alternative approaches to the architectural, transportation, communication, and attitudinal barriers confronting individuals with disabilities, particularly with respect to telecommunications devices, public buildings and monuments, parks and parklands, public transportation (including air, water, and surface transportation, whether interstate, foreign, intrastate, or local), and residential and institutional housing;

(6) determine what measures are being taken by Federal, State, and local governments and by other public or nonprofit agencies to eliminate the barriers described in paragraph (5);

(7) promote the use of the International Accessibility Symbol in all public facilities that are in compliance with the standards prescribed by the Administrator of General Services, the Secretary of Defense, and the Secretary of Housing and Urban Development pursuant to the Act commonly known as the Architectural Barriers Act of 1968 (42 U.S.C.A. 4151 et seq.);

(8) make to the President and to the Congress reports that shall describe in detail the results of its investigations under paragraphs (5) and (6);

(9) make to the President and to the Congress such recommendations for legislative and administrative changes as the Access Board determines to be necessary or desirable to eliminate the barriers described in paragraph (5); and

(10) ensure that public conveyances, including rolling stock, are readily accessible to, and usable by, individuals with physical disabilities.

(c) Additional functions; transportation barriers and housing needs; transportation and housing plans and proposals

The Access Board shall also (1)(A) determine how and to what extent transportation barriers impede the mobility of individuals with disabilities and aged individuals with disabilities and consider ways in which travel expenses in connection with transportation to and from work for individuals with disabilities can be met or subsidized when such individuals are unable to use mass transit systems or need special equipment in private transportation, and (B) consider the housing needs of individuals with disabilities; (2) determine what measures are being taken, especially by public and other nonprofit agencies and groups having an interest in and a capacity to deal with such problems, (A) to eliminate barriers from public transportation systems (including vehicles used in such systems), and to prevent their incorporation in new or expanded transportation systems, and (B) to make housing available and accessible to individuals with disabilities or to meet sheltered housing needs; and (3) prepare plans and proposals for such further actions as may be necessary to the goals of adequate transportation and housing for individuals with disabilities, including proposals for bringing together in a cooperative effort, agencies, organizations, and groups already working toward such goals or whose cooperation is essential to effective and comprehensive action.

(d) Investigations; hearings; orders; administrative procedure applicable; final orders; judicial review; civil action; intervention; development of standards; technical assistance to persons or entities affected

(1) The Access Board shall conduct investigations, hold public hearings, and issue such orders as it deems necessary to ensure compliance with the pro-

visions of the Acts cited in subsection (b) of this section. Except as provided in paragraph (3) of subsection (e) of this section, the provisions of subchapter II of chapter 5, and chapter 7 of Title 5 shall apply to procedures under this section, and an order of compliance issued by the Access Board shall be a final order for purposes of judicial review. Any such order affecting any Federal department, agency, or instrumentality of the United States shall be final and binding on such department, agency, or instrumentality. An order if compliance may include the withholding of suspension of Federal funds with respect to any building of public conveyance or rolling stock found not to be in compliance with standards enforced under this section. Pursuant to chapter 7 of Title 5, any complainant of participant in a proceeding under this subsection may obtain review of a final order issued in such proceeding.

(2) The executive director is authorized, at the direction of the Access Board—

(A) to bring a civil action in any appropriate United States district court to enforce, in whole or in part, any final order of the Access Board under this subsection; and

(B) to intervene, appear, and participate, or to appear as amicus curiae, in any court of the United States or in any court of a State in civil actions that relate to this section or to the Architectural Barriers Act of 1968 (42 U.S.C.A. 4151 et seq.).

Except as provided in section 518(a) of Title 28, relating to litigation before the Supreme Court, the executive director may appear for and represent the Access Board in any civil litigation brought under this section.

(3) Repealed.

(e) Appointment of executive director, administrative law judges, and other personnel; provisions applicable to administrative law judges; authority and duties of executive director; finality of orders of compliance

(1) There shall be appointed by the Access Board an executive director and such other professional and clerical personnel as are necessary to carry out its functions under this chapter. The Access Board is authorized to appoint as many administrative law judges as are necessary for proceedings required to be conducted under this section. The provisions applicable to administrative law judges appointed under section 3105 of Title 5 shall apply to administrative law judges appointed under this subsection.

(2) The Executive Director shall exercise general supervision over all personnel employed by the Access Board (other than administrative law judges

and their assistants). The Executive Director shall have final authority on behalf of the Access Board, with respect to the investigation of alleged noncompliance and in the issuance of formal complaints before the Access Board, and shall have such other duties as the Access Board may prescribe.

(3) For the purpose of this section, an order of compliance issued by an administrative law judge shall be deemed to be an order of the Access Board and shall be the final order for the purpose of judicial review.

(f) Technical, administrative, or other assistance; appointment, compensation, and travel expenses of advisory and technical experts and consultants

(1)(A) In carrying out the technical assistance responsibilities of the Access Board under this section, the Board may enter into an interagency agreement with another Federal department or agency.

(B) Any funds appropriated to such a department or agency for the purpose of providing technical assistance may be transferred to the Access Board. Any funds appropriated to the Access Board for the purpose of providing such technical assistance may be transferred to such department or agency.

(C) The Access Board may arrange to carry out the technical assistance responsibilities of the Board under this section through such other departments and agencies for such periods as the Board determines to be appropriate.

(D) The Access Board shall establish a procedure to ensure separation of its compliance and technical assistance responsibilities under this section.

(2) The departments or agencies specified in subsection (a) of this section shall make available to the Access Board such technical, administrative, or other assistance as it may require to carry out its functions under this section, and the Access Board may appoint such other advisers, technical experts, and consultants as it deems necessary to assist it in carrying out its functions under this section. Special advisory and technical experts and consultants appointed pursuant to this paragraph shall, while performing their functions under this section, be entitled to receive compensation at rates fixed by the Chairperson, but not exceeding the daily equivalent of the rate of pay for level 4 of the Senior Executive Service Schedule under section 5382 of Title 5, including travel time, and while serving away from their homes or regular places of business they may be allowed travel expenses, including per diem in lieu of subsistence, as authorized by section 5703 of such Title 5 for persons in the Government service employed intermittently.

(g) Reports to Congress; reports on transportation barriers and housing needs

(1) The Access Board shall, at the end of each fiscal year, report its activities during the preceding fiscal year to the Congress. Such report shall include an assessment of the extent of compliance with the Acts cited in subsection (b) of this section, along with a description and analysis of investigations made and actions taken by the Access Board, and the reports and recommendations described in paragraphs (8) and (9) of such subsection.

(2) The Access Board shall, at the same time that the Access Board transmits the report required under section 7(b) of the Act commonly known as the Architectural Barriers Act of 1968 (42 U.S.C. 4157(b)), transmit the report to the Committee on Education and Labor of the House of Representatives and the Committee on Labor and Human Resources of the Senate.

(h) Report to President and Congress on assessments of State expenditures to provide full access to programs and activities; grants and contracts to aid Board in carrying out its functions; report to Congressional committees on accessibility of Federally funded buildings; joint transmittal

(1) The Access Board may make grants to, or enter into contracts with, public or private organizations to carry out its duties under subsections (b) and (c) of this section.

(2)(A) The Access Board may accept, hold, administer, and utilize gifts, devises, and bequests of property, both real and personal, for the purpose of aiding and facilitating the functions of the Access Board under paragraphs (5) and (7) of subsection (b) of this section. Gifts and bequests of money and proceeds from sales of other property received as gifts, devises, or bequests shall be deposited in the Treasury and shall be disbursed upon the order of the Chairperson. Property accepted pursuant to this section, and the proceeds thereof, shall be used as nearly as possible in accordance with the terms of the gifts, devises, or bequests. For purposes of Federal income, estate, or gift taxes, property accepted under this section shall be considered as a gift, devise, or bequest to the United States.

(B) The Access Board shall publish regulations setting forth the criteria the Board will use in determining whether the acceptance of gifts, devises, and bequests of property, both real and personal, would reflect unfavorably upon the ability of the Board or any employee to carry out the responsibilities or official duties of the Board in a fair and objective manner, or would compromise the integrity of or the appearance of the integrity of a Government program or any official involved in that program.

(3) The Access Board shall, at the same time that the Access Board transmits the report required under section 7(b) of the Act entitled "An Act to ensure that certain buildings financed with Federal funds are so designated and constructed as to be accessible to the physically handicapped", approved August 12, 1968 (commonly known as the Architectural Barriers Act of 1968) [42 U.S.C.A. 4157(b)] transmit that report to the Committee on Labor and Human Resources of the Senate and the Committee on Education and Labor of the House of Representatives.

(i) Authorization of appropriations

There are authorized to be appropriated for the purpose of carrying out the duties and functions of the Access Board under this section such sums as may be necessary for each of the fiscal years 1993 through 1997.

Section 504 of the Americans with Disabilities Act of 1990

42 U.S.C. 12204

12204.   Regulations by the Architectural and Transportation Barriers Compliance Board

(a) Issuance of guidelines

Not later than 9 months after July 26, 1990, the Architectural and Transportation Barriers Compliance Board shall issue minimum guidelines that shall supplement the existing Minimum Guidelines and Requirements for Accessible Design for purposes of subchapter II and III of this chapter.

(b) Contents of guidelines

The supplemental guidelines issued under subsection (a) of this section shall establish additional requirements, consistent with this chapter, to ensure that buildings, facilities, rail passenger cars, and vehicles are accessible, in terms of architecture and design, transportation, and communication, to individuals with disabilities.

(c) Qualified historic properties

(1) In general

The supplemental guidelines issued under subsection (a) of this section shall include procedures and requirements for alterations that will threaten or destroy the historic significance of qualified historic buildings and facilities as defined in 4.1.7(1)(a) of the Uniform Federal Accessibility Standards.

(2) Sites eligible for listing in National Register

With respect to alterations of buildings or facilities that are eligible for listing in the National Register of Historic Places under the National Historic Preservation Act (16 U.S.C. 470 et seq.), the guidelines described in paragraph (1) shall, at a minimum, maintain the procedures and requirements established in 4.1.7(1) and (2) of the Uniform Federal Accessibility Standards.

(3) Other sites

With respect to alterations of buildings or facilities designated as historic under State or local law, the guidelines described in paragraph (1) shall establish procedures equivalent to those established by 4.1.7(1)(b) and (c) of the Uniform Federal Accessibility Standards, and shall require, at a minimum, compliance with the requirements established in 4.1.7(2) of such standards.

APPENDIX 11–B

You Have to Be Deaf to Understand

What is it like to 'hear' a hand?
You have to be deaf to understand

What is it like to be a small child
In a school, in a room void of sound—
With a teacher who talks and talks and talks;
And then when she does come around to you,
She expects you to know what she's said?
You have to be deaf to understand

Or the teacher who thinks that to make you smart,
You must first learn how to talk with your voice:
So mumbo-jumbo with hands on your face
For hours and hours without patience or end,
Until out comes a faint resembling sound?
You have to be deaf to understand.

What is it like to be curious,
To thirst for knowledge you can call your own,
With an inner desire that's set on fire . . . ,
And you ask a brother, sister, or friend
Who looks in answer and says, 'Never mind!'?
You have to be deaf to understand

What is it like to a corner to stand,
Though there's nothing you've done really wrong.
Other than try to make use of your hands
To a silent peer to communicate
A thought that comes to your mind all at once?
You have to be deaf to understand.

What is it like to be shouted at
When one thinks that will help you to hear;
Or misunderstand the words of a friend
Who is trying to make a joke clear,
And you don't get the point because he's failed?
You have to be deaf to understand.

What is it like to be laughed in the face
When you try to repeat what is said;
Just to make sure that you've understood,
And you find that the words were misread . . .
And what you want to cry out 'Please help me, friend!'?
You have to be deaf to understand.

What is it like to have to depend
Upon one who can hear to phone a friend;
Or place a call to a business firm
And be forced to share what's personal, and
Then find that your message wasn't made clear?
You have to be deaf to understand.

What is it like to be deaf and alone
in the company of those who can hear—
And you only guess as you go along.
For no-one's there with a helping hand,
as you try to keep up with words and song?
You have to be deaf to understand.

What is it like on the road of life
To meet with a stranger who opens his mouth . . .
And speaks out a line at a rapid pace;
And you can't understand the look on his face
Because it is new and you're lost in the race?
You have to be deaf to understand.

What is it like to comprehend
Some nimble fingers that paint the scene,
And make you smile and feel serene
With the 'spoken word' of the moving hand
That makes you part of the world at large?
You have to be deaf to understand.

Yes, you have to be deaf to understand!
(Madsen, in Corbet, 1996, pp. 88–89)

REFORMING THE WELFARE STATE

A "baby boomer" was elected to the White House, and once again liberal politics had a dramatic effect on the country. With Bill Clinton's election into office in 1992 came the call for dramatic welfare reform. The economy flourished, for the most part, and many Americans were happy with the changes brought about by the Clinton administration; but Clinton politics came at a horrendous personal cost to the man. From the day he declared his candidacy for the presidency, he—and to a lesser extent his wife Hillary Rodham Clinton—came under constant attack by the conservatives and the media.

This chapter tells the story of some of that welfare reform, along with other significant events of the time. For example, the assault on affirmative action and the O. J. Simpson verdict are discussed in the context of a country that remains racially divided. Excerpts from the mass media are presented to detail the language of reform and to tell part of the story of this era. Proposed changes in welfare and Medicaid are discussed from a strengths perspective.

President Bush was taken by surprise with the rising popularity of his presidential opponent, Bill Clinton. Bush felt secure in his stance on foreign affairs, especially the winning of the cold war, expelling Saddam Hussein from Kuwait, and bringing the troops home. He was thrown off guard when he finally realized that the American people cared more about the problems at home than those abroad and belatedly offered a promise for economic recovery. The economic package he proposed, for the most part, consisted of more of the same—capital gains tax cuts, lower interest rates, and a heavier dosage of supply-side economics, which had brought mainly a declining economy, a decay in public services, a rise in social disorder, and, most glaring, a growing disparity in the distribution of wealth between the rich and the poor (Trattner, 1999).

When that failed, Bush resorted to tactics that had served him so well four years earlier: attack politics (Trattner, 1999). As Trattner describes it:

> He attacked all sorts of "evil" forces that allegedly were conspiring against him—the "cultural elite," the "make-work" lawyers in their "tasseled loafers," the "lazy poor" who rioted in Los Angeles, the "nuclear freeze crowd," "tree-hugging" environmentalists, homosexuals, and the godless, who, Bush never tired telling the American people, "forgot to put the three letters G-O-D in their party platform." He talked about "family values," (a euphemism for his anti-abortion and anti–gay rights positions) and savagely attacked his opponent, "Slick Willy," as a "waffler," a draft-dodger, an overseas war protestor, and even as "Bozo the Clown," who knew less about foreign policy than Bush's dog Millie. Most of all, however, Bush and his supporters went after "liberals," especially those who pretended to be something other than traditional "tax and spenders." (p. 389)

WILLIAM JEFFERSON CLINTON

Clinton made welfare reform a major theme of his campaign, touting his successful implementation of the welfare-to-work program as governor of Arkansas. In his attempt to walk the line and please both conservatives and liberals, he mainly proposed setting a two-year limit on welfare benefits for the able-bodied. Clinton repeatedly said, "I want to erase the stigma of welfare for good by restoring a simple, dignified principle: No one who can work can stay on welfare forever" (Trattner, 1999, p. 390).

Clinton, however, did some waffling on his stand on welfare reform—for instance, denouncing New Jersey's decision to eliminate additional benefits to women who had more children while on welfare. He called for more spending on health and child care, education, and public service employment, if necessary. During the campaign, the debate over welfare reform reflected agreement on some of the issues, such as that the existing system was not working and that it needed to be changed to do a better job of getting recipients off welfare and into the workforce, with significant differences between the candidates on how to achieve those goals and on what degree public officials should use welfare to control the personal lives of its recipients (Trattner, 1999).

Clinton's pattern of inconsistency, in welfare reform and other issues, can be explained by his evolution as a Democrat. In the wake of McGovern's defeat in 1972 as the presidential candidate (Clinton campaigned for McGovern), Democrats sought to move the party back to the center fearing that the party had been captured by special interest groups such as feminists, civil rights groups, and organized labor. This brand of Democrat was particularly opposed to affirmative action, liberal welfare programs, and the eclipse of the states's policy roles. In 1980, Clinton chose to identify with the moderate wing of the party by supporting Jimmy Carter over Teddy Kennedy for the presidential nomination. He then helped cofound the Democratic Leadership Council (DLC) in 1985, which sought to define a third way—a political platform that fell between traditional liberal and conservative positions. The traditional Democrats had favored redistribution of resources to the poor, civil rights legislation, affirmative action, and cuts in defense spending, whereas the new Democrats emphasized a narrower range of economic reforms such as job training, national standards in education, free trade, and infrastructure improvements. The traditional faction favored new spending on social programs and retention of existing spending; the new faction favored balanced budgets. The language was different too, with traditional Democrats referring to the obligations of citizens to help others and with the new Democrats emphasizing the responsibilities of citizens, for example, to seek work, raise families, and help their communities. Probably the most significant difference was that the new faction emphasized the economic needs of the middle class rather than low-income groups or racial minorities, partly because they attributed the Republicans' upsurge in the 1980s to the alienation of white voters who perceived the Democrats as beholden to feminists, civil rights activists, and gays (Jansson, 1997).

Clinton was seen as a chameleon long before becoming president, stemming, in part, from his intense ambitions and determination to win election in his southern state. He saw himself as a social reformer, but if he thought his political base was jeopardized he would backtrack on his social causes. For example, he repudiated former allies like organized labor or school teachers, sought tougher work requirements for welfare recipients, failed to seek civil rights legislation, and demanded that the national Democratic Party move to the center. Earlier fears by political observers were that he lacked conviction, and they questioned whether he possessed any core values. The concern was that he was overly eager to be liked by everyone and unable to take a strong, confrontive position when confronted with arch conservatives (Jansson, 1997). We know from history that his style remained pretty much the same throughout his presidency.

Clinton weathered the vicious attacks of his opponent, and, despite his shortcomings, he won the presidency with 370 electoral votes, 202 more than his Republican rival. The win was largely thanks to a battered economy, a deeply splintered Republican Party, and an ineffectual campaign. The results, however, indicated more; the American people wanted a president who was for something rather than someone who merely spawned numerous demons. *The Milwaukee Journal*'s response was apropos: "the triumph of vision over drift, of inclusiveness over meanness, of optimism over fear" (Trattner, 1999, p. 391). The president-elect responded on the night of his victory, "It was a victory for all the people who work hard and play by the rules, a victory for the people who feel left out and left behind but who want to do better. [The American people] want their future back. . . . I intend to help give it to them" (Trattner, 1999, p. 391).

After the inauguration, *The Washington Post* summarized the victory under the heading: Rebuilding the Party: Democrats' future rests with Clinton, "For the Democratic Party, the 1992 presidential election was less a full-scale victory than a tentative first step toward building a foundation strong enough to hold constituencies that have been divided by race, class and values. Bill Clinton remains the party's central pillar, and his presidency, more than anything else, will determine whether it succeeds in regaining majority party status, lost since the late 1960s" (Edsall, 1993, p. F3).

In the view of some of Clinton's key strategists, what was more important than the revived legitimacy of the Democratic party was the collapse of the conservative Republican coalition. It was, in part the disreputable position of the Republicans that created the status of the Democratic Party. Clinton's pollster, Stan Greenberg made reference to the public not looking to the Republicans for anything with the campaign which allowed Clinton to use a combination of rhetoric and carefully planned positions and tactics by which to construct a biracial coalition. But there was an element of realism in that his bids in office to strengthen this coalition would be dependent on real world results. There were specific factors of the campaign that helped pull white voters back into the Democratic fold, for example, rhetorical challenges to Jesse Jackson and Sister Souljah, along with a call for tough welfare overhaul. These factors combined with Clinton's encouragement to a rising generation of black leaders and his opposition to the conservative policies of the Reagan-Bush years served to maintain an 8-to-1 Democratic margin among African Americans. Not since Lyndon B. Johnson's campaign in 1965 was the process of coalition building through governance used so effectively by a Democratic president. Furthermore, before Clinton, no Democratic presidential nominees have been the least bit effective, with the possible exception of Jimmy Carter in 1976 (Edsall, 1993).

The Clinton victory did seem to pave the way for real change, but whether or not he would give the American people "their future back" remained to be seen. He and his wife Hillary, an influential figure and a well-respected lawyer, indeed had been very active in matters of social welfare, especially in promoting education and children's rights. Hillary had chaired the board of directors of the Children's Defense Fund, which broadened her husband's appeal to liberals. The president-elect also had a Congress controlled by his own party with its composition having more new faces than at any time since 1969, and more African Americans, Hispanics, and women than ever before in American history. There seemed every indication that Clinton would make good on his promises to change the way things worked in Washington and to be president to all the American people (Trattner, 1999).

Clinton did not support civil rights legislation in Arkansas, but he appointed many African Americans (and women) to governmental posts (Jansson, 1997), and black Americans were clearly interested in the outcome of the election. They seemed to see in Clinton and Gore, also a southerner, an interest in their problems that had not been evident during the Reagan and Bush years. Ron Brown, who had managed Jesse Jackson's campaign in 1988, had become chairman of the Democratic National Committee and was a powerful force in attracting African Americans to the Clinton-Gore ticket. The African American voter turnout in November was approximately 8% of the total voter turnout, with 83% of black voters supporting Clinton and Gore. Also, in Illinois, Carol Mosely Braun defeated U.S. Senator Alan Dixon in the Democratic primary and went on to win the Senate seat in November. She became the only African American in the 20th century, besides Republican Edward Brooke of Massachusetts, to go to the upper house and the first woman to sit in the U.S. Senate (Franklin & Moss, 1994).

USA Today, under the headline "Dems owe victory to blacks," reports:

> Three weeks ago, Democrats made history. Last weekend, some of them tried to rewrite it. The election of Bill Clinton ended the Republican Party's 12-year hold on the presidency, a victory that was due largely, if not decisively, to support from black voters. But when state Democratic Party officials gathered here for their annual meeting, they got a briefing on Clinton's victory that did not mention the record turnout of blacks. More than a simple oversight, this faulty analysis threatens to deny African Americans the credit—and rewards—they deserve. To assess Clinton's victory without considering the black vote is like a military historian looking only at Saudi army tactics to explain the outcome of the Persian Gulf war. . . . Much of the credit for [the] rise [in black voter turnout] belongs to

Jesse Jackson, who Clinton quietly turned to in the final weeks of the campaign
to ensure a large black voter turnout. (Wickham, 1992, p. 12A)

Because of congressional redistricting, along with several attractive and
politically adroit candidates, 16 African Americans—11 men and 5 women—
gained new seats in the House of Representatives. This brought the number of
African Americans in the lower house up to 39, a record high for all time. Eight
of those new House members represented five states that had not sent any
African Americans to Congress in the 20th century. Some of them were Earl
Hilliard of Alabama; Corrine Brown, Alcee Hastings, and Carnie Meek of
Florida; Eva Clayton and Melvin Watt of North Carolina; Jim Clyburn of South
Carolina; and Bobby Scott of Virginia. In Texas, Eddie Bernice Johnson was
the first African American ever to sit in Congress from that state (Franklin &
Moss, 1994).

There were 40 African Americans in the 103rd Congress, putting them in
a position to exert considerable influence in decision making. Many had
already had legislative experience; for example, Cleo Fields of Louisiana had
been chairman of the committee in his state legislature that passed on all
major appointments, and Carnie Meek of Florida had been chair of a major
appropriations committee in the Florida senate (Franklin & Moss, 1994).

Clinton's campaign comment that his administration "would look like America" began by the appointment of Vernon Johnson, a prominent Washington
attorney and former president of the National Urban League, as chairman of his
transition team. Maya Angelou read her poem "On the Pulse of Morning" at
Clinton's inauguration. She wrote the poem for the occasion.

Angelou begins her poem with the lament, "A Rock, A River, A Tree/Hosts
to species long since departed, . . . Is lost in the gloom of dust and ages," and
then eloquently takes us through the ages with a tale of the struggles of a
nation over time with hope for the future:

> Each of you, a bordered country, . . .
> Your armed struggles for profit
> Have left collars of waste upon
> My shore . . .

and then she offers the challenge:

> Lift up you eyes
> Upon
> The day breaking for you.
> Give birth again
> To the dream. . . .
> Mold it . . . Sculpt it into . . . a new beginning . . . The horizon . . .
> Offering you space to place new steps of change.

Here, on the pulse of this fine day . . . have the courage
To look up and out and upon me. . . .
And into your sister's eyes,
Into your brother's face, your country
And say simply
Very simply
With hope
Good morning.

For his cabinet, Clinton selected Ron Brown as secretary of commerce; Mike Espy, U.S. representative from Mississippi, secretary of agriculture; Hazel O'Leary, executive vice president of the Northern States Power Company of Minnesota, secretary of energy; and Jess Brown, executive director of Disabled American Veterans, secretary of veterans' affairs. No other president had had more than one African American on his cabinet. Other African Americans named in the early days of the Clinton administration were Joycelyn Elders, surgeon general of the United States; Clifton Wharton, deputy secretary of state; Walter D. Broadnax, deputy secretary of health and human services; Terrence Duvernay, deputy secretary of housing and urban development; and Drew Days, solicitor general of the United States. There were more African Americans in other departments who became undersecretaries and assistant secretaries. Thus, African Americans were satisfied that the president had made a significant beginning toward making his administration look like America (Franklin & Moss, 1994).

Franklin and Moss (1994) state:

> Looking back on almost four centuries of residence in the Western world, African Americans could correctly visualize themselves, from the beginning, as an integral part of the struggle for freedom. At times they were passive symbols of the struggle that was carried on by others. Frequently, however, they were active participants in the valiant warfare to destroy bigotry, repression, and subjugation. Studying carefully their role in the growth and development of the United States, they could see that they were more than very important contributors to the economic, political, and social development of their country. They had also been important factors in the ageless struggle between freedom and slavery. They had been the nation's constant reminders of the imperfection of its social order and the immorality of its human relationships. They had witnessed a nation dedicated to liberty move toward the brink of destruction in the struggle to settle the question of freedom. They had seen that same nation compromise its position in the family of nations because of its inability to face squarely the problem of freedom for all at home. (p. 570)

African Americans had undergone a rich experience, moving together with other peoples into another era in the final years of the 20th century, giving evidence of greater maturity. Having been an integral part of Western culture and civilization, their fate was inextricably connected with it. They were doubtlessly wounded by the rejections that they had suffered, but such treatment also gave them a perception and an objectivity that others had difficulty achieving.

Therefore, they could point out more clearly than some others the inherent weaknesses in Western civilization (Franklin & Moss, 1994).

In spite of all the early fanfare, Clinton got off to a bad start when it was discovered that his attorney general designate, Zoe Baird, had hired illegal aliens as domestic servants and failed to pay their legally required Social Security taxes. The same fate fell on his second nominee, Kimba Wood, which meant that the Justice Department remained leaderless for some time while the search continued for a third candidate. He then ran into more troubled waters when, with stiff opposition from the military brass and powerful legislators, he announced his intention to lift the ban on gays in the armed forces, a campaign promise. Another campaign pledge that he hinted he probably would not be able to follow through on was to cut taxes on the middle class. Later, he was highly criticized by many citizens when they learned that air traffic at the Los Angeles airport came to a standstill while he had his hair trimmed aboard the presidential airplane by a Beverly Hills hairdresser (for $200). There was a scandal in the White House travel office; due to conservative opposition, the president withdrew his nomination of longtime friend Lani Guinier to head the Justice Department's Civil Rights Division; and he hired a veteran of the Nixon and Reagan White House, David Gergen, to help refurbish his sagging public image (Trattner, 1999). There was more. The president delayed unveiling his plans for revamping the nation's health and welfare systems, put aside his promise to push for an increase in the minimum wage, hinted at his willingness to compromise on the issue of gays in the military, and did so with a plan that would make gay conduct rather than homosexual status incompatible with military service. His proposal for the plan was a "don't ask, don't tell, and don't pursue" policy. It is no wonder that the people's faith in his judgment and competency was shaken, and not that of liberals. Public opinion polls in 1993 showed only a 36% people approval of Clinton's handling of the presidency. Clinton was nothing if not resilient and was able to bounce back from these political setbacks when he scored some important political victories (Trattner, 1999).

Clinton's credibility began to rise when he got Congress to pass a Family Leave Act, which he quickly signed into law. Additionally, he lifted the ban prohibiting federally subsidized family planning clinics from discussing abortion with clients who were pregnant, called the nation's pharmaceutical industry on its "shockingly high prices," launched a campaign guaranteeing free immunizations of all American children, and persuaded Congress to extend unemployment compensation to people most affected by the prolonged recession. Reform of the health care system was also one of Clinton's earlier pursuits (Trattner, 1999).

Clinton had realized, long before his presidential campaign, that the American health care system was full of flaws. The existing system revolved around employers and private insurance companies and tended to work well for those who were covered by it. Vast numbers of people lacked coverage, however, because of unemployment, because of employers who chose not to offer health coverage, or because of chronic or catastrophic conditions that had exhausted their benefits. In addition, the system was extraordinarily costly, absorbing about 15% of the GNP in 1992, compared with less than 10% in other industrialized nations. Costs were increasing at such an astronomical rate that experts predicted it would reach 20% of the GNP soon after the turn of the century. Costly technology and drugs, along with the endless stream of innovations from huge biotechnology and pharmaceutical firms, drove costs up at one end of the spectrum; and on the other end were the tens of millions of poor and uninsured Americans who lacked access to primary care and prevention services seeking care only after their medical conditions had become gravely serious (Jansson, 1997).

Not only were there political barriers to reform to surmount, there were many entrenched interests such as private health insurance companies, physicians, hospitals, and pharmaceutical companies who would resist reform that curtailed their profits or autonomy. Nonetheless, Clinton chose to prioritize health reform, not just for moral reasons but also in the hope of enhancing his political fortunes like the educational reform in Arkansas did. In 1993, he placed Hillary Rodham Clinton in charge of this endeavor, along with the assistance of Ira Magaziner, a liberal aide (Jansson, 1997).

Controversy existed within the administration from the beginning, with the first being that of the scope of health reform. After much debate and opposition from key advisors, Hillary and Magaziner, with the president's blessing, chose universal coverage as the central goal, dismissing the warnings of the president's economic advisors. Clinton's foes of the plan played on the fears of many Americans that they would pay more for health insurance under the plan. Providers and Republicans opposed the plan, and, in the end, neither liberals nor conservatives rallied to the plan. Along with all the other problems, there were complications with the logistical problems of enacting health care in the Congress where several committees would have jurisdiction, three in the House and two in the Senate; and the plan began to lose momentum (Jansson, 1997).

While some were quick to back Clinton's plan for health reform, it remains unclear whether any plan would have gained support from the Congress in 1994. The defeat was a painful, crushing blow to the president. He had gambled that the enactment of his plan would occur just prior to the congressional elections of 1994. The defeat, however, once again made him look ineffectual and renewed the public's distaste for government gridlock. The Republicans jumped on the defeat, portraying Clinton's plan as a bureaucratic, big-government scheme, persuading many voters that he was a traditional liberal and eroded Democrats' support in moderate and conservative districts (Jansson, 1997). In terms of health care, what did happen for the country was the expansion of managed health care in an attempt to contain the rising cost of medical care.

MANAGED CARE

Managed care was designed to control costs and is defined as "a complex health and behavioral health care services delivery system." This system has evolved over a lengthy period of time, and the current managed care "revolution" is, therefore, more appropriately termed an evolution (Weeder & Pebbles-Wilkins, 2001, p. 1). Its structural complexity is further complicated by the potential for its two stated goals of cost efficiency and service delivery effectiveness to work at cross purposes or to be in direct competition for the scarce allocation of resources. For example, it could be that the most efficient cost-controlled methods of delivering services may in fact not be the most effective in terms of providing quality service solutions to those who suffer from severe and persistent health and behavioral health problems (Weeder & Pebbles-Wilkins, 2001).

The Los Angeles Times reported on a study done by Harvard University and the Kaiser Family Foundation on attitudes toward managed care and found that 51% of respondents said managed care had lowered the quality of medical care for the sick, compared to 32% who said it had improved the quality. Another 55% said they were worried that if they became ill, their managed care plan would be more interested in saving money than in providing the best medical treatment. At its best, managed care is perceived as a system in which appropriate structure, control, and accountability allow the most efficient use of resources to achieve maximal health outcome. At worst, it is perceived as a system in which no real dollars are saved with money being diverted to administrative operations and profits at the expense of needed patient services (Jackson, 1995).

Already, vast sums of federal money such as Medicare and Medicaid were flowing through private, for-profit managed care organizations by the time national health reform efforts collapsed in 1994. States began to develop contracts with managed care organizations to manage all or part of their Supplemental Security Income and Aid to Families with Dependent Children and, later, Temporary Assistance to Needy Families. This meant that the gainfully employed as well as older adults, people with serious and persistent mental illnesses, people with disabilities, and economically disenfranchised people had become legitimate targets for this growing industry. The rationale was, as long as federal and state governments would pay, managed care organizations would take the risk of covering oppressed and vulnerable populations (Davidson, Davidson, & Keigher, 1999).

Policy Directs Practice

Managed care is another example of how social policy dictates practice. Not only did the practitioners have to adapt their service delivery to align with managed care, social work educators had to educate students for a changing health care environment as well as new market realities. See Figure 12.1.

Social workers are also trying to affect policy. They helped stage a demonstration in the Capital in April 2000 to thrash managed care. The protestors demanded that the management of health care by profit-driven corporations be replaced with another approach such as the single-payer system, not unlike what the Clinton reformers had purposed. They said that managed care "costs too much, covers too little and excludes too many." One of the spokeswomen said, "This industry was going to take advantage of both mental health patients and professionals. They're literally destroying psychotherapy." She said figures show that between 1985 and 1995, managed care reduced medical spending 7% but mental health spending 54%. Furthermore, under managed care, patients have lost choice, privacy, and control over decisions. As a result of these concerns, the Coalition of Mental Health Professionals and Consumers was formed and currently boasts 1300 members. It is an interdisciplinary coalition (Slavin, 2000, pp. 1 & 10).

A REPUBLICAN VICTORY IN CONGRESS

The Republican Party won a dramatic victory in the 1994 congressional elections by securing control of both houses of Congress (for the first time in 40 years), and other misfortunes befell Clinton. There were problems for the president and his wife over financial dealings that involved their alleged plot to cover up those activities, which came to be known as Whitewater. There had also been charges of sexual harassment against the president while he was governor of Arkansas; all of these issues produced the image of a president lacking in character and leadership. The new Congress proclaimed a mandate to totally remake the federal government, including deep tax cuts, a balanced budget, a constitutional amendment to ban abortions, and the like. The newly elected conservative pledged to dismantle social policies and programs that extended back to the New Deal of the 1930s. Clinton's vetoes and threats of vetoes, however, helped to stymie most of their more extreme efforts; through this process, some of Clinton's popularity returned (Trattner, 1999).

With the presidential elections of 1996 ahead of him, Clinton was determined to uphold his claim of being a "centrist" and to deliver on his long-delayed promise to "end welfare as we know it," something the public was still calling for. History has told us that since the mid-1960s public sentiments on poverty and the welfare issue had shifted. The country went from viewing poverty as the result of social and economic conditions over which the needy had little or no control—because of things like a shortage of adequate jobs and child care facilities, poor education, ill health, racism, and so

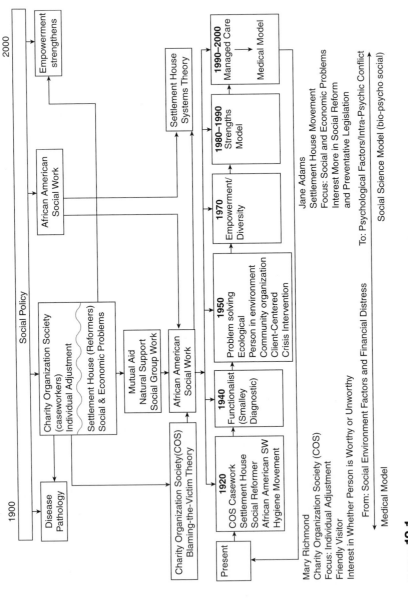

FIGURE 12.1

This is the final illustration depicting how policy drives practice. We see that, with the advent of managed care, our policies have gone full circle back to the medical model.

on—to blaming the poor and the nation's public welfare programs for their problems. It was argued by the critics of the system that AFDC, more than any other welfare program, encouraged laziness and other negative personal values and thus kept the poor mired in cycles of dependency. The critics claimed that this was especially true in the nation's inner cities where unemployment, drug usage, crime, violence, and teenage pregnancy seemingly had become epidemic (Trattner, 1999). For example, John Goodman, a fellow at the Barry Goldwater Institute claimed, "Poverty is a matter of choice. . . . We'd have very little poverty if young people would do these things—finish high school, get married before having babies, and get a job, any job" (Trattner, 1999, p. 396).

Whatever President Clinton's views might have been about these beliefs, he was willing to go along with them for political purposes. He granted waivers to several states that allowed them to terminate AFDC payments to women having additional children while on relief, along with approving a number of other restrictive measures designed by the states to force recipients off the welfare rolls. This was followed by the congressional Republicans taking the initiative in revamping the entire system with his approval. The president did veto two measures that they proposed, forcing them to come forward with one that was slightly less punitive, which he signed into law in August of 1996. This was done despite vigorous opposition from liberal Democrats and others and the omission of funds for work training and a guarantee of health insurance and jobs for welfare recipients, breaking his earlier promise (Trattner, 1999). Trattner explains that

> The Personal Responsibility and Work Opportunity Reconciliation Act, as it was titled, was a dramatic and very controversial measure that brought an end to, or reversed, six decades of federal social policy—that of guaranteeing at least a minimum level of financial assistance, or some sort of safety net, to the nation's destitute and dependent citizens, especially its young people. (p. 397)

Aid to Families with Dependent Children was abolished by the measure and replaced with a system of grants to the states that were to decline by some $55 billion over the following six years. The states were allowed to establish most of the rules of eligibility but were required to end welfare to all recipients after two years, with or without jobs (Trattner, 1999).

MEDICAID

The Republicans' Budget Resolution also called for a savings of $182 billion from Medicaid, but the details were not spelled out for how this should be done. Medicaid is the health care program for low-income individuals. Under the block grants for the states, a cap on the federal government's contribution reduced payments from 50% to 40% under the new formula. Like AFDC, states were given extraordinary latitude in designing their programs and the government would only require coverage of children and pregnant women falling beneath specific income guidelines. It was iffy whether states would choose to fund medical care for poor people at reasonable levels due to budgetary constraints. This worry came on top of the already inadequately funded program in which beneficiaries had to endure extended waits for care of uncertain quality in antiquated facilities (Jansson, 1997).

A story in *The St. Louis Post-Dispatch* in 1996 under the headline "Neither Healthy Nor Wealthy" reported:

> Health is wealth, the saying goes. When you're both ill and poor, you've got two strikes against you and cannot afford a third. Many of the men, women and children who are the *Post-Dispatch's* 100 neediest cases this year suffer from a chronic, acute or terminal illness—or several. The sickness often arises out of their impoverished condition and, in any case, greatly accentuates and complicates it. With the new push for welfare reform, these families' meager incomes now often disqualify them for Medicaid, which would at least cover their medical expenses. . . . All three members of the B family—both parents, who are in their mid-40s, and their 10-year old son—have serious medical problems. They moved to St. Louis recently for the little support their extended family could give them. . . . The family needs to [move] because . . . [of] major safety problems. The oven catches fire . . . and water is dripping through the overhead kitchen light. Complaints to the landlord have been fruitless. (Vollard, 1996, p. 1E)

And:

> Mrs. W is a 37-year-old mother caring for five children ages 3 to 12 while her husband is in prison. Cancer she thought she had licked has returned and repeated chemotherapy treatments have left her weak and depressed. . . . She is a caring and concerned parent but the future is grim and uncertain. The family has many unfilled needs, such as no living room furniture and not enough beds for the children . . . [and there were many more]. (Vollard, 1996, p. 1E)

The law brought further restrictions: a lifetime limit was set on assistance at five years; legal immigrants who had not yet become American citizens were barred from receiving food stamps and Supplemental Security Income; and the states were given the authority to end Medicaid payments to legal immigrants as well. It was pointed out that by eliminating any national entitlement to welfare, the measure reflected a resurgence of a number of fundamental themes of colonial poor law—that it was more unworkable or at least had unfair and punitive provisions, namely, local responsibility—as well as the restrictions on providing aid to "strangers" and the "work or starve" mentality for the able-bodied (Trattner, 1999). An example of how this affected a group of immigrants in California was reported in *The Los Angeles Times* in 2000 under the headline, "Looming Welfare Cuts Put O.C.'s Poor in Worry Mode," dateline, Fullerton:

> Every afternoon for two years, 40-year old Suong Nguyen and 43-year old Nga Phan have chatted in front of Richman Elementary School while waiting for their children. Lately, their conversations . . . have been filled with anxiety about how their families are going to survive without government aid. . . . The two women, both immigrants from Vietnam who depend on welfare, commiserated with each other. "I just don't know how we go about preparing for this," Nguyen said, sighing. Her friend shook her head and replied, "I worry too. I don't know where we could go to find jobs. I feel helpless. I don't know what to do." (Richardson, Dizon, & Reyes, 1996, p. A1)

The fear expressed by the women is characteristic of the mood in their south Fullerton neighborhood. Some residents worry about poverty while carrying on with daily routines like child care, shopping for food, and doing the laundry. The new federal welfare laws will change life in this neighborhood while many residents eke out a living with a boost from the government. This Fullerton community is typical of the pockets of low-income areas throughout the county and across the state and nation where new welfare laws will cause dramatic changes (Richardson et al., 2000):

> Welfare reforms already require counties to shut off all federal aid to legal immigrants, although Orange County welfare officials have yet to act, waiting to see if a court challenge will overturn the regulation. . . .
>
>   A local Circle K store owner has already felt the hard times, saying his immigrant customers have told him they now fear the state's anti-immigrant mood. Dozens of Latino immigrants with green cards are not spending as much these days and are hoarding what little they do have. (Richardson et al., 1996)

But not everyone in this community is fearful of welfare reform. A 44-year-old mother of six said she and her husband make do with his salary and no government help. She said that "if we can do it, they can too" and believes that the government is too lenient, making it too easy to get on welfare, that just because you moved in from another country does not mean you are deserving of welfare. The school principal disagrees, saying, "We probably have a lot of people who will be affected by the reforms, but even if some people do receive welfare, many if not most of my students' parents also work. I don't see people just lazing around, collecting welfare. The people I see are working hard, maybe two jobs trying to make it" (Richardson et al., 2000, p. A3).

If we go back to Clinton's presidential campaign promise to "end welfare as we know it," we see that he had set into motion the forces that led to this "reform." Others took the initiative and secured a far different and much more punitive measure than Clinton had originally envisioned. He was urged by many people not to sign the measure into law, but he had his eye on the presidential election only months away and did not heed their advice. In spite of vast criticism, Clinton remained unapologetic for his action as he prepared for his reelection bid (Trattner, 1999).

Stunned, critics were outraged at the president, estimating that the new law would push some 1.2 million children into poverty, along with another

1.5 million adults who would be denied food stamps and SSI. Meanwhile, state and local officials all across the nation scrambled to try to understand the complicated measure and how to implement it. Among the opponents of the measure was Peter Edelman, Clinton's assistant secretary for planning and evaluation in the Department of Health and Human Services who resigned in protest over what he referred to as this "mindless measure"; he wrote in an article in *The Atlantic Monthly* that it was "The Worst Thing Bill Clinton [Ever] Has Done." Edelman's wife, Marian Wright Edelman, who was the founder and head of the Children's Defense Fund, called it "a moment of shame" (Trattner, 1999, p. 398).

"Jobs aren't always way out of poverty, magazine reports," was the headline from the Associated Press for an article printed in *The Times Picayune* in 1999. The article reported:

> Leaving welfare is no guarantee that a family will escape poverty. One third of all poor children live in families where parents work, researchers state in a report on the working poor. The report, by the firm Child Trends, notes that the overhaul of the nation's welfare system was meant to both increase work by parents and decrease child poverty. But imposing a strict work requirement does not guarantee that a family will escape poverty, it warns. Twenty percent of all American children—or about 14.2 million youngsters—lived in families with incomes below the poverty line in 1996. That meant less than $16,000 a year for a family of four. Five million of those poor children—35%—had working parents. . . . In the meantime, researchers are recommending that states provide health insurance and child care subsidies after families leave welfare before they can afford it on their own. (Meckler, 1999, p. A3)

LESSONS FROM HISTORY: THE MOVE AWAY FROM HELPING THE POOR

We have learned that, beginning in the early 1960s, social workers started moving steadily further from social policy, due primarily to the shrinking funding for public-sector casework. The shrinkage led social workers to the search for paying clientele, which diminished our historic collective sense of responsibility for poor women and children. Our numbers did not decrease as much as other professions, and, as Gordon (1998) reminds us, "Few professionals are so well positioned to grasp the not-so-hidden injuries of being a poor single mother, or being stigmatized by the very programs that are supposed to help" (p. 11).

One important lesson from history is the power of language. We have seen through the chapters of this book that there has been a tendency for centuries to vilify the poor and to begrudge them help. Along with this, however, has been a countertendency, with periods where there was the impulse to help and to expand democracy; and language helped create both. The term *welfare* referring only to means-tested programs like AFDC is not a neutral colloquialism but a fundamental aspect of how antiwelfare public opinion was created. With mystifying language, it becomes possible for vast sectors of people to believe wild fabrications and to hold contradictory opinions. For example, at least 80% of federal social welfare spending goes to the nonpoor and 50% of the U.S. population receives direct government benefits such as unemployment insurance, medicare, SSI, social security pensions, aid for farmers, school aid, public health–infectious disease, all social insurance. These programs are often so invisible and so taken for granted that we do not know when we are the beneficiaries (Gordon, 1998).

One of the biggest myths held by many Americans is that cutting welfare is a way to cut the deficit. This is dead wrong; AFDC accounted for about 1.2% of the federal budget, and the reality is that it takes cutting big-ticket items to reduce the deficit. It seems that Americans are equally ambivalent about balancing the budget, with 79% saying they supported it; but only 32% did so if it meant cuts in Social Security. When it comes to helping the poor, 75% said they supported cuts in welfare, but they did not want to cut support for poor mothers and children (Gordon, 1998).

It is particularly sobering for many liberal Democrats that it was Clinton, not the Republicans, that began the attacks on welfare in his 1992 campaign; then the Republicans zeroed in on AFDC for a vastly higher proportion of cuts than any other federal program, and Clinton went along with it. The stark reality of these cuts is the elimination of the only program designed for poor children and mothers, as well as the idea of public assistance altogether. The federal government has abjured any responsibility for the poor, meaning that poor parents and children no longer have any citizenship right to help. With the states now responsible, it has given rise to a race to the bottom with states competing with each other to drive the poor out by offering the stingiest amounts of help. The claim that state governments are closer to the people bears no evidence, and, in fact, the state governments are far more vulnerable to business threats of disinvestment and flight. History tells us that the state governments have done a poor job of protecting women and minorities, with these groups having to look to the federal government for their rights (Gordon, 1998).

From *The New York Times* Service, the following article was printed in *The Times Picayune* in 1999 under the headline, "As welfare dies, burden on Grandma grows: Older relatives are pressed into action as children left alone":

> As Wisconsin drives its welfare rolls to record lows, the number of grandmothers pressed into action is reaching unexpected highs. Unwilling or unable to work for public aid, many of the state's most troubled mothers have lost their benefits, often en route to drug clinics, jail cells, shelters, or the streets. And grandmothers . . . are being left to care for the children abandoned along the way. The story of Wisconsin's beleaguered grandmothers is just one chapter of the complex

treatise on social change being written by welfare's end. And like most aspects of Wisconsin's daring experiment, it is drawing national, even international, attention from a world eager for glimpses of the post-welfare future. No anti-poverty idea has animated the past decade as much as "ending welfare." And no state requirement has cut the cash welfare rolls by an astonishing 91% [like Wisconsin]. The food stamp and Medicaid rolls also are declining. . . . President Clinton and his Republican adversaries have celebrated the dwindling rolls—in Wisconsin and across the country—as evidence of clear success. Skeptics warn that families are suffering out of sight and that a flagging economy may yet leave them sleeping on grates. . . .

Grandmothers . . . have long served as pillars of poor communities. . . . Nationally, the Census Bureau reports that the number of children in their grandparents' care has risen more than 50% in the past decade alone. If Wisconsin's experience is an indication, the nation's tougher welfare laws will push the number even higher . . . [and as] the number of children falling into relatives' care has exceeded state projections, [it has] created waiting lines for aid and touched off a new safety-net debate. (DeParle, 1999, p. A32)

Looking back at history again, in June 1961, the city manager of Newburg, New York, a town of 31,000 up the Hudson from New York City, announced a plan to overhaul the city's welfare system. It began by imposing a three-month limit on assistance and excluded any children born out of wedlock while on welfare. The plan proceeded to include a new, lightly coded language that blamed the city's poverty on the influx of black immigrants and focused on black mothers' immorality, while hardly mentioning the children. The city manager went so far as to claim that welfare was attracting trollops and the dregs of humanity from the South. Even before the plan was implemented, it engendered the largest national discussion of welfare to that date and a Gallop poll showed that 80% of the public supported it (Gordon, 1998). "What produced this backing was neither racism nor sexism alone but the deadly *association* of black women and sexual/reproductive immorality and irresponsibility. Newburgh was the direct ancestor of the bipartisan welfare repeal of 1996" (p. 10).

It was easy to attack AFDC for a variety of reasons; its constituency may be one of the politically least powerful groups in the country—not a high voting record, and they are often hidden from the prosperous who avoid the ghettos and rural areas where they are concentrated. The very shame attached to their status by the incessant pounding of pejorative rhetoric, in fact, induces welfare recipients to try to be unnoticeable—the very opposite of what is necessary to exert political power (Gordon, 1998).

In her book *So You Think I Drive a Cadillac?*, Seccombe (1999), through personal interviews, puts faces and voices on welfare. Amy, a 23-year-old white mother of one, who attends university full-time, says:

It's a very humiliating experience—being on welfare and being involved in the system. You are treated as though you are the scum of the earth. A stupid, lazy, nasty person. How dare you take this money? It's a very unpleasant experience. I'd avoid it at all costs. But unfortunately, I can't avoid it right now. (p. 59)

Keisha, a 33-year-old African American woman with two children, says:

> A phone? No. That's an extra bill I can't afford right now. I had one, and that was
> a bill I had to let go. My parents, especially my mom, say, "Why don't you get a
> phone?" Well Mom, I can't afford a phone right now. (p. 110)

Kim, a 29-year-old African American woman with three children, says:

> Okay, first I have to get a money order to pay my rent—it's due on the fifth. I wait
> on my light bill . . . so I know how much I'm going to spend and how much I
> have left over. Like a budget. I don't never go over my budget. Well, this month
> I bought my kids some clothes with the telephone money. You do what you have
> to do. (p. 115)

Molly, a middle-aged white woman with three children, says:

> When I was taking my sociology class [at a community college], we had this talk,
> and it sickened me some of the things people were saying. They were not true.
> You can't generalize and say that everyone is the same. "She has babies so she can
> have this extra money to live on!" I don't think I've met anybody who wanted to
> be on welfare. (p. 66)

Mandy, a 20-year-old African American woman with two young children, says:

> They say you lazy. They say you lazy and don't want to work. You want people to
> take care of you. You want to sit home and watch stories all day, which I don't.
> And they say it's a handout. (p. 51)

From the community, Beth, a 27-year-old white woman with one child, says:

> Oh they say silly stuff, "The black people are getting it so we might as well—you
> might as well go ahead and get it too while you can. They're driving Cadillacs,"
> and this and that. It just shows how ignorant they are—to me. (p. 53)

This attack on welfare is based on the premise that government neither
can nor should try to improve its people's well-being or to solve social and economic problems. The western and midwestern militias and other groups
attacking federal workers such as park rangers are also part of this movement.
This is a campaign funded by huge corporate fortunes, conservative tax-free
foundations, and a well-organized right wing attempting to rig one of the most
massive transfers of resources from the poor and the middle class to the rich
in America. Often, this movement is also supported by grassroots waves of
anger, which takes us back to the robber-baron ideology that markets are natural and supreme and their consequences irresistible. This Republican legislative program, which the Clinton New Democrats support, at least tacitly,
would strip government of the capacity to reduce the extremes of inequality,
regulate economic instabilities, and curb business excesses. This is not unlike
the attack on affirmative action, resting on the notions that only the market
should determine who gets jobs and education and that discrimination cannot
be challenged by regulating the market (Gordon, 1998).

The meaning of all this on gender and race is central. Large corporations have always had the tremendous influence over the state; however, conservatives are right to see that popular movements such as labor, women, and minorities have been able to force government to intervene on the side of the subordinated. The use of the democratic state to move people closer to social, political, and economic justice has historically been a central part of the labor, civil rights, and feminist programs. The antigovernment rhetoric put forth by the conservatives is a direct repudiation of these traditions (Gordon, 1998).

This attack is, in part, preeminently a racial attack. The same racial agenda is behind both welfare cutbacks and affirmative action, often coded in language of "no special rights," as if people of color were currently equal and asking for privileged treatment. The callousness toward children, with welfare repeal, is surely conditioned by the fact that so many of these children are not white, nor does the labor market need them. What is at issue with the Personal Responsibility and Work Opportunity Reconciliation Act of 1996 is feminism, family, and sexual morality. It is, in part, a backlash against the unorthodox, experimental, secular, and feminist values of progressive social movements. The beginning lines of the welfare law are, " The welfare repeal attempts to use support for children as a means of changing their mothers' sexual and marital behavior—something tried for centuries and always a failure" (Gordon, 1998, p. 13).

As we read more and more about the sufferings caused directly and indirectly by making welfare a dirty word, we can only hope for a counterreaction to this reform act of 1996. As a society, we must not lose sight of the fact that welfare is about real mothers and real children and that caring for children is hard and important work, very difficult for one parent alone and virtually impossible for low-wage earners without child care or medical insurance (Gordon, 1998).

The Associated Press reported the findings of a recent study that blamed welfare reform for the uninsured:

> Nearly a million low-income parents have lost their Medicaid coverage and probably are uninsured as a consequence of welfare overhaul. . . . Families USA examined Medicaid figures in 15 states with most of the uninsured low-income population and found that 945,880 adults with children had been dropped from the program from 1996 to 1999, a decline of 27%. More than 2.5 million were enrolled in Medicaid in the 15 states at the end of last year. The study . . . blamed the problem on states, saying they mismanaged the 1996 welfare reform law and improperly kicked people off of Medicaid once they left welfare, created barriers for people to sign up and set income eligibility requirements too low. "The basic thrust of welfare is to move people to jobs, but unfortunately when they do so they are considered to have too much income for Medicaid so the reward of moving off welfare is getting no health insurance," said Ron Pollack, executive director of Families USA. In Louisiana, for example, a family of three earning more than $3,168 a year would be ineligible for Medicaid. (Gullo, 2000, p. A3)

CLINTON'S SECOND TERM

The second term of the Clinton presidency was overshadowed with scandal; the most lethal was his affair with Monica Lewinsky. This affair, and all that surrounded it, led to his impeachment hearings. The president denied having lied under oath, denying the affair, but confessed to having an "inappropriate sexual relationship."

Clinton knew his admission would leak to the public, and he decided to tell the nation about his sexual relationship with Lewinsky. The following is a draft of the speech he was to deliver at 9:00 P.M., August 17:

> My fellow Americans:
>
> No one who is not in my position can understand the remorse I feel today. Since I was young, I have had a profound reverence for this office I hold. I've been honored that you, the people, have entrusted it to me. . . . I have fallen short of what you should expect from a president. I have failed my own religious faith and values. I have let too many people down. I take full responsibility for my actions— for hurting my wife and daughter, for hurting Monica Lewinsky and her family, for hurting friends and staff, and for hurting the country I love. None of this ever should have happened.
>
> I never should have had any sexual contact with Monica Lewinsky, but I did. I should have acknowledged that I was wrong months ago, but I didn't. . . . What I did was wrong—and there is no excuse for it. I do want to assure you, as I told the Grand Jury under oath, that I did nothing to obstruct this investigation.
>
> Finally, I also want to apologize to all of you, my fellow citizens. I hope you can find it in your heart to accept that apology. I pledge to you that I will make every effort of mind and spirit to earn your confidence again, to be worthy of this office, and to finish the work on which we have made such remarkable progress in the past six years.
>
> God bless you, and good night. (Torricelli & Carroll, 1999, pp. 435–436)

This speech, however, ended up being replaced by one that was less contrite and sterner in tone (see Torricelli & Carroll, 1999, pp. 436–437).

Like so many times before, Clinton was able to rebound and left the office he served for eight years with one of the highest job approval ratings of any president leaving office. In an editorial written for *The Washington Post*, Reich (2001) critiques Clinton's presidency by recognizing that his time in office showed the longest economic expansion in history and the lowest rates of joblessness and inflation in nearly 20 years. Crime rates were down, teenage pregnancy was down, welfare rolls were slashed, and the budget was balanced. All this along with peace in the Balkans, near-peace in Northern Ireland, and freer trade with Mexico and China, as well as the rest of the world. In the final assessments, however, little of all this seems to matter. What we are left with is the melodrama from the Clinton years, ranging from the wild ride that lurched from near-disaster to narrow triumph, and back to death-defying crisis narrowly averted and back to victory. Reich sums it up as, "Gays in the military: Oops! The first budget: By a hair! Hillary-care: Collapse! . . . Whitewater: Watch out! . . . The showdown and shutdown: Amazing! . . . The reelection: Incredible! Monica: This is surely the end! The senate vote on impeachment: Saved! . . . (p. B7)

While this editorial was meant to be tongue-in-cheek, and some may agree or disagree, Clinton does get top marks for his commitment to and work with the problems facing the minority communities. In an editorial, Teepen (2001) reports:

> President Clinton devoted one of the strongest statements in his long recessional . . . to the challenge race still presents to the nation. He called for an end to racial profiling, for criminal justice reforms that would mitigate the gross racial disparities in sentencing, for replacing old, unreliable voting systems that are concentrated in minority precincts, for increased research into diseases that affect minority communities more heavily than others. . . . Throughout his presidency, Clinton has shown rare understanding of the imperative for racial justice. . . . (p. B7)

Before we move on to review affirmative action during the last several years, we will bid adieu to President Clinton, our 42nd president, with a few words from one of his farewell speeches. This comes from a sermon he delivered at the Foundry United Methodist Church, where he and his family attended services during their time in Washington, D.C.:

> In the years ahead, America may have presidents who do this job better than I have. But I really doubt we'll ever have another one who enjoyed it more than I have. . . . I look forward to finding out whether John Quincy Adams was right when he said there is nothing so pathetic in life as an ex-president, or whether, instead of his words, the life of John Quincy Adams and the life of Jimmy Carter prove exactly the reverse. (Therolf, p. A7)

AFFIRMATIVE ACTION

Even in the wake of the worst urban uprising in American history, the Los Angeles race riots, this occasion was not used by politicians to develop far-reaching proposals to help the largely African American and Latino populations of the nation's inner cities. Demonstration empowerment zones were developed under Clinton for some major cities, but this was a relatively small response to such large problems (Jansson, 1997). Even as our nation was steeped in the 2000 presidential election campaign, there was no serious discussion of race. *The Washington Post* commented on this in an editorial that ran in *The Times Picayune* under the headline, "Candidates must address racial ills."

According to the Brookings Institution race was placed first among eight forums focusing on the election pertaining to policy matters. The issue that rose to the top, over and over again was that of the divisions between black and white. So great are the divisions that even civil rights leaders have been surprised. Roger Wilkins, a professor and former assistant attorney general, evoked Thurgood Marshall, saying the late Supreme Court justice thought long ago that "all the schools in the United States would be desegrated in about five years, and the whole country would be desegregated by the 100th birthday of the Emancipation Proclamation." That would put the hoped for change at 1963, which we know did not happen. The lesson here is that racism is unyielding, and denial remains ever present. The presidential candidates of 2000, Gore, Bush, McClain, Bradley, barely mentioned it (Overholser, 2000).

Another top issue was crack cocaine use and the grievous damage it has done to family structures. Joyce Ladner, a senior fellow at Brookings, said, "People were poor, but they didn't have this feeling they would never get out of it. At least we had the optimism that upward mobility was possible, now there is a poverty of the spirit in the underclass that blots out that optimism" (quoted in Overholser, 2000, p. B7). There were suggestion offered for change, for example, conversations about race using the language of education, health care and economics across racial lines, different ways to look at old problems. Overholser says, "Whatever your taste in tactics, the challenges facing American's black underclass, in particular, are profoundly real. No candidate can lay claim to leadership in America today without finding a way—direct or by proxy—to address them"(p. B7).

Around the country, affirmative action lost ground during the Clinton years as policies to help persons of color fell under attack. In California, Governor Pete Wilson had affirmative action rescinded in the University of California system and he supported a proposition on the California ballot in 1996 to end affirmative action throughout state government. The perception was that white claimants were being denied positions and opportunities, which prompted some public resentment (Jansson, 1997).

This was only the beginning of the effort to eliminate affirmative action. In Texas, the Hopwood ruling involved four white students who sued the University of Texas law school for discrimination because they were not admitted in 1992. *The Houston Chronicle* reports on the appeal of this case with the headline "State seeks Hopwood case reversal." The text reads, in part:

> State attorneys asked the U.S. 5th Circuit Court on Wednesday to dissolve a court ruling that effectively bans racial preferences in Texas public colleges, despite a 1996 decision by the same court that said such preferences were illegal at the University of Texas School of Law. Texas Solicitor General Greg Coleman told a three-judge panel on the 5th Circuit Court that the 1996 Hopwood ruling "was wrong" in saying race-based affirmative action should only be used to remedy discrimination, and not simply as a tool to achieve diversity. (Nissimov, 2000, p. 27)

The column went on to recount what the lawyer representing Hopwood and Carvell said, "It contradicts common sense for the state to claim the law school's affirmative action policy in 1992 was not the reason his clients were denied admission. At the time, the law school had lower academic requirements for black and Mexican American applicants. The four students had higher academic ratings than many black and Hispanic students who were accepted" (Nissimov, 2000, p. 27).

The Christian Science Monitor, in a column with the headline "Hour of Truth for Affirmative Action," reports on several affirmative action laws and bills. "One of the nation's most vexing affirmative action cases" that was to convene in October 1997 was brought by a white teacher in Piscataway, New Jersey, whose job was lost to an African American. This arises "anew a question at the heart of the American conundrum over race: Should diversity be taken into account in hiring?" (Marquand, 1997, p. 1):

> The cases come at a time of often confused soul-searching about America's old dilemma of establishing both justice and equality for all. . . . Liberals, urban leaders, and church groups show heightened concern about Americans' sensitivity to race issues, and warn of widening social divisions. Some conservatives argue that an emphasis on race-based remedies is itself divisive and contributes to, rather than cures, racial problems.

Furthermore:

> Efforts to end affirmative action programs are growing. A bill to drop nearly all federal set-asides for women and minorities, for instance, is moving forward in Congress; sponsored by Sen. Mitch McConnell (R) of Kentucky and Rep. Charles Canady (R) of Florida, the "Civil Rights Bill of 1997" could go to the floor next month. . . . Senator McConnell is also tying a measure that would end minority set-asides to a big highway bill moving through Congress. . . . In California, Proposition 209 will go into effect when the Ninth Circuit Court of Appeal issues, as early as Thursday, a mandate. The law bars preferential treatment based on race or gender in public employment, education, and contracting. Many cities, such as Los Angeles, have a "population parity ordinance" that asks officials to hire employees in numbers that roughly match the city's ethnic and racial makeup. Those would also end.

And, pertaining to the school case:

> The Piscataway case . . . is highly unusual in that Piscataway school board, having to cut one teacher in a 10-member department, relied on a seldom-used affirmative action policy instead of flipping a coin or finding other criteria. . . . Both Debra Williams, who is black, and Sharon Taxman, who is white, were hired on the same day in 1989 and had identical qualifications. Piscataway opted to promote racial diversity. . . . Ms. Taxman filed suit and won back a job, along with $144,000 in back damages, which have not been yet paid pending appeal by the school board. . . . Affirmative action to remedy past discrimination, when it is proved, is constitutional. In Piscataway, the question is whether promoting racial diversity is allowable as a public policy goal. . . . Advocates of a color-blind jus-

tice system say it is not. On the Supreme Court, those advocates appear to have four of the five votes needed to eliminate preferential treatment based on race. Justice Sandra Day O'Connor holds the fifth swing vote.

Cynthia Tucker (1999) writes for *The Atlanta Journal-Constitution;* in an editorial published in *The Times-Picayune,* she refers to Michael Adams, the president of the University of Georgia, who "shows a courage rare in the public domain these days" by standing up for affirmative action in admissions. Standing with him were Chancellor Robert Berdahl of the University of Berkeley and Lee Bollinger, head of University of Michigan:

> Last week, Adams announced that UGA, the flagship of Georgia's university system, will maintain its very modest affirmative-action program as it judges admissions for next year's class. He make the decision despite the fact that UGA's diversity effort has been challenged in court and is likely to face more lawsuits. . . . African Americans and Latinos admitted through affirmative action are by no means incompetent to handle the work. Critics of diversity efforts don't like to concede this, but most college affirmative action programs are quite modest. UGA, for example, admits about 85% of its students on the basis of college entrance exams and grades alone. Another 15%, with test scores slightly lower, are admitted on the basis of a complicated grid system that considers several factors including extracurricular activities, alumni in the family (also called legacy), and race. (Tucker, 1999, p. 5)

Tucker reports that those "affirmative action students who graduate from prestigious universities earn advanced degrees in professions such as medicine and law at the same rate as their white counterparts." She also notes:

> As black America becomes wealthier and more sophisticated, it will also become more academically competitive. The students admitted to college through affirmative action today will become parents whose children do not need affirmation action . . . [so] "if we can just buy some time for this generation . . . the problem will take care of itself" . . . based on the premise that supporters of affirmative action must admit that it cannot—and should not—last forever. (Tucker, 1999, p. 5)

William Raspberry (1999) is a columnist for *The Washington Post* who puts a little different twist on the issue of civil rights and affirmative action. He takes the stance that the struggle for justice of the civil rights phase is successfully over and it is time that attention be turned to the second phase which is already under way.

One needs to think of two present areas of contention in order to grasp the end of the first phase: college admissions and affirmative action. Raspberry challenges the believe that the main problem with college admissions is that university officials bar qualified applicants because of skin color. Applicants who could no doubt do reasonably well even though they may fall shy of their white counterparts in the admissions criteria. He ponders what the weapon is that is used to attack affirmative action, an attack so forceful that some find it frightening. To describe this phase, Raspberry uses the now infamous words of the California proposition that the government "shall not discriminate against, or grant preferential treatment to, any individual or group on the basis of race, sex, color, ethnicity, or national origin" (p. 5) He declares that that is the language of African Americans' that they worked to get adopted because they thought they would be better off if they could get the American majority to start to judge them by the "content of our character" as well as similar nonracial criteria.

Raspberry believes they are better off for it, even though he feels the black Americans are still, too often, judged by race. He contends that another part of the present-day reality is that color-blindness has not been enough to bring us to equality, let alone fundamental fairness.

The Times-Picayune, byline, Palo Alto, California, reports on a gathering at Stanford University of more than 200 leading scholars of race, who were mostly black, to consider the state of African Americans in the beginning of the new century. The column bears the headline, "Race and black history still matter, scholars say." The underlying theme of the conference was that it is up to the black intelligentsia to do a better job of refuting the notion that race no longer matters, with one of the participants, Paula McClain, a professor of government at the University of Virginia, imploring the audience to "resist the seduction of the color-blind language. . . . [P]ast opponents of racial equality and equal rights now cloak themselves in the tenets of the Civil Rights Act of 1964 and claim Martin Luther King as their patron saint—'People should be judged by the content of their character and not the color of their skin.' They argue that the external barriers to black social and political progress are things of the past and no longer exist. These are the ideas that have currency" (Tilove, 1999, p. 21).

The column also addressed comments by Harvard sociologist Lawrence Bobo, who said that "the new era is one of 'laissez-faire racism' in which Americans are content to view inequality as a fact of life and the free market, nothing to be disturbed or worried over—rather than as a consequence of the nation's racist history . . . at end of the Civil War black people controlled half of 1 percent of American's wealth; today, they control 1 percent"; and Eduardo Bonilla-Silva, a sociologist at Texas A&M University, who directed a project interviewing white people about their racial attitudes, said, "Most are unaware of the advantages of being white" (Tilove, 1999, p. 21). [For a compelling and insightful article on white privilege, see Peggy MacIntosh's article (2001).]

The O. J. Simpson Trial

Another illustration of how our nation remains racially divided is the O. J. Simpson trial that took place in 1995. Hacker (1995) writes about this trial in his book, entitled *Two Nations: Black and White, Separate, Hostile, Unequal,* and entitles the chapter "Two Nations, Two Verdicts" (1995, p. 207). He maintains that there were two trials and two verdicts in the O. J. Simpson case. The Los Angeles courtroom held the first trial with the jury's unanimous decision; and, as millions followed the proceedings across the county, the second "trial" went on. The public arena, however, was marked by disagreement, with the central cleavage being racial. The testimony and evidence were analyzed by black and white Americans in radically different ways. Even before the trial was over, "the two racial nations had reached two different verdicts" (Hacker, 1995, p. 207).

Hacker contends that to fully understand the outcome of the trial, the concentration needs to be on the jury: who they were; what they did; and their reactions to the trial in front of them, a trial the rest of us did not see as we formed our own verdicts. Because of the length of the full, daily coverage, it was impossible for everyone to watch every hour of the real trial; and those who did watch only saw what the camera showed. The jurors, on the other hand, were able to sense nuances of demeanor, which inevitably figured as they made their decisions. It must be kept in mind, too, that the jury was not allowed to see much of the "trial" witnessed by the rest of us. The jurors were sent out of the room frequently so lawyers could argue arcane points of procedure and admissibility; thus, the public was influenced by facts and allegations that had been withheld from the jury as they formed their verdicts. The most memorable were the recorded racial remarks made by Mark Fuhrman of which only a few reached the jurors' ears (Hacker, 1995).

It can only be speculated on just how carefully the "home jurors" evaluated the evidence. As the trial drew to a close, *Newsweek* did a survey showing that 74% of whites believed that O. J. Simpson committed the murders, while 85% of black Americans felt he was not guilty or that his guilt had not been established beyond a reasonable doubt. Hacker ponders the question, "Were white and black Americans watching the same trial?" In a literal sense, yes, especially as only one camera was in the courtroom. In reality, however, the words and images were sifted by both races through their own eyes and ears, thus explaining "why each race mustered a solid majority for its own verdict" (Hacker, 1995, p. 212).

Obviously, blacks and whites had differing images of the courtroom, let alone the trial. For blacks, the courtroom resembled a white fortress that was armed with the state's power to prove its official case. Although the presiding judge's grandparents were born in Japan, if people closed their eyes while watching him preside, his ancestry could not be detected. So, for African Americans, the courtroom and its proceedings represented a system in which they were still essentially outsiders. Moreover, it is a system that has brought grief to a major segment of the black population. This put the arrest and indictment of O. J. Simpson in a new light on the use and misuse of the nation's police power. Even African American professionals can tell of incidents of rudeness and discourtesy, of insults and humiliation upon encounters with police officers (Hacker, 1995).

A large majority of white Americans were convinced that Simpson committed the two murders, regardless of whether they followed the trial daily or only read accounts on occasion. Simpson had long been a white favorite as a professional athlete and then as a representative of products—most prominently, the car rental industry. Almost the instant he fell under suspicion, his preferred status began to evaporate and further deteriorated when he chose Johnnie Cochran to supplant Robert Shapiro as his lead attorney. White men felt that Simpson had betrayed them and no longer fit the description of the "model black man." The fact that he had a white wife did not set well with the white community, nor did the alleged physical abuse of her. Adding another dimension, whites reacted to more than just the verdict: the African American elation over the outcome. "The shouting, laughing, and crying were captured on every television channel. To white eyes, this was a victory celebration: if O. J. Simpson had won, so had all of his race" (Hacker, 1995, p. 221).

So what did this mean, the effects of the trial on racial America? Hacker (1995) states that whites will not riot in the street, but he believes the impact will be felt in small, subtle ways. He predicted that the public vote on whether to retain affirmative action in California would fail without the substantial white support at the polls, which it did. At the time, African Americans had recently augmented their political power, due to districts redesigned to give them lawmakers of their own race. Those seats were being challenged, and their survival was to be decided by white judges. Hacker closes by saying, "This is not to say that whites will consciously impose punishments for what one jury did. But minds and actions shift by degrees, and white Americans are not apt to forget that they have a defeat to make up" (p. 222).

There were also questions about 9 of the 12 jurors who were African American. Many whites doubted that those individuals could be impartial when called upon to judge a member of their race. There was also the suspicion that they would favor Johnnie Cochran's analysis because he was black. In many ways, the white reactions to the verdict were predictable. One was heard to say, "Here's what happens when you give blacks responsibility, with an obligation to be impartial," and others remarked "that the jurors would never convict, given that they would have to return to their home neighborhoods. Or that they didn't even realize that a case of this magnitude deserved at least several days of deliberation." Hacker says, ". . . [H]ere we are, yet again, hearing whites tell blacks that they should conduct themselves in ways that evoke white approval" (p. 221).

This has been a very broad sweep over the Simpson verdict, and the reader is encouraged to read the entire chapter by Hacker (1995) to gain a fuller insight into all the many ramifications of this high-profile trial and the impact of its verdict on society.

One headline—"The O. J. Simpson verdict; Radio callers show the same racial divide; Most blacks cheer the decision, but whites call it an injustice"— from *The Houston Chronicle* reported:

> Houston radio audiences rendered their own swift opinions Tuesday after the not guilty verdict in the O. J. Simpson double-murder trial. And, with few exceptions, views expressed about the trial's outcome depended on the race of the caller, reflecting results similar to that of last week's *ABC News* poll showing 77% of whites surveyed thought Simpson was guilty and 72% of African Americans believed him innocent. . . . Comments from . . . radio station KOCH-AM . . . were from a predominantly black listenership [and] included, "I'm just so happy. Chills ran through my body," and "My grandfather and uncle were killed by white men. Now they can rest in peace." Radio station KRBE-FM . . . has largely white listeners, and made these comments, "It goes to show you what a colossal mistake our justice system has become. It's a sad statement that if you've got money and possibly the fame you can make a perfect crime happen," and "It sends a terrible message about domestic violence."
>
> The DJ from a Latino station, Super Tejano, KXTJ-FM, said that his listeners ". . . had mixed feelings about the verdict, but most were negative. Many felt that race played too big a part in the trial." And, KMJQ-FM, an urban-contemporary music station said the calls mostly favored the verdict. One caller to gospel KYOK-AM put it, "We as a black race find peace." (Rust & Westbrook, 1995, p. 10A)

Unrelated to the O. J. Simpson trial, from *The New York Times* comes the recent story, "Race relations called good, yet distance persists":

> Thirty-five years after the dismantling of legalized segregation, a majority of Americans maintain that race relations in the United States are generally good, but black people and white people continue to have starkly divergent perceptions of many racial issues and remain largely isolated from each other in their every-day lives, according to a nationwide poll by *The New York Times*. The poll suggests that even as the rawest forms of bigotry have receded they often have been replaced by remoteness and distrust in places of work, learning and worship. The poll, which surveyed 2165 adults, detected some signs that both black and white people believe that race relations are improving. . . . And the percentage who said the country has made real progress in reducing racial discrimination . . . is about 25 percentage points higher for each group than in May 1992, just after the deadly rioting that followed the acquittal of four police officers in the beating of a black California motorist. But in question after question the poll also revealed a core of black people—about four in 10, many of them college educated—who find little to celebrate even today. . . . [T]hey thought that race relations were generally bad and that there had been no real progress in eliminating racial discrimination since the 1960s.
>
> On many questions, particularly those related to whether black people are treated equitably and whether race plays too large a role in the national discourse, black and white people seem to be living on different planets. Indeed, one of the few areas where black and white people are most in agreement is in their perception of racial hostility. Similar percentages—39% of white people and 45% of black people—said they think that either many or almost all white people dislike

black people. And 45% of white people and the same percentage of black people said they think that either many or almost all black people dislike white people. (Sack & Elder, 2000, pp. A1, 6)

SOCIAL WORK AND RACE IN THE 21ST CENTURY

As we learned from Chapter 11, social workers in the 1980s were portrayed as naive and superficial when it came to antiracist practice. We now look at where we stand, having recently entered the 21st century.

The present question is whether the social work profession has responded to the challenge put out by Allen-Meares and McMahon (1992) to shift its practice to social activism and social change through work for racial equality and social justice. Recently, Carlton-LaNey (1999) has argued that "many social workers today know very little about their African American clients and fail to see the importance of immersing themselves in African American history and culture" (p. 318). She claims that the profession continues to be silent about the inequities and social conditions that face African American families and that schools of social work have similarly failed African American faculty and students.

Allen-Meares and Burman (1995) found the same silence in the profession in its work with African American men. Despite the fact that social work has emphasized a person-in-environment perspective, "to enhance functioning and coping, to provide services and resources, and to act as a bridge between the individual and organizational systems . . . , [interventions with African American men] focus on individual pathology and antisocial activities, rather than the unfair and intolerable practices of larger systems and institutions that create dissension and corresponding malfunctioning" (Allen-Meares & Burman, 1995, p. 271). In doing so, "social workers are thought to be agents of social control instead of advocates for social change" (p. 271).

In addressing the needs of African Americans, Carlton-LaNey (1999) argues for the adoption of "the Africentric paradigm" (p. 318), which includes personalizing the professional relationship; emphasizing reciprocity and the client's strengths in the helping relationship; and recognizing the importance of organizations, institutions, and informal groups as empowerment sources. Allen-Meares and Burman (1995) also stress the importance of an Africentric perspective but further urge social workers to engage in an activist practice that empowers African American clients to "seek strategies to address policies and practices that promote advocacy, social justice, social change, and knowledge and education for empowerment while activating change at macro and micro levels" (p. 273).

Advocacy for an Africentric perspective and an activist practice seem to reveal the dominant themes as the social work profession has dealt with race and ethnicity. The first is indicative of the broader call for social workers to be culturally competent as they work with cultures other than their own. The second acknowledges the need for social workers to pursue change on a policy and environmental level to approach problems related to race from a structural viewpoint rather than looking at the problem as being manifested in the behavior of the individual client.

Ample evidence exists that the social work profession has struggled, and continues to struggle, with issues related to race and ethnicity from the policy statements adopted by the National Association of Social Workers (NASW) in 1996. Among the statements approved that year were those concerning racism; affirmative action; cultural competence in the social work profession; and gender-, ethnic-, and race-based workplace discrimination (NASW, 1997).

In explaining racism, the NASW recognizes that it is an insidious condition that is strongly embedded in societal privilege:

> Racism is the ideology or practice through demonstrated power of perceiving the superiority of one group over others by reason of race, color, ethnicity, or cultural heritage. In the United States and elsewhere, racism is manifested at the individual, group, and institutional levels. It has been institutionalized and maintained through educational, economic, political, religious, social, and cultural policies and activities. It is observable in the prejudiced attitudes, values, myths, beliefs, and practices expressed by many people, including those in positions of power. Racism is functional—that is, it serves a purpose. In U.S. society, racism functions to maintain structural inequities that are to the disadvantage of people of color.
>
> Organized discrimination against members of visibly identifiable racial and ethnic groups has permeated every aspect of their lives, including education, employment, contacts with the legal system, economics, housing, politics, religion, and social relationships. It has become institutionalized through folklore, legal restrictions, values, myths, and social mores that are openly supported by a substantial number of people, including those who maintain control of the major institutions of American society. (NASW, 1997, p. 263)

The NASW discusses cultural competence as a process "of becoming more attuned to how clients experience their uniqueness, deal with their differences and similarities, and cope with a sociopolitical environment which is less and less concerned with the welfare of its people, however diverse their needs may be" (NASW, 1997, p. 76). In this statement, the NASW attempts to recognize the relationship between individual and environmental conditions and, further, maintains that "social workers need sophisticated skills and abilities to advocate for clients against the underlying devaluation of cultural experiences related to difference and oppression" (p. 76).

The NASW (1997) policy statement on affirmative action puts the profession on record for a particular course of action on a specific issue related to race, one that is clearly related to underlying social work values. As the statement asserts:

The profession of social work is committed to equality and justice. NASW has always fought discrimination. Social work values, belief in the worth and dignity of each individual, history of practice, and advocacy on behalf of oppressed people require that social workers speak out at this critical juncture in our nation's history.

Although measurable gains have been made as a result of affirmative action, "color-blind" policies cannot survive racist biases still prevalent in U.S. society. Affirmative action has been an effective tool in forcing changes in entrenched patterns of segregation and prejudice. It is best understood as a tool with which to create change. Proportional representation, numerical quotas, women and minority set-aside programs, and other efforts are tools that can be used to implement affirmative action. . . .

The 1996 Delegate Assembly chose affirmative action as one of the four social policy priorities requiring aggressive action by NASW over the next three years. This formal policy statement declares NASW's commitment to affirmative action and enables social work practitioners to vigorously advance affirmative action programs. Although critics of affirmative action have questioned its effectiveness and even the continued existence of discrimination, social workers must not lose their way in this controversy. NASW stands in firm support of the mandated inclusions afforded by affirmative action. (pp. 13–14)

The problem with policy statements is that they are just that—statements. They do not necessarily translate into action. Gibelman (2000) posits that the social work profession "has not been an active contributor to the debate [on affirmative action] when compared to the disciplines of sociology, political science, and law" (p. 154). While acknowledging the profession's verbal commitment in policy statements and the *Code of Ethics*, Gibelman asserts that the NASW statements are politically naive and "lack the level of specificity and direction needed to serve as a guide to professional behavior" (p. 165). She argues that social workers must practice in a way that influences policy:

Social workers need to be able to actively apply social planning knowledge and policy development skills to identify new solutions. Further, social work must lend its expertise to the collection and analysis of the empirical data on the outcomes of past, present, and future approaches to end discrimination. The credibility of the profession in the affirmative action debate may well depend on being able to document, through our practice, the continued negative impact of discrimination and, conversely, the positive outcomes of anti-discrimination strategies. The profession must also be clear about its potential contributions to an interdisciplinary dialogue. (p. 165)

In Gibelman's (2000) argument, one can see the dynamic interplay between practice and policy. The current attacks on affirmative action policy lead to the need for practice that effectively deals with discrimination, which in turn may inform future policy directions. Gibelman also holds that the profession must look internally:

Social work can and should be a model for other professions. The ability of the profession to relate to the communities it serves suggests the imperative of a more diverse human services labor force. The composition of the profession must be brought more in line with the proportion of clients served by social workers who are racial minorities. The current profile of African Americans in the social work profession (at least in regard to NASW membership) reflects less than one half of the 11.8% that this group comprises of the U.S. population. . . . These numbers are unacceptable for a profession that would like to see itself in the vanguard of progressive social change. Strategies to recruit ethnic minorities into the profession deserve greater attention and resources. Schools of social work have an essential role to play in recruiting ethnic minorities through outreach and scholarships. This means reaching potential students earlier (perhaps in high school) and more effectively. "Marketing" social work as a career has never been more important. More concentrated efforts to promote diversity within social work will be a signal to others of our commitment in action as well as in words. (p. 169)

See Appendix 12–A for an example of a project at the St. Thomas Health Clinic (located in one of the Housing Projects) in New Orleans, Louisiana. St. Thomas is a community-driven clinic and receives its direction through active community membership on its board of directors, consultant services by community leadership, and community dialogue sessions. The clinic is developing a process for change in health care that includes the development and implementation of an antiracist culturally competent comprehensive curriculum for providers of services in the African American community. Also, one of this book's authors is developing curriculum content for an antiracist agenda for social work.

The Smith College for Social Work is an example of an institution that has taken on the challenge of deliberately transforming a well-intentioned desire into action. Since 1986, the school has consciously been working toward becoming an antiracist institution. The school faculty and students struggled with curriculum and student and faculty recruitment issues but would eventually clearly state that "Smith College School for Social Work has committed itself to becoming an antiracist institution. The School pledges to overcome racism in all of its programs" (Basham, Donner, Killough, & Werkmeister Rozas, 1997, p. 566).

The National Association of Social Workers has a policy statement on racism, stating that they ". . . support an inclusive society in which racial, ethnic, social, sexual orientation, and gender differences are valued and respected. Racism at any level should not be tolerated. Emphasis must be placed on self-examination, learning, and change to unlearn racist beliefs and practices in order to be fully competent to join others in full appreciation of all differences" (NASW, 1997, p. 264). See Appendix 12–B for the full policy statement on racism, as well as NASW's policy statement on cultural competence and their affirmative action statement.

A STRENGTHS PERSPECTIVE

Having read some of the previous chapters, you can see that welfare reform and the changes in Medicaid were about as far from a strengths model as one could perceive. The voices of the people that were affected were not heard in a way that would change their circumstances, nor was there any hint of "common human need." It took on the guise of "them" versus John/Jane Doe Public. The voice from the media offered straightforward reporting, reported facts, and, in some cases, expressed opinions; but, of course, that does not effect change—and we heard no cries of outrage from that sector. The counterreaction to the reform act of 1996 that Gordon hoped for did not happen. As social workers, we cannot give up the hope that that counterreaction is yet to come and that we will be a part of it.

When social policies and programs emphasize individual pathologies and deficits, they ignore structural barriers that many people face in getting ahead—poor educational preparation, lack of decent jobs, inadequate day care and health care, and poverty. When we continue to look at the individualistic nature of problems such as AIDS, pregnant teenagers, and truant children, we fail to examine the institutional nature of the social problems, especially the endemic, insidious repercussions of institutionalized racism, and may fail to see the potential of a community to address its problems when given the resources to assert itself.

Hundreds upon thousands of women and children in dire straits who were affected by the welfare reform of 1996 will undoubtedly experience suffering from more than their lack of food, clothing, shelter, and medical care. There is growing literature demonstrating that the effects of institutionalized racism—years of oppression, discrimination, poverty, and racism—cause ill mental and physical health (see Major & Perkins, 2000; Stewart, 1999). Every day, clinics around the country serving people of color see the physical health impact of depression upon their patients, as well as the mental health issues that accompany depression and that often overwhelm individuals, their families, and the community they are a part of (Major & Perkins, 2000; Stewart, 1999; see Appendix 12-A).

When people are provided with adequate physical and mental health services, it helps reduce disease, unwanted pregnancy, delinquency, school dropouts, and so on (Major & Perkins, 2000; Treadway, 2000). Social policymakers need to take this, along with the other important factors, into consideration when formulating policies that predominately affect people of color.

When speaking of race and ethnic sensitive social work practice, Pinderhughes (1989) says:

Agencies must be created that facilitate the efforts of practitioners to use helping strategies that validate people's culture and enhance their cultural identity. Services should be so organized that attempts to empower clients, to help them reduce their personal feelings of powerlessness, and to counteract denigration of themselves and their cultural groups do not leave practitioners trapped and overwhelmed with powerlessness themselves. Policies should be set that strengthen the health of the ethnic community and reinforce action, self-esteem, pride, self-assertion, and mastery among its members; that promote the ability to cope with the overwhelming problems stemming from their confusing and contradictory roles within the social system; and that facilitate the ability to embrace biculturalism as a strength, whereby they are able to function in the American mainstream and remain connected to the ethnic community if that is desired. (p. 202)

We saw none of this in The Personal Responsibility and Work Opportunity Reconciliation Act.

SUMMARY

Not since Harry Truman's confrontation with the Republican Congress in 1947 and 1948 has there been more conflict over social policy than in 1995. Hopes were quickly dashed for liberals who thought that Clinton, the first Democratic president since the end of the cold war, would reorient the nation's priorities toward domestic needs (Jansson, 1997). "[The] third year strongly resembled the politics of 1981, when Ronald Reagan had orchestrated huge cuts in domestic spending—except that the cuts in 1995 were orchestrated not by the president, but by the congressional leader" (p. 345).

As Gordon (1998) pointed out, the welfare reform act of 1996 was cut from the same cloth as the 1961 Newburg, New York, welfare overhaul, but the cuts went deeper, metaphorically, because we have gone backward rather than forward. The division between the haves and the have-nots is wider than it has ever been in American history, and social workers' concern should be "Who cares?" Who really cares enough to lead the counterreaction? Government turns a blind eye as it takes credit for having done a good thing, forcing so many people into a deeper, more abject poverty.

REFERENCES

Allen-Meares, P., & Burman, S. (1995). The endangerment of African American men: An appeal for social work action. *Social Work, 40,* 268–274.

Allen-Meares, P., & McMahon, A., (1992). Is social work racist? A content analysis of recent literature. *Social Work, 37*(6), 533–539.

Angelou, M. (1993). *On the Pulse of Morning.* New York: Random House, Inc.

Basham, K. K., Donner, S., Killough, R. M., & Werkmeister Rozas, L. (1997). Becoming an anti-racist institution. *Smith College Studies in Social Work, 67,* 564–585.

Carlton-LaNey, I. (1999). African American social work pioneers' response to need. *Social Work, 44,* 311–321.

Cross, T. L., Bazron, B. J., Dennis, K. W., & Isaacs, M. R. (1989). *Towards a culturally competent system of care.* Washington, DC: Child and Adolescent Services Program. Technical Assistance Center.

DeParle, J. (1999, February 21). As welfare dies, burden on grandma grows. *The Times-Picayune,* p. A32.

Edsall, T. B. (1993, January 20). Rebuilding the party: Democrats' suture rests with Clinton. *The Washington Post,* p. F3.

Franklin, J. H., & Moss, A. A. (1994). *From slavery to freedom: A history of African Americans* (7th ed.). New York: McGraw-Hill.

Gibelman, M. (2000). Affirmative action at the crossroads: A social justice perspective. *Journal of Sociology and Social Welfare, 27,* 153–174.

Gordon, L. (1998). How welfare became a dirty word. *New Global Development: Journal of International & Comparative Social Welfare, XIV,* 1–14.

Gullo, K. (2000, June 20). Welfare reform blamed for uninsured. *The Times-Picayune,* p. A3.

Hacker, A. (1995). *Two nations: Black and white, separate, hostile, unequal.* New York: Ballantine Books.

Jansson, B. S. (1997). *The reluctant welfare state* (3rd ed.). Pacific Grove, CA: Brooks/Cole.

Levine, M. L. (1996). *African Americans and civil rights: From 1619 to the present.* Phoenix, AZ: The Oryx Press.

Major, B., & Perkins, K. (1999–2000). *Culturally competent mental health curriculum for people of color: An anti-racist approach, Parts I & II.* Papers presented at the Diversity Conference sponsored by University of South Carolina, College of Social Work, Part I, Charleston, NC, Part II, Atlanta, GA.

Marquand, R. (1997, August 28). Hour of truth for affirmative action. *The Christian Science Monitor,* p. 1.

McIntosh, P. (2001). White privilege and male privilege: A personal account of coming to see correspondence through work in women's studies (1998). In *Race, Class, and Gender: An anthology* (4th ed.) United States: Wadsworth Publishing.

Meckler, L. (1999, February 25). Jobs aren't always way out of poverty, magazine reports. *The Times Picayune,* p. A3.

National Association of Social Workers. (2000). *Social work speaks: NASW policy statements.* Washington, DC: NASW Press.

Nissimov R. (2000, June 8). State seeks Hopwood case reversal. *The Houston Chronicle,* p. 27.

Overholser, G. (2000, January 27). Candidates must address racial ills. *The Times-Picayune,* p. B7.

Pinderhughes, E. (1989). *Understanding race, ethnicity, and power.* New York: The Free Press.

Raspberry, W. (1999, October 19). Civil rights movement moves on. *The Times-Picayune*, p. B5.

Reich, R. (2001, January 19). How the melodrama fascinated us. *The Times-Picayune*, p. B7.

Richardson, L. Dizon, L. & Reyes, D. (1996, October 21). Looming welfare cuts put O.C.'s poor in worry mode. *The Los Angeles Times*, p. A1.

Rust, C., & Westbrook, B. (1995, October 4). The O. J. Simpson verdict: Radio callers show the same racial divide; Most blacks cheer decision, but whites call it an injustice. *The Houston Chronicle*, p. 10.

Sack, K. & Elder, J. (2000, July 11). Race relations called good, yet distance persists. *The Times-Picayune*, pp. A1,6.

Seccombe, K. (1999). *So you think I drive a Cadillac? Welfare recipients' perspectives on the system and its reform.* Boston, MA: Allyn & Bacon.

Slavin, P. (2000, May). Demonstrators thrash managed care. *NASW News*, pp. 1 & 10.

Stewart, R. (199, September). "Dead on Arrival." *Emerge*, pp. 34–40.

Teepen, T. (2001, January 20). Bush fuzzy on racial justice. *The Times-Picayune*, p. B7.

Therolf, G. (2001, January 8). Clinton gives sermon at church. *The Times-Picayune*, p. A7.

Tilove, J. (1999, November 21). Race and black history still matter, scholars say. *The Times-Picayune*, p. A21.

Torricelli, R. (Senator), & Carroll, A. (1999). *In our own words.* New York: Kodansha International Ltd.

Trattner, W. I. (1999). *From poor law to welfare state: A history of social welfare in America* (6th ed.). New York: The Free Press.

Treadway, J. (2000, June 10). "Mental health services lacking for LA [Louisiana] children, official says." *The Times-Picayune*.

Tucker, C. (1999, October 7). College affirmative action buys time. *The Times-Picayune*, p. B5.

Volland, V. (1996, December 11). Neither healthy nor wealthy. *St. Louis Post-Dispatch*, p. 1E.

Veeder, N. W., & Peebles-Wilkins, W. (2001). *Managed care services.* New York: Oxford University Press.

Wickham, D. (1992, November 23). Dems owe victory to blacks. *USA Today*, p. 12A.

APPENDIX 12–A

Culturally Competent Mental Health Curriculum for People of Color: An Antiracist Approach–Part 1

Two Louisiana State University (LSU) Schools: LSU School of Social Work and LSU School of Medicine, along with a faculty member from Southern University School of Social Work (a historically black school), have formed a partnership with the St. Thomas Health Clinic for the purpose of developing a curriculum for culturally competent mental health service delivery. The Clinic, in New Orleans, is located in the African American community that it serves.

The model for the development of this curriculum was borne of the Clinic's executive director who has been doing community organization work for over 20 years from an antiracist vantage point. During those 20 years, she has also been affiliated with the People's Institute for Survival and Beyond: Undoing Racism. The People's Institute is a national organization of multicultural, antiracist, veteran community organizers who work with community groups nationwide who are struggling to face racism and empower community residents. Over a two year period, the People's Institute, along with mental health professionals, have been building a collaboration of mental health professionals, their agencies, and schools of social work. It is a shared belief that racism is a barrier that keeps agencies from being more effective in their work with ethnic communities. During those years, 4 trainings and 15 follow-up sessions focusing on mental health issues trained over 200 mental health professionals in New Orleans, each of whom serves countless children, youth, and families of color in the metropolitan area. The development of the mental health curriculum for service delivery is the logical next step to the ongoing Mental Health Undoing Racism training.

The curriculum model has three components: the community, service delivery, and the academy. In keeping with our antiracist philosophy, we took direction for the development of the curriculum from the community. The vision for the curriculum includes placing it not only in the Clinic but also in the local schools of social work and the medical school. The bigger picture, using these local facilities as a pilot, is to introduce cultural competency to other health systems in the New Orleans and Baton Rouge area, as well as nationally. We also hope to do the same with social work and medical education.

The challenges we faced putting this curriculum together were multifaceted for both the oppressed community we serve, the larger black and white community, as well as the white and black persons who deliver the services. The overriding challenge went beyond the actual system, or institutions, of service delivery and reached into the methods that are used to address the mental health issues. In other words, to address the racism that taints a dysfunctional system, both white and black folks need to address the many dynamics that are involved within that system. Moreover, we cannot view the black and white groups as separate entities but must consider the gravity of their interactions within the service delivery system. When it comes to race, both groups, black and white, have dual identities. These identities are also multifaceted; for example, the dynamic of the "victims and healers" is often a contradiction when the healers, or service providers, have some unresolved racial issues from their own background that impedes their work with the client.

Before we can really look at what might be wrong with an individual, we need to look at the historical development in America that has caused the current problem with blacks and whites as it relates to slavery. As a country, we ended the practice of slavery but not the practice of racism. To carry it a step further, the experience of African Americans historically has been that of a dual personality. Their roots are African, and history shows us that early on they were forced to become Americans, which has translated into them now striving to be Americans. Black Americans embrace their own culture while at the same time struggling to fit into mainstream society, to be "normal." This very process can cause mental anguish and is often misconstrued by their mental health providers as an illness. On the other hand, white Americans are so absorbed in their "white privilege" that they are frequently not aware of its existence. This privilege, or superiority, however, is fiercely protected. The protection of privilege can be unconscious and covert, or it can be well thought out and overt. One sure way of protection is to keep oppressed people down. None of this is said to cast blame or produce guilt. Both people of color and whites are indoctrinated and socialized in a manner such that we are all "prisoners of racism."

Unrecognized by most institutions is that their very existence is rooted in a white superiority model, and because of this they cannot lead the process for changing mental health care services to oppressed communities in America. It is the nature of institutions not to change. It is the community that must lead the change, and the institutions must follow that lead.

In many ways, this is a new way of thinking. Using history, we know that when the community (black/slaves) changes, the institutions (white/masters) will change. What we propose to do is to push—St. Thomas is pushing for the change in the delivery of mental health services, moving away from traditional toward the more nontraditional delivery of mental health services. There are several such nontraditional approaches. For example, one is tapping into the people's strengths, looking at what is right rather than what is wrong, and using this information to assist in the problem-solving process. Another is the process of collaboration with community, academe, and service delivery, with the community being the major informer. One of the end results that we are striving for is to send healthy people back to their respective communities with the tools necessary to apply what they have learned, enabling them, through self-empowerment, to live and work in the community collectively—to be interdependent with each other and not so reliant upon outside resources for their survival. Historically, we know that people are not poor (sick) because they lack services but because they have no power.

Culturally Competent Mental Health Curriculum for People of Color: An Antiracist Approach—Part 2

This is the second installment on the development of an antiracist culturally competent mental health curriculum for service providers. The first installment of this process was delivered at the Diversity Conference last year in Charleston.

The curriculum model has three components: the community, service delivery, and the academy. In keeping with our antiracist philosophy, we are taking direction for the development of the curriculum from the community. The second stage of the process moved from research, brainstorming, and conceptualization to "hands on" planning. At a day-long retreat, we broke into groups with the following assignment: service delivery was to talk about what services exist, what the values were within or implied by practice, policies, and regulations; and, for academe, what exists, and what the values were within content [of courses], with both groups then determining whether each was liberating, oppressive, or disempowering. For community, the assignment was what exists [what services are provided], are they liberating or oppressive, and what does community want, need, and demand [in the way of services].

Common themes were found among the three groups and were used for the drafting of the curriculum. These themes were discussed fully at the Diversity Conference. The next page provides an example of one of the identified areas.

APPENDIX 12–B

NASW Policy Statement on Racism

NASW supports an inclusive society in which racial, ethnic, social, sexual orientation, and gender differences are valued and respected. Racism at any level should not be tolerated. Emphasis must be placed on self-examination, learning, and change to unlearn racist beliefs and practices in order to be fully competent to join others in the full appreciation of all differences.

The association seeks the enactment of public social policies that will protect the rights of and ensure equity and social justice for all members of diverse racial and ethnic groups. It is the ethical responsibility of NASW members to assess their own practices and the agencies in which they work for specific ways to end racism where it exists. The basic goal should be to involve social workers in specific, time-limited educational and action programs designed to bring about measurable changes within provider agencies and within NASW national units, chapters, and local units. This is based on the premise that to engage in constructive intraprofessional relationships and to effectively serve clients, social workers must engage in self-examination of their own biases and stereotypes and work to develop an unbiased attitude. Racism is embedded in our society, and unless we identify specific instances

Community	Service Delivery	Academy
Not enough mental health services & centers in general or for crisis intervention* (O); Long waiting lists when services are accessible—because of sliding scale (D/O).	To access services, individual must be homicidal, suicidal, or gravely disabled (D/O); *Prevention and intervention not valued, operates in a crisis mode.*	*Practice:* Do not teach language of other cultures; content built by whites so people of color trained and acculturated to white content and practice (O); *Not reflecting with/for community, not effective with people of color.*
Community would like more community-based and faith-based mental health services, crisis intervention, and home visits—i.e., outreach crisis counselors, more resources ($$, Staff), larger facilities to accommodate more people, use facilities to teach.	Child and maternal health does not include mental health services, i.e., fragmentation or incomplete services (D/O); *Mental health & wellness not valued, medication over services; managed care puts mental health on the backs of primary care provider.*	*Policy:* History of social work taught from a "value neutral" (objective) perspective (D); *Needs critical perspective to see impact on community, e.g., personal responsibility act.*
Legend		*Diversity and Oppression:* Approach varies and typically taught by a person of color; *Can be empowering if done well.*
D = Disempowering		
E = Empowering		*Research:* Teach single-system design and program evaluation—standard academic approach, usually not very creative (D); *Not focused on issues of people of color or outcomes for people of color.*
L = Liberating		
O = Oppressive		
STHS = St. Thomas Health Clinic		
Explanation: An underlined and italicized statement in the column headed "Community" reflects a community desire, need, and/or demand associated with the statement(s) or expression(s) that precedes it; such statements in the column headed "Service Delivery" or "Academy" are associated comments and/or perceived underlying values for the statements or expressions that precede the underlined italicized part.		

This is a snap-shot of one segment of the process of identifying what the problems are in each area. For Community, there is also a statement of want/need.

and work to remove them we are part of the problem rather than a mechanism for the solution. The statement goes on to make specific statements under the following headings: Education, Employment, Housing and Community, Health Care and Mental Health Services, Public Welfare Services, Social Services, Criminal Justice System, Political Activity, Profession.

NASW Policy Statement on Cultural Competence in the Social Work Profession

Social workers have an ethical responsibility to be culturally competent practitioners, as the *NASW Code of Ethics* (NASW, 1996) suggests. The social work profession needs to clearly define what is meant by culturally competent social work practice. *Cultural competence* is a set of congruent behaviors, attitudes, and policies that come together in a system or agency or among professionals and enable the system, agency, or professionals to work effectively in cross-cultural situations. The word "culture" is used because it implies the integrated pattern of human behavior that includes thoughts, communications, actions, customs, beliefs, values, and institutions of a racial, ethnic, religious, or social group. The word "competency" is used because it implies having the capacity to function effectively. A culturally competent system of care acknowledges and incorporates at all levels the importance of culture, the assessment of cross-cultural relations, vigilance toward the dynamics that result from cultural differences, the expansion of cultural knowledge, and the adaptation of services to meet culturally unique needs (Cross, Bazron, Dennis, & Isaacs, 1989).

Cultural competence requires social workers to examine their own cultural backgrounds and identities while seeking out the necessary knowledge, skills, and values that can enhance the delivery of services to people with varying cultural experience associated with their race, ethnicity, gender, class, sexual orientation, religion, age, or disability. Furthermore, culturally competent practice is a critical component of professional social work expertise in all practice settings, whether urban or rural.

A policy statement alone cannot fully define the values, knowledge, and skills required for culturally competent practice. Cultural competency is an important ingredient of professional competency, as important as any component that forms the basis of the theoretical and clinical knowledge that defines social work expertise. This policy statement supports and encourages the development of standards for culturally competent social work practice, a definition of expertise, standards for culturally competent social work practice models that have relevance for the range of needs and services represented by diverse client populations. As advocates for the providers and consumers of social work services, social workers need to promote cultural competence by supporting the evaluation of culturally competent service delivery models and setting standards for cultural competence within the profession. Monitoring cultural competence among social workers should include establishing mechanisms for obtaining direct feedback from clients. The social work profession should be encouraged to take more proactive measures to ensure cultural competence as an integral part of social work practice and to make efforts to increase research and scholarship among its professionals (NASW, 1997, p. 77).

NASW Affirmative Action Policy Statement (1996)

The intent of affirmative action is to correct the present effects of past discrimination and exclusion from opportunities (Myers, 1995) and to achieve future parity. Its purpose is to provide opportunities to a class of qualified individuals who have either historically or actually been denied opportunities to prevent recurrence of discrimination (U.S. Commission on Civil Rights, 1977, 1981). Affirmative action has been effective in a broad spectrum of U.S. society's activities including, but not limited to, employment, education, housing, and federal contracting.

NASW supports affirmative action as a viable tool for upholding its ethical code to act to prevent and eliminate discrimination. NASW supports the following principles:

> Full endorsement of local, state, and federal policies and programs that give all people equal access to resources, services, and opportunities that they require—everyone should be given equal opportunity regardless of age, disability, gender, language, race, religion, or sexual orientation.

- Social workers joining others to denounce attempts to end affirmative action initiatives

- Changes in affirmative action that will strengthen practice and policy at ending discrimination and its impact

- A firm commitment to protect the gains realized by affirmative action

- Working with others to develop more effective and cogent policies and strategies to guide society and communities to that end (p. 14)

Name Index

Subject Index

345

Credits

Chapter 2. 26: Fig. 2.1: From *The Medieval Village,* by G. G. Coulton. Copyright © 1931 Cambridge University Press. Reprinted by permission.

Chapter 3. 38 and 44: Tables 3.1 and 3.2: From "Poverty and Poor Relief in Pre-Revolutionary Philadelphia," by G. B. Nash, in *William and Mary Quarterly, 33,* p. 9 and p. 23. Copyright © 1976 Omohundro Institute of Early American History and Culture. Reprinted by permission.

Chapter 4. 51 and 52: Tables 4.1 and 4.2: Adapted from "Federal Welfare for Revolutionary War Veterans," by J. P. Resch, *Social Service Review, 56,* p. 175 and p. 177. Copyright © 1982 University of Chicago Press. Adapted with permission.

Chapter 5. 76: Poems: From "The Colored Soldiers" and "The Unsung Heroes," by Paul Laurence Dunbar, in R. Marius (Ed.), *The Columbia Book of Civil War Poetry, 1994.* Copyright © 1994 Columbia University Press.

Chapter 7. 146: Table 7.1: From *FERA Monthly Report,* June 1935, p. 31.

Chapter 8. 153: Table 8.1: From *Public Relief 1929–1939,* by J. C. Brown, p. 302. Copyright © 1940 Henry Holt and Company. Reprinted by permission. **155: Fig. 8.1:** From Conference on Poverty, *Community Social Program Inventory.* Chapel Hill, N.C., September 1994. In *Social Welfare: Policy and Analysis,* Second Edition, by A. W. Dobelstein, p. 229. Copyright © 1996 by the Wadsworth Group, a division of Thomson Learning.

Chapter 9. 187: Table 9.1: Adapted from *Two Nations: Black and White, Separate, Hostile, Unequal,* Second Edition, by A. Hacker. Copyright © 1995 by Ballantine Books. Adapted with permission. **193: Poem:** Used with permission of George Bowering.

Chapter 10. 228 and 234: Tables 10.1 and 10.3: Adapted from *Two Nations: Black and White, Separate, Hostile, Unequal,* Second Edition, by A. Hacker. Copyright © 1995 by Ballantine Books. Adapted with permission. **246: Appendix 10-A:** From *NASW News,* June 1979, pp. 175–177. Copyright © 1979 National Association of Social Workers. Reprinted with permission from the National Association of Social Workers. All printed material is copyrighted.

Chapter 11. 257: Excerpt: From "U.S. Welfare Plan to Require Check on Family Assets," by R. Pear, 9/4/81, p. A1. Copyright © 1981 The New York Times. Reprinted with permission. **257: Excerpt:** From "Reagan-Era Welfare: Washington Gives Push to Self-Help," by L. Overbea, in *The Christian Science Monitor,* 1/26/82, p. 6. Copyright © 1982 Christian Science Monitor. Reprinted with permission. **257: Excerpt:** From Wires; from news services in *The San Diego Union-Tribune,* 3/31/84, p. A1. Reprinted with permission of The Associated Press and LexisNexis, a division of Reed Elsevier, Inc. **267: Lyrics:** Reprinted with permission from Sugar Hill Records. **271: Excerpt:** From "Voices from the Community," by A. Di Rado, 5/21/92. Copyright © 1992 Los Angeles Times. Reprinted by permission. **293: Poem:** From *Bad-mouthing: The Language of Special Needs,* by J. Corbet, pp. 88–89. Copyright © 1996 Falmer Press. Reprinted by permission of Taylor & Francis, Inc.

Chapter 12. 299: Excerpt: From "Dems Owe Victory to Blacks," by Wickham, 11/23/92, p. 12A. Copyright 1992, USA TODAY. Reprinted with permission. **300: Poem:** From "On the Pulse of Morning" by Maya Angelou, copyright © 1993 by Maya Angelou. Used by permission of Random House, Inc. **308: Excerpt:** From "Neither Healthy nor Wealthy," by V. Volland, 12/11/96, p. 1E. Reprinted with permission of the St. Louis Post-Dispatch, copyright 1996. **309: Excerpt:** From "Looming Welfare Cuts Put O. C.'s Poor in Worry Mode," by L. Richardson, L. Dizon, and D. Reyes, 10/21/96, p. A1. Copyright © 1996 Los Angeles Times. Reprinted by permission. **310: Excerpt:** From "Jobs Aren't Always a Way Out of Poverty, Magazine Reports," by L. Meckler, in *The Times Picayune,* 2/25/99, p. A3. Copyright © 1999 Associated Press. Reprinted with permission of The Associated Press. **311: Excerpt:** From "As Welfare Dies, Burden on Grandma Grows," by J. DeParle, 2/21/99, p. A32. Copyright © 1999 The New York Times. Reprinted by permission. **314: Excerpt:** From "Welfare Reform Blamed for Uninsured," by K. Gullo, in *The Times Picayune,* 6/20/00, p. A3. Copyright © 2000 Associated Press. Reprinted with permission of The Associated Press. **316: Excerpt:** From "Bush Fuzzy on Racial Justice," by T. Teepen, in *The Times Picayune,* 1/20/01, p. B7. Copyright © 2001 Cox News Publishing. Reprinted with permission. **317: Excerpt:** From "State Seeks Hopwood Case Reversal," by R. Nissimov in *The Houston Chronicle,* 6/8/00, p. 27. Copyright © 2000 The Houston Chronicle. Reprinted by permission. **318: Excerpt:** From "Hour of Truth for Affirmative Action," by R. Marquand, in *The Christian Science Monitor,* 8/28/97, p. 1. Copyright © 1997 The Christian Science Monitor. Reprinted by permission. **319: Excerpt:** From "College Affirmative Actions Buys Time," by C. Tucker, in *The Times Picayune,* 10/7/99, p. B5. Copyright © 1999 The Atlanta Journal Constitution. Reprinted by permission. **320: Excerpt:** From "Race and Black History Still Matter, Scholars Say," by J. Tilove, in *The Times Picayune,* 11/21/99, p. A21. Copyright © 1999 Newshouse News Service. Reprinted by permission. **323: Excerpt:** From "The O. J. Simpson Verdict; Radio Callers Show the Same Racial Divide; Most Blacks Cheer Decision, But Whites Call It an Injustice," by C. Rust and B. Westbrook, in *The Houston Chronicle,* 10/4/95, p. 10. Copyright © 1995 The Houston Chronicle. Reprinted with permission. **323: Excerpt:** From "Race Relations Called Good, Yet Distance Persists," by K. Sack and J. Elder, 7/11/00, p. A1, 6. Copyright © 2000 The New York Times. Reprinted by permission. **Appendix 12-B:** From: "Racism," in *Social Work Speaks,* 2000, p. 264. From "NASW Policy Statement on Cultural Competence in Social Work Profession," in *Social Work Speaks,* 2000, p. 77. From "NASW Affirmative Action," in *Social Work Speaks,* 2000, p. 17. Reprinted with permission from the National Association of Social Workers. All printed material is copyrighted.

PHOTO CREDITS

Page 1 © Bettman/Corbis; Page 19 © Gianni Dagli/CORBIS; Page 35 © Bettmann/Corbis; Page 49 © CORBIS; Page 67 © CORBIS; Page 99 © Hulton Archive; Page 131 © Minnesota Historical Society/CORBIS; Page 151 © CORBIS; Page 175 © Bettman/Corbis; Page 207 © Roger Ressmeyer/CORBIS; Page 213 © PhotoDisc; Page 216 © PhotoDisc; Page 249 © Peter Turnley/CORBIS; Page 295 © Leif Skoogfors/CORBIS.